# Form, Matter, and Mixture in Aristotle

Edited by Frank A. Lewis and Robert Bolton

T0385537

Copyright © University of Southern California 1996

ISBN 0 631-20092 4

First published 1996

Blackwell Publishers
108 Cowley Road, Oxford, OX1 1JF, UK.

and 350 Main Street,
Malden, MA 02148, USA.

All rights reserved. Except for the quotation of short passages for the purposes of criticism and review, no part of this publication may be reproduced, stored in a retrieval system, or transmitted, in any form or by any means, electronic, mechanical, photocopying, recording or otherwise, without the prior permission of the publisher.

Except in the United States of America, this book is sold subject to the condition that it shall not, by way of trade or otherwise, be lent, resold, hired out, or otherwise circulated without the publisher's prior consent in any form of binding or cover other than that in which it is published and without a similar condition including this condition being imposed on the subsequent purchaser.

*British Library Cataloguing in Publication Data*
Cataloguing in Publication data applied for.


*Library of Congress Cataloging in Publication Data*
Cataloging in Publication data applied for.


This book is a corrected version of special issue 76:3/4 (1995) of
*Pacific Philosophical Quarterly*.


Published by Blackwell Publishers on behalf of the
University of Southern California, Los Angeles

# CONTENTS

# CONTENTS

# PREFACE

This volume brings together papers by participants in the fourth annual USC/Rutgers conference in Aristotle, held at USC in December of 1992 on Aristotle's theory of matter. The details of Aristotle's fundamental hylomorphic hypothesis work out quite differently at the different "levels" at which he applies it: at the lower levels of matter in the account of the uniform or homoeomerous stuffs, which are mixtures of the elemental bodies; in the analysis of the individual substance as a compound of form and proximate matter; and in the explanation of psychological states. The opening paper by Michael Wedin asks whether Aristotle's account of human soul as form to the human body as matter is consistent with compositional plasticity, and investigates the sense in which the matter with which a given form can combine is included in the definition of that form. Frank Lewis addresses the unity of the substantial form and proximate matter in the individual substance, and explores the connection with Aristotle's notions of potentiality and actuality. A paper by Kit Fine takes up the topic of mixtures, produced out of the elemental bodies at a lower level of matter. Aristotle argues against the sceptic that the elements that enter into a given mixture are altered but not destroyed as the result of being mixed; Fine exploits a plasticity in the ways in which a homoeomer can be decomposed to explain how the elements can themselves be present in the mixture. It is fundamental to his account that we understand the form of a homoeomer as itself a "mixture" of the elemental forms. Other themes include latent and patent capacities; the question of how the initial ingredients can be recovered from the mixture, as Aristotle requires; and Aristotle's quantitative analysis of qualitative change. An alternative account of mixture, with a response to Fine, is offered by James Bogen; a second response to Fine appears in a paper by Alan Code. The final paper by Robert Bolton, surveying the account of substance in *Metaphysics* Book *Zeta* and its background in *Gamma*, attempts to bring Aristotle's account of compound material substances under the rubric of Aristotelian science as described in the *Posterior Analytics*.

# ABBREVIATIONS

| | |
|---|---|
| *An. Po.* | *Posterior Analytics* |
| *An. Pr.* | *Prior Analytics* |
| *Catg.* | *Categories* |
| *De An.* | *On the Soul* |
| *De Cae.* | *On the Heavens* |
| *De Int.* | *On Interpretation* |
| *De Sens.* | *On Sense* |
| *E.N.* | *Nicomachean Ethics* |
| *G&C* | *On Generation and Corruption* |
| *G.A.* | *Generation of Animals* |
| *H.A.* | *History of Animals* |
| *M.A.* | *Movement of Animals* |
| *Met.* | *Metaphysics* |
| *Meteor.* | *Meteorology* |
| *P.A.* | *Parts of Animals* |
| *Phys.* | *Physics* |
| *S.E.* | *Sophistical Refutations* |
| *Top.* | *Topics* |

# KEEPING THE MATTER IN MIND: ARISTOTLE ON THE PASSIONS AND THE SOUL

BY

MICHAEL V. WEDIN

Aristotle's psychology reserves for the person alone such things as thinking, desiring, and feeling pain. The soul itself is the subject of none of this. Nevertheless, only in virtue of the soul, more exactly certain of its parts, does the person manage to be in a given such state or to perform a given such act. So psychological explanation is a kind of levels explanation. What goes on at one level, the level of the person, is explained by what goes on at another, and lower, level of organization.[1] Although I may think the Pythagorean theorem in virtue of the content and operations of my mind, my mind does not think the theorem. *I* do. Moreover, higher level occurrences are effects of lower level occurrences, despite absence of standard casual relations between the levels. Levels causation, as we might call this,[2] is a kind of dependence. This gives rise to reflection about the nature of the dependence relation. One suggestion[3] is that levels causation involves the supervenience of higher level states or events on lower level states or events. In earlier works I develop this suggestion and, on the basis of *Physics* VII.3, examine the merits of a version of supervenience that is consistent with so-called compositional plasticity.[4]

The present paper worries mainly about compositional plasticity itself, specifically, about its fidelity to Aristotle's texts. To be exact, it worries about two texts only—*De Anima* I.1's discussion of anger and the notorious Young Socrates passage from *Metaphysics* Z.11. So its scope is nominally narrow. This is offset by the fact that both passages are prominent players in recent debate. Section I is devoted to anger and Section II to Socrates the Younger. The paper also looks at the relation between compositional plasticity and the proposal that matter is to be included in the forms of natural things. In this regard, the paper's parts

1

are distinctly complementary, with Section I focusing on definitions as they occur in physics and Section II worrying about the ultimate metaphysical reach of such definitions. In particular, I suggest that for the case of interest, the soul, establishing form's plasticity is tantamount to establishing the plasticity of psychological capacities and states.

## I. The Passions

### THE 'CANONICAL DEFINITION' OF ANGER

In the course of discussing those affections of the soul that involve the body (apparently all, to judge by 403a16), Aristotle offers an initial result concerning their definitions:

D. Hence, their definitions are such as, for example, being angry (*orgizesthai*) is a particular movement (*kinēsis tis*) of a body of a certain kind or a part or potentiality <of it>, <caused> by this and for the sake of that (403a26–27).

What this passage has to do with compositional plasticity comes by way of its use in recent discussions of Aristotle's alleged functionalism. Here the line has assumed an importance well exceeding its length. Kathleen Wilkes[5] uses the passage to buttess the fourth of eight parallels that, she argues, establish the essential identity of ancient and modern functionalism. Christopher Shields also appeals to the passage in his brief to make Aristotle the first functionalist[6] and, more recently, S. Marc Cohen[7] finds that the line evinces an openness to the sort of compositional plasticity that contemporary functionalists find congenial. Weighing in against this are a number of formidable figures including, famously, Myles Burnyeat (1992), as well as Alan Code and Julius Moravcsik (1992). The latter, for example, argue that 403a26–27 has nothing to do with compositional plasticity and that, in general, it is simply a mistake to press the functionalist reading of Aristotle.[8] My interest in the first part of the paper is in determining which camp has the better claim to 403a26–27 and the following few lines.

The cited line is something like a schema for defining those affections of the soul that, like anger, involve matter. The following lines exemplify the schema with the case of anger. We might translate these as:

E. But each of these<i.e. *pathe*> will be defined differently by the physicist and the dialectician; for example, what anger is—the dialectician would define it as desire for retaliation or something of this sort (*ti toiouton*), the physicist as the boiling of blood or hot stuff about the heart. One of these gives the matter and the other the form and principle (*to eidos kai to logon*) (403a29–b2).

To ask whether these passages support a functionalist reading is to ask what theses, essential to functionalism, (D) and (E) support and how. For present purposes I shall consider two standardly found in the literature:

(F1) $\psi$ is a psychological state $\rightarrow$ $\psi$ is defined in terms of its causal relations to input, output, and other psychological states,

and

(F2) $\psi$ is a psychological state $\rightarrow$ $\psi$ is compositionally plastic.

Dropping the reference in (F1) to other psychological states yields a stronger version of functionalism, namely, a version that aims to define psychological states in thoroughly non-psychologistic or non-mentalistic terms. So (F1) comports with what Shields (1989) calls weak functionalism. Because they define a psychological state by its functional role, that is, by its causal role in a system's behaviour or out-put, given in certain in-put and other states, neither weak nor strong functionalism places constraints on the kind of material such a state can be realized in. So (F2) is usually paraded as something of a necessary condition for (F1) or its strengthened version.[9]

So which thesis, (F1) or (F2), is supported by which passage and in which version? It will be useful to begin with Shield's recent claim that in (D) Aristotle "explicitly advocates the use of functional definitions" and that it contains Aristotle's "canonical definition" of anger.[10] This presumes that (D) supports (F1). In fact, Shields takes (D) to support strong functionalism. As it stands, however, (D) cannot manage this. First, (D) does not contain a canonical definition of anger at all. Rather, as indicated above, (D) is a general schema for defining all *pathē*; anger is simply the example. So if all *pathē* are defined as (D), then (D) can hardly give the canonical definition of anger. Rather, what is specified is the form of such definitions. And when, in (E), Aristotle turns explicitly to the case of anger, some sort of desire is to be included in the full definition. Yet, surely, desire is a psychological state. So it would appear that neither (D) nor (E) supports strong functionalism.

Passage (D) says only that an affection of the soul, at least those of the sort that anger is, is a certain movement (*kinēsis tis*) of a body caused by something and for the sake of something else. That is, where $\kappa$ is the movement and $x$ and $y$ are different, the affection satisfies the following:

(1) $\kappa$ is caused by $x$ & $\kappa$ is for the sake of $y$.

Immediately, Aristotle says that the physicist and the dialectician define anger differently—and now he is narrowing in on a definition of *anger*. Note that he does not indicate that one of these has better claim to match

(1). Rather, both the physicist and the dialectician are represented as putting forward instances of (1)[11]. Presumably, they do this in the course of offering their differing definitions of anger. So we can take Aristotle to be suggesting that the physicist includes

(1a) *boiling of the blood* is caused by $x$ & *boiling of the blood* is for the sake of $y$,

in his definition, whereas the dialectician includes

(1b) *desire for retaliation* is caused by $x$ & *desire for retaliation* is for the sake of $y$.

So because (E) considers two ways to instantiate the general schema (D) and because one of these involves desire for retaliation, it is hasty in the extreme to conclude that the general schema "provides a definition in wholly non-mentalistic terms."[12] Yet just this is required for strong functionalism. Moreover, (E) at least appears to recommend that *both* (1a) and (1b) are to figure in the canonical definition of anger and allied affections.[13] So, again, strong functionalism is not established.

The surveyed argument for the strong functionalism of (D) comes up short, in part, because it neglects (E). From this, however, it does not follow that (D) and (E) are hostile to a functionalist reading of Aristotle. Cohen 1992, for example, explicitly uses (E) in arguing Aristotle's openness to compositional plasticity, in effect, thesis (F2) above.[14] So it is in this way that the pair of passages welcomes functionalism. While anger must be realized in matter, it cannot be reduced to the boiling of blood about the heart because, according to Cohen, this is just its matter and, in general, form and matter are only contingently related. Thus, something other than boiling of blood about the heart could serve as matter for the psychological stage anger because, presumably, something other than the boiling of the blood could serve as matter for the *form* of anger. In this way the passage comes down on the side of compositional plasticity. As Cohen rightly stresses, the contingency of the relation between form and matter is clear in the case of artifacts (something Code and Moravcsik appear to accept). Moreover, artifacts are standardly adduced to illuminate more complex cases, including living things. Indeed, a point Cohen could press into service, the very passages we are considering go on, at 403b3–7, to liken the case of affections of the soul to the definition of a house. So the immediate context appears to buttress Cohen's claim that the form and matter of psychological states enjoy only a contingent connection.[15]

Code and Moravcsik (1992) give two grounds for rejecting any interpretation of (D) and (E) along these lines:

First, *kinesis* is not here to be construed as a physiological process as opposed to a psychological process. In the cases under consideration, a *kinesis* is simply the actuality of some potentiality possessed by the body, or one of its organs. It is the anger itself that is the *kinesis*, not some underlying physiological state that can be specified independently of the other two factors (agent and purpose). Secondly ... the boiling of the blood is not matter for the anger; rather the boiling is a *kinesis* of blood, the blood being a part of the body and hence matter. Thus, he is not indicating that creatures with very different physiologies could be in the same emotional state (anger) just so long as they have some physiological process that plays the right kind of functional role (loosely described as 'desire for retaliation').

Although not presented as a full-fledged interpretation, these remarks amply reward extended discussion. As the passage sits, the thrust of its argument may prove elusive to some. It will help to make explicit a central background assumption, namely, that for contemporary functionalists the matter that realizes a form or enformed process must be specifiable independently of the form or process itself.

Suppose we characterize this independence requirement as

(2a) $\kappa$ is a form or enformed process & $\kappa$ is functionally realized in $\varphi \rightarrow \varphi$ can be specified independently of $\kappa$.

From Code and Moravcsik's first ground we get something like

(2) $\kappa$ is a *kinesis* involved in psychological state $\psi \rightarrow \kappa$ just is $\psi$,

and

(2′) $\kappa$ just is $\psi \rightarrow \kappa$ cannot be specified in strictly physiological terms.

Theses (2) and (2′) are of a piece with Code and Moravcsik's correct point that for Aristotle the psychological and the physical do not constitute exclusive domains. Otherwise, psychology would not fall, as it does, under physics.

With the background assumption (2a), (2) and (2′) are supposed to yield

(2″) $\kappa$ is a *kinēsis* involved in psychological state $\psi$ & $\kappa$ is an enformed process $\rightarrow \neg \Diamond(\kappa$ is functionally realized in $\varphi$ & $\varphi$ is strictly physiological).

Proposition (2″) says that if you take a psychological state to be an enformed process, as Aristotle does, then it cannot be the case that the state is functionally realized in something that is strictly physiological. But just this is the central thesis of functionalism. So Aristotle's position cannot be combined with functionalism. It is important to note, however, that the inference to (2″) requires assuming, further, that what a psychological state is realized in must itself be something that is involved in the psychological state. Otherwise, (2) will lose its grip in the argument. But this is a loaded notion of involvement because it must support the claim, registered in the consequent of (2'), that the 'stuff' of realization cannot be strictly physiological. On the face of it, this appears simply to beg the question against the functionalist.[16]

Now everything said so far is consistent with finding in Aristotle a sturdier dichotomy between form and matter. Were, thus, boiling of the blood not an enformed process but simply the matter of anger, nothing would prevent its realizing, in a functional way, the psychological state of anger. Code and Moravcsik block this, as a reading of Aristotle, by arguing, in their second ground, that Aristotle denies that boiling of the cardio-blood is the matter for anger, in effect, holding

(3) $\kappa$ is boiling of the blood about the heart $\rightarrow$ $\kappa$ is an enformed *kinēsis* involved in a psychological state.

From (2″) and (3) it follows that anger cannot be functionally realized in boiling of the cardio-blood. Thus, even were form and matter contingently related, in a way friendly to functionalism, Cohen is wrong to suppose that this relation obtains between being angry and blood's boiling. So, at least, Code and Moravcsik.

Note, however, that what they conclude, on the basis of the two grounds, is only that Aristotle is *not indicating* that creatures differently constituted physiologically, may be alike psychologically. This, of course, is true. Friends of compositional plasticity will, however, insist that the question is, rather, what is allowed by what Aristotle explicitly says, not what he explicitly says is allowed. And, so far, nothing blocks the possibility that different matter may realize *both* the physical *kinēsis* and the psychological state. On this view what is essential to the physical *kinēsis* that the anger itself *is* (to adapt Code and Moravcsik's idiom) is the boiling rather than the blood. Other material might do, but boil it must.

To determine whether Aristotle's treatment of the formal and material features of anger excludes compositional plasticity, it will be useful to have in hand some formulations. Taking anger, with Aristotle, as a stock psychological state, we can generate a number of alternative interpretations of the definitional schema in (D). Code and Moravcsik take a psychological state just to be the movement and to be what is caused by something and what is for the sake of something else. So we might try the following as a representation of their view:

(4a) $x$ is psychological state $\rightarrow$ $(\exists y)(y$ is a *kinēsis* of some body & $y = x$ & $y$ is caused by something & $y$ is for the sake of something).

If, on the other hand, the psychological state is different from the movement, then two alternatives emerge:

(4b) *x* is a psychological state → (∃*y*)(*y* is a *kinēsis* of some body & *y* ≠ *x* & *y* is caused by something & *y* is for the sake of something)

and

(4c) *x* is a psychological state → (∃*y*)(*y* is a *kinēsis* of some body & *y* ≠ *x* & *x* is caused by something & *x* is for the sake of something).

On (4b) it is the movement (i.e., *y*) that is caused by something and that is for the sake of something; on (4c) it is the psychological state itself (i.e. *x*). There is no role for this distinction on (4a), where the psychological state and the movement are identified. For the moment I shall use (4a) to develop the analysis.

Immediately, (4a) runs into a slight complication. As a general schema it ought to mesh with Aristotle's example in (E). Now, 403a26–27, the text backing (4a), says that a psychological state is a movement of the body (*kinēsis tou toioudi sōmatos*). So Code and Moravcsik appear to be correct in distinguishing between blood as the body or matter and the boiling as a movement of it. On the other hand, Cohen appears to be on firm ground, for in (E) the physicist is said to give the matter (*ho men tēn hulēn apodidōsin*), when defining anger as the boiling of the blood. To ease the impression of contradiction it is sufficient to point out that not everything mentioned in "giving the matter" need be matter. Thus, it may be enough that the physicist's definition mentions matter, namely, blood, and eschews the form *favoured by the dialectician*, namely, desire for retaliation.[17]

Note, however, that on (4a) the psychological state can only be identified with the *kinēsis* that the physicist alludes to when he "gives the matter." Consequently, there is no room at all for the dialectician's identification of the psychological state with the desire. This is important in light of the fact that Aristotle appears to pursue an evenhanded strategy in the passage. The physicist and dialectician each have equal claim to the truth about anger, but not to the whole truth. The first identifies it with a movement caused in a certain way and for a certain end, the second with a desire for a certain end, resulting from a movement caused in a certain way. Moreover, were we to adapt (4b) or (4c) no room would remain for the physicist's identification of the psychological state with the *kinēsis*. So this is no better off.

What is needed is an account that gives equal footing to the material and the formal features of psychological states, in general, and anger, in particular. To get this, we might try replacing the schema (4a) with

(4d) *x* is in a psychological state *ψ* ≡ (∃*y*)(*y* is a *kinēsis* in or of *x*'s body & *y* is caused by something & *y* is for the sake of something).[18]

Note that (4d) does not require *identifying* the state *ψ* with any single

thing in the conditions. It thus promises to accommodate, on an equal
footing, the claims of the dialectician and the physicist. Applying the
general schema to the case of anger, we get something like the following:

(5) $x$ is angry $\equiv (\exists y)(\exists z)(y$ is a boiling of the blood around $x$'s heart & $z$ is a desire of $x$
for retaliation & $y/z$ is caused by an insult/injury & $y/z$ is for the sake of retaliation).

(5) is not, of course, a straightforward instance of (4d) but it is close
enough to count as an application. So psychological states, generally, and
anger, specifically, are given what might be called benignly reductive
accounts. The reduction is benign because the terms of definition include
other states of the same order—explicitly, in the case of anger, desire for
retaliation, and implicitly, beliefs of the agent about (or awareness of)
apparent insult or injury, etc.

Notice, however that (5) says nothing about the exact relation between
the boiling ($y$) and the desire ($z$). It makes do with the quite informal
slash notation '$y/z$' in attempting to preserve at least the appearance of
parallel roles for matter and form in the account of anger. But sustaining
this appearance is not entirely straightforward. We can see this by
revisiting our two initial descriptions of anger, (1a) and (1b), those of the
physicist and dialectician, respectively. (1a) might be thought odd because
of saying that boiling of the blood is for the sake of something. Surely,
one might object, it cannot be for the sake of *desire* for retaliation but
simply for retaliation. But how, then, can the physicist's description
parallel that of the dialectician, as (1b) suggests? For (1b) would have us
saying:

(1b) (i) *desire for retaliation* is caused by $x$ & (ii) *desire for retaliation* is for the sake of
retaliation,

and some will worry that (ii) installs a tautology where explanation
belongs.

We might try to put a happy face on this by insisting that, strictly
speaking, the boiling of blood about the heart corresponds to the desire
and that the desire itself is for something else, namely, retaliation.
However, this separates desire from its object—something Aristotle would
resist, even were it allowable *tout court*. For an identity condition on any
desire is that it be of this or that object. This suggests that (ii) must be
maintained.

In fact, however, (ii) is not a mere tautology. Desire for retaliation can,
indeed, be for retaliation, so long as this does not amount just to
specifying, as it were, the formal object or content of the desire (that is,
being a desire for retaliation and not a desire for, say, exercise). If the
mention of desire serves, rather, to specify its potential causal role in
*exacting* retaliation, then desire for retaliation will play a causal role in

explaining the agent's output—whether retaliatory action or simply a resolved disposition toward such action. Not only does this preserve the parallel between (1a) and (1b) but also it has the dialectician giving desire a causal role suspiciously like that favored by functionalists for internal states.

## SUPERVENIENCE AND PLASTICITY

The parallel between the dialectical and physical accounts appears to hold up. Still, as (5) is formulated, there need be no relation between the desire and the physical *kinēsis*. This problem does not arise for (4a) because there the desire and the *kinēsis* are identified.[19] But this can hardly count in favour of (4a) because, if anything is clear, it is that the desire ($z$) and the *kinēsis* ($y$) are related as form to matter;[20] yet no one would take Aristotle to identity form and matter. So if the identity of form and matter is rejected, we need an alternative account of the relation between desire and the boiling of blood.

Help may be forthcoming from the fact that the parallel between the physical and dialectical accounts must hold even when (1a) is taken to license the claim that boiling of the blood about the heart is for the sake of retaliation. For this encourages a proposal concerning the relation between (5)'s $y$ and $z$, namely, that the desire for retaliation ($z$) supervenes on the boiling of the cardio-blood ($y$). For we may say that the desire and the boiling are both for the sake of retaliation because the boiling is for the sake of retaliation and the desire supervenes on it. For the desire to be, casually, for the sake of retaliation (i.e, for it to be causally relevant to actualizing retaliatory behaviour), the desire must be materially realized. The boiling of the blood about the heart just is this material realization. This, I believe, is the reason Aristotle brings in the supposedly clearer case of a house at 403b3–9. For, if it is to be (*ei esti*), he says, the form of a thing must be in matter of a certain kind (*en hulēi toiaidi*). On the approved definition, a house is the (a certain) form in matter of this sort (namely, stones, bricks and timbers) for the sake of these other things (namely, shelter from winds, rain, and heat): *en toutois to eidos heneka tondi*. The definition does not specify whether it is the form of the house that is for shelter or the house itself. But if the case is to provide a parallel for anger, it will be the form (at least)[21] that is for the sake of shelter.[22] Moreover, the form can be effectively, as opposed to formally, for the sake of shelter, only if it is realized in an appropriate arrangement of matter. The appropriate arrangement of matter just is its material realization. And, analogously to the case of anger, we can say that the form is effective in actualizing shelter because an appropriate arrangement of matter is effective in actualizing shelter and the form supervenes on it. And, in the letter of Charles 1989 and the spirit of Lewis 1989,[23] the form says what the materials are *for*. So the form suffers no reduction in its explanatory role.

This way of looking at (D) and (E) brings the case of anger much closer
to the cases from *Phys.* VII.3, discussed in Wedin (1993a), where form is
held to supervene on matter. And because that discussion entertained a
version of supervenience that explicitly allows for multiple realizability,[24]
we need to press further Aristotle's openness to the possibility that anger
is compositionally plastic. Can, that is, the form of anger, namely, desire
for retaliation, be realized in matter other than blood or boiling of blood?
In short, is (5) compatible with compositional plasticity?

Cole and Moravscik argue against compatibility on the grounds that
the boiling of the blood cannot be specified independently of its cause
and purpose. This is so, presumably, because for them anger just is the
*kinēsis*, boiling of the blood. Of course, unlike (4a), which they favor,
(5) does not share this presumption. But even if one follows Code and
Moravcsik and identifies anger with the physical *kinēsis*, one need not
follow them on compositional plasticity. What is correct here is that one
can not plausibly specify a given *kinēsis* as *anger* unless one specifies it
relative to an appropriate cause and purpose. But because the blood yields
to independent specification so must its boiling. So *qua* boiling of blood
the *kinēsis* is independently specifiable, *qua* anger, or perhaps, retaliatory,
desire, it is not.[25]

Still, it might appear that compositional plasticity is ruled out by the
very formulation of (5). For, assuming it to be universally closed, (5)
counts the boiling of the blood about the heart as a *necessary* condition
for anger.[26] Thus, a psychological state realized in materially different
stuff or underwritten by a physiologically different process would not be
anger. There are two responses available to friends of plasticity. First,
Aristotle says that anger will be desire for retaliation or *something of this
sort (ti toiouton)*. So if the *kinēsis* that turns out to be anger just is the
desire for retaliation, then Aristotle allows room for something else to
play its role. Hence, compositional plasticity remains alive. (This assumes
that "*ti toiouton*" is in the text not merely to connote the provisional
nature of the "desire for retaliation" formula[27]). But even if this response
is rejected, possibly on the grounds that (5) does not expressly identify
the *kinēsis* (i.e., $y$) and the desire (i.e., $z$),[28] a second is at hand. For, as
Code and Moravscik rightly insist, Aristotle simply "is not indicating that
creatures with very different physiologies could be in the same emotional
state ...." That is, on their view, the passage simply does not address this
issue. But precisely because of this, (5) cannot *exclude* compositional
plasticity. For the thesis of compositional plasticity promotes the in-
principle *possibility* of psychological invariance across physiological
variation: Tralfamadoreans, as well as Earthlings, may exhibit anger. To
exclude this, (5) must be a necessary equivalence. But it is not. Hence, it
is consistent with compositional plasticity. Moreover, if the relation
between form and matter is everywhere contingent, as Cohen urges, then
(5) may positively welcome plasticity.[29]

Finally, there is a natural connection between a (5) open to compositional plasticity and versions of supervenience that are friendly to functionalism. Recall that for Code and Moravcsik boiling of the blood is not the matter for anger, but a *kinēsis* of the matter, namely, blood. The version of supervenience assayed in Wedin (1993a)[30] accommodates this by taking boiling to be a property of the matter of the supervenient base and desiring of retaliation to be a property supervening on it. Thus, the boiling of the blood at *t* is sufficient for occurrence of the desire at *t*; moreover, it is sufficient on its own, without the instrumentality of form.[31] But this is necessitation without explanation. In order to explain *what* the boiling of the blood is or is *for*, we need the form. That is, to explain the role of the boiling, we must connect it up with the desiring of retaliation. Aristotle would do this by saying that the desiring is the form imposed on the boiling. We do it by saying that the desiring supervenes on the boiling, or alternatively, that the boiling subserves the desiring. When these relations obtain, we have anger.[32]

WORRIES ABOUT SUPERVENIENCE

This use of supervenience will not, however, please everyone. Burnyeat (1992), for example, argues that Aristotle cannot allow that the desire for retaliation supervenes on the boiling of the blood because this would require "that determination is 'from the bottom up'," something Aristotle would flatly deny. Although Wedin (1993a) has already quarrelled with this for the case of *Phys.* VII.3, Burnyeat's argument calls for an independent appraisal because he finds Aristotle's denial to be alive and well in *De An.* I.1 itself, indeed, in the very portion of the chapter we have been discussing. He says (1992, 23): "Thus when one is angry, the blood boils, but that is merely a necessary, not a sufficient condition for anger; hence one's body, as he [Aristotle] puts it, can be agitated and in the state is is in when one is angry without one's actually being angry (403a21-2). The extra element needed is that an occasion for retaliation should be noticed by the agent."

There is a textual point and a conceptual point here. The textual point is best made by supplying the context of the cited line:

A sign of this <that all affections of the soul are with matter> is that (i) sometimes severe and striking affections (*pathēmata*) occur without our being provoked to exasperation or fear, while at other times (ii) we are moved by what is slight and barely noticeable—when the body is agitated and in the sort condition is in when we[33] are angry (*hoton orgai to sōma kai houtōs echē hōsper hotan orgizētai*, a21-22).[34] And this is even clearer, (iii) for many may come to have the affections of one who is frightened even though nothing frightening occurs (403a19-24).

So Burnyeat's cited line, 403a21-22 gives the middle of three cases, all of which are supposed to provide grounds for the central thesis, given earlier at 403a16–17, that all affections of the *soul* are with the body (*ta tēs psuchēs pathē panta einai meta sōmatos*).

It is difficult to see how 403a21–22 could support such an embodiment thesis, if the lines say that one can be in the physical state standardly realized when one is angry and yet not be angry. This reading does not render the lines incompatible with the embodiment thesis but it does make them irrelevant to it. Besides, the lines may not say quite what Burnyeat says they say. In particular, to say that the body is in a state like the state it is in when the person is angry does not *entail* that the person not be angry. Aristotle's point is rather that whenever the body is aroused and is in the state it is standardly in when one is angry, then a very slight provocation can elicit an outburst. And nothing here entails that the agent is not angry.[35] This, I submit, is simply irrelevant to 403a21–22's function in the passage, which is to give a case where the person's physical state matters in a way that shows how the affections (*pathē*) are not without the body.[36] It is precisely angry persons who strike out at the slightest provocation and they do so precisely because they are in the requisite physical state. Hence, psychological states or affections are not 'without matter.' Likewise, the person whose body is not agitated will be considerably less susceptible to provocation. But such a person is in a calmer *psychological* state; and were his bodily condition not calm, then he would not be in this state, that is, in the state that explains his reserved response.

Nor is it clear to what extent, or even whether, the agent must "notice an occasion for retaliation" in order to react with anger. The canonical definition of anger, (5), requires only that something cause the desire for retaliation, and phenomenologically speaking, nothing prevents this from arising straightaway without any special 'noticing.' So the cases appear to suggest that appeal to the physical state of the body is sufficient to explain this. Moreover, although the cases require that something cause the response, causes may be invariant across widely variant responses and so difference in response is to be explained primarily by the physical state of the agent. These cases aim to show, then, that the physical condition of the body is central to explaining a person's responses and, hence, to explaining what psychological state he is in. Thus, they underscore the point, made some eight paragraphs back, that for desire to have causal punch relevant to retaliation (as it must if it is to count as anger), it must be materially realized.

What the cases do not show is that a person can be in the physical state standardly associated with a given psychological state without being in that psychological state. Neither, however, do they rule this out. This brings us to the conceptual point that anger requires something more than a physical state, namely, the agent's belief that this state is caused by something deserving of retaliation. Here Burnyeat is quite correct. Moreover, this is hardly something we could deny, since it is, in effect, entailed by our canonical definition (5). But we need to be careful in asking what this correct conceptual point shows. It does not, at least not obviously, show that one can be in the same physical state one is in when one is angry without being angry. Not, at least, if one holds with Code and Moravcsik that the anger just is the *kinēsis*. For by (5) the anger will be identical with a movement that is caused by something and that is for the sake of something else. But the same holds even if the anger is not identified with the movement, so long as the movements that are relevant to psychological states are individuated by causes and effects. And in any event the claim we are trying out is that the *form* of the psychological state supervenes on the movement thus specified.[37]

So the cases discussed at 403a19–24 cannot be used to establish that psychological states are independent of correlated physical states.[38] This does not, of course, entail that they supervene on such states, but it is consistent with such supervenience. In fact, however, there may be reason to take the cases as favouring the stronger reading. We can see this by revisiting the point that all three cases are introduced as evidence for the embodiment thesis, namely, the thesis that psychological states come with the body (*meta sōmatos*). Initially introduced at 403a16–17, the thesis is held to be entailed by the fact that psychological states such as anger and fear occur at the very moment that the body is affected in a certain way (*hama gap toutois paschei ti to sōma*, 403a17–19).[39] So the occurrence of a psychological state is simultaneous with the occurrence of a physical state. Then come our three cases, followed by a general remark about the sorts of things psychological states are:

If this is how things are, it is clear that the affections are enmattered formulae (*logoi enuloi*) (403a24–25).

Finally, it is because affections of the soul are just such enmattered structures that we are to define them as required in (D), the passage cited at the beginning of the paper.

Since we have argued that the schema given in (D), along with its exemplification in (E), is consistent with the supervenience reading, it would not be surprising to find this reflected in the three cases discussed in 403a19–24. Consider, in particular, the third case. Aristotle says that a man can have the *affections* proper to one who is afraid, even though nothing fearful has actually occurred. Now this is supposed to support not only the embodiment thesis, but also the claim that fear and the like occur simultaneously with the occurrence of certain physical states, as well as the claim that they are just are a certain kind of structure in a certain kind of matter. And this, we have seen, is reflected in their appropriate definitions, definitions such as (5). At the moment, however, the point I wish to stress is that it is arguable that the third case can support the embodiment thesis and, especially, the thesis that affections are enmattered structures, only if the psychological state itself *supervenes* on the correlated physical state(s). For, if psychological states are independent of physical states, that is, if they are not determined by the occurrence of the physical state, it is hard to see why Aristotle would regard them as enmattered structures of any kind.[40] And, if they depend on some physical state(s) without supervening on them, then it is hard to see why he would describe them as enmattered *formulae (logoi enuloi)*. So it is at least arguable that psychological states, as enmattered items of a certain kind, are superveniently dependent on the correlated physical state(s).[41]

The affections one has when one is afraid (to stay with case (iii) discussed above) are, presumably, matched by the affection(s) one has when one is angry (to revert to the canonical definition), that is, by desire for retaliation. It is because anger is an enmattered item of this short that its definition must mention the matter (i.e,. the physical *kinēsis*) as well as the form (the desire for retaliation). Anger itself, will, in the first instance, supervene on the desire and the physical *kinēsis*. Only because of the supervenience between these latter two items can the anger itself be said to supervene on the physical *kinēsis* proper. Just this was suggested by the case of affections appropriate to fear in the absence of something fearful. But even if the supervenience of form (desire) on matter (the *kinēsis*) is denied, we still have a kind of partial supervenience for anger. Moreover, it is consistent with this that the form and, hence, the desire be realized in different sorts of matter. Hence, denial of full supervenience for anger is consistent with its compositional plasticity.

## II. The Soul

At this point it is natural to object that, in characterizing anger as so much boiling of the blood. Aristotle is giving a *definition* of anger. Hence, as a matter of definition, anger *could not* be realized in anything other than blood. So compositional plasticity falls by the wayside. This is a tempting maneuver, but one that ought to be fundamentally resisted. For the definitions recommended for purposes of investigation in physics are definitions in a reduced sense only, *precisely because they involve matter*. Because of his stake in actual, matter-of-fact explanation, the physicist had better well focus on psychologically real models when he addresses the question of what structures realize psychological functions. Here possible realizations are no more relevant than they would be for today's neurophysiologist. Not so for the metaphysician, who is concerned with the modal properties of form. His definitions, definitions in the metaphysically strict sense, are purely formal and, as such, they alone provide the testing ground for what is essentially a modal issue, namely, what sorts of stuff could realize a given form. By the same token, here is where the debate over compositional plasticity is to be decided.

KEEPING THE MATTER IN MIND

The fact that *De An.* I.1, 403b3–7, uses the definition of house to illuminate cases such as anger further recommends scrutiny of the role of form proper in definition as a means to clarifying the plasticity of psychological states. Nonetheless, some might object that anger is not a substance anyway and so could not have a strict definition and from this they might conclude that discussion of the modal properties of form proper is simply irrelevant to the possible plasticity of psychological states. But this miscasts the issue. It is common now to cast questions about the plasticity of the mind, for example, in terms of the plasticity of mental states. This is a point of principle and so can be applied to Aristotle's discussion: if the soul (the lead case of the form of a substance) is compositionally plastic, then so must be its chief faculties. But the latter makes sense only if the functions of such facilities, in turn, enjoy plasticity. And this, in turn, would make sense only if the states correlated with such functions are themselves realizable in more than one sort of material. So the compositional plasticity of states such as anger is something of a necessary condition for the plasticity of the soul itself. To this extent, establishing the soul's plasticity establishes the plasticity of psychological states. This would complement the results of the first part of the paper. So it is pretty clear that we should take a closer look at the object of metaphysically fit definitions, namely, form itself.

## METAPHYSICS Z.11 ON THE PURIFICATION OF FORM

In two passages of *Met.* Z.11 Aristotle appears, first, to raise, and then, to dash hopes for a compositionally plastic reading of form's relation to matter. The first of these, 1036a31–b7, I call, for reasons soon to be apparent, the Thought-Experiment passage; the second, 1036b24–32, is the notorious Young Socrates passage.

Suppose we begin with the uncontroversial claim that psychological functions ($\psi$ings) are linked to physical structures in something like the following way:

(6) $x$ $\psi$s → there is a form or definable structure in virtue of which $x$ $\psi$s.

Now even if the form in question is the structure of a certain portion of the matter of $x$'s body, it does not follow that (6) embraces a kind of materialism friendly to compositional plasticity. At least not according to Code and Moravscik (1992),[42] who insist that such a reading of (6) would require attributing to Aristotle the more controversial thesis that *whatever* enables a subject to $\psi$, regardless of its material realization, is the functional equivalent of say, the organ of sight. The trouble, according to Code and Moravscik, is that debates about compositional plasticity, in anything approaching contemporary guise, proceed largely by means of thought experiments, a device alien to ancient disputation.

In one critically placed passage, however, Aristotle appears to don modern dress, namely, in what I am calling the Thought-Experiment passage. It reads as follows.

[TH] Whatever is found to occur in things that are specifically different, as the circle is found to occur in bronze and stone and wood, it seems to be clear that these are no part of the substance of the circle, neither the bronze nor the stone, because it is separated from them. Whatever is not seen to occur separately, nothing prevents things from being similar in these cases, just as were all circles that had been observed bronze; for it would no less be the case that the bronze is no part of the form. But it is hard to separate this in thought. For example, the form of man (*to tou anthrōpou eidos*) is always found in flesh and bones and parts of this sort. Are these, therefore, parts of the form and the formula (*ar' oun kai esti tauta merē tou eidous kai tou logou*)? No, rather they are matter (*ē ou all' hulē*, b5) but because it <the form> does not also occur in something else we are unable to separate it (*alla dia to mē kai ep' allōn epigignesthai adunatoumen chōrisai* (1036a31–b7).

As it stands, the Thought-Experiment passage appears designed precisely to make the point that a form is not to include matter, not even that matter, if any, in which it is always and characteristically realized. The pure reading, or PURITY as I shall call it, takes "*ē ou*" at 1036b5 to initiate an answer to the original question rather than to continue it. So I read it in the above translation. Here I follow Ross (1924) and Frede and Patzig (1988). But if the question continues to the end of the passage, a quite different reading suggests itself. Burnyeat and others (1979, 88–89), for example, paraphrase 1036b5–7 as follows: "Are the flesh and bones in which we always find the form of man themselves part of the form and the definition, or are they (inessential) matter which, like the bronze of the hypothetical bronze circles, we find ourselves unable to separate because it is never actually found separate?" This paraphrase will prove inviting to proponents of the impure reading. For IMPURITY, as I call their view, has Aristotle rejecting the claim that the matter characteristically realizing a form is mere matter and accepting the claim that is part of the form.[43]

My remarks will focus mainly on the pure reading because even here it remains an open question whether compositional plasticity is forthcoming and this is our immediate concern. The pure reading also strikes me as more likely, for three reasons. First, the impure reading appears to reverse, or at least to occlude, the order of explanation indicated in the text. For now the thought experiment (all circles being bronze) serves to explain a case that is hardly in need of this sort of analogical explication. On IMPURITY itself, the form of man is already and unproblematically realized in a specific sort of matter, namely, flesh and bones. To explain this it would hardly make sense to appeal to a hypothetical, indeed, counter-factually hypothetical case. So on IMPURITY the analogy has no real work to do, contrary to Aristotle's indication. Second, the impure reading says that flesh, bones and the like are not mere matter but belong to the form. But if any matter is fit to be smuggled into the form, it would have to be functional matter—fingers, legs, and the like. But in *Met.* Z.10 and 11 this matter is *contrasted with* flesh and bones and these are remnant matter, the matter into which an organism is resolved upon passing away.[44] This matter can exist without the form and, hence, can hardly be part of the form, as IMPURITY requires. Finally, it should be pointed out that the impure reading is not required, even if "$\bar{e}$ *ou*" at 1036b5 of [TH] is taken to continue the question.[45] For the question could be, simply, whether flesh and bones are part of the form or whether, rather, they are matter but we are unable to separate the form from the matter because the form does not occur in any other matter. On PURITY the first is answered negatively and the second affirmatively. Moreover, the affirmative answer is made on the strength of the hypothetical case and, so, unlike the impure reading, PURITY gives the Thought-Experiment itself a central role in the argument.

For these reasons I shall restrict myself to the pure reading. Purists take the Thought-Experiment passage to assert

(7) (i) The circle is found in various material realizations → (ii) the matter is not part of the form of circle,

and compositionally minded purists might hold, in addition,

(8) The matter is not part of the form of circle → (iii) the form of circle can exist without a specific (kind of) material realization.

The difference here is not slight, for the generalization of (8) is equivalent to

(8') A form cannot exist without a specific (kind of) material realization → matter is part of the form

and this will be rejected by certain purists[46] even if affirmed by others.[47] Nonetheless, if nothing in [TH] blocks (8), the analogy between man and circle would allow us to move, on the basis of (7) and (8), to

(iii') The form of man can exist without a given material realization,

which will please compositionally liberal purists.

Now Aristotle says that even were (i) to fail, (ii) could hold—after all (i) is only a sufficient condition of (ii). And he seems to say just this about the form of man, that is, he seems to assert something like

(8*) ¬(The form of man, $f_m$, is realized in $m_m$ only → $m_m$ is part of $f_m$).

Notice that (8*) does not contradict (8') because the antecedent of the negated conditional in (8*) is weaker. So it might be thought that

(8!) The form of man can be realized in $m_m$ only → $m_m$ is a part of $f_m$

holds. But Aristotle does not assert (8!). Indeed, he says that even if we *can't* separate $f_m$ from $m_m$, the matter is still no part of the form. That is, he maintains

(8**) ¬(The form of man can't be conceived to be in anything but $m_m$ → $m_m$ is a part of $f_m$).

(8**) gives the cash value of the Thought-Experiment passage. Despite our inability to conceive of men being constituted of something other than flesh and bones, such matter is no part of man's form. And this is shown by the analogy with the circle. To put the point generally, even if one cannot conceive of a different (kind of) material realization for things of a given kind, still the matter will be no part of the form(s) of such things.

So far I am in agreement with purists such as Frede and Patzig. But the matter is slightly more complicated with respect to Code and Moravscik. As purists, they ought to be attracted to (8**). But (8**) appears to clash with (8'), which they find contained in the Thought-Experiment passage. In response they claim, first, that the Thought-Experiment passage is thoroughly aporematic and, hence, that Aristotle is not speaking in his own voice. Thus, presumably, he is setting up but not endorsing (8'). Further, they hold that when Aristotle does speak in his own voice, namely, in the Young Socrates passage, he officially rejects compositional plasticity. To some extent, then, the aporematic reading of the Thought-Experiment passage feeds off the perception of conflict between it and the Young Socrates passage. So if this perception can be removed, so can much of the motivation for the aporematic reading. One might do this by tinkering with the Young Socrates passage or by expelling (8') from the Thought-Experiment passage.

Before the proposed tinkering, what can be said about (8')? Well, one thing that is clear is the central position of (8**). Strictly speaking, however, it is not clear that it contradicts (8'), as Code and Moravscik seem to assume. For this requires the existence of an entailment, in either direction, between the impossibility of $x$'s existing without $y$ and the impossibility of conceiving of $x$'s existing without $y$. And it is not obvious that there is such an entailment. Although this undercuts the attraction of the aporematic reading, it will not please those purists who object to (8').[48] Such noncompositional purists can, however, challenge (8) itself. For if all agree that (8**) plays a central role in the Thought-Experiment passage, it is not clear that (8) even makes an appearance there. Throughout, they may insist, Aristotle is concerned with what is conceptually possible not with what is metaphysically possible. This at least appears to be the explicit force of his remarks, and accordingly, (8') may be set aside. Therefore, the Thought-Experiment passage appears to come down on the side of PURITY, albeit noncompositional purity, concerning the relation of form to matter.

Notice, however, that noncompositional purity is compatible with compositional plasticity. For in rejecting (8) noncompositionalists simply deny that there is any *entailment* from matter's not being part of the form to the possibility that the form exist without that specific sort of matter. This leaves it open whether the possibility might be urged, or rejected, on other grounds. And, indeed, this is exactly where the possibility remains when we arrive at the Young Socrates passage.[49]

SOCRATES THE YOUNGER ON THE SOUL OF MAN

If the Thought-Experiment passage is neutral on compositional plasticity, the Young Socrates passage is decidedly not. This, at least, is the dominant opinion among Aristotle's commentators. For impurists this is unsurprising: inclusion of matter in the form is deemed sufficient to exclude the form's compositional plasticity. But as we have just seen, noncompositional purists could join the ranks on this point, arguing that matter's exclusion is consistent with denial of form's plasticity. Despite such agreement, it seems to me that the text establishes neither the impurist nor the purist case against compositional plasticity.

The Young Socrates passage is introduced by four lines that claim to summarize some portion of the proceeding discussion falling between it and the Thought-Experiment passage. Here is the summary text, as I shall call it, followed by the Young Socrates passage itself.

[SU] That there are some difficulties concerning definitions, and why this is so, we have discussed. Hence (*dio*), to reduce everything in this way (*to panta anagein houtō*, b22) and to leave out the matter (*aphairein tēn hulēn*) is useless, for some things are probably (*isōs*) a this in a that (*tod' en tōid'*) or <the> that in a particular state (*hōdi tadi echonta*) (1036b21–24).

[YS] And the comparison (*parabolē*) that Socrates the Younger used to make in the case of animal is not happy, for it leads away from the truth (*apagei apo tou alēthous*) and makes one suppose that there could be a man without the parts, as there can be a circle without the bronze. But these are not similar, for an animal is a certain perceptible thing (*aisthēton ti to zōion*, b28)[50] and cannot be defined without movement (*aneu kinēseōs ouk estin horisasthai*) nor, thus, without the parts being conditioned in a certain way. For not in any old way is a hand a part of man but only when it is capable of exercising its function, thus, only when it is ensouled. If it is not ensouled, it is not a part (*mē empsuchos de ou meros*) (1036b24–32).

I shall raise two questions about the pair of passages. First, (Q1), do they show, as many hold, that Aristotle's official position is that the matter of man is part of the form of man? If not, (Q2) does it follow that the form of man is after all compositionally plastic?

We may begin by noting that the *'dio'* at 1036b22 in [SU] suggests that the mentioned difficulties for definitions are connected with a distinctly anti-reductionist sentiment on Aristotle's part. That is,

(A1) Reducing everything in this way and eliminating the matter,

is useless because

(A2) Some things are no doubt a this in a that or a that in a certain state.

So it appears that (A2) is sufficient to defeat (A1). But what exactly is the target of attack? This will depend, on part, on how we read 'in this way' (*houtō*) at 1036b22. Where, in short, has the (A1) reduction occurred? At first glance, it would not seem to be in the Thought-Experiment passage, for that passage says nothing about eliminating matter. Even supposing its "separation in thought" (*aphelein tēi dianoiai* at 1036b3) to match the notion of elimination in the Summary text (*aphairein tēn hulēn* at 1036b23), the Thought-Experiment passage presses the difficulty of separating the form from the matter but the Summary text worries about separating or eliminating the matter.

More likely, the reference is to the Pythagoreanizing underway in the intervening text, 1036b7–20. If so, then (A1) probably is not to be taken as a unit. Rather, its first part, the reduction of everything "in this way", would refer to the intervening text's reduction of all things to numbers (note the parallel language at 1036b12: *anagousi panta eis tous arithmous*), and, presumably, to the extension of this to all things' being one in form and, hence, to everything's being one. How, then, does the second part of (A1), the elimination of matter, fit into the picture? Well, if we assume that numbers, as mathematical objects, are non-material then the reduction of all things to numbers would entail the elimination of at least perceptible matter and this latter is precisely the stuff of human beings.[51]

Code and Moravcsik, on the other hand, accommodate the worry about eliminating matter by reading it as a worry eliminating matter from the definition. The implicit endorsement here, that form is to include matter, will please impurists but it can hardly be sustained in view of the fact that Aristotle's worry about (A1) is based on (A2) alone and this is simply not enough for the wanted endorsement.[52]

In effect, Aristotle's qualms about (A1) amount to the point that both form and matter are needed to account for at least some things, saliently, of course, natural things. Hence, no more than one could get by simply with matter can one get by simply without matter.[53] But this does not require that matter be mentioned in the definitions of such things or that it be part of their form(s). So far as the Summary text is concerned, then, a negative answer to Q1 is still open. Thus, purists are free to read the Thought-Experiment passage as eliminating matter from the definition without threat from the Summary text. Of course, this will amount to little, if the requirement is established in the Young Socrates passage proper. So we come finally to it.

Socrates the Younger suffers mention elsewhere,[54] but only *Met.* Z.11 addresses his philosophical views. And here we are told very little, only that he was fond of a certain comparison involving animal (the YS-comparison):

(9) Animal is compared to something, $x$.

We are also favored with Aristotle's opinion of the view, namely,

(9a) The YS-comparison leads away from the truth,

and

(9b) The YS-comparison makes one suppose there could be a man without the parts.

Now, presumably, (9b) explains (9a). Our question, then, concerns the intended value of $x$, in (9), such that (9b) results. Although not explicit on the point, the text does provide grounds for an educated guess because Aristotle expands (9b) as

(9b) The YS-comparison makes one suppose there could be a man without the parts as there could be a circle without the bronze.

We may plausibly infer from this that the $x$ in the YS-comparison is the or a circle. So (9) is completed as

(9') Animal is compared to $x$ & $x$ is the/a circle.

As it stands, (9') has three interpretations, all attested at different places in *Met.* Z.10–11: $x$ may be a perceptible circle, a mathematical (noetic) circle, or a purely formal item, namely, the form itself. Because (9b)'s anomalous result concerns the existence of *a man* without parts, Aristotle is not even entertaining the question whether the *form* could exist without parts let alone without matter. So the comparison in (9') must be to the perceptible or to the mathematical circle, both of which are concrete particulars. But since the parts that are mentioned are bronze segments (presumably) rather than noetic segments, the YS-comparison is clearly to the bronze circle.

We may begin, then, by asking how the circle can exist without the bronze. And here there are two cases:

(A) The circle may exist as a concrete circle in some perceptible matter other than bronze;

and

(B) The circle may exist as a concrete circle in noetic, rather than, perceptible matter (such as bronze).

On (A), bronze is a specific determinate kind of perceptible matter; on (B), it stands in for any perceptible matter whatever. So if (A) is the contrasting case, then it would appear that Socrates the Younger is faulted for suggesting that the form of man is compositionally plastic. If, however, (B) is the contrasting case, then the fault would lie with the implication that the form of man could exist in something like noetic matter. In faulting this, nothing need be said about the form's compositional plasticity (in any interesting sense) but simply about its being in perceptible rather than noetic matter. But note, further, that on option (A) is still does not follow that matter is part of the form. For the most this option inveighs against is that *a man*—a concrete particular—should exist without its parts.

It is quite natural for Aristotle to continue by saying that an animal is a *perceptible thing*, thereby enabling us to retain 1036b28's *aisthēton* rather than adopting Frede and Patzig's popular emendation, *aisthētikon*.[55] More to the point, an animal is that sort of concrete thing that, unlike the concrete circle, can only be a perceptible thing.[56] This suggests that (B) is the intended point of contrast and so this would be the first dissimilarity between men and circles. Moreover, man is the sort of perceptible thing that is defined by a certain kind of motion. This, I take it, is the second and more critical dissimilarity.

So we get[57]

(10)  $\neg\Diamond(x$ is an animal & $x$ is defined without mention of motion),

or, perhaps, more perspicuously for our purposes,

(10′)  $\Box(x$ is an animal $\rightarrow x$ is defined by reference to motion).

(10) and (10′) record unusual brevity, even by Aristotle's standards. But it is not unreasonable to suppose that in mentioning motion, they in effect bring in *De Anima's* notion of a second actualization (actualization$_2$).

Then (10)/(10') amount to the claim that an animal is defined by certain characteristic activities or exercises of functions or movements involving these. On this reading, for the parts to be in a certain state is just for them to be capable of exercising these actual$_2$ functions. Aristotle gets this by, in effect, extending the consequent of (10'):

(11) $x$ is defined by motion → $x$ has parts & $x$ is defined by its parts being in a certain state.

From (10') and (11) we get

(12) $\Box(x$ is an animal → $x$ is defined by reference to $x$'s parts being in a certain state).

Now if we take (12), reasonably, to contrast with (9b) above, then we get

(13) $x$ is defined by reference to $x$'s parts being in a certain state → $\neg\Diamond(x$ is an animal & $x$ can exist without its parts),

as something like the grand upshot of the passage.

Were the consequent of (11) to assert only that $x$'s parts are to be in a certain state, the definition of animal would not need to mention the parts at all, but simply the characteristic functions. If, on the other hand, the parts' being in a certain state is actually mentioned in the definition, then it is incumbent on Aristotle to say something about *how* an animal is related to its parts, such that they are mentioned in the definition. The fact that Aristotle proceeds to address just this point suggests that he prefers this second alternative, which is encoded in (11).

But notice that, even if the parts are somehow included in the definition, (13) still does not say that matter is to be included in the form nor that Young Socrates' mistake was to exclude it. In fact, it does not even say that a man cannot exist without matter, although this is doubtless true. So exactly how matter enters the picture is somewhat unclear.[58]

Now (12) is supposed to distinguish the case of the circle from that of man. But clearly the consequent, as it stands, does nothing in this service. For one could argue that the segments of a thing, treating these as its parts, must be in a certain state if the thing is to be a circle. Now, of course, one might point out that the circle is not defined in terms of its parts being in a certain condition. This is simply because the circle is not defined in terms of its constituent parts at all. But from this it would not follow that man and circle are contrasted on the point that the first is defined in terms of certain *material* parts and the second in terms of nonmaterial parts. Rather, the crucial point is that the parts be *conditioned* in some way. So we must understand the clause in the way we have suggested, as saying that the parts must be in a state that enables the animal to move, that is, that enables the animal to exercise its characteristic functions. The parts of a man, so characterized, do follow from the definition, but the parts of the circle, whatever their make-up or characterization, do not.[59]

This explains why (13) does not have the impure consequence that matter belongs to the form. For there are two versions of the claim that is crucial to (13):

(13a) $x$ is defined by reference to $p_1...p_n$ & $p_1...p_n$ are remnant parts $\rightarrow$ $x$ cannot exist without $p_1...p_n$.

and

(13b) $x$ is defined by reference to $p_1...p_n$ & $p_1...p_n$ are functional parts $\rightarrow$ $x$ cannot exist without $p_1 ...p_n$.

Thesis (13a) is pretty clearly false[60] but (13b) may well be true. In any case, it is the version Aristotle wants. This is clear from the support offered for (12).

The support does not amount simply to reiterating the familiar cant that the hand separated from the man is a hand in name only. Aristotle says, more emphatically, that it is not a part at all of the man. In short order, we get

(14) $x$ is a hand and a part of a man $\rightarrow$ $x$ is capable of functioning in hand-like ways.

(14') $x$ is capable of functioning in hand-like ways $\rightarrow$ $x$ is ensouled,

and, so,

(15) $x$ is a hand and a part of a man $\rightarrow$ $x$ is ensouled.

According to (15) nothing can be both a hand and a part of a man unless it is ensouled because no such thing can function in its characteristic ways unless it is ensouled. In effect, Aristotle here follows the practice, familiar from the psychology, of defining faculties (and antecedently their organs) in terms of functions and explicating the latter in terms of the form of the system as a whole. On my reading, (14') commits Aristotle to just this.

Now, however, we face a slight anomaly. For (12) insists that an animal is to be defined in terms of its parts being in a certain state. Suppose, as purists, that we enforce here Z.10–11's insistence that only the form and formal parts are to be mentioned in definitions (adding, perhaps, that definitions be allowed to apply to concrete particulars because these are definable insofar as their forms are definable). Then it ought to follow, as (12) reports, that man is defined in terms of his parts so long as these are something like formal parts. So, by (12), man is defined by reference to certain parts; but, by (15), these parts themselves are defined by reference to the whole system (the form of the man). This has the look of an uncomfortably close circle.

Perhaps, however, the idea behind (12), is that when one has properly specified *all* the parts that are definable in the sense of (14)–(15), then one has, in effect, given a specification of the form of man. Propositions (14)–(15) concern only particular parts or functions. While the form is not defined in terms of any single such part or function, when all have been properly specified so has man's form. So what looked like a circle might turn out to be only a closed curve in semantic space, particularly if the individual functions can be specified without actually mentioning *man*.[61] This solution works, of course, only because the parts mentioned in (12) are functional parts. So regardless of our preference for (A) or (B) above as the official reading of the YS-comparison in (9'), we are stuck with parts that are functional parts.

How, then, does (12) bear on our question (Q1)? Does form include matter after all? A number of more global considerations make it convenient for Aristotle to answer this question negatively.[62] Here, however, my concern is with the possibility of a pure reading of just the Young Socrates passage. On one quite attractive suggestion, due to Frede and Patzig (1988), in the Young Socrates passage Aristotle continues to hold

(16a) The definition (of man) is not to include matter,

and so champions a purist reading of the relation of form to matter. Closeness of fit between form and matter is, rather, to be explained by

(16b) The definition (of man) displays, by itself, what kind of matter can realize the form.

As something of a corollary to (16b), they add

(17) Only one kind of matter can realize the form (of man).

For purists the general thrust of Frede and Patzig's solution will be hard to resist, particularly (16a) and (16b).[63]

## THE CASE AGAINST PURITY

Not all commentators see PURITY in the soul of Socrates the Younger. Indeed, for some the Young Socrates passage is prime evidence for form's IMPURITY. So a closer look at the impure reading is in order. It will be useful to begin with Whiting's recent critique of Frede and Patzig's purist reading.[64] I shall argue that the attack fails to touch the heart of their position and, to that extend, that it does not advance the cause of IMPURITY. Although on some points I shall part company with Frede and Patzig, in the end PURITY emerges unscathed.

Suppose we begin with Whiting's worries about (16a). Purists go wrong in failing to appreciate the parallel between *Met. Z.*11 and E.1. So Whiting begins with

(18) Z.11 parallels E.1

She next looks at *Met.* E.1's distinction between objects of physics and objects of mathematics: "... Aristotle distinguishes the objects of physics (which include souls) from the objects of mathematics by arguing that the essences of physical objects contain perceptible matter in a way in which the essences of mathematical objects do not" (1992, 627). Let us enter this as

(19) The way essences of objects of physics contain perceptible matter differs from the way objects of mathematics contain perceptible matter.

Now there does appear to be some support for (19). Concerning the objects of physics, Aristotle says, at 1026a2–3, that "none of them can be defined without reference to motion... rather they always have matter (*outhenos gar aneu kinēseōs ho logos autōn, all' aei echei hulēn*)." Moreover, he goes on to say that all objects of physics, including animal in general, are to be defined like the snub (*to simon*). This gives the cash value of his admonition that we should not overlook *how* their essences and their definitions are (*dei de to ti ēn einai kai ton logon pōs esti mē lanthanein*, 1025b28–29).

From (19), thus supported, and (18), Whiting concludes

(20) Z.11's form contains matter.

Whatever its eventual success, (20) is not established by the parallel between *Met.* Z.11 and E.1. This is not to deny that there is a parallel between the two chapters, for just as *Met.* E.1, 1025b31–32, distinguishes between the *ti esti* and definition of the snub (*to simon*), on the one hand, and concavity (*to koilon*), on the other hand, so *Met.* Z.11 distinguishes concavity (*hē koilotēs*) from the snub nose and says that the latter is the sort of thing that contains matter (*hoion rhini simēi...enestai kai hē hulē* at 1037a30–31). But this parallel does not advance the impurists' cause. For the snub that, in E.1, is an object of physics because of containing matter must be what Z.11 opposes to concavity (*hē koilotēs*). But in Z.11, at 1037a27–33, concavity deputizes as the sort of form that is the primary substance and it is likened to the soul, whereas both the snub nose and snubness are barred from this role. So (20) can hardly be thought to follow from Z.11 and E.1. Moreover, *Met.* Z.4–6 concedes only that the snub and its ilk have definitions in a derivative sense but remains adamant in denying them definitions in the sense required for primary substance. Since the form under discussion in Z.10–11 is primary substance, (20) renders Z itself internally inconsistent.[65]

Fortunately, we need not swallow such bitter tonic. Note, first, that Aristotle contrasts, in (19) above, the way objects of physics and objects of mathematics contain matter. Neither of these, however, are objects of first philosophy. So it is unclear how (19) bears at all on the identity of those forms that are the objects of metaphysical inquiry. Second, and related, recall that E.1 says that we must not overlook *how* or *the way* (*pōs*) the essence is and notice that the question is asked in the course of discussing how the student of physics ought to proceed. This allows room for the possibility that the essence of *x*, *qua* object of physics, will be investigated differently than the essence of *x*, *qua* object of metaphysics. And, parallel to the treatment of embodied passions (such as anger) in *De An.* I.1, one and the same form may be investigated, once, *qua* object of physics, in which case the material realization is ineliminable, and, once *qua* object of metaphysics, in which case the material realization, if any, is eliminable. In short, *Met.* E.1 articulates a notion of definition and essence that will be of use to the physicist and such definitions are not meant to enjoy the full metaphysical reach of their purely formal counterparts. So there need be no clash between it and a strictly pure reading of Z.10–11.

If the attack on (16a) can be met, how does (16b) fare? Whiting objects that Aristotle does not alert the reader to the distinction between what is explicitly mentioned in a definition and what is only implied by what is mentioned. If this is essential to sustaining (16b), then Frede and Patzig's version of PURITY is not yet out of the woods. Here, I think, purists can respond that 1036b29's constraint against the definition of man proceeding *aneu kinēseōs* signals just the sort of implication Whiting is looking for. But what is not fully explained on Frede and Patzig's account, and what Whiting wants an account of, is how Aristotle could have held both (16a) and (16b), for the latter ties form to *matter*.[66]

Whiting herself rejects (16a) in favour of (16b) on the grounds that the forms of natural things just contain characteristic matter. With the purist camp, we would argue that this line of interpretation fails. But Whiting is quite correct to press for the purist explanation of (16b). One response will not work. Suppose that matter is introduced by the notion of something's having parts that are in a certain state (e.g., in [11] above). Suppose, further, that the '→' in (10)–(12) marks some kind of entailment. Then, it would appear to follow that the definition *entails* that the form involve a certain sort of matter—supposing that definitions contain nothing but form. Moreover, if with Frede and Patzig, one holds (17), then it is hard to see why matter should not be included in the definition. It will not do to say that (10) does not mean to *define* animals in terms of motion. For Aristotle uses *"horisasthai,"* which surely has canonical force in this context. So the problem is that on one account of what it means to say that $A$ entails $B$, $B$ is contained in $A$. Moreover, this account is not without some attraction for Aristotle. One might, for example, say that the conclusion of a syllogism is contained in the premises or that a superordinate element in an essence (e.g., animal) is contained in a subordinate element (e.g., man) and so is 'entailed' by it. So if we allow that specific characteristic matter is 'entailed' by a given form, how can we bar the form containing matter?[67]

Purists are advised, then, not to hold both that (10)–(12) express entailments and that the consequent of (11) mentions matter. So (10)–(12) cannot be where (16b) is located. Nonetheless, Frede and Patzig are, I believe, on the right track. The crucial move is to deny that (10)–(12) mention matter at all. Thus, let the definition, $D_f$, specify the functions anything is to have should it instantiate the form $f$. This agrees with our proposal at the end of the previous section for reconciling (12) and (15). On our suggestion, (12) alludes to a definition in the strict sense but the parts in question are functional parts and these are specified at a sufficiently abstract level of description to count as nonperceptible parts— in the sense that the materials in which such parts are realized is neither needed for nor relevant to the fully articulated definition of the form of the animal in question.

Roughly, the idea is that these functions, which are somehow aspects or elements in the definition, exhaust the constraints on matter but do not, by themselves, say anything about what specific sorts of materials might realize the functions.[68] So we have:

(21) c is an object of physics & $c = f + m$ & $D_f$ is the definition of $f \to m$ is not mentioned in $D_f$ & $D_f$ specifies the functions of $c$.

On this view, specifying $c$'s functions amounts to specifying $c$'s functional parts. To describe a part as a hand, for example, is already to locate it at a comfortably abstract level (for purists, that is), namely, at a level where mention of realizing material is as inappropriate as mention of stone or iron would be in the case of an axe. So far as (21) is concerned, then, form constrains matter by way of the functions that constitute the form. The most that follows from this, however, is the relatively weak

(22) $D_f$ constraints $m$ to *whatever* can realize the functions of $c$.

Because there is no 'entailment' relation from form-constituting functions to matter, the form cannot by *itself* establish specific material constraints on its realization. And it is especially difficult to see what grounds there are in Z.11 for holding (17). Had form contained matter of a sufficiently specific sort, then it might have been plausible to argue that only this matter can realize the form. By suitably neutralizing (16b), we can, as purists, accept (16a) but we must do so without thinking that (17) comes along for the inferential ride. Rather, cashing (22) is an empirical matter or, to use more current jargon, a production problem. For even if it is a deep natural fact about the world that the form of man is realized in flesh, sinew, and bone, the matter still is no part of the form itself. Exactly this is what Aristotle appears to have believed. And nothing here, to return to our question (Q2), excludes compositional plasticity; nor, on the other hand, is compositional plasticity entailed. It is simply left as an open question.[69] But then the thesis of compositional plasticity must be consistent with the Young Socrates passage as well as with the Thought-Experiment passage. If consistency of the latter sort is unsurprising, consistency of the first sort is not.

## III.   Conclusion

In arguing above that (10)–(12) need not be taken to mention matter, I am committing the Aristotle of *Met.* Z.11 to the claim that the definition of man does not mention matter. It may, of course, still be the case that man is always and only found in characteristic sorts of matter. So there are two ways in which man might be tied to specific material parts: (i) such parts may be mentioned in or may be entailed by the definition of man or (ii) such parts may follow from certain facts about the natural world. I have argued that Z.11 fails to establish (i) and so leaves us with nothing stronger than (ii). However, if giving the form of man is just to give the definition of man, then something stronger can be said. For now not only is option (i) not established in the Young Socrates passage, but also it appears to be excluded at the outset of Z.11. There definition is *of* the form (*tou eidous*) and it is this notion that is said to be involved in defining *each* thing. So Z10–11's exclusion of matter and material parts from the form would seem to imply that the *definition of man* cannot contain anything of a material nature.

Notice, however, that even were (i) embraced by Aristotle, it still would not follow that the *form* of man contains material parts. This is because one could grant that to be a human being is just to be a member of a determinate biological species and so to have a very specific material nature and yet insist that the form of such creatures be realizable in quite different sorts of matter. Creatures so constituted would not be human beings but they would be entities with similar functional capacities and states. In short, they would still be persons. From the point of view of philosophy of mind what matters are the psychological capacities, functions, and states characteristic of persons. Just what these are is determined by a form—the form that happens to be realized in human matter. (It is this latter that will exercise the Aristotelian physicist). So even were *man* itself defined in terms of such material, the *form* of man would not be, and thus, would retain its plasticity.[70] This would be enough to support the plasticity of anger and other psychological states of the sort discussed in section I of the paper. For, as we pointed out at the beginning of section II, if the form of man is compositionally plastic, so are the associated psychological states and capacities.

Let me end, finally, with some speculation on the sources of the Young Socrates' 'error' and a pair of projections.

To begin with the speculation, recall that the Young Socrates passage speaks of defining man (*ton anthrōpon*), whereas the Thought-Experiment passage speaks of defining the form of man (*to tou anthrōpou eidos*). This makes it doubtful that the Young Socrates passage was meant to answer the Thought-Experiment passage. Neither, thus, is it likely that Socrates the Younger erred simply by reasoning:

(23a) circle: parts of a circle :: man : parts of man,

(23b) The/a circle can exist without its perceptible parts,

therefore,

(23c) The/a man can exist without his perceptible parts.

The mistake may well be more complicated, for we argued above that

(23b) is grounded in the fact that

(23b') The/a circle can consist of (just) noetic parts,

so that one might think that man could exist without his perceptible parts
because the analogy to the circle suggests

(23c') The/a man can consist of (just) noetic parts,

and such parts are nonperceptible. The complication in (23c') is that man
has no constituent noetic parts. What is, however, correct is that noetic
parts, in the case of the circle, are the analogues of functional parts, in
the case of a man, despite the fact that they are not actually *noetic* parts.
Although functional parts, as answering to parts of the definition, are
purely formal, in certain cases they can constitute parts of a particular
entity, but only if they are realized in material stuff. Such is the case with
man but not with the circle. So whereas the functional part analogues in
the case of the circle can be noetic, the functional parts of man cannot.
And this, to press the speculation, may underlie what was misleading
about Socrates the Younger's comparison. For, so construed, the analogy
would suggest that there could exist a man with just such parts much as
there can be a (mathematical) circle with noetic parts only. And this,
presumably, is precisely why Aristotle insists at Z.11, 1036b28, that an
animal is a *perceptible object*.[71], Moreover, this is the sort of mistake one
might make, if having given up the claim that the functional parts of man
are material, one thought that the only alternative was to make them into
noetic parts. Aristotle's corrective at the end of the Young Socrates
passage, then, amounts to insisting that as functional parts, heads, hands
and the like resist simple classification as noetic or material parts.[72]
Functional distinctions cut across the noetic and material boundary.

   The projections are, in effect, pointers for further research. One begins
with the observation that the issue of compositional plasticity is something
of a red herring. For whether plasticity is embraced or rejected. Aristotle
takes it that the forms of natural entities are, as a matter of fact, realized
in quite specific kinds of matter. Moreover, this is a deeply entrenched
fact about nature. Nonetheless, it is not a fact that is *explained* by facts
about the forms of natural things. So, on our analysis, the "Aristotelian'
question to press is how it can be a fundamental natural truth that man
is realized always and only in flesh, sinew, and bone despite the fact that
this is not forthcoming from truths about the form of man. It will not do
simply to invoke, for example, hypothetical necessity because this gets us
no further than (22). What we need an account of is how, in the case of

man, (22) itself is to be limited to just those constraints called for by the fundamental natural truth that the matter of man is always flesh, sinew, and bone. And *this* is an account that belongs in the province of physics.[73]

The second projection concerns the currently popular claim that for Aristotle determination cannot be "from the bottom up." The claim aims to do justice to the autonomy and the causal role of form. As such it takes the crucial question to be "How can form transform matter?" Indeed, this question has received the lion's share of attention from Aristotle scholars. Although it harbors no presumptions incompatible with compositional plasticity (imagine that it asks what kinds of stuff a given form *can* transform), the question does appear inhospitable to answers friendly to supervenience. Suppose, however, we take the crucial question to be "How can matter transmit form?" Answers to this question may include exhibits from partisans of supervenience as well as friends of compositional plasticity. The claim, standard with supervenience theorists, that the physical facts determine all the facts, including formal or psychological facts, is often taken to denigrate form in some way. But if supervenience is allied with compositional plasticity, this is not obvious. For although "determination from the bottom up" may compromise the causal role of form, that fact that form is not welded to a single sort of matter affords it a measure of autonomy from matter and, more importantly, provides it with genuine explanatory space. Whatever the ultimate verdict on the Aristotelian credentials of the notions of supervenience and compositional plasticity,[74] the second question itself is one that we ought to be addressing.[75]

## NOTES

[1] This involves, at increasing depth, thoughts, images, and ultimately, physical states or processes. For some suggestions on how this works see Wedin (1989), (1993a) and (1993b).

[2] To follow Wedin (1989), (1993a) and (1993b)

[3] Floated in Wedin (1989).

[4] Wedin (1993b), and especially, (1993a).

[5] Wilkes (1978), 118–121.

[6] Shields (1989), 24–5 and 28–9.

[7] Cohen (1992).

[8] Code and Moravcsik (1992), Frede (1992), 104, also appears to take this line.

[9] In fact, however, (F1) can be held independently of (F2). So it is not at all obvious that compositional plasticity is essential to the notion of a functional state. It is, of course, consistent with this that compositional plasticity, as part of a campaign against identity theory, may well provide sufficient grounds for taking psychological states to be functional states.

[10] Shields (1989), 25 and 28.

[11] In fact, as we shall see, neither of these attempts meets the requirements of (1), when properly drawn out.

[12] Shields (1989), 28.

[13] I am assuming that (D) requires a verb. With Ross (1961), I supply 'caused' and take

it to pick up *kinēsis* at a26 and reflect this in (1), (1a), and (1b). Some might insist, however, that the verb picks up *orgizesthai* and that (1), (1a), and (1b) should be changed accordingly. But if (1a) and (1b) are part of the project of *defining* anger, then they should explain but not themselves mention anger. This means, as Lewis has pointed out, that the form and matter of anger, which may be considered its causes, in turn have efficient causes. Although this might strike some as exceeding the spirit of the *Physics*, it is the sort of thing we get in *Phys.* VII.3's account of the generation of form and the extension of this to psychological states. On this see Wedin (1993a).

[14] Shields (1989) joins Cohen (1992) in finding compositional plasticity in Aristotle but, unlike Cohen, he does not locate it (at least, not explicitly) in (D) or (E). Rather, he offers independent considerations in favor of compositional plasticity. One of these concerns what I call the Thought-Experiment passage. It receives extensive treatment in the next section. See Note 69 below for comment on Shield's remaining pair of considerations.

[15] Notice that one could have contingency without plasticity, reading contingency as form's capacity to exist apart from matter. For even, if when realized, a form is realized always and only in a specific sort of matter, the connection would be contingent so long as the form can exist without any matter at all. No doubt this ripple in the parallel between contingency and plasticity loses interest in light of Aristotle's principled resistance to such a disembodied mode of being (for forms of material things). See Further Note 69 below.

[16] And, perhaps, against the functionalist reading of Aristotle.

[17] Bolton has expressed some skepticism about this resolution of the contradiction, urging that Aristotle would want to exclude just such an option.

[18] Probably, (4d) should be weakened to a conditional; but I shall not worry about that here.

[19] The problem does, of course, arise for (4b) and (4c) as well as for the mixed cases, where the *kinēsis* is caused by something and the desire is for the sake of something and where the desire is caused by something and the *kinēsis* is for the sake of something.

[20] Bolton has suggested that while the desire and the kinesis are related as formal and material *cause*, this may be a broader relation than that of form to matter—at least if one thinks of the form-to-matter relation as found in standard cases of compound substances.

[21] The caveat in parentheses, admits that, properly, what is for the sake of shelter is the actual house, that is, the compound substance.

[22] I am indebted to John Malcolm for reminding me that there is a certain tension here. *Met.* H.3, 1043a32–33, counts *covering(skepasma)* as the form (*eidos*) or second actuality (actuality$_2$) (*energeia*) of a house and so seems to support our reading. *Met.* H.2, 1043a16–18, on the other hand, appears to give, as the actuality (*energeia*), *covering for sheltering possessions and bodies*. Plugged into our reading, this would yield the decidedly uninformative result that a covering for shelter is for the sake of shelter. Note, however, that the H.2 passage reports that those who give the definition of house as *a covering for shelter of possessions and bodies* "speak of the actuality" (*tēn energeian legousin*). Form is not explicitly mentioned. So, perhaps, Aristotle need not be taken to say that the form itself includes the sheltering of possessions and bodies. This seems correct because the sheltering is the end and, in the case of a house, the end can be specified independently of the form. This may not necessarily hold of living systems, where form and function are especially intimately connected.

[23] And pressed into service in Wedin (1993a).

[24] Namely, SUP: A family $\Psi$ of properties supervenes on a family $\Phi$ of properties$\equiv$necessarily, for any property $\psi$ in $\Psi$, if $x$ has $\psi$ then there is a property in $\phi$ in $\Phi$ such that $x$ has $\phi$ and, necessarily, whatever has $\phi$ has $\psi$. See Caston (1993), who finds a weaker version of supervenience in *Phys.* VII.3.

[25] There is, thus, a parallel between boiling of the blood and the body in general. From *Met.* Z.10–11 it is clear, that *qua* functional matter, the matter of an organism cannot be specified independently of the organism's form but that, *qua* remnant matter, it can be so specified. I say more about this in Section II of this paper. I am inclined (at this point) to see in this distinction commitment, not to two different matters, but only to different

descriptions of the same matter. (The hedging apparent in the last sentence is prompted by a remark of Lewis's).

²⁶ This possibility appears to be overlooked in Shields (1989), perhaps, as a result of focusing exclusively on (D).

²⁷ This assumption will have to deal with the testimony of *Met.* H.2, 1043a16–18, which says that those who define a house by proposing that it is a covering for shelter of possessions or bodies, *or something else like this (ē ti allo toiouton)*, define it by speaking of the actuality. For here the "*ē ti allo toiouton*" frame is clearly a marker for the provisional nature of the formulation of the form. Here, again, I am indebted to Malcolm.

²⁸ Of course, it does not exclude this either.

²⁹ This will be so even if the contingency holds only for matter characterized in a form-free way. Whether the contingency of form and matter is indeed global cannot be settled here.

³⁰ Namely, SUP, for which see Note 24 above.

³¹ Here I am admittedly provocative. For some justification see Wedin (1993a).

³² There is a final point of interest concerning (5). It indulges in the convenience that both the physicist's boiling and the dialectician's desire are caused by the same thing (insult/injury) and are for the sake of the same thing (retaliation). But if, as I hold, the physicist works at a different level, won't he describe these causes and ends in language appropriate to that level? *M.A.* VII suggests that the boiling is caused by various 'vascular' contractions and expansion and that it is for the sake of readying the limbs and internal organs for movement. And here one might, I suppose, consider whether the perception of insult or injury supervenes on the contractions and expansions and whether the retaliatory behavior supervenes on the readied state of the body. No doubt a strictly physicalist account would have to say something about this. But Aristotle himself insists that the physicist too must be concerned with form. This is probably required to ensure, at least, that he be able to ask which physiological structures and processes underlie which psychological states and processes. So Aristotle is not insisting that the physicist provide analyses that preserve the *meanings* of psychological terms. He need only *explain* the occurrence of the correlated psychological phenomena. This relieves some of the anxiety occasioned by the leveling in (5). Here I am indebted to a worry and a suggestion put by John Ferguson Heil.

³³ Hamlyn takes the body to be the subject of *orgizētai* and so translates: "... when the body is aroused and is as it is when it is anger." But for Aristotle persons are angry, not their bodies. In any case, the subject of the verb is omitted and, has Hicks suggested, is best taken to be a personal subject. On this point, Burnyeat's translation of the line seems exactly right.

³⁴ Hicks translates the parenthesized Greek, "when the blood is up and the bodily condition is that of anger." Doubtless, the body is agitated in just this way, when it is in the condition standardly associated with anger, but the Greek is entirely bloodless. In this Hicks appears to follow Wallace, who opted for a more robust vertion of the sanguine reading: "the body being at such times boiling full and in the same state of excitement as in anger." Here I am indebted to a remark of Bolton's.

³⁵ Taking, perhaps, the slight provocation to be the efficient cause, as required by (5).

³⁶ Lewis has suggested that it is, indeed, relevant whether the agent is angry or not. On his view, slight provocations do not ordinarily elicit anger at all; but when the bodily state is suitably disturbed, then such provocations might well produce anger. Until the provoking, however, there is not yet any anger. Although appealing, the last sentence overstates the case. The most that is certain is that until the provocation, there is no *expression* of anger. It remains a moot point whether we should say that the person responded to the slight provocation because he *was* angry, or not. Saying so would, of course, require that the suitable disturbance be appropriate for attribution of the *dispositional* state of anger and not merely be a state like fatigue. But I need not insist on this reading because I take the status of the agent's specific psychological state to be additional to the main point at issue in the passage. Lurking here is an important question about the nature and of identity

conditions for psychological states, namely, whether those who come to have the affections of one who is frightened, in the absence of any actual thing to fear, are in fact frightened. The question, which is invited but not answered by Aristotle's subtle language, is one I cannot go into here.

[37] So we have here an instance of what is called systemic supervenience in Wedin (1993a).

[38] Where the correlated physical state is the one standardly realized when one is in the psychological state in question.

[39] I do not take 403a17–19 to issue a standard logical conditional but rather to give us a statement of simultaneity. So it is not obvious that occurrence of the physical state is not sufficient for occurrence of the psychological state. (Here I attempt to cope with a worry put by Lewis.)

[40] This is, perhaps, too strong. What ought to be said is that this is arguably the most plausible explanation of his view that they are enmattered structures.

[41] Adopting the standard reading, *'enuloi'* against E and T's *en hulēi* Although the latter is common in Aristotle and the former confined to this occurrence, editors and commentators are virtually one in adopting *'enuloi'*. This may not be irrelevant, if *'enuloi'* is meant to convey something stronger than the fact that something is *in* matter, that is, something stronger than the claim that matter is only a necessary condition. For the latter idea is adequately expressed by *'en hulēi'* and, thus, adoption of ET's text might give less support to reading the relation between form and matter as a supervenience relation.

[42] Indeed, they deny (1992, 133) that "(a) the elements that enter into the specification of the form and structure are properties ... of matter that (b) can exist outside of the realization of some enlivening potential." On this basis, they would deny that (6) is materialist at all. I shall have more to say on this later.

[43] As court reporter to the London Reading Group, Burnyeat himself is under no obligation to embrace their impurity. Indeed, as he made clear at the 1993 Oriel Aristotle Conference, he is in substantial agreement with our reading of the passage.

[44] Lewis takes this contrast to clash with Aristotle's usual line on flesh and bone. For the moment, I shall simply register the point.

[45] Here I am prompted, again, by a remark of John Malcolm's.

[46] For example, Code and Moravcsik (1992) and Frede and Patzig (1988).

[47] For example, Shields (1989).

[48] E.G., Frede and Patzig (1988).

[49] Moreover, this is precisely where it ought to remain. Shields tries to get more out of the Thought-Experiment passage. Despite the fact that we do not see the form of man in material other than flesh and bone, nothing hinders it from being like the form of circle, which (we see) is realizable in various kinds of material. Shields routinely concludes that human beings are compositionally plastic. Although this passage may be consistent with compositional plasticity, much more needs to be said. For, as we have seen, when Aristotle says that "nothing hinders them (i.e., the things that are not seen in separate matter) from being similar to these (i.e, the things that are seen in separate matter)" he may just mean that in both cases the matter does not belong to the form, despite the fact that this is difficult to grasp in the case of human beings. And this, we saw, is consistent with denial as well as affirmation of compositional plasticity. Furthermore, even were the form of man compositionally plastic, it would not follow that *human beings* "can be realized in any functionally suitable matter" (Shields 1990, 23) but only that there could be functionally similar creatures, arguably, of an entirely different species. See below for more on this.

[50] I comment below on the fashionable substitution of *aisthētikon* for *aisthēton* at b28.

[51] It may be worth noting that, as Frede and Patzig (1988) nicely show, the reduction of all things to numbers happens in part because some take certain parts that are in fact material parts to be formal parts and, in this way, they eliminate the matter.

[52] This is not a problem for Code and Moravcsik because they take Aristotle still to be operating in the dialectical mode and, hence, not committed to the implicit endorsement that matter is to be included in the definition.

<sup>53</sup> It should be noted that Ross's translation at (A1), "And so to reduce all things thus to forms and to eliminate the matter," reads form into the phrase "*to panta anagein houtō*", whereas I take it to refer, in the first instance at least, to the intervening reduction to numbers. It is in this way that the nonmaterial enters the story.

<sup>54</sup> A fellow mathematician and contemporary of Theatetus, he is mentioned by Plato at *Theaetetus* 147D, *Sophist* 218B, and possibly, at 358D in the XI *Letter*. He also takes the stage as an interlocutor in the *Statesman*.

<sup>55</sup> Also proposed by Irwin (1988), 569 Note 39 and Whiting (1992), 627.

<sup>56</sup> By a concrete thing, I mean (perhaps, nonstandardly) a particular compound of form and matter—whether the matter is perceptible or noetic.

<sup>57</sup> Getting to (10) in this way gives us what Frede and Patzig want out of the emendation, *aisthētikon*, namely, a connection with the discussion of motion and, implicitly, perceptual functions. The motivation for emendation is certainly correct, so I would be happy to follow Frede and Patzig should the current proposal fall short.

<sup>58</sup> Certainly, it seems to me, less clear than as represented in Burnyeat and others (1978), where (10′) is held to require that matter be mentioned in the definition. Bear in mind here Note 43.

<sup>59</sup> In this paragraph, I am indebted to a remark of Bolton's.

<sup>60</sup> That is, a given localizable portion of matter, part of Smith at a given moment, may, at some later time, exist apart from Smith without prejudice to Smith's existence. So long as, of course, other suitable matter has, in the appropriate manner, found its way into Smith's body.

<sup>61</sup> As is suggested by Aristotle's fondness in the biology for accounts of faculties and functions that apply across species.

<sup>62</sup> Principally having to do with the kind of explanatory role he assigns to form in the central books of the *Metaphysics*. For this see Wedin (in progress).

<sup>63</sup> The corollary, (17), seems to me to be another matter and I turn to it below.

<sup>64</sup> In her helpful and stimulating review (Whiting 1992) of Frede and Patzig (1988) and Furth (1988).

<sup>65</sup> In an glaringly non-Geachian way (see Michael Woods 1991 for deciphering).

<sup>66</sup> Propositions (16a) and (16b) are difficult to reconcile, only if (16b) makes matter part of the definition. But, as Lewis has reminded me, this is not obvious.

<sup>67</sup> The force of this difficulty might be thought mitigated by *Top.* 102a18–19, where Aristotle says a proprium is "that which, while not revealing the essence <of the subject>, belongs to it alone and is counterpredicable of it." But this says nothing about the connection between the proprium and the definition. Indeed, the exact nature of this relation is notoriously difficult to specify.

<sup>68</sup> *Pace* Frede and Patzig (1988), vol. 2, 213.

<sup>69</sup> Shields (1989) tries out two additional arguments in favor of the compositional plasticity of form. First, he offers *De An.* 414a25–27: "For the actuality of each thing comes about naturally in what holds in potentiality and in the appropriate matter (*hekastou gar hē entelecheia en tōi dunamei huparchonti kat tēi oikeiai hulēi pephuken egginesthai*)." This is held to establish that the only constraint on the matter of a thing is that it be functionally suitable. But, without further argument, the lines are neutral on compositional plasticity. For as it stands, the passage is consistent with holding that capacities are irreducible and essential properties of certain quite specific kinds of matter. Reading "appropriate matter" this way would appear to give us a version of 414a25–27 that does not require compositional plasticity. The second argument depends on facts about thought. Thus, while my thought of Socrates is achieved by way of images, God's thought of Socrates is not. Hence, concludes Shields, Aristotle must accept the multiple realizability of the mental. But this presupposes that Aristotle's God thinks of the same things we think of. This is hardly obvious. Indeed, it is not even clear that God's thought is propositional (see Wedin (1988), especially, Appendix C, "The Return of the Unmoved Mover"). Besides, insofar as Aristotle is offering a psychology adequate for persons, appeal to the behaviour of transcendent entities is not

of much interest. What we need to see is whether compositional plasticity is a feature adopted from within Aristotle's naturalistic stance.

[70] So even if (16a) turns out to be false, we can remain purists about form and compositionally-minded ones at that.

[71] Hence, adding weight to retention of *aisthēton*, the manuscript reading, as against *aisthētikon*, the emendation suggested by Frede and Patzig (1988).

[72] This suggestion has the virtue of explaining why Aristotle says, not that the Young Socrates's comparison itself is false, but only that it misleads one. It is also the sort of suggestion that might come easily to a mathematician, the reported occupation of Socrates the Younger

[73] This is, to repeat, because it is a metaphysical question whether the *person* is always realized in such stuff, assuming that men just are human beings. For to be a human being is just to be a member of a biological species, even, some would argue, a historically bounded species. So, arguably, nothing could belong to the species unless composed of human flesh and bone. Persons, on the other hand, may well appear in rather different dress.

[74] Despite the initial guise of neutrality at the paper's outset, the reader will detect sympathy for approaching Aristotle's texts informed by current work on functionalism and supervenience. Some of this given voice in Wedin (188) and (1993a). There is, of course, a lively and articulate opposition. In addition to Code and Moravcsik (1991) and Burnyeat (1992), one might also mention Robinson (1983), Granger (1990) and (1994) and Wardy (1990).

[75] In addition to the somewhat unruly crowd at the December 1992 USC-Rutgers Conference. I am indebted to the participants in the July 1993 Oriel College Conference on Aristotle's *De Anima* for spirited and constructive discussion of the paper. More narrowly, thanks are due, as usual, to John Malcolm as well as to John Ferguson Heil for very helpful remarks on a earlier version of the paper. Warm thanks are due also to Rob Bolton and Frank Lewis for extensive written comments on the penultimate draft. Malcolm alone accepts responsibility for any remaining errors.

## REFERENCES

Burnyeat, M. 1992 "Is an Aristotelian Philosophy of Mind Still Credible?" In Nussbaum and Rorty, 1992: 15–26.
Burnyeat, M. and others 1979. *Notes on Book Zeta of Aristotle's 'Metaphysics'*. Oxford: Sub-faculty of Philosophy.
Caston, V. 1993. "Aristotle and Supervenience." In *Ancient Minds: Spindel Conference 1992*, ed. John Ellis, *Southern Journal of Philosophy*, Supp. vol. 31: 107–135.
Charles, D. 1988. "Aristotle on Hypothetical Necessity and Irreducibility." *Pacific Philsophical Quarterly* 69: 1–53.
Code, A. and Moravcsik, J. 1992. "Explaining Various Forms of Living." In Nussbaum and Rorty, 1992: 129–45.
Cohen, S. M. 1992. "Hylomorphism and Functionalism." In Nussbaum and Rorty, 1992: 57–73.
Frede, M. 1992. "On Aristotle's Conception of the Soul." In Nussbaum and Rorty, 1992: 93–107.
Frede, M. and Patzig G. 1988. *Aristotle's 'Metaphysik Z'*. Text, Übersetzung, Kommentar. 2 vols. Munich.
Furth, M. 1988. *Substance, Form, and Psyche: An Aristotelean Metaphysics*. Cambridge.
Hamlyn, D. W. 1968. *Aristotle–De Anima, Books II and III*. Translation with an introduction and notes. Oxford.
Hicks, R. D. 1907. *Aristotle: De Anima*. Cambridge.
Horgan, T. (ed.) 1983. *The Concept of Supervenience in Contemporary Philosophy:* 1983 Spindel Conference. *The Southern Journal of Philosophy* 22, Supplement.
Irwin, T.H. 1988. *Aristotle's First Principles*. Oxford.
Kim, J. 1984. "Epiphenomenal and Supervenient Causation." *Midwest Studies in Philosophy* 9: 257–70.

38     MICHAEL V. WEDIN

Kim, J. 1978. "Supervenience and Nomonological Incommensurables." *American Philosophical Quarterly* 69: 54–98.
Lewis, F.A. 1988. "Teleology and Material/Efficient Causes in Aristotle." *Pacific Philsophical Quarterly* 69: 54–98.
Manuwald, B. 1971. *Das Buch H der aristotelischen 'Physik': Eine Untersuchung zur Einheit und Echheit. Beiträge zur klassischen Philologie* 36. Meisenheim.
Nussbaum, M.C. and Rorty, A.O. 1992. *Essays on Aristotle's De Anima.* Oxford.
Ross, W.D. 1924. *Aristotle's Metaphysics.* A revised text with Introduction and Commentary. 2 vols. Oxford.
Shields, C. 1990. "The First Functionalist." In *Historical Foundations of Cognitive Science,* ed. J.-C. Smith. Dordrecht.
Wallace, E. 1882. *Aristotle's Psychology in Greek and English.* With introduction and Notes. Cambridge.
Wardy, 1990. *The Chain of Change: A Study of Aristotle's Physics VII.* Cambridge.
Wedin, M.V. 1988. *Mind and Imagination in Aristotle.* New Haven.
Wedin, M.V. 1989. "Aristotle on the Mechanics of Thought." *Ancient Philosophy* 9: 67–86. Reprinted in *Aristotle's Ontology. Essays in Ancient Greek Philosophy,* vol. 5, eds, J. Anton and A. Preus, Albany, 1992.
Wedin, M.V. 1993a. "Content and Cause in the Aristotelian Mind." In *Ancient Minds*: Spindel Conference *1992,* ed. John Ellis. *Southern Journal of Philosophy,* Supp. Vol. 31: 49–105.
Wedin, M.V. 1993b. "Aristotle on the Mind's Slef-Motion." In *Self-Motion: From Aristotle to Newton,* ed. M.L. Gill and J. Lennox, 81–116. Princeton.
Wedin, M.V. 1996. "Aristotle on How to Define a Psychological State." *Topoi* 15: 11–24.
Wedin, M.V. (in progress). *Word and Object in Aristotle.*
Whiting, J. 1991. "Metasubstance: Critical Notice of Frede-Patzig and Furth." *The Philosophical Review* 100: 607–39.
Wilkes, K.V. 1978. *Physicalism.* London.
Woods, M.J. 1991. "Particular Forms Revisited." Review of Frede and Patzig (1988), *Phronesis* 36: 75–87.

# ARISTOTLE ON THE
# UNITY OF SUBSTANCE

BY

FRANK A. LEWIS

Given that a thing has many parts, Aristotle asks, what makes for its unity? For Aristotle, I take it, the parts in question are real parts, and what makes for unity too really is something about the thing itself—some real metaphysical constituent of the thing. So I shall set to one side "constructivist" or "projectivist" interpretations of Aristotle, according to which the analysis of individual substances as in some sense compounds of form and matter, or as wholes composed of many material parts, is an artifact of our way of looking at them, and not a feature they exhibit "in the real order."[1] On the contrary assumption, that the parts of a thing are its real parts and not merely our creations, the question about unity encourages the further question, What is the true structure of the thing? In addition to Aristotle's positive answer to these questions, advanced in *Metaphysics* H6, there are two wrong answers he is especially anxious to discredit. One mistake, discussed in Z17, is to think that what is responsible for the unity among the obvious material parts, or elements (*stoicheia*), that make up a thing is *yet another element*, or is *composed of elements*; this suggestion invites an infinite regress of elements, so that there can be no single definite answer to questions about the true structure of the thing. To avoid these embarrassments, Aristotle supposes that the source of a thing's unity is not an element or elements, but rather a form, which is a *principle* (*arche*) but not an element, and which he identifies as the substance of the thing and the cause of its being.

The second mistake Aristotle argues against is to think that there is a single definite answer to the question about the true structure of the thing, but that it requires introducing a *special connecting relation*, the same in all cases, in addition to the obvious material parts and the form. This option is left open by the regress argument in Z17, but it comes under attack in the second half of H6. A crucial ingredient in Aristotle's argument here is what I shall call the Content Requirement, which

39

connects the role of a given form as the principle of *unity* for a thing to
its role as what he calls the cause of the thing's *being*—that is, the causal
role the form plays in the analysis of the membership by the thing in its
kind. As we shall see, the account of kinds takes precedence: it is *because*
a form is the cause of the being of the thing—that is, its being a member
of its proper kind—that the form can also figure in the explanation of its
unity.

Aristotle's positive view is that the unity of a thing is to be traced to
its matter and, especially, its form, and to nothing more than these. So
he must be able to say what it is about the matter and, especially, the
form *by themselves* such that the compound material substance that results
from them is indeed a unity. This project is also under way in the second
half of H6.

The two mistakes in answering questions about the unity and true
structure of a thing are discussed in Sections II and III respectively, and
Aristotle's positive answer to these questions is the subject of Sections
IV, V and VI. By way of a preliminary, Section I takes up the connection
between Aristotle's discussion of unity in the second part of Z17 and his
account of kinds earlier in the chapter.

## I. Kinds and Unity in Metaphysics Z17

Two items are on Aristotle's agenda in Z17: questions about how an
individual substance is a member of a kind, and questions about how it
is a whole of parts. The two topics are linked by way of the Content
Requirement already noted, which suggests that we will not be able to
settle questions about the unity of a thing independently of a solution to
questions about its kind.

In the first half of Z17, Aristotle sets about analyzing a central feature
of the metaphysical theory in the *Categories* that is never properly
explained there. What is it for an individual to be a member of a kind?
In Z17, the inquiry into kinds fills out the connection Aristotle postulates
between the notion of *substance* that is his main target in *Zeta* and the
notion of a *cause*. Aristotle argues that substance is the *cause of being*
(*aition tou einai*) for a thing— that is, the cause of its being a member of
a kind, for example, of this being flesh, or this a syllable (1041b26–7). In
particular, the cause of being of an individual substance will be the
substance *of* that substance.

Aristotle's account proceeds in two stages. First, the proper question
about a thing's kind is not, Why is this, that is, this man, a man? but
rather, Why does this matter, this body in this state, constitute a man?[2]
The second step—modelled after the analysis of event-types in the
*Posterior Analytics*—is to introduce *form* as a middle term: the matter
constitutes a thing of a given kind thanks to the relevant form.[3]

The second topic on the agenda in Z17 involves the *unity* of the compound material substance. If a thing is to be a unity, Aristotle suggests, it must be not only its material parts, or "elements," but also something else (1041b16–19). This new factor again is both the cause of being, and also the substance, of the thing (b26–31, cf. b7–9); and as before (b8), presumably, it is a form. This role for form allows Aristotle to hold that there is a single definite answer to the question, What is the true structure of the thing, such that its *many* parts (*ek tinos suntheton*, b11) make up a *single* whole? The correct answer, according to Aristotle, involves the obvious material parts or "elements," together with a single unifying form or "principle." Aristotle argues in Z17 that the unifying form is not itself a further element: a policy of adding new elements to explain a thing's unity is a sure recipe for having the list of constituents of the thing grow infinitely long.

How are the two topics of Z17 connected? What ties together the account of being a member of a kind, and the account of being a unified whole of many parts? One thought is not relevant here. It is often said that things are one, that is, countable, only insofar as they fall under some covering concept that gives a criterion for counting.[4] But countability and the availability of some suitable covering concept are far wider notions than proper Aristotelian unity and belonging to a genuine Aristotelian kind. For example, the suitable covering concept allows us to count not only one or more oak trees or sand castles, but also one or more piles of leaves or heaps of sand. But only things of the first sort are good candidates for being members of Aristotelian kinds (and not all equally good candidates at that); and only things of the first sort are plausible candidates for being Aristotelian unities, as opposed to the piles and heaps of the second list.[5] However close the connection between falling under a suitable covering concept and being one in the sense required for counting, this will not explain the tie Aristotle sees between genuine Aristotelian unities and membership in a genuine Aristotelian kind.

Aristotle suggests that the source of the connection is instead *causal*. At 1041b26–31, as his discussion of unity progresses, he reminds us of his results earlier in the chapter, in particular, the causal role (*kai aition ge*, b26) that gives form a place in the account of a thing's kind and makes it the substance of a thing and the primary cause of its being.[6] As I understand Aristotle, his view is not just that the notions of unity among a thing's material parts and membership by the thing in its kind are materially equivalent. They are equivalent with good reason, for they *have the same cause*, namely, the relevant form.[7] More than this, it is no accident that they have the same cause: it is *because* form has the causal role it does in the analysis of kinds that it can also be a cause of a thing's being a unified whole of many parts. I will formalize these various ideas as the Content Requirement:

*Content Requirement.* A form plays the role it does as the principle of unity among the different parts of a given thing if and only if, and *just because*, it is also the substance of the thing and the cause of its being [= the cause of its being a member of its lowest kind].[8]

I shall suppose that Aristotle accepts the Requirement in full, so that for him, success in questions about a thing's unity is possible only given an answer to the prior question about membership by the thing in its proper kind.[9] More than this, answers to questions about the thing's kind involve the *content* of the relevant form, which is the *substance* of the thing and the *cause of its being*;[10] and it is the reference to content that makes these answers to questions about the kind suitable also as answers to questions about unity.

Aristotle has one further point in mind when he picks one and the same form as both the substance and cause of being of a thing, and also the principle thanks to which its material parts constitute a unity. Strikingly, there is exactly *one* such form or principle for each thing, in addition to its elements. The point is one Aristotle simply takes for granted in Z17. But clearly, his view is that the relevant form or unifying principle *will* be unique. This follows immediately from the claim that this form will be the substance of the thing and the cause of its being: Aristotle will hold that Socrates (say) has one *and only one* substance, and one *and only one* cause of his being. Partly, this means to exclude competing lowest kinds—Socrates will not be a tiger as well as a man, and so on. But Aristotle also means to exclude other undesirable possibilities. For example, there is no new entity in addition to the substance of a thing that is the substance of that substance.[11] Very much along the same lines, as we shall see, he also holds that there is no need for any special "connecting relation" beyond the initial unifying form involved in the constitution of the thing. For example, it is the *order* or the *arrangement* of the letters, *A* and *B*, thanks to which they make up the syllable, *BA*; there is no further connecting relation, no special tie, such that the syllable is composed of not only the letters *A* and *B* and the appropriate arrangement, but also the tie that holds together those letters and that arrangement.[12]

It is sometimes suggested that Aristotle rejects any special connecting relation in addition to the initial unifying form of the thing and the material parts, on the grounds that if he allows in one such relation, then he will be committed to allowing in infinitely many, so that the thing will have infinitely many constituents. Aristotle objects openly elsewhere to the idea that there can be infinitely many components in the essence or definition of a thing,[13] and he would also find the idea of infinitely many connecting relations intolerable. But contrary to what is sometimes supposed,[14] the regress argument already at work in Z17 does not support the slide from *one* connecting relation to *infinitely many*. The regress argument in Z17 introduces an infinite sequence of *elements* in the construction of a thing, but it has no consequences one way or the other for whether the thing contains a single unifying principle identical with the form of the thing, or whether it contains a special connecting relation on top of the thing's elements and the initial form, or even contains a whole string of such connecting relations. I will argue in Section III that a better source for the "single principle" or "no connecting relation" view is not the threat of a regress, but instead the Content Requirement for the principle of unity for a thing: as we shall see, in H6 Aristotle rejects the idea of a special connecting relation in addition to the form on the basis of a *reductio* argument in which the Content Requirement plays a major role. Meanwhile, it is also worth getting straight on the regress argument of Z17; in Section II below I argue that Aristotle shows that the form that unifies a thing cannot be another element or composed of elements, on pain of a regress, but his argument is neutral on the question of a special connecting relation.

## II. The Regress Argument in Z17

In Z17, Aristotle asks how a collection of material parts, or elements, can be unified so as to constitute a genuine whole. His answer is that there exists some further item that unifies the matter in the required way. But, he argues, we must not think that what does the unifying is itself an element, or composed of elements. If it is composed of more than one element, how are these a unity? Alternatively, if the unifying factor is a single element, then as before, we will need to appeal to yet another element to explain how the original unifying factor and the original elements themselves fit together, and so on, *ad infinitum* (1041b19–25).

The regress Aristotle has in mind suggests that if we take something—this syllable, or flesh (b16–19)—to be a unity, there can be no final answer to the question, What is the true structure of the thing? Our first thought may be that it is composed of just two elements, $e_1$ and $e_2$. But, we are to suppose,

(1) For any i (i > 1), elements $e_1$, ..., $e_i$, make up a unity thanks to the presence of some further element, $e_{i+1}$.

So the initial answer citing just $e_1$ and $e_2$ must be corrected to allow for the new element, $e_3$, and the thing contains three constituents. But this answer too cannot be right. For $e_1$, $e_2$, and $e_3$ in turn make up a unity only if we also allow for the presence of the further element, $e_4$. And so on, to infinity. To defend against the regress, Aristotle introduces a distinction between what does the unifying—in fact, a *form*—and the material parts it unifies: the form is a *principle* in contrast to the material parts, which are *elements* (b31). (1), then, is false, and in its place, Aristotle is committed to the following principle:

Principle 1. If all of a number of items are to be unified into a genuine whole by means of
some additional item, and if all the original items are elements, then that additional item
is a form, and it must not be an element, but a principle.

So much is relatively uncontroversial. Difficulties enter in when one turns
from the question of how the material parts "fit together" thanks to a
given form, to ask instead how—if at all—the form and the material parts
themselves "fit together." Aristotle insists that the form is not just one
more material part. If he is consistent, then, he cannot think that the form
and the material parts "fit together" on exactly the same terms that the
material parts do so. Is he barred from thinking that they "fit together"
at all? Having put form clearly on the side of what *does the unifying* in
contrast to the material parts that get unified, can he still entertain the
idea that matter and form themselves "fit together," now apparently
counting form among the items suitable for *getting unified*?

Sceptics on this issue may point to the example in Z17, where the items
to be unified are all material parts, or elements, and conclude that in
general, in Aristotle's view,

Principle 2. If all of a number of items are to be unified into a genuine whole, the items
themselves must all be elements.[15]

Principles 1 and 2 together suggest that form can unify the material parts,
not only because it is a principle if they are all elements (Principle 1), but
also because in fact all the parts unified *are* elements (Principle 2). As for
the material parts and the form itself, these are not all elements, since the
form is instead a principle; accordingly, Principle 2 rules out their "fitting
together," or "making a unity," in any way. Given Principle 2, the question,
How do form and matter "fit together"?, simply should not arise.[16]

But there are good reasons for dissatisfaction with Principle 2. If
Aristotle has 2 in mind in Z17, so that the issue of form and matter "fitting
together" is just a non-question, he apparently backslides in H6 and
elsewhere by seeming to raise and answer this very question.[17] Worse,
Aristotle routinely flatly assumes that in some sense form and matter *do*
"fit together" or "make up a whole": witness the phrase, "the compound
substance," *he sunole ousia*, for the individual substance.[18] Against this,
it is sometimes suggested that Aristotle is not serious in talking of the
individual substance as a compound of form and matter.[19] Doubts
about compounding are especially at home in the "projectivist"' or
"constructivist" interpretation of Aristotle. Sellars, for example, asks
about the sense in which a compound material substance is a composite
or "whole" which (on Sellars' view) has an individual form and an
individual piece of matter as its "parts": his answer is that

the individual matter and form of an individual substance are not *two* individuals but *one*.
The individual form of this shoe is the shoe itself; the individual matter of this shoe is *also*

the shoe itself, and there can scarcely be a real distinction between the shoe and itself ... the "parts" involved are not incomplete individuals in the real order, but the importantly different parts of the formula
(piece of leather) (serving to protect and embellish the feet)
projected on the individual thing of which they are true.
Sellars, (1967), p. 118, his emphasis.

This projectivist picture makes quick work of questions about the unity of form and matter in the compound material substance, but I remain unconvinced that Aristotle's apparatus of form and matter has anything in common with the "as if" or "pseudo" ontology that projectivism recommends.[20] More broadly, I shall continue to suppose that Aristotle means seriously his talk of individual substances as *compounds* of form and matter, and that his questions about how the form and matter of a thing combine into a unity genuinely invite an answer.

Despite this, it may seem that dropping Principle 2 on Aristotle's behalf loses important ground in a modern dispute begun by Bradley. Given Principle 2, the fact that the material parts are elements but the form a principle rules out any Bradleian *tertium quid*, any connecting relation that itself in turn must stand between them. The material parts and the form cannot be combined in the first place; *a fortiori*, then, they cannot be combined by a *tertium quid*. As far as Bradley is concerned, however, even for opponents of a Bradleian *tertium quid* Bradleian skepticism may seem a cure that is no better than the original disease. In any case, the modern parallels are not all on the side of Principle 2. Aristotle's distinction between elements and principles is sometimes compared to Frege's distinction between a function, which is "incomplete" or "unsaturated," and objects, which are "saturated" or "self-sufficient."[21] It is certainly the orthodox Fregean line to deny the necessity for any *tertium quid* to explain how an $n$-ary function can apply to its $n$-many arguments (as we shall see, however, this falls far short of showing there *cannot* be any *tertium quid* that stands between them). It is also certain, however, that Frege would flatly deny any counterpart to Principle 2. For example, from "On Concept and Object," we read, "not all the parts of a thought can be complete; at least one must be 'unsaturated,' or predicative; otherwise they would not hold together."[22] That is, the thought is composed of parts of *different* logical type, and the difference in logical type explains how they "hold together" to make a unity.

If Principle 2 seems too restrictive, we may consider instead this weaker principle:

Principle 3. If all of a number of items are to be unified into a genuine whole *by means of some additional item* or *form*, the original items themselves must all be elements.

Unlike Principle 2, Principle 3 does not stand in the way of unifying form and matter into a whole. At the same time, 3 also ensures that if the material parts and the form are elements and a principle respectively, as Aristotle supposes, there can be no question of introducing any *additional* form—no question of any *tertium quid*—to say how the original form and matter can make up a single whole. So Principle 3 has the appropriate anti-Bradleian consequences, but without the negative features of Principle 2.

Although Principle 3 fits Aristotle's purposes far better than its precedessor, it still obscures some important detail. The point this time is not textual but philosophical, and has to do with the horror of a *tertium quid* excited by the threat of a Bradley-style regress. In fact, there is not that much wrong with the introduction of a *tertium quid*, if it is handled correctly. Bradley's regress comes from supposing that to explain how *Rab*, there *must* be a new relation *R'* such that *R'* holds between *R*, *a*, and *b*. But no regress follows just from the assumption that where *Rab*, *in fact* there is some *R'* such that *R'* holds between *R*, *a*, and *b*. In terms of the familiar "rope around the tree" argument: to tie a rope of sufficient length around the tree, it is not the case that one *must* first have an intermediate piece of rope to join the original rope and the tree, and then yet another piece of rope, and so on. But equally, it's not the case that, given one piece of rope adequately long for the task, one *cannot* insert an intermediate piece of rope, or indeed as (finitely) many pieces as one pleases.

In Fregean terms, our problem was how to explain the notation of application of function to argument. The extreme anti-Bradleian stance in Principle 3 commits us to saying that we cannot eliminate any case of this notation in favor of the name for a function, on pain of the kind of regress Aristotle avoids. But this motivation is not correct. For any $n$-ary function, the connective for application of that function to its $n$-many arguments can be eliminated by introducing the name of an associated $n+1$-ary function. For any such connective you please, nothing stands in the way of eliminating that connective by using instead the name of the associated (higher-order) function. Admittedly, you cannot eliminate *all* connectives in this way, and if you cannot eliminate them all, why eliminate any? That is, why ever replace the notation for application of function to argument by the name of an associated (higher-order) function? In this reasoning, however, the distinction between function and argument in itself plays no part. The distinction does not stand in the way of introducing the name of a higher-order function to replace the logical connective for application of function to argument. Nor does it play any role in the reasoning that not all logical connectives can be replaced in this way.[23]

For reasons of this sort, in place of Principle 3 we might prefer Principle 4:

Principle 4. If all of a number of items are to be unified into a genuine whole without the resort to some additional item or form, then at least one of the original items is an element, and at least one a principle.

According to Principle 4, by Modus Tollens, if the items to be unified are all elements, then their unity must be the work of some further entity, as Z17 predicts (1041b20–22). (Principle 1, which is still in force, then tells us that this further entity is a principle, and not an element.) But if at least one of the items to be unified is an element, and at least one a principle, then Principle 4 has no advice on the necessity or otherwise of a further entity to do the unifying. Given at least one principle and at least one element, Principle 4 does not require a *tertium quid*, but it does not prohibit it either.

On this last point, Principle 4 is significantly weaker than Principle 3, which requires that a difference between element and principle among the items to be unified *rules out* any possibility of a *tertium quid*. At the same time, where the items to be unified are all elements, 3 is silent on how they are to be unified. By my score sheet, then, in contrast to Principle 4, Principle 3 is too strong in ruling out a *tertium quid* in certain cases, and too weak in not requiring some further unifying entity in others.

Finally, adopting Principle 4 in preference to 3 leaves us free to halt the sequence of forms at any point we wish—at its very beginning, if we so choose—but for reasons that lie outside Principle 4 altogether. (But we can have the freedom we need and still retain Principles 1 and 4, for the sake of the hope they offer of a reasonably systematic account of unification: 1 for the role it gives to form as an external principle of unity for the material parts of a thing, 4 for the room it leaves for form as an internal principle in a componential account of unity: see Note 8 above.) Setting out the new reasons for an early halt to the sequence of forms brings us to the Content Requirement and the argument of *Metaphysics* H6.

## III. The Rejection of a Connecting Relation: H6 and the Content Requirement

Aristotle holds that the sole constituents of a thing are a given set of material parts[24] together with the form thanks to which the parts make up a unity. In particular, there is a *single* unifying form or principle, and no special "connecting relation" to connect that form with the material parts. The argument against a connecting relation is not generally recognized, but it appears in the middle of *Metaphysics* H6:

Owing to the difficulty about unity some speak of 'participation' (*methexin*), and raise the question, what is the cause (*aition*) of participation and what is it to participate; and others speak of 'communion' (*sunousian*), as Lycophron says knowledge is a communion of knowing with the soul; and others say life is a 'composition' (*sunthesin*) or 'connexion' (*sundesmon*) of soul with body. Yet the same account applies to all cases (*ho autos logos epi panton*); (b12) for being healthy, too, will on this showing be either a 'communion' (*sunousia*) or a 'connexion' (*sundesmos*) or a 'composition' (*sunthesis*) of soul and health, and the fact that the bronze is a triangle will be a 'composition' (*sunthesis*) of bronze and triangle, and the fact that a thing is white will be a 'composition' (*sunthesis*) of surface and whiteness (b16). The cause (*aition*) is that people look for a unifying formula, and a difference, between potentiality and complete reality (*dunameos kai entelecheias* ... *logon henopoion kai diaphoran*). (H6, 1045b7–17, after Ross' translation)

The last sentence is especially cryptic. Aristotle suggests that the mistaken talk criticized in the rest of the passage results from the quest for "a unifying formula, and a difference, between potentiality and complete reality." Perhaps his thought is this. *If* there is a "difference" between potentiality and actuality, or between form and matter, as people allege, then some unifying formula will be needed to connect them. And *if* again some unifying formula is needed, then we will resort to the talk of *sunthesis, sundesmos*, and the like, highlighted in the earlier parts of the passage. In reality, however, no difference of the kind alleged exists, and the unifying formula, and the consequent talk of *sunthesis* and the rest, are unneeded solutions to an nonexistent problem.[25]

What is the "difference" people see between the matter and the form, and how are they mistaken? According to some readings, Aristotle's solution to the unity of matter and form is that in fact these are one entity, not two; so the difference mistakenly found between them must be *numerical* difference. The proposed correction, that the matter and the form of a thing are identical, pitches us directly into the projectivist reading of Aristotle already criticized in Section II. Alternatively and, I think, preferably, Aristotle's solution in H6 argues that a thing's matter and form are *alike* in a way that people had not expected, so that the difference people wrongly see must be *qualitative* difference.[26] On this account, it is common ground to those who find a difference between the matter and the form of a thing and to those who do not that the matter and the form are straightforwardly nonidentical. The view that a difference exists between the matter and the form takes these to be two items or natures, with no relevant similarity possible between them. The view is corrected, not by supposing that the matter and the form are identical; rather, they are *two* items or natures, but they can after all exhibit some relevant similarity. As we shall see, the matter and the form of a thing are alike in the way that in general the potential and the actual are alike.[27] In particular, as Aristotle points out more than once in H6, if I am about to make a bronze sphere, its matter is already potentially a sphere, and the form is actually the very same thing, that is, a sphere.

This clears the way for the positive story to come on how matter and form do in fact "fit together." But Aristotle also has the negative goal of discrediting the move to a special connecting relation or *logos henopoios*. If people exaggerate the difference between matter and form, he may have room to argue that the *logos henopoios* is at least unnecessary. What supports the further view that it is outright objectionable? The Content Requirement is a key player in the argument for this result. On Aristotle's ordinary theory, the syllable *BA*, for example, is composed of the appropriate form or arrangement and the relevant letters:

$BA$ = arrangement $(A, B)$.

I take the brackets-and-comma notation '$(\,,)$' here to be syncategorematic: it is *not* the name of some connecting relation between the arrangement and the letters $A$ and $B$. Aristotle holds that the arrangement is the unifying form or principle of *unity* for the syllable; by the Content Requirement, it is also the substance of the syllable and the cause of its *being*.

Suppose now that, contrary to what has just been suggested, we cannot understand how the letters and the arrangement go together to make up the syllable without introducing some connecting relation to join them:

$BA$ = arrangement $(A, B)$ = *sunthesis* (arrangement, $A, B$).

On this view, the principle of unity for the syllable turns out to be not the arrangement after all, but rather the new connecting relation of *sunthesis*.[28] But according to the Content Requirement, the principle of unity for the parts of a thing is also the thing's substance and the cause of its being; accordingly, *sunthesis* is also the substance and the cause of the being of the syllable. The argument in H6 fastens on what happens when we generalize this result. Suppose that we have two things, a bronze triangle (say), which is a *sunthesis* of bronze and triangle, and a white surface, which is a *sunthesis* of surface and whiteness (b14–16). As Aristotle points out, the bronze triangle and the white surface are unities. thanks to the use of the *same* notion, *sunthesis*, in both cases. A possible, but weak, reason for finding this objectionable might be a general distaste for solutions that apply in common to every case, cutting them all from the same cloth.[29] Aristotle's misgivings gain far more point, however, if they address the issue of *content*. By the Content Requirement, if *sunthesis* is the principle of unity for the bronze triangle and for the white surface alike, it will also be the substance and the cause of being for both.[30] And in general, if we give up the idea that what unifies the parts of the thing is the form that we take to typify the kind, and appeal instead to some purely contentless notion, *sunthesis* (say), which is the same for all cases, then every unity will have the same substance and the same cause of its being. That is, the same unifying principle is common to members of quite different kinds, and the same account—that is, the same *definition*—applies vacuously to them all.[31] Or as Aristotle characterizes a comparable result in Z11, "there is a single form of many things whose form is clearly different," so that eventually "all things will be one."[32]

This gives the true nature of the *reduction ad absurdum* that commentators have seen in the passage.[33] The Content Requirement is a crucial assumption of the argument. In line with the Content Requirement, if each kind of thing has a distinctively different definition as Aristotle's larger theory demands, it will also have a distinctively different principle of unity. But the use of a single connecting relation, be it *sunthesis* or *sundesmos* or *methexis* or whatever, to explain how each and every thing alike is a unity, assigns the *same* definition to each thing, no matter what its kind. So the theory of a special connecting relation, the same for all, must be rejected.[34]

## IV. The Positive Story (I): The General Shape of the Problem in H6

What, then, is it that makes man one, and why is it one and not many, for example, animal and two-footed, especially if there are, as some say, animal-itself and two-footed-itself? Why is not man those-themselves,[35] and men will exist by participation not in man, nor in one thing but in two, animal and two-footed, and in general man would be not one but more than one thing, animal and two-footed?

(a20) Clearly, then, if people proceed in this way in their usual manner of definition and speech, they cannot answer and solve the difficulty. But if, as we say, the one is matter, and the other form, and the one <is> potentially, the other actually, (a24) the object of our inquiry would no longer seem to be a puzzle. For this puzzle is the same as would arise if 'round bronze' were the definition of 'cloak'; for this word would be a sign of the definitory formula, so that the object of inquiry is, What is the cause of the bronze and the round being one? (a28) It is evidently no longer a puzzle, because the one is matter, the other, form. What, then, is the cause of this—of what is potentially being actually—except for the agent, in the case of things of which there is coming-to-be? (a31) For nothing else is the cause of the potential sphere's actually being a sphere,[36] but this was all along the essence of each of the two (a33) ... (b17) But as has been said, the proximate matter and the form are the same and one, the one potentially, and the other actually. Therefore it is similar to ask what is the cause of the <thing that is> one, and <to ask the cause> of its being one [= these come down to the same question]; for each thing is *one* thing of a certain *kind* (*hen gar ti hekaston*, b20), and the potential and the actual are somehow one. Therefore nothing else is the cause here, unless there is something which caused the movement from potentiality into actuality. H6, 1045a14–33, b17–22[37]

We have seen that Aristotle rejects any special connecting relation, any *logos henopoios*, in favor of the view that the true structure of a thing includes its matter and its form, but nothing more. A primary component of his argument is the Content Requirement, which suggests that the form is the principle by which the material parts make up a unified thing *in virtue of the content* of that form. In what follows, I shall argue that the Content Requirement also governs Aristotle's approach to the unity of form and matter themselves (see Note 8 above); as we shall see, the appeal to content is what sets his treatment apart from other, perhaps more familiar, accounts on which the unity of a thing is again to be traced solely to the items to be joined, but without reference to the content of either.

One clue to Aristotle's overall approach to the problem of the unity of form and matter and to the difficulties that follow if this problem is not addressed comes from what he regards as the related problem of the unity of *definition*. What makes all the parts produced by definition by division—two-footed and animal, for example, in the definition of man—into the needed unity? On a conventional approach to definition, especially one wedded to a Platonic ontology, the puzzle is intractable; but it apparently evaporates, given an ontology of matter and form, and the attendant apparatus of potentiality and actuality. That is (continuing to paraphrase Aristotle), the puzzle evaporates because it is the same as the puzzle about the unity of the compound material substance. One feature common to the two puzzles is that failure to resolve them gives rise to similar problems. In H6, Aristotle spells out one consequence if the unity of definition fails: if man is defined in terms of *two* things, animal and two-footed—if man just is "those-two-themselves" (a17)—we may wonder how Socrates (say) is just one kind of thing, (a) man, rather than two, (an) animal and also two-footed (a18–19, cf. B6, 1003a9–12). (The obvious answer is that the one is subordinate in some way to the other: but we need some account of animal and two-footed, beyond just that they are two, in order to make this answer stick.) The problem regarding definition has a counterpart at the level of the compound material substance: how is a given particular bronze sphere, a compound of form and matter, a single kind of thing, rather than equally bronze and (a) sphere?[38] A constraint on the solution to either of the two unity questions is that it should provide an answer to these questions about how to classify the whole.

Aristotle suggests that the puzzle over definition is especially vivid given a Platonic view of the nature of genus, differentia, and species (a15–17). The Platonic form Man, for example, is defined in terms of the forms Animal and Two-footed, so that one substance in actuality, the form Man, is apparently composed of two substances, each of which again exists in actuality, contrary to Aristotle's strictures in Z13–16. On this account, Animal and Two-footed are equally substances. Worse, given the connection Aristotle argues for between the notions of substance and substance *of*, both forms are equally the substance of the species, Man; similarly, both are equally the substance of the individual men that fall under the species. Small wonder, then, that on Plato's theory, as Aristotle complains, Socrates' being a man—that is, by definition, his being a two-footed animal—seems to make him not one (kind of) thing, but two.

Aristotle's own view of genus and differentia involves identifying the differentia with the form of the thing, and comparing—some would say, "identifying"—the genus with the matter. But I take it to be a basic feature of Aristotle's account that the solution to the unity of genus and differentia can be properly understood only *after* we have a solution to comparable questions about the unity of the compound material substance.[39] In the latter case, Aristotle himself believes that the bronze sphere, for example, has two constituents, its matter and its form, each of which is a nature and is a candidate for the nature *of* the thing. Does it follow that the sphere is equally bronze, thanks to its matter, and (a) sphere, thanks to its form? Aristotle has already argued in the *Physics* that of the two, the matter is *less* the nature of the thing than the form.[40] A passage in *Metaphysics* θ7 takes for granted that the contributions of the two natures will not be in competition. According to θ7, a sphere is not equally bronze (thanks to its matter) and (a) sphere (thanks to its form), since we say that it is not bronze but bron*zen*, in the style appropriate to attributes. Being bronzen and (a) sphere is like being (a) sphere and also red (but not red*ness*). No one supposes that a thing's attributes compete with its kind; in fact, the matter does not do so either.[41]

But *how* can can we knit form and matter together so that they make one thing and not two? The passage quoted at the head of this Section conveys Aristotle's proposal that something about the matter and the form *by themselves* suits them for "holding together" in the finished individual substance. But what features are they of the form and the matter by themselves that allow the two together to make up a unity? Aristotle's account is at first sight conspicuously Fregean.[42] On a Fregean account, a function is "unsaturated," as opposed to an object, which is "saturated," and the two together make up a "complete whole." Aristotle's distinction between element and principle in Z17, for example, can seem a direct, if more prosaic, counterpart of Frege's contrast between saturated and unsaturated.[43] The discussion in H6 directly contradicts these expectations. Frege's distinction has to do with "formal" rather than what might be called "proper" features of the items to be unified:[44] it has no interest in the *content* of the items to be joined together. By contrast, for Aristotle, the question of how the matter and the form "fit together" in the thing has everything to do with their content. Aristotle calls on the notions of potentiality and actuality to explain how the matter all along is potentially (a) sphere, and how under certain circumstances it, like the form, is actually (a) sphere and together with the form makes up a unity. In contrast to Frege, then, Aristotle's solution essentially involves the content of the items to be joined.[45]

The move to content in Aristotle's account is not surprising. The Fregean view, which relies on *formal* features of the items to be joined, is too permissive for Aristotle's purposes. For Frege, a wide variety of functions and arguments can "fit together" to produce a value. As Aristotle repeatedly emphasizes, however, matter and form must be suited for each other, so that any story for how they are united in a given compound material substance cannot be based solely on some purely formal feature of each, which holds across the board, for all choices of form and matter regardless of content; his approach instead must be piecemeal, letting the content do the work in each case, if he is to be true to his own theory.[46]

I have suggested that Aristotle's solution to the unity of matter and form runs in terms of the *content* of these two, and is tailored to avoid the problem of dual classification—to show how the sphere can be harmlessly both bronze (or bronzen) and (a) sphere. In both respects, his conception of the problem is distinctly unFregean, and part of the interest of Aristotle's discussion of unity in H6 is how it can take the—for us relatively unfamiliar[47]—route through the content of the form and the matter of a thing in order to answer what in Fregean or Bradleian terms can seem a purely "formal" problem, which has no bearing on the content of the items to be joined together. This difference, however, should not blind us to the fact that Aristotle's unity problem is still cast in essentially the same mould as the puzzle discussed by Frege and Bradley. For example, Aristotle is not in H6 concerned with the physical puzzle of what keeps the elements in the physical composition of the thing from following their natural tendency to move to their proper place and pulling the compound material substance apart.[48] Again, the appeal to content should not make us think that Aristotle is pursuing here a different question about potentiality and actuality: why is it that when the potentiality of the potentially healthy thing has been realized, the result is that the thing is healthy and not musical (say)?[49] This question is on the right track, since it leaves behind questions about ordinary efficient causes, but again it is not the question addressed in H6.

I have suggested that the issues Aristotle means to address in his discussion of unity do not involve ordinary efficient causes. It is tempting to speculate that those issues do not involve first-level causes at all, but are instead in our terms *metatheoretic*. The question with which Aristotle begins, "Why is the bronze (a) sphere?" obviously lends itself to answers in terms of ordinary first-level efficient causes and the account of how the bronze *came to be* a sphere: the craftsman made the bronze into a sphere (more informative accounts will mention his knowledge of the relevant form, and his desire to realize that form in a given matter). But the issues Aristotle has in mind concern *being* rather than becoming (a) sphere (I argue this point in more detail two paragraphs below), and they are *metaphysical* rather than causal in the ordinary sense. What is it about the bronze and the form of a sphere, that the bronze can be (a) sphere? We know from *Physics*. B1 that the matter of a thing and its form together determine the nature of the thing, and in B7 Aristotle explains how this fact about them is foundational to the theory of four causes. In line with this, the general thrust of Aristotle's argument in *Phys*. B is that a thing's constitution as a compound of form and matter is *prior to* the official theory of causes. So the question, How is it that form and matter fit together in the thing? is one that it is beyond the resources of the theory itself to answer. In this sense, Aristotle's question about unity is *about* rather than *in* the theory of causes, and there is no *first-level* causal answer to the question as Aristotle intends it.

One final general issue remains. In our discussion so far, we have assumed that the unity of substance is a legitimate topic of inquiry in the first place, and this is controversial. We have seen that Aristotle turns his question about the unity of a bronze sphere into a question about the cause thanks to which the potential sphere is actually (a) sphere. But his discussion of the cause gets off to a decidedly rocky start. Some have concluded that there is *no* cause: conspicuous among the sceptics are the projectivists, already mentioned in previous Sections.[50] Aristotle's text here is more than usually laconic. His first move, as I understand him, is to set aside any efficient-causal story in telling how it is that a potential so-and-so actually constitutes a so-and-so.[51] He asks: "What, then, is the cause of this—of what is potentially being actually—except for the agent, in the case of things of which there is coming-to-be?" (a31). That is, apparently, there is *no* cause for the potential sphere's actually being a sphere unless we count the efficient cause, relevant only in cases of becoming, which are not his target here.[52] Aristotle is not much interested here in how potential spheres are turned into actual ones, but rather in how a potential sphere actually *is*—that is, it actually *constitutes*—(a) sphere. He mentions cases of becoming, which require an efficient cause, at a31 only to bracket them; they are after all irrelevant to issues of the unity of *definition* which prompted the move to questions about the unity of the individual substance.

Once efficient causes are bracketed, what is left? Aristotle continues: "For nothing else is the cause of the potential sphere's actually being (a) sphere, but this was all along the essence of each of the two" (a31–3). One of the many uncertainties here is Aristotle's "nothing else." On one reading, he means there is no cause other than the agent, already dismissed in the previous sentence: on this showing, the count of causes still stands at zero, and the skeptics are right. But the second part of his remark, "but this was all along the essence of each," seems to suggest that there is a cause of unity after all[53]—so does unity have a cause or not?[54] An intriguing alternative possibility is that by "nothing else" Aristotle means that there is no cause *over and above the actual and the potential spheres themselves* that might explain why they are one.[55] On this reading, Aristotle tacitly assumes that the efficient cause has already been excluded; once it has been set to one side, however, only the actual and potential spheres—that is, the form and the matter—remain as the cause of unity. In this way, no *outside* factor explains why the matter and the form make up a unity. In particular, as Aristotle will argue later in the chapter (b7–17, see Section III), there is no special "connecting relation" standing between them. It is consistent with this, of course, that there *is* a cause of their unity, but this must be something intrinsic to the matter and the form themselves. In the next Section, I argue that in fact this is exactly the way things turn out: the matter and the form fit together thanks to features that are essential to the matter and the form themselves, and without the benefit of any special connecting relation, or *logos henopoios*, to stand between them.

## V. The Positive Story (II): H6 on How the Matter and the Form are One

For the most part, Aristotle's positive account of the unity of form and matter in H6 begins and ends in the middle of the full story, with two versions, weak and strong, of what I shall call the *correspondence thesis* governing the form and matter of a given thing. I will divide the details of the larger story into four parts, beginning in (i) with the different versions of the Correspondence thesis, together with their basis in Aristotle's text. Discussion of the theoretical background and of the consequences for unity then follows in (ii)–(iv) below. The results of the Section are also formalized in the Appendix.

(i) *Weak and Strong Correspondence: How the form of a sphere is actually (a) sphere, and how the matter may be potentially or actually (a) sphere.* I begin with the weaker version of correspondence, which may hold between the matter and the form of a sphere (say), even before any compound sphere exists:

*Weak Correspondence.* The matter and the form of a sphere *weakly correspond* to each other: that is to say, it is in the essence of the matter and of the form that the matter is potentially (a) so-and-so and the form is actually (a) so-and-so, where each is potentially or actually the same so-and-so, i.e, (a) *sphere*.

According to Weak Correspondence, the matter and the form are each in their own way (a) sphere. In the text, Aristotle approaches the point in a variety of ways, not all of them utterly clear. Barring the efficient cause, according to Aristotle, "there is no other cause of the potential sphere's actually being (a) sphere, but this [= being (a) sphere?[56]] was all along the essence of each of the two" (a31–33). Each of the two, then, the matter or potential sphere and the form or actual sphere, has an essence in a way that helps solve the unity problem. But they will not have exactly the same essence.[57] I take Aristotle's point to be that it is essential to the matter and the form alike that it *is (a) sphere*, but each is (a) sphere *in its own distinctive way*.

What are these different ways? The answer comes twice, towards the beginning of Aristotle's discussion, and in the difficult lines at the end of the chapter. First (a23–4), "the one is matter, and the other form, and the one <is> potentially, and the other <is> actually"—that is, in terms of the sphere example, the matter is potentially *(a) sphere* and the form is actually *(a) sphere*.[58]

Again, "the proximate matter and the form are the same and one, the one potentially, and the other actually ... each thing is one thing of a certain kind, and the potential and the actual are in a way one" (b17–19, 20–21). The difficulty here is the grammar, which is quite different from what is usually thought.[59] Aristotle is not claiming that the matter is the same and one as, much less identical with, the form. Rather, he is saying that there is one and the same thing, in fact, one and the same kind $k$, such that the matter is potentially (a) $k$, and the form is actually (a) $\underline{k}$.[60] For example, the matter is potentially a sphere, the other is actually a sphere.

Weak Correspondence is concerned only with certain preconditions for the existence and unity of the compound material sphere. Aristotle is clear that for the compound sphere to exist, we need Strong Correspondence, which posits that the matter is not only potentially but also *actually* a sphere:

*Strong Correspondence.* The matter and the form of the sphere *strongly correspond* to each other: that is, the form is actually (a) so-and-so (as before) *and the matter too is actually (a) so-and-so* (a30, 32—3, b22), where each is actually the *same* so-and-so, i.e, (a) *sphere.*

Once Strong Correspondence is satisfied, a compound material sphere exists. What remains is to show that the terms on which it exists also guarantee that it is a unity. This in turn requires that we understand better the grounds on which claims of Weak and Strong Correspondence are based. Once we have a handle on the theoretical background for the different kinds of correspondence, we will be better placed to see how, if the form and matter of the sphere strongly correspond to each other in the sense spelled out, there will exist a compound sphere that is a unity of the desired kind.

*(ii) The Theoretical Background: Form-As-Actuality, and Telelological Dominance and Dependence.* A crucial component in both versions of Correspondence is Aristotle's "Form-As-Actuality" assumption—the assumption that the form of a sphere, for example, is itself actually (a) sphere (a23–4, b17–19, see (i) above). I take it that being actually (a) sphere is an intrinsic, or nonrelational, property of the form. It is also explanatorily basic in Aristotle's theory: there is no more fundamental fact on which this feature of the given form is based.

The idea that the form of a sphere *is actually (a) sphere* is perhaps something we would express by saying that the form of a sphere has a certain *content*. The form is the form *of* a thing that has the (here unspecified) defining properties of a sphere. The form "brings" its content to a given compound sphere, and it is presumably thanks to its content that the form of a sphere is, as Aristotle says, the *actuality of* the compound sphere.

A second fundamental ingredient in Aristotle's metaphysical theory is essentially relational, and involves a pair of asymmetric relations linking the form and the relevant matter. The idea is not explicitly mentioned in either Correspondence assumption, and our source for it is not H6, but the discussion of potentiality and actuality in the later chapters of *Metaphysics* Θ. According to Aristotle in Θ8, the matter exists *for the sake of* the form. I interpret this in terms of notions of *teleological dominance* and *dependence*:

*Teleological Dominance and Dependence.* The matter stands in one relation or another of *teleological dependence on* the form or actuality as goal (*telos*), while the form is in one way or another *teleologically dominant* with respect to the matter.

Teleological dependence is a special case of the larger notion of *ontological dependence*, which I take to be a basic notion for Plato as well as for Aristotle. Sensibles, for example, are ontologically dependent on (Platonic) forms in Plato (this I suspect is a case of ontological dependence that also involves teleological dependence), while in Aristotle's own theory in *Categories.* 1–5, everything that is not an individual substance is ontologically dependent on individual substances. In the present case, matter or potentiality is not just ontologically but also teleologically dependent on the appropriate form or actuality. Teleological dependence has teleological dominance as its converse; teleological dominance is the notion of priority in substance that is the subject of Θ8. Aristotle argues in Θ8 that actuality is prior in substance to potentiality; his arguments depend in part on the idea that the potentiality is *for the sake of* the actuality, so that the actuality or goal is the *principle* (*arche*) of the potentiality in the matter. The idea that the actuality is the principle of the relevant potentiality suits not only Aristotle's conclusions about priority in substance in Θ8, but also the claims about the relations of teleological dominance and dependence between form and matter.

Teleological Dominance and Dependence and the Form-As-Actuality assumption together give the basic explanatory schema for how the matter is potentially (a) sphere:

*Schema I.* The matter *m* is *potentially* (a) sphere, *because* (i) *m* is teleologically dependent on the form and (ii) is *actually* (a) sphere.

It follows from schema I that the form and the matter weakly correspond to each other in the sense explained in (i) above. The schema employs a pattern of explanation that goes back to Plato, who will say that a sensible, Socrates (say), is (a) man (he Has man, in the Code-Grice jargon of Izzing and Having[61]), thanks to a relation of teleological as well as ontological dependence on the (Platonic) form man, which too is (= Is) (a) man.

The explanatory force of schema I is due in part at least to the *causal* role it assigns to form—the idea that the form is the cause of the matter's being potentially (a) sphere. The sense of 'cause' here is not an easy one.

Aristotle has in mind at least that the form is the final cause of the matter: according to Θ8, "the matter is potentially *because it would come into the form*" (*elthoi an eis to eidos*, 1050a15); again, everything that comes to be "proceeds towards a principle" that is also an end, so that the potentiality is *for the sake of* that end or actuality, and the end or actuality is *the principle of* the relevant potentiality.[62] On top of the "goal directedness" brought out in this talk, there is the additional idea that the matter is ultimately *assimilated* to the form.[63] The assimilation is prepared for in schema I, which establishes that the matter is potentially (a) sphere; the assimilation is completed in schema II below. The causal relation schema I brings to light embodies the familiar Aristotelian idea that a cause itself exhibits to some special degree, or in some privileged way, the feature which it transmits to the effect. This causal assumption is one that schema I shares with the Platonic scheme for the dependency of sensibles on (Platonic) forms.[64]

Next, what happens when—going beyond being a potential sphere— the matter actually is (constitutes) a sphere? This is the problem case addressed in H6. The schema for actually being a sphere involves a deepening of teleological dependence, but is otherwise the same as before:

Schema II. The matter *m* "actually is" (a30, 32–3, b22) (a) sphere, *because* (i) *m* is fully teleologically dependent on the form ψ and (ii) ψ is actually (a) sphere.

It follows from schema II that the form and the matter strongly correspond to one another, so that a compound material sphere in fact exists (see (i) above). In II, as in I, one or another relation of teleological dependence holds between *m* and the form ψ, while at the same time ψ is actually a sphere. The dependence relation in II is just an intensification of the relation in I; the analysans in II and that in I would be identical, but for the fact that dependence and dominance come in different degrees. As predicted, II brings to light a strong *similarity* between the matter and the form; they differ, however, in that the matter actually is (a) sphere thanks to some *other* entity, namely the form, while the form *in itself* is actually (a) sphere.[65]

The notion of teleological dependence, no less than the idea that teleological dependence can come in different degrees, is, I believe, central to both Plato's and Aristotle's metaphysics. Both ideas are highly mysterious, and I am still trying to understand them. But I am encouraged by the fact that they are at least consistent with a more familiar component in the interpretation of Aristotle. This is the idea that the form exists *at a higher degree of actuality* when the matter is actually (a) so-and-so (teleological dominance by the form is here at its fullest); but it has been present all along at a *lower* level of actuality even when the matter is only potentially (a) so-and-so (here, simple teleological dominance is in effect). As best I can tell, however, the two sets of views are not equivalent.[66]

(iii) *The Subordination of Matter to Form, and the Account of Unity.* I have suggested that the Form-As-Actuality assumption together with the different relations of Teleological Dependence and Dominance explain the claims of Weak and Strong Correspondence that are central to Aristotle's discussion in H6. It remains to show that if the conditions obtain on which the matter is actually (a) sphere, so that a compound material sphere exists, that sphere is also a unity.

It will be useful to begin with a reminder of what I have argued is Aristotle's own conception of the problem of unity. His discussion of unity in H6 has as its starting-point the idea that a thing is a *compound* of matter and form, where the form belongs to, or is predicated of, the matter. How, then, is the thing a unity? Aristotle interprets the question of how the matter and the form "fit together" in the thing as a question about their *content.* Does the compound of the two have a single, unified nature? How is it that the bronze sphere is not subject to competing classifications—both bronze and equally (a) sphere—thanks to the different natures of the matter and the form that it incorporates? The key to a solution, in Aristotle's eyes, is to show that under the conditions sufficient for the existence of a given form-matter compound, the matter is appropriately *subordinate to* the form. If the compound of matter and form exists, and if the matter is subordinate to the form in the required way, then the objections to the unity of the two will have been removed.

Like Correspondence, subordination too is rooted in Dependency. Schemas I and II above suggest how the subordination is done. According to schema I, the matter in itself is potentially (a) sphere thanks to the fact that the matter is teleologically dependent on the form, which in itself is actually (a) sphere. Schema II now shows that the bronze is incorporated into the whole, so that the bronze is now actually (a) sphere, as the result of a deepening in the degree of teleological dependency by the matter on the form. The teleological dependence by the matter on the form, required by both schemas, is unremitting, so that the contribution the matter makes to the whole is subordinate throughout to that made by the form. So the matter and the form are distinct ingredients of the finished substance, but the compound is not a "heap" of the two but a member of a single unitary kind, thanks to the form.[67]

The causal role of form here is crucial. Where the matter is actually (a) sphere, the form is fully dominant, while the matter is fully dependent, so it is appropriate to think of the *form* as the cause of the matter's being actually (a) sphere. But if the form is the cause of the thing's *being*—its belonging to the kind sphere—and if the form also harnesses the contribution by the matter, subordinating it to the contribution the form itself makes, then the form is appropriately the cause of *unity* of the form and the matter in the compound sphere as well.

(iv) *The Role of Essences in Aristotle's Account.* Aristotle claims that it is
*essential* to the matter that it is potentially (a) sphere; it follows by I that
dependence on the form to some degree is essential to the matter all along,
and the full dominance of the matter by the form in II is only an
intensification or deepening of a connection with the form that is integral
to the matter from the very start. At the same time, it is *essential* to the
form that it is actually (a) sphere; in fact, then, the form is actually the
very so-and-so, namely (a) sphere, that the matter is potentially, and the
feature that makes the form dominant over the matter is one that is
essential to the form all along.

In itself, then, the matter is potentially (a) sphere, thanks to its
dependency on the form, which in itself is actually (a) sphere; and the
matter too will be actually (a) sphere (but not *in itself* actually (a) sphere)
when it is fully dependent on the form. In this way, the matter actually
is (a) sphere, thanks chiefly to the causal role of the form, which totally
dominates the matter, but due also to facts about the matter, which has
been potentially (a) sphere and, hence, dominated by the form to some
degree right from the start. The solution to the problem of unity, then,
requires the notion of the intensification of teleological dependence and
otherwise, as promised, nothing beyond the resources of the matter and
the form by themselves.

It is not possible, however, to reduce teleological dependence by the
matter on the form to facts about the form and the matter each taken by
itself. There is no hope that either of the (asymmetric) relations of
dominance and dependence is (in a later jargon) an *internal* relation,
reducible to intrinsic properties of each of its terms.[68] Relations of
teleological dominance and dependence, then, between the form and the
matter are irreducible ingredients in the foundations of Aristotle's
metaphysical theory.

## VI. Conclusion

According to a central idea in Aristotle's discussion of the unity of form
and matter, there is no cause for the unity of the compound material
sphere beyond the form and the matter themselves. Having characterized
the matter as all along potentially (a) sphere, and the form as all along
actually (a) sphere, however, he has no more to say about how the unity
of the two is achieved. But how is the reference to potentiality and
actuality any less mysterious than the claims about the unity of form and
matter it seeks to explain? I have suggested that the relation of potential
spheres to actual ones should be understood ultimately in terms of the
assumptions of Form-As-Actuality and of the different degrees of
Teleological Dominance and Dependence between the form and the
matter. With these assumptions in force, we can argue that the conditions

under which, according to Aristotle, the matter is actually (a) sphere, so that the compound sphere exists, are also conditions under which the contribution made by the matter to the whole is subordinate to that made by the form, so that the compound sphere is a genuine unity.

But are the assumptions of Form-As-Actuality and Teleological Dominance and Dependence themselves any less mysterious than the claims they are used to support? The only answer here must be that in the last analysis, Aristotle's solution is possible, only given the role these various assumptions are stipulated to have at the foundations of his metaphysical theory. Without the assumptions his explanations appeal to, the theory itself would not be possible, and there is no support to be found for them within the theory except, perhaps, abductively: the very power of the theory that he builds on these foundations is sufficient argument for finding them appropriate.

The idea that the matter is potentially (a) sphere is mysterious in yet another way, however, for it is not obvious that the bronze is any more potentially (a) sphere than it is potentially (a) cube, or (a) statue, or (a) rear fender.[69] If in the last analysis the potentiality in the bronze amounts to nothing more than sheer malleability, how does this make the union of the bronze with the form of a sphere any kind of unity at all? Aristotle's choice of an artifact—the bronze sphere—as an example is quite misleading in this regard.[70] In nature, the potentialities in the matter are frequently limited to one: this matter, for example, is feline matter, and if it develops at all, the result will be a cat. Even in art, however, the range of possibilities for a given matter is not always that large (think of the Hermes in the marble). And there seems no reason why it should be "up to" the matter alone to determine which of its potentialities should get realized; causal intervention by the agent selects for one given form in preference to its possible rivals, and this can quite appropriately determine which of the potentialities in the matter is realized. Even where competing potentialities in the matter do exist, it is not clear that they undercut Aristotle's account of how, *once one of these potentialities is selected for*, the result is a unity.

Still, it may seem troubling that before the sphere is made, there is a whole raft of possibilities facing the bronze—a whole variety of different forms it is teleologically dependent on. The very variety of rival dependencies weakens the dependency in any one given case: the dependency by the bronze on the form of a sphere, for example, like its dependency on the form of a cube and the rest, must be very slight. This weakening in the dependency by the matter on the form is in fact an advantage. Plausibly, the weakness in the initial dependency by the matter on the form also weakens the degree of unity of the matter with the form in the eventual sphere (if this is the form the craftsman chooses to impose on the matter). And in general, the degree of unity of the form and matter in the finished thing varies inversely with the number of alternative forms the matter is matter for. It is tempting to think that competing dependencies by a single matter on multiple forms is typical of lower-level matter, and of the matter of artifacts; if so, then we have an explanation for the weaker degree of unity Aristotle sees in these kinds of case.[71]

This last point brings out one more facet of the difference between Aristotle's account of unity and the Fregean view. On any solution to Aristotle's problems about unity along Fregean lines, content plays no role in the account of unity, and the range of possibilities open to a given matter will be irrelevant. Never mind how many different ways a given matter might have developed—into a cube instead of a sphere, and so on—the sphere that exists in the actual world has the same degree of unity, on a Fregean view, as any other form-matter compound. For Aristotle, by contrast, the unity of the form and matter in a thing varies with the kind of the thing—whether it is a living thing, or an artifact, for example, or how far below the level of substance it comes in the hierarchy of form-matter compounds.[72] I have speculated on Aristotle's behalf that the degree of unity that a given compound enjoys is determined by whether *alternative outcomes* are available for its matter, and if alternatives are available, how many. For example, if feline matter can only develop into a cat, then the degree of unity of feline matter and feline form when the cat finally comes into existence is quite high; but if bronze can be worked up into a variety of shapes, or if a man may be pale, or dark, or a variety of shades in between, the unity of the whole is correspondingly less.[73] Suppose next that it is determined by the *content of a given form* whether the compound of a given matter with that form is the sole available outcome for the matter, or whether the form will tolerate a variety of different outcomes on the part of the matter. This is a question of the "grip" the form of (a) sphere, for example, has on the bronze in advance of the craftsman's work, when the bronze is only potentially (a) sphere: is its grip sufficiently weak, for example, to allow competing forms—of a cube, or a rear fender—an equal or even a stronger claim? If a story along these lines can be made out, then ultimately for Aristotle the degree of unity of a thing varies with, and is determined by, the content of the relevant form.

Other questions about Aristotle's account remain. One question involves a variation on the problem of dual classification. I have argued that there is no conflict between being bronzen (thanks to the matter) and being (a) sphere (thanks to the form), since the contribution the bronze makes to the whole is subordinate to that made by the form: the bronze in the finished substance is actually (a) sphere, thanks to the form, which itself is actually (a) sphere and is dominant with respect to the matter. But this solution to how a single compound sphere can be both bronze (better: bronzen) *and* (a) sphere—apparently *two* things—comes at the price of a new way in which the sphere appears to be two things, not one: how can one and the same compound sphere be *two spheres*, the matter and the form? Even worse, how can it be two *actual* spheres?—since, as we have seen, the form and the matter in the finished thing are each actually (a) sphere. Or, on a still less favourable count, we now have *three* actual spheres to contend with, one cobbled together out of two others.

These problems have a close relative in Aristotle's insistence in Z13–16 that no substance can be composed of actual substances.[74] Pellegrin suggests usefully that Aristotle's rule must be indexed according to the level of the substances involved. With the proper indices in place, according to Pellegrin, the rule requires that "No substance of level $n$ be composed of substances themselves of level $n$"—but the compound substance, for example, which is of level 2, can be composed of form (of level 1) and matter (level 3).[75] This leaves us free to think that within the compound material substance, the substantial form is a substance, and also perhaps a unity, *in the fullest sense.* By the same token, the form is also *actually (a) sphere* in the fullest sense—it is actually (a) sphere thanks to itself and to nothing else; the matter, however, is actually (a) sphere thanks to something *else*, namely, the form, which is an *external* principle with respect to the matter. (Similarly, the compound sphere is actually (a) sphere thanks again to the form, which is an internal principle to, but a proper part of, the compound itself.) So there are different levels of being actually (a) sphere, and the form is actually (a) sphere at a level *higher than* that at which either the compound sphere, or its matter, is actually (a) sphere. Conflict between the different spheres will arise, however, only if (what is not the case) all were spheres *at the same level of actuality.*

A last objection takes up the *scope* of Aristotle's discussion in H6. In the chapter, Aristotle explicitly restricts questions about the unity of the compound material substance to questions about its proximate matter and (substantial) form (1045b18). So his account of the unity of the bronze sphere considers only how the bronze and the form of a sphere combine to make a unitary whole. But there are further questions about unity that this leaves unaddressed. We know that the bronze is itself a compound of matter and form, and that that matter too, no doubt, is a compound of still other matter and form, and so on all the way down (perhaps) to prime matter (cf. Note 24 above). Pretend now, with Aristotle, that the bronze sphere is a genuine substantial unity. Aristotle represents this as a problem about the relation of the proximate matter $m$ (the bronze) and substantial form $\psi$ (the form of a sphere). But it is far from clear that we will get the same account of unity for other levels of matter and form, *below* the level of $m$ and $\psi$.[76] Even without this complication, however, difficulties threaten. We may suspect that the proximate matter $m$ of the sphere—the bronze—is *less* of a unity, and *its* proximate matter $m^1$ even less of a unity still, and so on down the line (see Z16, 1040b5–10). How then can we get a substantial unity—a unity in close to the strongest sense—if the thing is worked up out of a string of matters whose unity becomes less and less the further down we go? At first blush, one might think that in general, the degree of unity of a whole compounded from parts $x$ and $y$ cannot exceed the degree of unity of each of the parts, $x$ and $y$, separately. If so, then Aristotle's story in H6 about the unity of $m$ and $\psi$ is apparently subverted by the thought that $m$ itself is a compound of $m^1$ and some other form $\psi^1$, where $m$ has less unity than the initial compound of $m$ and $\psi$ is supposed to have. At the same time, the matter $m^1$ of $m$ in turn is compounded out of yet another layer of matter and form, $m^2$ and $\psi^2$, and $m^1$ has less unity than $m$, and $m^2$ less unity still; and so on all the way down.

To put the problem in only slightly different terms: Aristotle's appeal to the idea that the matter is potentially (a) sphere apparently only pushes our initial problem one stage back. If there is doubt about how the compound sphere can be a unity given its composition out of form and matter, how does the bland assurance that the matter in itself was all along potentially (a) sphere answer doubts about whether the matter itself is a unity, given its composition as bronze on the one hand, and its potential for being (a) sphere on the other?

Perhaps Aristotle would answer that in the special case of compounds of substantial form and proximate matter, the degree of unity of the parts—the form and, especially, the matter—taken separately will not undercut the unity of the whole. As for the form, we already know that it is a unity *par excellence* (see Note 67 above). At the same time, Aristotle may think that the substantial form $\psi$ "reaches down" at least a certain distance through the lower orders of matter, and makes matter at each level more of a unity than it would be by itself.[77] Thus, while $\psi^1$ is the *intrinsic* principle of unity for the proximate matter $m$ (itself a compound of $m^1$ and $\psi^1$), $\psi^1$ is superseded by the substantial form $\psi$, which is an intrinsic principle of unity for the finished substance compounded from $m$ and $\psi$, but also an *extrinsic* principle of unity for $m$ by itself. But in unifying $m$, $\psi$ will also unify each of the (upper-level) coincident matters that make up $m$: is (perhaps) also an extrinsic principle of unity for $m^1$ (itself a compound of $m^2$ and $\psi^2$), and for $m^2$ (a compound of $m^3$ and $\psi^3$), and the rest.[78]

The unifying influence of the substantial form extends down only so far, however. Aristotle most often thinks of the uniform parts of an animal as matter *for* an animal of that kind—feline flesh, feline bone, and the like[79]—and it may seem that the solution of H6 for proximate matter and substantial form will work equally well to show that the uniform parts can be part of a genuine whole, thanks again to the extended downwards reach of the substantial form. If the account given in the previous paragraph applies here as well, two assumptions must be satisfied. First, the substantial form $\psi$ can unify a given set of uniform parts so that they make up a genuine whole, only if each part itself has a degree of unity no less than that of the whole. Second, each uniform part itself has the required degree of unity *thanks again to* ψ, which again acts as an extrinsic principle of unity for that part. It is not clear, however, whether this second assumption is correct and hence, also unclear whether the story told in the previous paragraph can be adapted to show how together the uniform parts too can be parts of the living thing as a genuine whole. The uniform parts are the result of Aristotle's technical notion of *mixis* or "mixture." Any result of mixture in Aristotle's sense has the four elements as its initial ingredients, or pre-existing matter, and Aristotle is explicit that in this case the pre-existing matter does not persist in what I take to be the standard way: instead, the initial ingredients, earth, air, fire, and water, exist only *potentially* in the result of mixture. Whatever the details of this admittedly difficult proposal, it is reasonable to think that each uniform part is a unity to the degree that it is for reasons that cannot be properly understood apart from details distinctive of the theory of mixture. For similar reasons, any account of how together the uniform parts can be parts of a genuine whole is also intertwined with the account of mixture. It is more than possible, then, that Aristotle's solution to questions about the unity of the compound material substance in H6 applies at best only at the upper reaches in the composition of a thing, and that a different story will be needed for the lower-level cases where the theory of mixture is also in play.[80]

## *APPENDIX. The Formal Account of Unity*

It may be useful to set out the main steps in the argument I attribute to Aristotle in Section V above. Let ψ be the form of a sphere, and $m$ be the bronze that is its matter. We start with two assumptions:

(A1) ψ is actually (a) sphere.   [The Form-As-Actuality Assumption]
(A2) $m$ is teleologically dependent on ψ.   [Teleological Dependence]

Given (A1), (A2), and in light of Schema I, we know that

(T1) $m$ is potentially (a) sphere,

so that by (A1), (T1), and the definition of Weak Correspondence,

(T2) $m$ and ψ correspond weakly to each other. [Weak Correspondence]

Suppose now that the degree of teleological dependence is increased, so that (A2) is superseded by the stronger assumption that

(A3) $m$ is fully teleologically dependent on ψ. [Full Teleological Dependence

By (A1) and (A3), and in light of Schema II,

(T3) $m$ is actually (a) sphere,

so that by (A1), (T3), and the definition of Strong Correspondence,

(T4) $m$ and $\psi$ correspond strongly to each other.

[Strong Correspondence]

From (T4), it follows that in fact

(T5) The compound of $m$ and $\psi$ exists.

By (A3), we can also show that

(T6) m is subordinate to $\psi$.                    [Subordination]

By (T5) and (T6), then,

(T7) The compound of m and $\psi$ is a unity,

as required. As before, the causal role of form is expressed in (A2) and its stronger version, (A3), which set out the different degrees of Teleological Dominance by the form over the matter. (T7) rests on (A1) and (A3) as assumptions.

## BIBLIOGRAPHY

Ackrill, J. L. 1972–73. "Aristotle's Definitions of *Psyche*," *Proceedings of the Aristotelian Society* 73, pp. 119—33.

Annas, J. 1976. *Aristotle's Metaphysics: Books M and N*. Oxford.

Anscombe G. E. M., (1959), *An Introduction to Wittgenstein's Tractatus* (New York).

Austin J. L., (1968). *The Foundations of Arithmetic* by Gottlob Frege (English translation of Frege, 1884)) (Evanston, Illinois).

Balme, D. (1987). "Aristotle's Biology Was Not Essentialist," in Allan Gotthelf and James Lennox, *op. cit.*

Bradley F. H., (1893), *Reality and Appearance* (London).

Burnyeat, M. et al. (1984). *Notes on Eta and Theta of Aristotle's Metaphysics*. Oxford.

Charles, D. (1988). "Aristotle on Hypothetical Necessity and Irreducibility," *Pacific Philosophical Quarterly* 69, pp. 1–53.

——, Gill, M. L. and Scaltsas, T. (1994), editors, *Unity and Identity: The Principles of Aristotelian Substances* (Oxford).

——, (1994), "Matter and Form: Unity and Identity," in Charles, Gill, Scaltsas, *op. cit.*

Church, A. 1956. *Introduction to Mathematical Logic*, Volume I. (Princeton).

Code A., (1986), "Aristotle: Essence and Accident," in Richard Grandy and Richard Warner, editors, *Philosophical Grounds of Rationality: Intentions, Categories, Ends*, pp. 411–39. (Oxford).

——, (1987), "Soul as Efficient Cause in Aristotle's Embryology," *Philosophical Topics* 15, pp. 161–9.

Irving M. Copi (1958) (= [1966]). "Objects, Properties, and Relations in the *Tractatus*," *Mind* 67, pp. 145–65, reprinted in Copi and Beard (1966), pp. 167–86.

—— and Beard, R. W. (1966). *Essays on Wittgenstein's Tractatus* (New York).

Devitt, M. (1991). *Realism and Truth*, 2nd edn. Oxford.

Frege, G. (1884). *Die Grundlagen der Arithmetic*, translated into English in Austin (1968).

—— (1893), *Grundgesetze der Arithmetic*, excerpted and translated into English in Geach and Black (1980), pp. 117–38.

Furth, M. (1985). *Aristotle Metaphysics Books Zeta, Eta, Theta, Iota.* (Indianapolis).

—— (1988), *Substance, Form, and Psyche: an Aristotelean Metaphysics* (Cambridge).

Geach, P. and Black, M., eds. (1980), *The Philosophical Writings of Gottlob Frege*, 3rd edn. Oxford.

Gill, M. L. (1989). *Aristotle on Substance: The Paradox of Unity.* (Princeton).

Gotthelf, A. and Lennox, J., eds. (1987). *Philosophical Issues in Aristotle's Biology.* (Cambridge).

Graham, D. W. (1987). *Aristotle's Two Systems.* (Oxford).

Granger, H. (1986). "*Metaphysics Z. 17* and H. 6: On the Unity of the Composite Substance," unpublished paper read at the Pacific Division meetings of the American Philosophical Association, Los Angeles, CA.

—— (1990) "Aristotle and the Functionalist Debate," *Apeiron* 23, pp. 27–49.

Grice, P. (1988). "Aristotle on the Multiplicity of Being," *Pacific Philosophical Quarterly* 69, pp. 175–200.

Halper, E. (1984). "*Metaphysics Z12* and H6: The Unity of Form and Composite," *Ancient Philosophy* 4, pp. 146–59.

Hartman, E. (1977). *Substance, Body, and Soul: Aristotelian Investigations.* (Princeton).

Haslanger, S. (1994). "Parts, Compounds, and Substantial Unity," in Charles, Gill, and Scaltsas, *op. cit.*

Keyt, D. (1964) (= [1966]). "Wittgenstein's Picture Theory of Language," *Philosophical Review* 73, pp. 493—511, reprinted in Copi and Beard (1966), pp. 372–92; references here are to the 1966 reprinting.

—— (1971). "The Mad Craftsman of the *Timaeus*," *Philosophical Review* 80, pp. 230–5.

Kirwan, C. (1971). *Aristotle's Metaphysics Books , Γ, Δ, E ,* (Oxford).

Kosman, L. A. (1987). "Animals and Other Beings in Aristotle," in Gotthelf and Lennox, pp. 360–91.

Kretzman, N., Kenny, A. and Pinborg, J., eds, (1982). *The Cambridge History of Later Medieval Philosophy* (Cambridge).

Kung, J. (1981). "Aristotle on Thises, Suches, and the Third Man Argument," *Phronesis* 26, pp. 207–47.

Lear, J. (1987). "Active *Episteme*," in A. Graeser, ed, *Mathematik und Metaphysik bei Aristoteles: X Symposium Aristotelicum*, pp. 149–74. Bern.

Lewis, F. A. (1984). "What Is Aristotle's Theory of Essence?" *Canadian Journal of Philosophy* suppl. vol. 10, pp. 89–131.

—— (1991). *Substance and Predication in Aristotle.* (Cambridge).

—— (1994) "Aristotle on the Relation Between a Thing and Its Matter," in Charles, Gill, and Scaltsas (1994).

—— (1995) "Substance, Predication, and Unity in Aristotle," *Ancient Philosophy* 15, pp. 521–49.

Lloyd, A. C. (1976). "The Principle that the Cause is Greater Than the Effect," *Phronesis* 21, pp. 146–51.

Loux, M. J. (1991). *Primary Ousia. An Essay on Aristotle's Metaphysics Z and H.* (Ithaca).

—— (1995). "Composition and Unity: An Examination of *Metaphysics* H6," in May Sim, ed, *The Crossroads of Norm and Nature. Essays on Aristotle's Ethics and Metaphysics.* (Lanham, Maryland).

Mourelatos, A. P. D. (1967). "Aristotle's 'Powers' and Modern Empiricism," *Ratio* 9, pp. 97–104.

Peck, A. L. (1953). *Aristotle Generation of Animals* (Cambridge, Mass).

Pellegrin, P. (1990). "Taxonomie, Moriologie, Division. Réponses à G. E. R. Lloyd," in *Biologie, Logique et Métaphysique chez Aristote*, Paris, pp. 37–47.

Pickard-Cambridge, W. A. (1928) Translation of Aristotle *Topica* and *De Sophisticis Elenchis*, in Volume I of the Oxford Translation, ed. W. D. Ross (Oxford).

Rist, J. M. (1989). *The Mind of Aristotle: A Study in Philosophical Growth. Phoenix* Supp. Vol. 25 (Toronto).

Rorty, R. (1973). "Genus as Matter: A Reading of *Metaphysics* Z-H," in E. N. Lee, A. P. D. Mourelatos, and Richard Rorty, eds, *Exegesis and Argument: Studies in Greek Philosophy Presented to Gregory Vlastos. Phronesis*, suppl. vol. 1 (Assen).

Ross, W. D. (1924). *Aristotle Metaphysics*, 2 vols (Oxford).

Russell, B. (1903). *The Principle of Mathematics* (London).

—— (1910) "Some Explanations in Reply to Mr. Bradley," *Mind* 74, pp. 373–8.

Scaltsas, T. (1994). "Substantial Holism," in Charles, Gill, and Scaltsas, *op. cit.*

Schwegler, A. (1847). *Die Metaphysik des Aristotles* (Tubingen).

Sellars, W. (1967). "Aristotle's Metaphysics: An Interpretation," in *Philosophical Perspectives*, pp. 73–124 (Springfield, Illinois).

Stenius, E. (1960). *Wittgenstein's Tractatus: A Critical Exposition of Its Main Lines of Thought* (Oxford).

Whiting, J. (1992). "Living Bodies," in Martha C. Nussbaum and Amélie Oksenberg Rorty, eds, *Essays on Aristotle's De Anima.* (Oxford, 1992).

# NOTES

[1] The constructivist viewpoint in the interpretation of Aristotle is discussed in Section II below. For criticism of constructivism in general, see Devitt (1991), and for criticisms of the view in the interpretation of Aristotle, see also Lewis (1994), Charles (1994), and, most recently, Loux (1995), which contains the most effective review yet of the constructivist reading of *Metaphysics* H6 on the market.

[2] Strictly, this formulation of Aristotle's question is anachronistic; the question in the form Aristotle asks it is, Why is this matter, this body in this state, man?, with *is* instead of *constitutes*, and with no indefinite article, see also Note 41 below.

[3] In the *Posterior Analytics*, we are to suppose that there is a syllogism from which we can read off the definition of thunder:

(i) Noise belongs to extinction of fire.

(ii) Extinction of fire belongs to the clouds.

Hence,

(iii) Noise belongs to the clouds.

Here, the extinction of fire is the middle term, and noise is present in the clouds *thanks to* the extinction of fire there. That is, extinction of fire is the *efficient cause* of the phenomenon under investigation. Accordingly, thunder is defined as noise present in the clouds due to the extinction of fire there.

Aristotle appears to suggest in Z17 that there exists a parallel syllogism for substantial being, put together out of the three claims that (i') the kind, $k$, is typified by the form,$\psi$, and (ii') $\psi$ belongs to (*huparchei*, b6) a given matter, $m$, so that (iii') $m$ constitutes a $k$. The middle term in this account is the form, $\psi$, which is here the *formal/final* cause of the individual substance in question. We conclude that $a$'s being a $k$ is for a given matter $m$ to constitute a $k$, thanks to the appropriate form, $\psi$.

The parallel with the causal syllogism involving thunder in the *Analytics* is not terribly strong, see Lewis (1991), pp. 177–80 with Note 12. But an adaptation of an argument from Charles (1994) suggests how Aristotle may want to use the parallel to argue that in the account of substantial being in *Metaphysics* Z17, there cannot be any special "connecting relation," a *tertium quid*, to explain the connection between the matter of a thing and its form. In the thunder case from the *Analytics*, the major premiss is an immediate proposition; extinction of fire is the cause of noise in the clouds but, on the scheme Aristotle has in mind, there is no intervening cause to explain why noise accompanies the extinction of fire (the minor premiss, however, is apparently not an immediate proposition). Charles suggests that (i') and (ii') in the account of substantial being are *both* intended to be immediate propositions. That is, the form is the cause of the matter's constituting a thing of a given kind, but the relations between the kind and the form and between the form and the matter are not subject to explanation by the presence of any further middle term. It seems to follow that any explanation Aristotle may want to give of the connection between the matter *m* and the form $\psi$ cannot be by causal syllogism—it cannot proceed by introducing some further item, *t*, such that $\psi$'s belonging to *m* is understood in terms of $\psi$'s belonging to *t* and *t*'s belonging to *m*. In particular, then, there will be no special "connecting relation" joining $\psi$ and *m*, such that the individual substance *a* consists not just of $\psi$ and *m*, but also the connecting relation as well.

⁴ See Aristotle, *Metaphysics* I2, 1053b28–1054a13, and Frege, *Die Grundlagen der Arithmetik*, §§46 and following, cf. his *Grundgesetze der Arithmetik*, pp. 120, 130–1.

⁵ On the covering concept idea in Aristotle, it is worth noticing that piles of leaves or heaps of sand get such unity as they have from their *matter*, Δ6, 1016a17 ff, cf. Kirwan (1971), p. 136, rather than from the notion of one pile or one heap. Notice also the cautions in Annas (1976), p. 38, on whether Aristotle succeeds in maintaining a distinction between being one of something and being unitary: she cites M1, 1077a20–4 as a case in point, see her note on the passage, pp. 145–6.

⁶ In detail, Aristotle reminds us of the existence of an entity that is the cause of this being flesh, this a syllable (b26–27, cf. b7–8), and is the substance of each thing (b27–30, cf. b8–9), and is a principle (*arche*, b30–31, cf. a9–10). We are told at b8 (but not later in the chapter) that the entity that plays these different roles is a form.

⁷ Aristotle also discusses the role of form in both the unity of a thing and its membership in its appropriate kind at *De An.* B1, 412b5–9, quoted and discussed in Note 67 below. On the coextensiveness of being and unity, see *Topics* Δ1, 121b7—8, and *Metaphysics* Γ2, 1003b22–1004a2, I2, 1054a13–19; the passage from Γ2 is also discussed in Note 67. It is notoriously difficult, however, to be sure of the sense of 'is one' that Aristotle has in mind in a given passage.

⁸ This formulation generalizes beyond what is strictly allowed by the discussion in Z17, which has to do with the source of unity for the *material* parts of a thing. On the view I attribute to Aristotle, a form is an *external* cause of the unity of the material parts of a thing; but if we count as parts of a thing not only its matter but also the form, then the form is an *internal* principle of unity for those parts, since it is itself one of the items it unifies, and the account of unity is a *componential* one, see Haslanger (1994), p. 164, and Note 78 below. As I formulate the Content Requirement, it does not distinguish between these two options; the intent is that it should apply equally to both.

The right-hand side of the Content Requirement pairs the notion of the *substance* of a thing with that of the *cause of its being*: the pairing is fundamental to the argument of Z17, for example, and for present purposes we can assume that the notions are definitionally equivalent. It is also worth saying that the Requirement applies in the first instance to the unity of individual substances; it will also apply, however, to unities of lesser degree—form-matter compounds below the level of individual substances, for example, even accidental compounds (compounds of an individual substance with an accident) and artifacts. In these kinds of case, still lower-grade notions of the substance *of* relation will be in order (even the application of the relation to give the substance of a compound material substance is not the primary case of the relation: see Lewis (1984), p. 96, Note 14, and pp. 121–2).

⁹ The direct evidence for the (italicized) explanatory claim in the Content Requirement is only slight. At b25–7, Aristotle remarks that

It would seem that this [= the unifying factor] is something and <is> not an element, and <is> in particular the cause (*kai aition ge*) of this being flesh, and that a syllable. I take it that the *kai ... ge* at least hints that the form's place as the principle of unity for the material parts of a thing is *to be explained by* its causal role in the account of the membership by the thing in its appropriate kind. In later Sections, I try to explain why the role of a thing's form in the account of its kind also makes the form an appropriate principle of unity for the thing—not just of its material parts, but also *of the matter together with the form itself* (Note 8 above): see Sections IV and V, especially the summary at the end of Section V (iii).

[10] For the role of form in explaining the membership by a thing in its kind, see Lewis (1991), chapter 7, cf. Loux (1991), chapter 5 (but for a different account of the argument of *Met.* Z17, on which these accounts are based, see Bolton in this volume). I will have more to say about the content of a form in Section IV below.

Bolton (in correspondence) asks how identifying the form as the cause of being of a given man (say) can be consistent with Aristotle's view that, as standardly in his theory of causes, a man has *four* causes (see, for example, *Met.* H4, 1044a32—b3). A short answer will point to Aristotle's willingness to privilege the formal (or firmal/final) cause over its partners; a longer answer, which I cannot develop here, will explain the grounds of the privilege, in particular, the role Aristotle assigns to the form in determining the remaining causes, including the efficient and material causes (but for an opposing view, see Bolton (in this volume).

[11] In the theory of substance, *only primary substances*, that is only *forms*, have a substance in the primary sense of 'substance of.' Here, the substance of the form $\psi$ is identical with $\psi$ itself: it follows immediately that if two forms $\psi^1$ and $\psi^2$ are the substance in the primary sense of $\psi$, $\psi^1$ and $\psi^2$ are identical with $\psi$ and with each other. But a form is the substance of an *individual substance* in only a "reduced" sense of 'substance of.' The reduced substance-of relation has somewhat different properties from the primary version—in particular, where the form $\psi$ is the substance of the individual substance a in this reduced sense, a and $\psi$ are quite evidently distinct. Exactly as in the primary case, however, I claim that if two forms $\psi^1$ and $\psi^2$ are the substance of a single individual substance, then $\psi^1$ and $\psi^2$ are identical. And $\psi^1$, that is, $\psi^2$, has a substance in the primary sense of 'substance of,' and the substance of $\psi^1$ ($= \psi^2$) is just $\psi^1$ ($= \psi^2$) itself. For further details, see Lewis (1984) and (1991), Chapter 11.

[12] For the idea of a special connecting relation or tie, see Section III below, especially Notes 28 and 34.

[13] Aristotle requires both that a definition be finite and that it be well-founded (that is, not be open to an infinite regress). In the *An. Po*, he argues that if definition is possible at all, it must be finite in length. It follows that the elements in the essence of the thing being defined are finite in number: "if it is possible to define, or if the essence is knowable, but it is not possible to go through infinitely many things, then it is necessary that the things in the what <a thing> is be finite" (*An. Po*. A22, 82b37–83a1, cf. 84a25–26). This is of a piece with the view in *Met.* α2 that there cannot be an infinite sequence of causes. In particular, there cannot be an infinite sequence of essences, and a definition cannot be expanded *ad infinitum* to produce an infinite sequence of partial definitions (that is, it must be well-founded): "But neither can the essence be reduced (*anagesthai*) to another definition, expanded by means of a logos (*pleonazonta toi logoi*)" (994b16–18). That is, as Alexander remarks in his comments on the passage, Aristotle shows that "in the case of cause in the sense of form too, that is, essence, we do not proceed to infinity, as though whatever form or definition is taken, there is always again another definition and some other form" (Alexander in *Met.* 160.30–161.1). Aristotle again rejects the idea of an infinite sequence of essences in *Met.* Z6, 1032a2–4.

[14] Scaltsas (1994), see Note 34 below.

[15] Granger (1990), p. 41, appears to endorse a principle of this sort.

[16] Granger (1990), p. 41: "This [= what unifies the material parts] must be something of an altogether different nature from the material parts, so much so that the very question of its unity with the material parts could not possibly arise."

[17] On this, compare the discussion in the last two paragraphs of Section IV.

[18] References are in Lewis (1991), Chapter 6, Section 3. There is other supporting evidence. For example, Aristotle thinks there is a problem about the "unity of definition": if we define a species by reference to its genus and last differentia, these two must themselves "fit together" in some appropriate way into a single whole, else what is being defined itself turns out to be not one thing, but two. Aristotle tries to resolve this problem in Z12 and in H3, as well as in H6, by identifying the last differentia with form, and comparing (some would again say, "identifying") genus with matter; he then appeals to the way matter and form "fit together" to make up a unity, in order to show how genus and differentia can do the same. It is hard to think that the final moral of all this is that both problems of unity are in the last analysis non-questions. Finally, at the end of Z13, Aristotle suggests that you cannot make one substance out of two substances both present in actuality, but he does not say—going one step further with Democritus, and embracing the second horn of the dilemma at the end of the chapter—that a substance can have no (metaphysical) parts at all (1039a3–23).

[19] See, for example, Ackrill (1972–3), p. 124, controverted in Lewis (1991), p. 158, cf. Charles (1988), pp. 36–7. Instead of taking matter and form as in some sense constituents of the thing, Ackrill recommends that we think of the material 'aspect' of a thing, or of "a composite *qua* material or in its material aspect" (p. 125). The force of this, however, is weakened by his further assertion that to speak thus is "to refer to some material whose identity as that material does not depend on its being *so* shaped or informed"; as best as I can tell, to refer to this entity is to refer to something straightforwardly nonidentical with the thing, and the shading Ackrill is attempting by talking of the material *aspect* of the thing, or of the thing *qua* material, is lost. In general, I think, it is hard to know what to make of talk of "aspects" in interpreting Aristotle's notions of matter and form outside of outright projectivism, discussed briefly in the main text immediately below. "Aspect" talk appears also, for example, in Graham (1987), p. 260.

[20] Aristotle's remarks that the difficulty of unity "disappears," (this is Ross' perhaps misleading translation of H6, 1045a29, *ouketi de aporia phainetai*, "there is evidently no longer a puzzle"), or that it "is not necessary to inquire" about the unity of matter and form (*De An.* B1, 412b6), suggest not that there is no real question to ask, as the projectivist holds, but that the question is no sooner asked than answered, cf. Gill (1989), p. 7, Note 15. This hypothesis explains not only his apparent conviction that the question really has an answer (see, for example, *Met.* H3, "the argument is the same, and the substance is one in the way we have indicated (*houtos*)," 1044a7, Furth's translation), but also the telegraphic nature of the answer when he gives it, not only in H6, but also in H3 and in *De An.* B1 (see Note 67). But I doubt that the answer is as quick as the projectivist hypothesis suggests. For other reasons for objecting to the projectivist position—for example, Aristotle's insistence in the first two books of the *Physics* (for example, A7, 191a10—14) that matter and form are *principles (archai)* of the compound material substance—see Charles (1994), cf. Loux (1991), p. 57.

[21] The comparison is directly made in Granger (1986). Less directly, Kung (1981) suggests that the *element—principle* distinction in Z17 is a descendant of Aristotle's *this—such* distinction (p. 237), and that this in turn is a type-distinction comparable to Frege's distinction between "saturated" and "unsaturated" (p. 209).

[22] Geach and Black (1980), p. 54, cf. "the argument ... goes together with the function to make up a complete whole," from "Function and Concept," Geach and Black, p. 24.

[23] The argument I have just given that the notation for application of function to argument can if we want be replaced by the name of an associated function, comes from the modern Fregean, Alonzo Church (1956, pp. 34–6). But there are passages in Frege himself suggesting that such moves are not automatically ruled out, for example, at the end of "On Concept and Object" (Geach and Black, 1980, pp. 54–5).

The correct conclusion is that to start a regress, we need not only a tertium quid, but also the right recursive principle. An Aristotelian account of the structure of a given item *a* begins with two assumptions:

(2) $a$ is a unity composed of elements, $m_1, ..., m_n$.

(3) For any i (i > 1), elements $m_1, ..., m_i$, make up a unity, only with the addition of some further item, $\psi^1$, which is not an element, but a principle.

How now to generate a higher-order form, $\psi^2$, to say how $\psi^1$ can apply in this way to $m^1$ and the rest? One suggestion runs as follows:

(4) For any i (i > 1) and for any j (j ≥ 1), elements $m_1, ..., m_i$, and principles $\psi^1, ...,$ $\psi_j$, make up a unity (a *mixed*-order unity), only with the addition of some further item which is not an element, but a principle.

(4) has the right recursive structure to set a regress well in motion. And any such regress is stopped dead in its tracks by Principle 3, which says in effect that you can apply an additional item or form only to a *same*-order collection, containing all elements but no principles. Strictly, however, all that is needed to halt a regress of higher-order forms is the denial of assumption (4): we assume simply that

(5) There is some mixed-order collection of items that make up a unity *without* the addition of some further principle or form.

(5) will halt the regress at any point we wish. In particular, we may suppose that (5) is satisfied by the *first* mixed-order collection in the sequence the regress tries to construct: that is, it is satisfied by the collection comprising the original material parts $m_1$ and the rest and the original form $\psi^1$. And in fact, Aristotle has a principled reason for stopping here: see the discussion of the Content Requirement in Section III below.

²⁴ Perhaps the parts of those parts are also included, and *their* parts, and so on: I ignore this complication here, but see Section VI below.

²⁵ While Aristotle here denies that there is any "difference" (*diaphora*) between potentiality and actuality, from a different point of view, the word *diaphora* can properly describe the contrast between potentiality and actuality, see *Met.* Θ6, 1048b4–6. Note also that on the account offered in the main text, Aristotle is not concerned with a *diaphora* in the technical sense of "differentia," as Furth (1985), p. 58, supposes (? "... a differentia <to distinguish> what is potentially <a unity> from what is actually <a unity>," in line with a suggestion by Bolton (in correspondence)?).

²⁶ For this use of the noun, *diaphora*, at b17, compare the similar use of the adjective at *G&C* A7, 323b6–7, *ta anomoia kai ta diaphora*, "things that are unlike and different." I use the term, 'qualitative difference,' somewhat loosely in application to form and matter; ordinarily, *individuals* are taken to be qualitatively the same or different.

²⁷ "Alike in the way that in general the potential and the actual are alike": see *De An.* B5, 417b3–5, cf. *G.A.* A19, 726b15–22. In the account of *acting on* and *being acted on by* in *G&C.* A7, before one thing acts on another, the two are unlike in species, but alike in genus. When action takes place, however, the agent *assimilates* the patient to itself (to *poietikon homoioun heautoi to paschon*, 324a9–11), so that where before the patient was unlike the agent, they now are alike (*De An.* B5, 417a20, cf. 4, 416b6–7). In this story, initially the agent is actually what the patient is only potentially (417a18); at the end, however, they are both actually one and the same thing. These features of Aristotle's account are especially to the fore in the discussion of unity in *Met.* H6. The same explanatory schema is taken over and adapted to fit the account of perception and (with even further modification) thought in the *De An.*; see, for example, B5, 416b33–417a2, a14–20, 418a3–6; 4, 429a13–15, b22–6, 29–430a2.

²⁸ Wittgenstein is sometimes held to have argued for the existence of a single connecting relation along these lines in the *Tractatus*, see Stenius (1960), chapter 7. Stenius's view is controverted in Keyt (1964 =1966), pp. 382–4; Keyt's own conclusion is that the view in question is confined to Wittgenstein's pre-*Tractatus* period. The views of the *Tractatus* are also relevant to what I take to be the account of unity Aristotle accepts: see especially Note 45 in Section IV below.

²⁹ *koinon ge kata panton kai suntomon*, Z17, 1041a20, cf. *heis logos kai mia aitia epi panton*, a17.

³⁰ For the application of the Content Requirement to cases of this sort, see Note 8 above.

[31] *ho autos logos epi panton*, 1045b12. The Content Requirement entails that the unifying principle for a thing is also the substance of the thing and its *aition tou einai*. There are reasons of theory, then, and not a mere play on words, behind the shift from *logos* in the sense of 'explanatory story'—so that the same connecting relation is at work in the case of the bronze triangle and the white surface alike—to the sense of 'definition'—the triangle and the surface have the same definition in common.

[32] Z11, 1036b17-18, 20; the context is a discussion of various "mathematizing" Platonists, who "reduce everything to numbers," in effect minimizing the content of the form, and putting the differences between things of different kinds on the side of matter, see 1036b7-20, esp. 17-20. Aristotle also warns in the *Topics* about the perils for definition in an underspecified, even contentless, notion of *sunthesis*: "for it is not enough to say it is a composition (*sunthesin*), but you should also go on to define the kind of composition: for these things do not form flesh irrespective of the manner of their composition (*hoposoun suntethenton*), but when compounded (*suntethenton*) in one way they form flesh, when in another, bone," *Top.* Z14, 151a25-6, translation by Pickard-Cambridge, cf. a20-5.

[33] See, for example, Ross (1924), vol. II, p. 239, on b12-16.

[34] I emphasize that the use of the Content Requirement at 1045b7—17 to reject a special connecting relation is not idle. Scaltsas (1994) argues that a substantial unity cannot be a "related whole" (a "whole of interrelated distinct things"); I have reservations about his "distinct" here (see Note 65 below), but I take it that the rejection of "related wholes" at least includes the conclusion urged here, that a substantial unity cannot contain some special connecting relation in addition to the obvious ingredients, its matter and form. Contrary to Scaltas, however, the regress argument in Z17 cannot establish this result (a similar remark goes for Scaltsas's "trope overlap" argument). Aristotle argues in Z17 that introducing a further element to unify the existing elements of a thing leads to a regress. It follows that a substantial unity cannot be an aggregate of elements, but not that it also cannot be a "related whole," where some special connecting relation secures the unity of the thing (see Section II above). Contrary to Scaltsas, then, the regress argument in Z17 is not what motivates the project in H6 of showing how the substantial form unifies the elements *without* some further unifier and given only the resources of the form and the matter by themselves: some further argument—on my account, the argument at b7—17—must do the needed work.

On the account I give, Aristotle objects to a *logos henopoios* because it presents us with a *contentless* solution to the problem of unity, in violation of the Content Requirement. His rejection of a *logos henopoios* is sometimes construed quite differently, as a (covert) attack on his own notion of (metaphysical) predication deployed in the earlier chapters of ZH, and also later in Θ (see, most recently, Gill, 1989); this interpretation is controverted in Lewis (1995) and Loux (1995).

[35] The translation is in line with Schwegler's, as against Furth ("Why aren't those-themselves man ...?," 1985, p. 56) and Ross, who also takes *ekeina auta* as subject in preference to *ho anthropos*.

[36] "For there is no other cause of the potential sphere's *becoming* actually a sphere" (Ross, my emphasis). *Pace* Ross, however, Aristotle does not use the language of becoming in the chapter except to bracket such cases at a31 (*en hosois esti genesis*). So Aristotle's puzzle is not one about how the matter *becomes* (a) sphere, but about how it *is* (a) sphere. Ross's view that Aristotle is concerned with questions of becoming in H6 is in line with his larger thesis that, by contrast with Z, in H Aristotle "passes from the static consideration of substance to the dynamic consideration of change," (1924) Vol. I, p. cxxiv.

[37] The translation follows Ross, but with corrections especially in the translation of a30 and 32 (see Note 36) and b19-20.

[38] For the parentheses here, and the facts about Greek that make this question more compelling for Aristotle than it is for speakers of contemporary English, see Note 41 below.

[39] Here, I stand in direct opposition to Gill (1989), who supposes that the unity of genus and differentia provides the paradigm after which the unity of the compound material substance is to be modelled, so that the direction of explanation in H6 runs *from* the genus-

differentia case *to* that of the compound material substance (see, for example, Gill, pp. 139–41). In fact, however, Aristotle is explicit that the direction of explanation runs the other way: the unity of genus and differentia is no longer a puzzle, *because* (*gar*, a25) this is the same puzzle as that over the unity of the compound material substance, addressed in the discussion of potential and actual spheres in the balance of the chapter. According to Gill, the unity of genus and differentia is *assumed* in H6, where Aristotle explains the unity of matter and form in terms suggested by the genus-differentia case. In fact, however, neither kind of unity is assumed in H6. Here, Aristotle explains the unity of matter and form in the compound material substance in order to discharge a debt incurred in the discussion of the unity of genus and differentia in Z12. In Z12, the problem of genus and differentia is worked out largely by means of an assimilation of the genus to the role played by matter in the compound material substance; H6 now supplies what was merely taken for granted in Z12 by saying how Aristotle's view of form and matter guarantees the unity of the compound material substance, as required.

⁴⁰ *Phys.* B1, 193b6–12, cf. *Met.* Δ4, 1014b35 ff, where Aristotle argues that the form of a thing and its nature strictly so-called are one and the same.

⁴¹ *Met.* Θ7, 1049a18–b3 (a very different reading of this passage appears in Gill (1989), pp. 151–5, and is discussed in Lewis, 1995). The appeal to the language of accidents to explain the relation between a thing and its matter is part of Aristotle's apparatus for drawing the distinction an English-speaking philosopher might put in terms of different uses of *is* to express constitution and to express classification. In English, we can say of a thing that it is a sphere (its classification), or that it is bronze (its constitution). Putting the point as English naturally does, however, may underestimate Aristotle's difficulties with spheres. Greek has no indefinite article, so that where in English the sortal is the marked form (we mark it by the indefinite article: *a sphere*), for Aristotle, the term introducing the accidents of a thing or its matter is the marked form: hence, *red* and not *redness*, or *bronzen* and not *bronze*. (Here, his 'is bronzen' mimics his 'is red,' which exhibits the characteristic "change of inflection," as opposed to 'is redness,' see his discussion of paronymy in *Catg.* 1 and elsewhere.) The best I can do to reproduce his 'is sphere' in recognizable English is to use parentheses around the indefinite article: 'is (a) sphere.' Even this minimal use of the indefinite article, however, can disguise the fact that at bottom, Aristotle's problem of unity is a problem about apparently competing classifications of something we take to be one thing and not two.

⁴² An evident exception is Frege's tolerant attitude towards metaphor, which notoriously Aristotle does not share: this is no doubt part of the point at H6, 1045b7–16, cf. *An. Po.* B13, 97b37–39 with Barnes, p. 239, *ad loc*, G&C. A10, 327b13–22, and *Met.* A9, 991a20–22, 992a26–29, Z14, 1039b5–6, M5, 1079b24–27.

⁴³ To the references in Note 21 above, should now be added Loux (1995). Loux takes a straight Fregean line in interpreting Aristotle: "The central idea ... is that matter and form *have categorial features* such that their compresence is necessarily both necessary and sufficient for the existence of the composite entity whose constituents they are" (p. 271, my emphasis, and correcting the "categorical" of Loux's text, cf. his "matter and form have distinctive categorial features" later on the same page). His remarks put Loux in the camp of those who trace the unity of a thing to what I am about to call formal rather than proper features of the items to be joined. Despite this, he insists that content plays an essential role in Aristotle's account of unity, in contrast to what he calls the "neutralist" conception inherent, for example, in Lycophron's *logos henopoios*: but I have not understood his account of how we can get from the purely formal features of matter and form which on his account make for their unity, and which must remain the same across the board, to the details of content, which will vary with the kind to which the resulting unity belongs ("for each distinct kind of complex, there will be a distinctive predicative structure ...," p. 271, cf. p. 275, "predication itself varies with the content of forms").

⁴⁴ The "formal"-"proper" terminology is from Keyt (1971), although the context in which he uses the distinction is Platonic metaphysics.

[45] Tractarian friends (Michael Wedin, Kit Fine) remind me that Frege's essentially "contentless" approach stands in opposition not just to Aristotle's, but also to that attributed to Wittgenstein by some interpreters of the *Tractatus*. On the similar accounts due to Copi (1958) and Anscombe (1959), for example, for Wittgenstein, "relations go over into structure," and the device that achieves the unity of a given state of affairs is also partly responsible for its content; at the level of the proposition, correspondingly, an *n*-place predicate is replaced in Wittgenstein's "picture language" by the spatial arrangement of the *n*-many names. Copi's and Anscombe's interpretations are helpfully discussed in Keyt (1964) = ([1966]).

[46] See, for example, *De An.* A3, 407b13–26, B2, 414a21–8, P.A. A1, 642a10–14.

Kit Fine points out to me that while it is central to my account that the principle of unity for Aristotle have *content*, there are still "formal" features of the form that fit it for its unifying role: form is the right kind of thing to be a principle of unity—for example, it has content of the appropriate sort at the appropriate level of actuality, see the Form-as-Actuality assumption in Section V (ii) and the remarks about indexing in Section VI and Note 75 below.

[47] But see Note 45 above.

[48] Gill (1989), pp. 166–7, 169–70. This is not to say that Gill's puzzle is not one that occupies Aristotle elsewhere: see, for example, *De An.* B4, 416a6–9.

[49] *De Cae.* Δ3, esp. 310b16-24. This is the question, for a potential *F* that becomes actually (a) *G*, why *F* = *G*. The question is answered by the Correspondence Thesis in Section V (i) below. This is not a question Aristotle does or should find "absurd," as Mourelatos suggests (Mourelatos (1967), p. 102, esp. n. 23); but it is not an ordinary efficient-causal question either. (I suspect that in fact the question is not a *first-level* causal question at all, but instead is metatheoretic: see the paragraph immediately following in the main text.)

[50] For projectivism, see Note 1, the quotation from Sellars in Section II with Note 19, and the brief remarks towards the beginning of Section III. Other sceptics include Burnyeat et al. (1984), p. 43 (see Gill (1989), p. 7, Note 15, and p. 169, Note 48) and Graham (1987), p. 260. The idea that there is no cause and that questions about the unity of form and matter are pointless, is fuelled especially by the thought that 1045b17–23 commits Aristotle to the *identity* of proximate matter and form, see Section V and especially Note 59.

[51] Aristotle's topic is *not* how it *comes about that* a potential so-and-so constitutes an actual one, even though translators sometimes inject questions about becoming a sphere into the text; see, for example, Ross on a33, and Note 36 above, and Gill (1989), p. 170 and *passim*. Similar comments tell against the suggestion in Rist (1989), pp. 239–41, that the mention of moving causes and bronze spheres in H6 is prologue to the discussion of unmoved movers and the eternal movement of the heavenly spheres in Λ8: as I see it, moving causes, 'higher' or lower, are never really relevant in H6 at all.

[52] Commentators are hardly unanimous in taking Aristotle to exclude the efficient cause, however: along with the references in Note 51 above and 54 below, see now Loux (1995), p. 262 and passim.

[53] Aristotle writes: "*this* was all along the essence of each of the two" (my emphasis). Furth (1985) and Charles (1994) both gloss 'this' by 'the cause'; Schwegler (1847) goes so far as to incorporate this interpretation into his translation: "sondern die Ursache ist der Begriff eines Jeden" (Vol. 2, p. 147). On this reading, apparently, *the essences of the matter and of the form* are the cause of unity. A different view, which I shall develop below, is that there are features essential to the matter and features essential to the form that qualify *the matter and the form themselves* as the cause of unity. On this reading, 'this' refers back to the preceding clause, and is supposed to convey the *content* of the essences in question. Philosophically, the point is (roughly) that it is the essence of the matter to be potentially a sphere, and the essence of the form to be actually a sphere, so that (given the right intervening story) the matter and the form are the cause of their own unity. Grammatically, things are even less obvious. I take it that 'this' picks up the last two words, "being (a) sphere," from the preceding clause, so that it is essential to both the matter or potential sphere and the form or actual sphere that each *is a sphere*. This, however, does not commit

Aristotle to the view that the matter and the form will have precisely the same essence (this is the view attributed to him in Charles, 1994), for each will not be a sphere in precisely the same way: it is essential to the matter that it is *potentially* a sphere, and to the form that it is *actually* a sphere. As on the Schwegler-Furth-Charles view, the existence of these essences is taken to be causally relevant to the potential sphere's becoming an actual one; on the present reading, however, Aristotle does not expressly say that *they* are a cause.

It is also worth noticing the competing view that Aristotle's 'this' recapitulates the entire phrase, 'the potential sphere's actually being a sphere'; this reading again purports to give the content of the essences in question, so that on this reading, for a potential sphere, its essence is *becoming* an actual sphere, and for an actual sphere, *coming* from an actual one: the interpretation and the language of becoming (see Note 36 above) are both from Ross (1924), Vol. II, p. 238. Without the language of becoming, finally, this reading can be adapted to support the account that takes matter and form, or potentiality and actuality, to be abstractions, defined by their contribution to the unified substance, in the manner sketched—but not endorsed—in Charles (1994).

[54] One remedy is to suppose that the efficient cause has not been dismissed after all, see for example, Rorty (1973), p. 410, Graham (1987), p. 260, Loux (1991), p. 271, to which should now be added Loux (1995), p. 262 and passim. The stock of causes can be increased, if we suppose that in addition to the efficient causes, the facts about potentiality and actuality that are intrinsic to the matter and the form also contribute to the account of unity; in this vein, Gill argues that talk of potentiality and actuality fleshes out the efficient-causal account, Gill (1989), p. 169.

[55] The implication of the previous sentence too, then, (a30–1) must be not that there is no cause *tout court* aside from the agent, but that the agent is the only obvious extrinsic cause. A similar interpretation will apply to Aristotle's summary at b21–2: "nothing else is the cause here, unless there is something which caused the movement from potency into actuality"; similarly too for the cryptic claim at $\Lambda$10, 1075b34–7, which on the face of it flatly contradicts the view I am arguing for that the efficient cause is irrelevant to the kind of account Aristotle means to give. After earlier drafts of the present paper were written, I was pleased to find much the same interpretation of b21–2 had been reached independently by Charles (1994), pp. 88–9: "there is no cause of unity of substance *distinct* from the relevant actuality and potentiality, because these encapsulate all the causal features required to explain the unity of the composite substance" (his emphasis).

"this was all along the essence of each of the two": see Note 53 above.

"the essence of *each of the two*": that is, the essence of the matter and of the form—I assume that matter and form are the two items under discussion throughout the passage, contra Alexander, quoted in Ross (1924), Vol. II, p. 238.

[56] Cf. Note 53 above.

[57] Contra Charles (1994), cf. Note 53 above.

[58] Aristotle's remarks are elliptical at important spots, but the context makes the supplements I have given more than plausible. Aristotle asks, "What, then, is the cause of this—of what is potentially being actually?" (a30), and looks twice for an answer in the idea that the matter is potentially, and the form is actually (a23–4, b19), or even that the potential and the actual are somehow one (b20–1). But at a31–3, he is concerned with "the cause of the potential sphere's being an actual *sphere*" (my emphasis); I take it that this expansion of the original question at a30 allows us to supplement phrases of the form 'what is potentially' and 'what is actually,' or 'the potential' and 'the actual' elsewhere in the chapter with a reference to the kind of thing the potentiality or actuality is the potentiality or actuality *for*: 'what is potentially a *sphere*, 'the actual *sphere*,' and so on.

[59] In fact, there are a variety of options for understanding the claim that $x$ and $y$ are one, or that they are one and the same thing: (i) $x$ is the same as, or even identical with, $y$, see for example Peck (1953), pp. xii, xlvii, 111 (note on A20, 729a34), Sellars (1967), p. 118, Rorty (1973), p. 394, Hartman (1977), p. 99, Note 11 ("somehow identical"—apparently in a way that stops short of "full identity," pp. 75-80), Kosman (1987), p. 378, Balme (1987),

p. 295, Gill (1989), p. 8 ("somehow identical"), Charles (1994) ("in some way identical")—but this sameness relation cannot be symmetric, if we are to make sense of Aristotle's immediate qualification, "the one potentially the other actually"; (ii) unusefully here, each of *x* and *y* is one, or is one and self-identical; (iii) unusefully again, since it is the problem of unity that Aristotle is here trying to explain, *x* and *y* together make up a unity (perhaps a more promising variation on this reading is Loux's, "make up one <*k*>," Loux, 1995, p. 273); (iv) there is something *z* such that *x* and *y* both are *z* (for example, Aristotle and Speusippus are one and the same thing, viz. philosophers); or even (v) *x* and *y* are genidentical: they are different development stages of one and the same thing (so Schwegler)—but it is unclear how this answers questions about the synchronic unity of matter and form. I argue below for reading (iv), in preference to the usual (i).

⁶⁰ A parallel to this construction appears at *Met.* B4, 999a24—29: *hei gar hen ti kai tauton, kai* [= i.e.] *hei katholou ti huparchei, tautei panta gnorizomen*, cf. Alexander in *Met.* 211. 2–5; Aristotle is saying that two things are understood insofar as there is one and the same thing they both are, i.e, a single universal under which they both fall, not that they must be identical. The same construction appears also at *Met.* I8, 1057b36: *genos kalo hoi ampho hen tauto legetai, me kata sumbebekos echon diaphoran*. See also the discussion of the ways in which two or more things can be one (there is one thing—one genus, or one definition or essence—they all are, for example, they all are men) at Δ6, 1016a24 ff, cf. b3–6.

⁶¹ The Code-Grice terminology of Having (also sometimes rendered "Hazzing") first appeared in print in Code (1986). It is also used in Grice (1988). The dual of Having is Izzing, and the "Izzing-Having" jargon is discussed further in Lewis (1991), pp. 6–13 and *passim*.

⁶² "Everything that comes to be proceeds towards a principle (*ep' archen badizei*) that is also an end (*telos*) (for *that for the sake of which* is a principle, and the coming-to-be is for *the sake of* the end); but the actuality is an end, and the potentiality is acquired for the sake of that end" (1050a7–10). Aristotle argues parenthetically that in general if one thing is for the sake of another, the second is the *principle* (*arche*) of the first; given this, if the coming-to-be is for the sake of the end, then the end is the principle of the coming-to-be. (This idea, that if something is the *end* of what comes to be, then it is also its *principle*, is presumably the point of Aristotle's opening remarks before the parenthesis, see Ross (1924), vol. II, p. 262.) If, then, the actuality is an end, and the potentiality is *for the sake of* that end or actuality, then the end or actuality is the *principle* of the potentiality, so that (finally) the actuality is *prior in substance* to the potentiality. For the idea that the matter is for the sake of the form, see also Aristotle's view in P.A. A1 that the matter and the earlier stages in the production of a house come about and are for the sake of the end (639b27 ff.) and claims that cases of *natural* coming-to-be are no different; the "top-down" view of matter is also discussed in Lewis (1991), pp. 249–52.

⁶³ See the references in Note 27 above.

⁶⁴ As suggested at the end of the previous paragraph in the main text, Socrates, for example, is a man (Has man, in the jargon of Izzing and Having), thanks to a relation of dependency on the form man, which is (Is) a man; on this story, *Having* man is the way open to sensible men of doing what the form man does—their way of *Being* (a) man. There is further discussion in Lewis (1991), Chapter 2, Section 1.

It is important to notice that the Platonic form *is* a man "in a privileged way" (it Is (a) man): this puts considerable distance between Plato and the "paradigmatism" often attributed to him. A similar qualification applies in the case of Aristotle as well. The claim that the form is actually (a) sphere (better, perhaps, *Is* actually [a] sphere) indicates that the form has the definitional content appropriate to a man (see three paragraphs back in the main text); this is quite different from the way in which either the compound sphere or the bronze is actually (a) sphere (in both cases, in the last analysis, the matter is fully teleologically dependent on the form, or, equivalently, it Has the form in question).

For the place of assimilation in the causal story, see Note 27 above, and for the related principle that a cause is greater than its effect, see Lloyd (1976). Again, however, I suspect (but cannot argue here) that assimilation and the causal principle are both open to interpretation in a way that will distance Aristotle's views from the "paradigmatism" mentioned above.

⁶⁵ The idea that the matter is actually a sphere as a result of an intensification in an existing dependency by the matter on the form runs contrary to the position in Scaltsas (1994). Scaltsas argues that the components (matter) of a thing undergo "reidentification" upon being incorporated into the whole: once incorporated into the whole, the components "lose their distinctness" (from the form? from each other?), and become "identity-dependent" on the form. This radically overstates the difference it makes to the matter when it is united with the form in the finished substance. Scaltsas cites the dependence by the matter on the substantial form as grounds for his conclusions. As we have seen, however, this dependence is not newly acquired, taking over only when the matter is incorporated into the whole, but is in effect to a lesser degree from the start. The proximate matter is bound to the finished whole *prospectively*: the (proximate) matter is essentially matter *for* the finished product—equine matter is matter for the horse; bricks and beams, matter for the house—even before the horse or house exists.

At the same time, I have doubts about what "losing their distinctness" on the part of the material components, becoming "identity-dependent" on the form, and the rest, really come to. Scaltsas expressly says that once the form has been incorporated into the thing, it and the thing are identical; and depending on how we understand "losing its distinctness" on the part of the matter, there may even be a three-way identity between form, matter, and thing. With regard to the matter, Scaltsas says that the components of a thing "emerge," only when we divide the thing, either physically or by abstraction; they "do not exist in the substance, but only potentially." I am uneasy, however, with the thought that the matter is or is not identical with the thing depending on what *we* do, whether by physical division or by abstraction: is this projectivism all over again (see Section II above)?

⁶⁶ See Code (1987), p. 166, cf. Lear (1987), pp. 152 ff. The two views are not equivalent: different degrees of dependence and dominance might be reflected, not in the presence or absence of the form at a lower or a higher degree of actuality, but in stronger or weaker relations of dependency by the matter with respect to a form that exists at only a single "level of actuality". In addition to his view that a form can exist at various degrees of active potentiality, Code also supposes that the matter can exist at various degrees of passive potentiality. This last notion has been put to work in an account of Aristotle's solution to the problem of unity in Haslanger (1994), which she kindly sent me after the present paper was written; according to Haslanger, Aristotle's solution uses the notion of *differing degrees of passive potentiality for a given substantial form* on the part of the matter, all the way up to *maximum passive potentiality* (equivalent to my full teleological dependence) in the case of the matter that is an ingredient in the compound material substance.

Finally, it is worth remarking that the discussion in the main text is concerned exclusively with the potentiality in the matter for *being* a thing of a given kind $k$, so that it is silent on whether in addition to this potentiality there exists a distinct potentiality for *becoming* a thing of kind $k$. In particular, my account is neutral on whether when a $k$ comes to be, two distinct potentialities (the potentiality to become a $k$ and the potentiality to be a $k$) are realized by a succession of different forms (this is the medieval *fluxus formae* view, see Kretzman, Kenny, and Pinborg (1982), pp. 527–8), or whether a single potentiality for being a k is realized successively, first incompletely and later completely, by one and the same form (the *forma fluens* view). The latter is apparently the view adopted in Code (1987), p. 166 and Note 19.

⁶⁷ Notice that even if the contribution made by the matter is subordinated to that made by the form in the way suggested, Aristotle must assume that the form itself is a unity in the appropriate sense—that it has a unitary content, or that it typifies a coherent unitary kind, and is not itself a "heap" in the proscribed sense—before he can conclude that the compound material substance which that form characterizes is itself a single kind of thing, and free from the problem of competing classifications. Aristotle does not exactly advertize this assumption, but he may have it in mind in an especially cryptic passage in *De An.* B1:

For this reason it is not necessary to inquire whether the soul and the body are one, any more than whether the wax and the shape < are one>, or in general whether the matter of each thing and that of which it is the matter [= the form] <are one>; for while there are many ways in which we speak of unity and being, the actuality is the most properly <so spoken of>. 412b5–9.

Aristotle suggests not that the question about the unity of a compound material substance is flatly a non-question, but that it is no sooner asked than answered (see Sections II and IV). The second part of the passage sketches how the answer will go. Aristotle contrasts the general run of applications of being and unity, and their application to the actuality or form of a thing. There are many kinds of thing of which we say that it *is* and that it is *one*. But the actuality or form is what is *primarily* one, and what *primarily* is. If, however, by calling the form preeminently one, Aristotle means that it is preeminently a unity, then presumably it expresses a unitary kind; on this assumption, if a given compound material substance is a member of a given kind thanks to that form, it is classified as *one* kind of thing, and is not a hodge-podge of kinds.

The passage from the *De Anima* might be thought to suggest, rather differently, that for all things of whatever kind, their form is one or a unity in the primary way, and each of them too is one or a unity *derivatively* from this primary case (cf. the remarks about the transmission principle of causality earlier in this Section, and see perhaps the "focal meaning" account of *one* at Met. Δ6, 1016b6–9). This puts the Aristotle of the *De Anima* much closer to the Fregean line rejected on Aristotle's behalf in Section IV, for it suggests that being a unity is a formal property that all forms share, and that the form transmits to the compound material substance. But this cannot be Aristotle's view, for it pays no attention to the point that not any old form and any old matter can fit together. As noted in the previous paragraph in the main text, any account of how matter and form are united in a given compound material substance must take into account the *content* of both the form and the matter.

Finally, it may be that the point that the form or actuality is a unity in a privileged way is also made in the body of H6 itself, if Halper is right that 1045a36–b7 deals with the essences or forms of sensibles (Halper, 1984, pp. 154–5), and not just summa genera, as Ross (1924), Vol. II, p. 238, supposes; see also b23. This view also appears in Charles (1994). On this reading, Aristotle concludes that comparably to his conclusions for the compound substance in the surrounding parts of the chapter, in the case of the substantial form too, nothing *else* stands as the cause of its unity: instead, the form is "immediately" one, without falling under the genus *one*, and without our having to suppose that there exists a Platonic form of one (with Ross op. cit, p. 239, I supply an understood *tou ontos kai tou henos* with Aristotle's *oud' hos choriston onton* at b7, contrary to the translation in Furth, 1985, p. 57). In other respects, the message of a36–b7 is even harder to decipher. It is tempting to read the passage in the light of Γ2, 1003b22–34 (cf. I2, 1054a13–19), where Aristotle objects that it cannot be part of the content of a given form that it is the form of a thing that it . . . *and that it exists*, or of a thing that it . . . *and is one*. For H6, the moral is presumably that while we must look to the *content* of the form for a solution to the unity of form and matter, Aristotle rejects the easy solution, that being one is simply *included* in that content. At the same time, however, we may wonder whether the sense of *one* is the relevant one here: in Γ2, at any rate, the issue seems to be individuation—whether we have one item of a given kind, or two or more—and not whether the form expresses a unitary kind, and not whether the form and matter in the thing make up a unity.

[68] I have in mind the use of 'internal' (as opposed to 'external') at work, for example, in Bradley (1893) and in Russell (1903) and (1910). The theory of internal and external relations in these works concerns whether a relation can be wholly explained in terms of "intrinsic" or nonrelational properties of its relata (an internal relation), or not (an external relation). For the relevance of asymmetry in this connection, see, for example, Russell (1903), pp. 221–6.

⁶⁹ This objection was pressed by James Bogen in correspondence, and in discussion by David Bostock. A version of the objection appears in print in Loux (1991), pp. 269–70. Loux also objects on the basis of *Phys.* Γ1, 201a31–4, that Aristotle will deny that "the potentiality for actualization by a given form is written into the essence of whatever serves as matter for that form" (Loux, p. 269, cf. 180). Perhaps this difficulty can be answered by noting that the *Physics* passage is concerned with the potentiality *for kinesis*—for *becoming* a so-and-so—while the claim in the main text is that the bronze has the potentiality for *being* a sphere. Note also that Aristotle has no objection in general to thinking that a potentiality is a part, or even all, of a thing's essence; thus in the *De Anima*, he has no objection to saying that *nous* ("mind") "has no nature but this, that it is capable (*dunaton*)," 4, 429a21—2; or that it is the nature (*phusis*) of colour to be capable of exciting change (*kinetikon*) of the actually transparent, B7, 418a31–b2, or that this is the essence of colour (*touto ... en autoi to chromati einai*, 419a9–11).

⁷⁰ Artifacts are in any case not fully-fledged substances and, hence, not fully-fledged unities, cf. *Met.* Δ6, 1016a4, Δ26, 1023b34–6. Other lesser unities include accidental compounds, musical Coriscus, the one approaching, and the like. But here too, plausibly, an analogous solution will hold, with the *content* of the relevant differentia (*Met.* H2) or form-analogue doing the work. On differentiae and form-analogues in H2, see Lewis (1994), Section 5.

⁷¹ A similar explanation will hold for why musical Socrates is not a prime case of unity: being musical is only one among umpteen possibilities for Socrates.

⁷² In Lewis (1995), I argue that it is a constraint on Aristotle's account of unity that a thing is a genuine Aristotelian unity if and only if it is a "basic individual"—an instance of a genuine substance sortal—in more or less the sense at work in the "commonsense" framework of the *Categories*, cf. Loux (1991), p. 256. So our account must be able to explain how Socrates (say) is a genuine unity, while pale man or "cloak" is not; at the same time, it must also allow for the existence of members of lower-grade kinds—bronze spheres, pale men ["cloaks"], and the like—that exhibit correspondingly lesser degrees of unity.

⁷³ We may speculate that the degree of unity in a form-matter compound is at its highest when the form and the matter are uniquely appropriate for each other; this, however, falls well short of the kind of mutually faithfully monogamous relationship required in Whiting (1992), where the existence of genuine substantial unities is tied to a doctrine of individual forms: that is, a substantial unity exists just in case the matter cannot exist without the form and, equally, the form cannot exist outside that particular matter.

⁷⁴ *adunaton ... ousian ex ousion enhuparchouson energeiai*, Z13, 1039a3–4, cf. 4–23; see also the application to the construction of a Platonic species-Form out of genus- and differentia-Forms in Z14, and to an animal and its parts in Z16. The lack of express mention of indexing on Aristotle's part is not a real difficulty, since he is notably lax with qualifications of this kind; his own summary at the end of Z16, for example, tells us simply that "no substance is composed out of substances" (1041a4–5), leaving off the crucial qualification supplied in Z13: "... composed out of substances *existing in actuality*."

⁷⁵ Pellegrin, pp. 43–4. Pellegrin's version of Aristotle's rule is tailored to show that the living animal, which is itself a substance, is composed of nonuniform and (at a still lower level) uniform parts, which are also substances to differing degrees. But from the metaphysical point of view the compound substance has its form as (in some sense) a part as well as its matter; Pellegrin's assignment of levels in this latter case correctly suggests that Aristotle is committed to the conjunction of the revised rule,

No substance of level *n* can be composed of substances themselves of level *n*,

with the further requirement that

Exactly one component of a substance will be a substance at a level *higher than* the level of the whole.

In the case of a compound material substance, then, its constitutive form gets assigned to the highest level, followed by the compound material substance itself, followed in turn by its proximate matter. (As Fine points out to me, however, there will be complications in the account of the proximate matter: if it is of level 3, for example, as Pellegrin suggests, and if it has its own constitutive form, what level are we to assign to that form? Not, presumably, level 2, since that is the level of the original compound material substance; but not level 3 either (= the level of the proximate matter), since that is too low by the further requirement.)

[76] *Meteor.* Δ12, for example, suggests that the needed potentialities may not be present at the lower levels of matter; at the same time, Aristotle's account of *mixis* ("mixture") suggests a quite different model for explaining unity, see the discussion at the close of this Section.

[77] The extent of the "reach" that I attribute here to substantial form is uncertain: *Meteor.* Δ12, 390b2–14, for example, might seem to suggest that it does not extend beyond the non-uniform parts of the living animal, while *GA.* B1, 734b31–735a5, suggests that it will include the uniform parts as well. The phenomenon of "reach" is discussed also in Furth (1988), p. 88.

[78] For the distinction between *intrinsic* and *extrinsic* principles of unity for a thing at work in this paragraph, see Lewis (1994), Sections 5 and 6, and Haslanger (1994), Section VII.

[79] See Notes 62 and 76 above.

[80] This paper was first read at a conference at Boston University in January 1992. I am grateful also to James Bogen and Dennis Plaisted for help with an earlier version of the paper, and to Robert Bolton and Kit Fine for comments on the penultimate draft. Responsibility for the mistakes that remain is mine alone.

# THE PROBLEM OF MIXTURE

BY

KIT FINE

For Aristotle, the everyday world contains three main kinds of things: the elements, the homogeneous mixtures, and the heterogeneous substances. The topic of mixture was vigorously debated in medieval times (see Maier (1982): 142). But contemporary interest has focused on the objects at the extremes of his ontology—the elements and the substances—while the topic of mixture has been relatively neglected. This is unfortunate. For not only is the topic of great interest in its own right, it is also important for a wider understanding of Aristotle's scientific and metaphysical views.

The intrinsic interest of the topic largely arises from the difficulty in seeing how a non-atomistic conception of matter is to be reconciled with a plausible view of mixture. The exegetical interest has perhaps two main sources. The first resides in the special position occupied by mixtures in Aristotle's ontology. For all substances are composed of mixtures; and all elements compose mixtures, in so far as they compose anything at all. Thus the mixtures provide the cushion, as it were, between the elements and the substances; and any account of the role of the elements or of the nature of the substances should deal with the relationship of each to the mixtures.

The other source of exegetical interest lies in the relevance of the topic of mixture to other, more general, topics—principally, potentiality and change. Just as mixtures occupy a kind of midpoint between the elements and the substances, so mixing occupies a kind of midpoint between accidental and substantial change; and the potentiality of the ingredients in a mixture is one of the more important and problematic forms of potentiality for Aristotle. Thus no exegesis of his views on either change or potentiality can be considered complete unless it takes into account his views on mixture.

82

We now know that Aristotle's views on mixture are mistaken, and badly mistaken at that. In rejecting atomism he made a critical (though understandable) error; and when one combines the rejection of atomism with the antiquated belief in the four elements, it is easy to conclude that his views are purely of scholarly interest with no real relevance to contemporary concerns. But even though his views may be much further removed from reality than those of modern science, they are much closer in many ways to common sense. In the laboratory we do not suppose that every part of some butter is butter. But in the kitchen we do; and it is convenient, though erroneous, assumptions of this sort that guide us in our everyday life. This therefore suggests that we treat these views of Aristotle as having their most direct bearing, not on the nature of reality, but on the structure of common sense.

There have been recent attempts in cognitive science to formalize the content of folk or naive physics; such a physics is meant to provide the principles that would enable one to construct a robot that could deal with the everyday world in much the same way as we do. If I am not mistaken, the contemporary interest of Aristotle's scientific views may lie as much in their connection with these developments within cognitive science as it does with the content of the established sciences. I might add that the recent attempt to rehabilitate the notion of capacity by Cartwright (1989) and others also gives a topical interest to Aristotle's general views on capacities and on the way they might compose or interact within a mixture.

The paper is in six sections. In the first, I state the problem with which Aristotle opens his discussion of mixture in *Generation and Corruption*: how is mixture possible? Aristotle thinks he has a solution; and *our* problem is to understand what that solution is. In the next section, I consider three interpretations of his views on mixture, those of Sharvy (1983), Gill (1989) and Bogen (1995), and find all of them wanting. The main defect with these proposals, from my own point of view, is that they do not take Aristotle's hylomorphic outlook sufficiently seriously. In the third section, I provide a sketch of that outlook and set out the two main accounts of mixture that are in conformity with it, Leveling and Ascent; one places mixture at the same level as the elements, the other at a higher level. The next two sections are the heart of the paper and constitute a sustained argument in favor of Leveling. It is shown how two doctrines— the doctrines of intermediates and of derived parts—enable Aristotle to avoid the apparently insuperable difficulties that lie in the way of its acceptance. The final section considers the problem of how mixing, as opposed to mixture, is possible and argues that Aristotle is also in a position to solve this problem.

No substantive exegetical work on Aristotle is complete without some general remarks on method; and so let me mention two major respects in which my approach differs from that of others. In the first place, my approach is strongly realist; I take Aristotle's primary concern in his metaphysical and physical writings to be with the nature of reality rather than with the nature of language. I am rarely tempted, when Aristotle appears to be talking about things, to construe him as saying something about words; and, in particular, I take his primary concern in *Generation and Corruption* to be with the phenomenon rather than with the vocabulary of change.

This realist approach has led me to take literally what other philosophers would regard as fanciful ways of expressing linguistic facts. A good example is his doctrine of hylomorphism. Aristotle takes sensible things to be 'compounds' of matter and form. This form of expression suggests that he is thinking of items in the world and that he is taking each such item to be composed of matter and form; and this is how I construe him. But others think that what he really has in mind are compound expressions, such as 'the bronze statue', whose components are parts of speech, such as 'bronze' and 'statue', rather than items in the world. There is only one worldly item, on their construal, but three wordly ways of getting at what it is.

In the second place, I see him as a philosopher whose metaphysical preconceptions are often radically different from our own. Others have been more inclined to see him as 'one of us;' and this has made them much less willing to consider interpretations that make him appear too outlandish by our own lights. So whereas I have had no difficulty in supposing that a compound is literally composed of matter and form and, indeed, regard it as a characteristic Aristotelian doctrine, others have shied away from attributing to him anything so extreme and have attempted instead to soften the sense in which something may be said to be a compound, either through a linguistic construal of what is meant or in some other way.

The value of an approach lies largely in its results. But let me here express my opinion that the linguistic and conservative approaches are prone to make Aristotle seem much more banal and obscure than he really is. Rather than being seen as a philosopher who expresses extraordinary thoughts in an ordinary way, he is seen as a philosopher who expresses ordinary thoughts in an extraordinary way. The interest of such an interpretation lies more in the ingenuity by which certain views are imputed to Aristotle than in the views themselves. I hope the present investigation will help reveal the value of a more realist and radical approach, in regard to both the plausibility of the interpretation and its interest.

## I. The Problem

### 1. THE PUZZLES

Aristotle states two puzzles concerning mixture (*mixis*) in chapter I.10 of *Generation and Corruption*. The first (at 327a33–327b10) concerns the existence of the ingredients as they are mixed and may be stated as follows. Take any one of the ingredients. Either it continues to exist once it has been mixed, or it does not. If it still exists, then it must have remained unaltered in the process of mixing and hence cannot properly be said to have been mixed. If it no longer exists, then it must have been destroyed in the process of mixing and so, again, cannot properly be said to have been mixed.

The other puzzle (stated at 327b31–328a16) concerns the division of the ingredients as they are mixed. There are two models of how the division might go. Under the first, the ingredients will be divided into pieces, i.e. bodies which are further divisible, any piece of one being placed alongside a piece of the other. Under the other, the ingredients are divided into particles, i.e., bodies which are not further divisible, any particle of one being placed alongside a particle of the other. Now the pieces will be finite, the particles infinitesimal. The first model is therefore to be rejected on the grounds that a mixture should be uniform or 'homoeomerous'; "just as a part of water is water so it is with what has been mixed" (328a10–11). For at the level of the pieces, the mixture will not be uniform, the parts will not "have the same proportion as the whole" (328a8–9). The second model is to be rejected on the grounds that the supposed division into the particles is impossible.[1]

Mixing is a process in which two or more things become one. We might see these puzzles as arising from the demand that mixing be distinguished from other processes of this sort. In the first puzzle, it is required that mixing be distinguished from a process in which the antecedent materials are destroyed and something completely new is created. As Aristotle himself puts it, "Now what this argument is after seems to be to clarify the difference between mixing and coming to be or ceasing to be, and between a mixture and a thing that comes to be or ceases to be" (327b7–9). In the second puzzle, it is required that mixing be distinguished from a mere aggregation of the antecedent materials; the result of one, a 'gel' (*mixis*), must be distinguished from the result of the other, a 'jumble' (*synthesis*).

It is absolutely clear that Aristotle believes that he has a solution to both puzzles. Thus at 328b14–14, after his discussion of the puzzles, he concludes: "From what has been said, therefore, it is clear that there is such a thing as mixing, what it is, and what causes it." However, it is not at all clear from his discussion what mixing is supposed to be. His response to the first puzzle is that "each of the things which were, before they were mixed, still is, but potentially, and has not been destroyed" (327b25–26). But this is, at best, a solution *scheme*; for it leaves one in the dark as to what the potential form of existence might be or how it might account for the ingredients in the mixture being altered, in the relevant sense, and yet not destroyed.

His response to the second puzzle is that the two ingredients accommodate themselves to one another: "each changes from its own nature in the direction of the dominating one, though it does not become the other but something in between and common to both" (328a27–30). But it is not clear how this response avoids the dilemma posed by the puzzle. For even if the ingredients accommodate themselves to one another, why should this not be compatible with the pieces of each ingredient being placed side by side—the only difference from the standard case of aggregation being that each piece of one ingredient will be modified in the direction of a piece of the other ingredient as it is placed by its side. The resulting aggregate will indeed be uniform in kind. But it will still not, for Aristotle, be a mixture of the original two ingredients; for a sufficiently small part of it will only contain one of the original ingredients, though in a modified form.

It should also be noted that even if the present response succeeds in solving the second puzzle, it is still unclear why it succeeds in solving the first—and, after all, what we require is a simultaneous solution to both puzzles. For why should the process of mutual accommodation result in the ingredients achieving a potential state of being of the sort required by a solution to the first puzzle? Why should we not say, instead, that each of the two ingredients is destroyed?

The basic problem with the text, at these points, is that it does not provide us with a specific enough conception of mixing to see how the puzzles are to be solved. The process of mutual accommodation must somehow secure both the required alteration in the ingredients and their required unification. As Aristotle himself puts it at the close of *G&C.* I.10, "mixing is the unification of the things mixed resulting from their alteration." But it is unclear from his description how the required alteration-cum-unification is to be achieved.

What we need to do is to construct a fuller account of what Aristotle might here have had in mind on the basis of what he says in the rest of *Generation and Corruption* and elsewhere in his works. To this end, it will be helpful to distinguish between two rather different aspects of the problem, one dynamic and the other static. The dynamic problem is to say what *mixing* is; the static problem is to say what *mixture* is. The first concerns the nature of the *process* by which mixtures are formed and relates to what happens over time. The second concerns the nature of the *results* of mixing and relates to what happens at a time. The second problem would have application in a universe in which the mixtures came 'ready-made' and were not the result of mixing, though the first would not.

The puzzles can be taken to concern either the static or the dynamic version of the problem. Thus the skeptical challenge can be posed either in the form, "How is it possible for there to be mixing?", or in the form, "How is it possible for there to be mixtures?". Of these two questions, it is clearly the second that is primary: for we cannot ascertain what mixing is, or whether it is possible, without first ascertaining what mixture is, and whether *it* is possible.

As is evident from the passage cited above ('Now what this argument is after seems to be to clarify the difference between mixing and coming to be or ceasing to be, and between a mixture and a thing that comes to be or ceases to be' (327b7–9)), Aristotle is aware of the distinction between the two aspects of the question and thinks of the puzzles as relating to both. However, dynamical and static considerations are often run together in his thinking; and it will be important for us to be much more careful than he is in keeping them apart. We shall therefore deal first with the static aspects of the question and only then turn to the dynamical aspects.

In attempting to ascertain Aristotle's views, it will be helpful to set down a list of requirements to which any reasonable account of those views should conform. Some of these requirements will emerge from his statement of the puzzles, some from his solution to them, and others from his general metaphysical beliefs. In setting out the requirements, I make no claim either to be comprehensive or to be completely rigorous.

Let us begin with a reassessment of the two puzzles. Each may be seen to have its origin in certain requirements on the nature of mixture. The point of the puzzle is then to show that these requirements cannot be met and that mixture is therefore impossible. The requirements are taken to be evident and perhaps even constitutive of the concept of mixture. The puzzles thus take the form of a skeptical argument against the existence and perhaps even against the very notion of mixture. Any satisfactory account of mixture for Aristotle should therefore show how the evident requirements can be retained while the skeptical conclusions are resisted.

Two such requirements emerge from his discussion of the first puzzle. For the puzzle may be presented as being based upon four assumptions concerning the status of an ingredient, once it has been mixed: the ingredient is altered; it is not destroyed; if it exists, it is unaltered; if it does not exist, it is destroyed. From these assumptions a contradiction then follows. Now it is clear from his response to this puzzle and from what he says elsewhere (e.g. 327b26 and 328a19–20) that he does not wish to challenge the first two assumptions; his only concern is to show that the last two assumptions do not hold for an unequivocal sense of 'exists.' Thus his discussion of the puzzle leads to the requirements that the first two assumptions should be true: the ingredients of the mixture should be altered, but not destroyed.

In formulating the requirements in this way, we face head on the distinction between the static and dynamical points of view. Let us distinguish between the notion of a *concurrent* ingredient, one which the mixture is currently *of*, and the notion of an *antecedent* ingredient, one which the mixture is *from*. The requirement that the ingredients be altered but not destroyed is naturally taken to concern a change in the status of the antecedent ingredients. But it may also be taken to concern the status of the concurrent ingredients; they should be in that state that is characteristic of things that have, in the appropriate way, been altered

but not destroyed. The static version of the puzzle, which is what we are
after here, relates to the concurrent ingredients, the dynamic version to
the antecedent ingredients. Thus in the one case, we are asking how it is
possible for the concurrent ingredients to *be* altered and not destroyed;
and in the other case, we are asking how it is possible for the antecedent
ingredients to *become* altered and yet not destroyed.

Turning to the second puzzle, two further requirements emerge. One,
explicitly stated and affirmed by Aristotle, is that any mixture should be
uniform—it should be through and through the same, with each part
being like the whole (*G&C.* I.1, 314a20; I.10, 328a10). However, it is not
altogether clear what this requirement comes to. One aspect of what is
required is that a mixture should be of the same kind throughout; any
part of the mixture should be a mixture of the same kind as the mixture
itself and, in particular, the ratio of the one kind of ingredient to the other
should not vary from part to part (or from part to whole).

But something more definite is also part of this requirement, viz., that
any part of the mixture of the concurrent ingredients should be a mixture
of particular parts of those ingredients. Indeed, uniformity in the process
of mixing would seem to require that this more stringent form of
uniformity should hold of the mixtures themselves. For in a uniform
process of mixing, every part of the mixture will derive from parts of the
antecedent ingredients; and so, given that the antecedent ingredients of a
mixture are also its concurrent ingredients, it will follow that each part
of the mixture will be *of* those parts. It was implicitly because of this more
stringent requirement, that we were led (on Aristotle's behalf) to reject
the model of mixing in which small pieces of the two things to be mixed
were transformed into a common kind of thing while remaining disjoint.[2]

The other requirement is merely implicit in the statement of the second
puzzle. It is that the mixture should 'contain' the ingredients, that each
ingredient should be 'in' the mixture. Such as assumption seems central
to our conception of mixture. For how could a mixture be *of* its ingredients
and yet not contain them?

There is, however, a significant ambiguity in the notion of containment
or inherence. For the notion can be understood either mereologically or
topologically. To say that one thing contains or is in another can mean
either that it is part of the other or that its location is included in that of
the other.

But significant as the distinction may be, it is hard to see how an
ingredient could be in a mixture in the one sense and yet not in the other.
For suppose that one of the ingredients is part of the mixture. Then surely
it has a location; and given that it has a location, surely that location is
included in the location of the mixture. Suppose now that the location of
the ingredient is included in that of the mixture. Then what could account
for this other than the ingredient being part of the mixture?

It seems, in any case, to be clear that containment in at least the spatial sense is presupposed in the formulation of the second puzzle. For why is it supposed that, in any mixture, each of the ingredients will be divided into pieces or particles that lie alongside one another? The thought must surely be that the ingredients are spatially included in the mixture and that the only possible way for them to be so included is through their division into pieces or particles.

It also seems clear from his response to the first puzzle that Aristotle does not wish to challenge this presupposition. For he believes that the ingredients are not destroyed in the process of being mixed. But how can the ingredients enter into the formation of the mixture, not be destroyed, and yet still not be part of the mixture? (Conversely, it is hard to see how the ingredients could be destroyed and yet still be part of the mixture.)

There is a additional consideration that weighs heavily in favor of Aristotle's commitment to containment. For suppose the point of his account of mixing in terms of mutual accommodation was simply to make clear that two things could become a third, intermediate in nature between the two others, but not to establish that the ingredients were actually part of the mixture. Could not the skeptic justifiably retort that he was well aware of this possibility, which is, after all, a matter of common observation. *His* point is that unless the two things actually are part of the third, there is no reason to suppose that it is a mixture of the two things and not some other thing altogether. Thus if Aristotle's account is to provide a satisfactory response to the skeptic, it must be assumed that it is an account in which the ingredients figure as part of the mixture.

There is another, more general, reason for supposing that Aristotle believed that a mixture should contain its ingredients or, at least, should contain its elemental ingredients. For he repeatedly states that homoeomerous mixtures are composed of the elements. So, for example, at *G.A.* I.1, 715a9–11, he writes: "and the material of animals is their parts—of every whole animal the anhomoeomerous parts, of these again the homoeomerous, and of these last the so-called elements of bodies" (cf. *G&C.* II.8, 334b31 and P.A. II.1, 646a12–24). Some commentators take the elements to be the antecedent matter from which the homoeomers are formed. But here surely they are taken to be the concurrent matter; and they are explicitly taken to be parts.

An additional requirement is worth noting, even though it is a consequence of Uniformity and Containment and of other, relatively unproblematic, assumptions. It is that the ingredients in the mixture should coincide; their location should be the same. To see how this follows from the other assumptions, suppose, for purposes of reductio that the two ingredients do not coincide. There must then be a part of the location of one of the ingredients that is disjoint from the location of the other ingredient. Take now the part of the mixture which is at this sublocation. Then it contains only the first ingredient and none of the second and hence is not uniform with the mixture as a whole.[3]

Given that the location of the mixture must be included in the combined locations of the ingredients, it follows that the location of the ingredients and of the mixture must be the same, even though they themselves are not the same. Thus at the location of any mixture, there will be three distinct but coincident objects—the two ingredients and the mixture itself. I am not sure that there is any place where Aristotle explicitly draws this conclusion, but it follows fairly directly from what he seems to take for granted and by considerations of much the same sort as he uses in arguing against the model of mixtures as mere aggregates.

Let us summarize the requirements obtained so far. They constitute what might be called the *basic* problem of mixture and should be met by any satisfactory solution of the puzzles as Aristotle conceives them:

(1) *Alteration:* The ingredients of a mixture must be (appropriately) altered;
(2) *Non-destruction:* The ingredients must not be destroyed;
(3) *Uniformity:* The mixture must be uniform;
(4) *Containment.* A mixture should contain its ingredients;
(5) *Compresence:* The ingredients of a mixture should be compresent.

The first two requirements, which arise from consideration of the first puzzle, constitute what might be called the *transformational* aspect of the problem of mixture; and the last three, which arise from consideration of the second puzzle, constitute what might be called the *mereological* aspect. It is not hard to see how the requirements in the first subgroup might be satisfied. Indeed, requirements (1), (2) and (4) might reasonably be taken to be satisfied by the present-day atomistic conception of mixture as a form of chemical compound; for the atoms in such a mixture are all part of it, they are altered (through chemical bonding), and yet are not destroyed. It is much harder to see how the requirements from the second subgroup are to be satisfied, if only because they entail Compresence. But in demanding that all five requirements be met, Aristotle has posed a problem of enormous difficulty, one whose solution was not evident then and is not even evident today.

2. SOME FURTHER REQUIREMENTS

Aristotle believes he has solved the puzzles, and the solution he provides enjoys some additional features of its own. They are perhaps not required of an *arbitrary* solution to the puzzles, but they are required of a satisfactory account of *his* solution. Let us consider what they are.

One arises from the way he interprets the requirement that the mixture should be altered and yet not destroyed in his solution to the first puzzle at 327b23–26. For he interprets the alteration in the ingredients as a form of non-existence and their non-destruction as a form of existence. If it were in the same underlying sense of 'exists' that existence and nonexistence were required, then an immediate contradiction would ensue. There must therefore be two senses of 'exists', with nonexistence in one sense being compatible with existence in the other. Let us call the sense of existence excluded by alteration *strong* and the sense required by non-destruction *weak*. Aristotle then wishes to align the distinction between strong and weak existence with—or, rather, with one way of making—the distinction between actual and potential existence. The ingredients will be altered in the sense of not actually existing and they will fail to be destroyed in the sense of potentially existing.

There is another aspect of his solution that emerges from his discussion of the first puzzle. For he says "the things that are mixed, manifestly, both come together from formerly having existed separately and are capable of being separated again"(327b27–8). This suggests that the (antecedent) ingredients of any mixture should be recoverable; whatever went in can be got out.

But the requirement, as so formulated, is ambiguous between a generic and a singular reading. Under the first, what is separate before the mixing and capable of separation after the mixing are kinds of stuff—Water and Earth, we might say; while under the second, they are particular things— particular water, particular earth. Suppose that e and w are the particular earth and water that enter the mixture, i.e. the antecedent ingredients, and that e' and w' are the particular earth and water that leave, what might be called the *succeedent* ingredients. Then, under the one reading, e' is the same kind of thing as e, both are earth, and w' is the same kind of thing as w, both are water; while under the other reading, e' is the very same thing as e, w' the very same thing as w. The requirement is unproblematically correct under the generic reading; for no one is going to dispute what kind of thing it is that goes in or out of a mixture. But its truth is somewhat problematic under the singular reading; for even if it is clear that it is water or earth that goes in and out, it may still not be clear that it is the very same water or the very same earth.

The singular reading is the more natural and is, I suspect, what Aristotle has in mind. For the fact that the earth and water can be separated out is meant to show that their potentiality is preserved (327b27–30). But suppose that the particular earth and water that go into a mixture are not the same as the particular earth and water that come out. Then all that separation shows is that the potentiality of the outgoing earth and water is present—or, perhaps, of earth and water in general. But it would not show that the potentiality of the incoming earth and water was in any significant sense preserved; and it is this that is in question.

I am not sure that the view I have ascribed to Aristotle is essential for answering the skeptic, but it is hard to see how it is to be avoided. For suppose again that the antecedent and succeedent ingredients are not the same. Then on what basis do we say that the mixture is of the antecedent rather than of the succeedent ingredients? There is an awkward asymmetry here and no apparent basis upon which it can be resolved.

One might adopt a view according to which a particular mixture was of water and earth in a generic sense, though not of any particular water and earth. Or one might take the mixture to be of its own water and earth, distinct both from the water and earth that enter into the mixture and those that exit from it. But these are not options that would satisfy the skeptic's demand that a mixture be of the things that are mixed and nor are they options that Aristotle appears willing to embrace. He therefore has little choice but to accept the natural view that the antecedent, concurrent and succeedent ingredients are all the same.

We might add that acceptance of the identity of the antecedent and succeedent ingredients makes it all the more plausible to suppose that they are currently *in* the mixture, i.e. that they are  the concurrent ingredients. For if they were not, they would presumably not exist or have a location during the time that the mixture exists; and so there would be a gap in their temporal career. But given such a gap, it is not clear on what basis we could conclude that the antecedent and succeedent materials are the same. Earth is placed in a 'container,' the mixture; earth is then removed from the container. But without the assumption that the earth remains, it is hard to see why we should conclude that the earth we take out is the same as the earth we put in.

Of course, none of this goes any way towards showing that the antecedent and succedent ingredients *are* the same. The skeptic can conclude that water and earth go in and out of the mixture and yet, for all that Aristotle has said, still deny that it is the same water and earth. Indeed, in the somewhat analogous case of elemental transformation, Aristotle sides with the skeptic. When water changes into air and then back to water, Aristotle's view is that the two waters are not the same (*G&C.* II.11, 338b15–18). But why, the skeptic might ask, should the case of mixtures be any different?

In addition to the requirements that arise from Aristotle's own solution to the problem of mixture, there are some others that arise from his general metaphysical beliefs. Aristotle subscribes to a doctrine of hylomorphism, according to which every sensible thing is a compound of matter and form. In the special case of non-elemental homoeomers, he took the form to be a ratio of elements. So, for example, in discussing Empedocles' view that "bone exists by virtue of the ratio in it," he remarks that it "is similarly necessary that flesh and each of the other tissues should be the ratio of its elements, or that not one of them should" (*Met.* II.10, 993a16–20); and of these two alternatives, it is clear that he prefers the first.

It should be remarked, however, that Aristotle is not altogether consistent on this point. For he is sometimes inclined to uphold the doctrine of homonymy for flesh and the like: flesh on the butcher's block is not, properly speaking, flesh (*G.A.* II.1, 743b24–735a26). But it is hard to see how such a view is compatible with the form of the flesh being a ratio of elements. For the 'flesh' on the block is surely a homoeoemer and the ratio of its elements surely remains the same as it was before. It should therefore still be flesh.

There is tension here in Aristotle's thought. It may be resolved by distinguishing between two kinds of flesh, one essentially inanimate and the other essentially animate. Flesh of the first kind will have a 'rational' form; and it will be matter for flesh of the second kind, which will possess some sort of functional form superimposed upon the rational form (cf. Lewis (1994): 264–5). It is plausible to suppose that flesh of the second kind will not result directly from mixing but will be obtained from flesh of the first kind by an essentially different process. Thus, under the proposed resolution, it will be denied that every non-elemental homoeomer is a mixture (even though every mixture will be a homoeomer).

Another general doctrine of metaphysics of relevance to Aristotle's more particular views on mixture concerns potentiality. Things have the potentiality both to affect and to be affected. But it is not just actual existents that have potentialities, potential existents may have them as well. An especially clear illustration of this possibility occurs at *Met.* VIII.5, 1044b29–1045a6 (cf. *De An.* II.4, 416a6ff and *De Cae* II.6, 288b15–18). He is there envisaging a situation in which wine turns to vinegar; and he asks whether it is the wine or the water in the wine that is potentially vinegar (he also asks the corresponding question of whether it is the wine or the water that is the matter of vinegar). His answer is that it is the water, not the wine, that is potentially vinegar.

Now wine is a typical mixture, water a typical ingredient; and the example therefore suggests that it is generally true that an ingredient can have potentialities independently of the mixture in which it resides. There is, of course, a sense in which the wine is also potentially vinegar. But the potentiality of the wine, in this respect, is derivative. For what underlies the potentiality of the wine is the potentiality of one of its ingredients.

It is tempting to suppose that among the potentialities of the ingredients, as they occur in the mixture, is the potentiality to be actual. This is how Aristotle expresses himself. It is not the mixture itself that enjoys the potentiality to separate; rather, it is the "things that are mixed" that are "capable of being separated" (327b27–8). (Somewhat similarly, at *Met.* IX.8, 1050a15–17: "the matter exists potentially because it may attain to its form; and when it exists actually, then it is in its form."). If this is so, then the potentiality of the ingredients, in their potential state, to be actual (or separate) will provide a common basis for their potential existence (in the sense required for non-destruction) and their recoverability.

This potentiality, it should be noted, is not simply to *become* something actual, but to *be* actual. Thus the potentiality is only realized if the actualized thing is the same as the thing with the potentiality to be actual. Such an understanding of the potentiality will therefore immediately exclude the possibility that the ingredients extracted from the mixture might be different from the ingredients already in it.

Let us summarize the second set of requirements on a mixture and its (concurrent) ingredients. These requirements constitute what might be called the *broader* problem of mixture and should be met by any satisfactory account of Aristotle's own solution.

(1') *Non-actual Existence*: The ingredients of the mixture do not actually exist;

(2') *Potential Existence*: The ingredients potentially exist;

(6) (a) *Recoverability*: The ingredients of any mixture are recoverable;
     (b) *Derivability*: Any mixture can be derived from its ingredients;

(7) *Proportionality*: The form of a mixture is a ratio, or proportion, of elements;

(8) *Latent Potentiality*: The ingredients can have potentialities that do not derive from the mixture to which they belong.

Derivability has been listed along with Recoverability, since it is hard to see how Aristotle could believe in the one and not the other. Indeed, given his general views on the plenitude of possibilities (see, e.g., *De Cae.* I.12, 281b25ff), he may well believe that any mixture must always have been formed from its elemental— or, close-to-elemental—ingredients and must always separate into those ingredients.

It should be noted that the two requirements under (6) also have a dynamic aspect. For although the possibility of separating or forming the ingredients relates to the current state of the mixture, what it is for a given ingredient to be separated or formed involves considerations of identity over time. However, it is only in the last part of the paper that these further considerations will be addressed.

## 3. SOME PERIPHERAL REQUIREMENTS

Aristotle's discussion of mixing and change gives rise to some problems whose solution may be somewhat incidental to the puzzles stated above but is still essential for a full understanding of his views.

(9) *Elemental Underdetermination*: Aristotle believes that the nature of any homoeomerous mixture can be determined on the basis of the primary contrarieties, hot/cold and dry/wet. But to different ratios of the elements may correspond the same degree of hot/cold and of dry/wet. The first problem is to reconcile Aristotle's view on the determinative role of the primary contraries with his view that the form of the homoeomerous bodies (or mixtures) is a ratio of elements.

(10) *Unity*: The treatise *Generation and Corruption* is a general account of the different kinds of change that objects can endure. The second problem is see the account of mixing as a coherent part of this general account. It is necessary in particular, as Aristotle himself emphasizes, to explain how mixing differs from growth, creation, and destruction.

(11) *The Quantum Effect:* The third problem is a special case of the second. Aristotle holds the extraordinary view that when one mixes a middling amount of wine with water one gets a mixture of wine and water, but that when the amount of wine is sufficiently small one gets, not a faint mixture of wine and water, but water. What would otherwise be a case of mixing becomes a case of growth. We may call this the 'quantum effect', since it is only when there is a sufficient amount of wine that the 'jump' to a mixture takes place. Any account of the difference between mixing and growing should explain why mixing is subject to such a threshold and why growth occurs when the threshold is not reached.

## II. Some Proposed Solutions

### 4. SHARVY

Sharvy's paper (1983) is an interesting attempt to accommodate Aristotle's views on mixture within the framework of contemporary mereology. He presupposes throughout his paper that a mixture be construed as a mereological sum of its ingredients. He therefore takes his task to be that of distinguishing mixture from other forms of mereological sum. To this end, he draws attention to the above noted consequence of being homoeomerous, viz. that the ingredients must be compresent.[4] This then leads him to characterize a mixture as a mereological sum of compresent quantities (pp. 445–50). (I here use his term, 'quantity'. The term is unfortunate since it suggests that there must be a measure of how much of the stuff there is; my preferred term, to which I later revert, is 'parcel'.)

The great advantage of Sharvy's account is that it satisfies requirements (3)—(5) above (Uniformity, Containment and Compresence), and hence provides a solution to the second puzzle. We should also note that it satisfies the sixth requirement concerning Derivability and Recoverability, and the eighth requirement concerning Latency. Unfortunately, it fails to satisfy the other requirements; and for the purposes of constructing a more satisfactory account, it will be helpful to see where the failings of his own account lie.

Some derive from the way Sharvy conceives of compresence. He proposes a multi-dimensional model of how two, possibly scattered, quantities can be compresent (pp. 451–3). According to this model, compresence occurs through the two quantities occupying different regions within a fifth dimension. So just as one quantity can be spatially on top of another, it can be aspatially compresent with another. He is not, of course, asking us to take seriously the idea that Aristotle believed in a fifth dimension. The model is intended as no more than that—a model or way of seeing how compresence *might* be possible.

However, the model suggests a metaphysical picture, which Sharvy does seem to want to endorse. It is a picture in which two quantities being compresent need involve no more than their sharing the same location. Accordingly, the process of two quantities becoming compresent need involve no more than a change in their location. The quantities do not change in themselves; or, if they do, this is incidental to their becoming compresent. In this respect, the process of becoming compresent is not essentially different from the more ordinary forms of movement. Just as two quantities can pass by one another without any change in their intrinsic features, so they can pass through one another without any such change.

It is hard to be certain that this is the picture that Sharvy has in mind. But if he has any other view, he gives no indication of what it might be. Thus to the extent that he provides us with a definite conception of what mixing is, it must be one which involves no intrinsic change to the ingredients.

There are various different reasons why this view of mixture cannot be Aristotle's. In the first place, he would not have thought that compresence of the sort required by Sharvy was possible. There are many passages in which he expresses hostility to the idea of compresence. Sharvy himself (p. 450) mentions *Phys.* IV.1, 209a6, 213b18–20, 7.214b7, and *G&C.* I.5, 321a8–10; while we might also mention *Phys.* IV.8, 215a28–b23, *De Cae.* III.6, 305a19–20, and *De An.* I.4, 409b3, II.3, 418b13–18.

Now Sharvy does not take this evidence to be decisive and, in a way, he is right. For there are two cases in which Aristotle appears to allow compresence. One is that of a thing and its concurrent matter—a man and his body, let us say; the two are distinct and yet compresent. The other is the present case of a mixture and its ingredients. Somehow the conflict between the cited passages and the apparent counter-examples must be resolved.

The obvious way out is to suppose that the ban on compresence is not meant to be universal, applying regardless of the existential status or type of the objects in question. And, indeed, when we survey the texts, a natural restriction suggests itself. The ban is only meant to apply to two things when they *actually* exist, not when one or both of them *potentially* exist. Understood this way, the restriction accounts both for the passages, which involve only actual existents, and for the counter-examples, which involve at least one potential existent.

This way out, however, is of no help to Sharvy. For the two ingredients in the compresent sum, as he conceives it, actually exist. And, in fact, he suggests a different restriction, viz. that the ban is to apply to bodies (*somata*), but not to quantities of matter.[5]

It is very doubtful that the term 'body' will carry the weight that he wishes it to bear. But, in any case, when we examine some of the passages in question, we see that the ban they enjoin will apply directly to the kinds of things that mix.

For example, at *Phys.* IV.1, 209a6, Aristotle argues that "the place cannot be body; for if it were there would be two bodies in the same place." Take now a quantity of (actually existing) matter and suppose that it can be compresent with another quantity of matter, as required by Sharvy's account of mixing. Then surely we should allow that it can be compresent with what one might call 'a quantity of place,' given that there is such a thing, contrary to what the argument requires.

Or again, consider *G&C.* I.5, 321b15–16 (a related passage is at 321a8–10). He there writes, "nor do two objects possessed of size occupy the same place;" and this is meant to exclude the possibility of a thing growing by becoming compresent with that by which it grows. But if Aristotle believes that things can mix by becoming compresent, then why does he not concede in these passages that they might grow by becoming compresent? Indeed, in the present case it is clear that it is the same kind of things that mix and grow. For when a small of amount of wine is added to water we have growth, while when a large amount is added we have mixture (*G&C.* I.10, 328a23–30).

In addition to the direct evidence, there are considerations of a less direct sort against the required compresence. For Aristotle takes the elements to be combinations of contraries. But in that case, the compresence of two distinct elements would require the compresence of two distinct countraries—hot and cold, let us say; and it is hard to see how this could be possible on Sharvy's view.

I shall later argue that the prime matter of the elements in the mixture should be taken to be the same (assuming that they have any prime matter). But in that case, two contraries will (straightforwardly) attach to the same subject, a possibility expressly excluded by Aristotle at *Met.* IV 6, 1011b17, "contraries ... cannot belong at the same time to the same thing," and elsewhere (e.g., 1005b26–32, 1018a25–38, 1048a9–10). But even if we were to grant that the subjects of the two contraries could be different, it would still seem to be as difficult to make sense of as their simultaneously being attached to the same subject.

Sharvy is aware of this issue and likens the compresence of the elements to the compresence of heat and light or of sound and air (p. 451). But given Aristotle's conception of the elements, this is not the right analogy to make. The compresence of elements should be compared, rather, to the compresence of heat and cold or of wet and dry; and the suggested compresence of qualities across contrarieties gives us no help in understanding the required compresence of qualities within a contrariety.

But the problem is not simply over the possibility of compresence. Let us grant that compresence of the required sort is possible; and let us designate the envisaged process by which things become compresent as 'merging.' Then it would still not be correct to regard merging as a case of mixing. For the ingredients must reciprocally affect one another upon being mixed, each moving in the direction of the other (*G&C.* I.10, 328a19–21ff). But after merging, as it has been envisaged, the ingredients "are no more mixed than they were before but are just the same" (327b1).

Thus our very first requirement (Alteration) will not have been met and no solution to the first puzzle will have been given. Sharvy can provide for the unification of the two ingredients. But it is *brute* unification. He does not explain how the ingredients become unified as a result of having been altered.

It is the need for reciprocal action that explains why Aristotle thinks things of like nature cannot mix. For like-natured things cannot affect one another (*G&C.* I.7, 323b30–324a7); there is no engagement, as it were. Thus, for Aristotle, the 'mixing' of water with water is essentially different from the mixing of water with wine; for, in the former case, we can only obtain an aggregate of the two waters or some water that is completely new.

Under Sharvy's account, however, it is hard to see why like things should not mix as easily, if not more easily, than unlike things. He does suggest that Aristotle might reject the 'mixture' of water with water as a genuine mixture on the grounds that the two waters cannot be separated (p. 447, fn.12). But if this had been Aristotle's view, it would have been much more appropriate for him to deny that likes can be separated rather than deny that they can be mixed.

This problem is part of the general problem (called 'Unity' above) of fitting mixing into a general account of change. For it is difficult to see what account Sharvy can give of growth that will make it through and through, like mixing, and yet distinct from mixing. Growth cannot consist in things becoming compresent, since then it would be indistinguishable from mixing. But what then can distinguish water growing upon the addition of a small amount of wine and its mixing upon an addition of a large amount? No hint of an answer is given in Sharvy (1983) or appears to be available.

Sharvy is aware of making no allowance for Aristotle's views on the potentiality of the ingredients in a mixture. But he finds these views "very mysterious and in conflict with Aristotle's general views on matter and potentiality" (p. 441). He reasons as follows (pp. 454–6). In order for the statue Hermes to have potential existence in a block of wood it must be possible for Hermes to be created from the wood or from part of the wood. By the same token, for some matter to have potential existence in a mixture, it must be possible for the matter to be created from the mixture or from something in the mixture. But matter, as the substratum of all change, is not the kind of thing that is created or destroyed; and hence it cannot have a potential existence

The objection, as stated, is not compelling. For the matter whose potential existence is here in question is not prime matter (if such there be), but elemental or homoeomerous matter; and this is a kind of matter that, for Aristotle, *is* capable of creation and destruction.

But a related difficulty remains. For, in order for Hermes to exist potentially in the block of wood, the statue cannot already be in the wood, since otherwise it would actually exist. By the same token, in order for the matter potentially to exist in the mixture, it cannot already be in the mixture. But then the matter cannot be one of ingredients. Thus the requirement that the matter be in the mixture is incompatible with the requirement that it potentially exist.

This is, indeed, a genuine worry; and we shall later see how it might be met. But even if we were to grant that Sharvy was right to ignore it, he would still be mistaken in taking a mixture to be the mereological sum of its ingredients. For the sum existed even before the ingredients were mixed and it will continue to exist once they are separated. But the mixture comes to exist only when the ingredients are mixed and ceases to exist once they are separated. Indeed, on the standard conception of mereological summation, the sum of the two ingredients will exist at any time at which only *one* of the ingredients exists.

It is important, in this connection, to recall the distinction between mixing, which is a certain process, and mixture, which is a result of that process. In identifying the one we do not thereby identify the other. Thus even if we grant that a mixture will have been formed when its ingredients become compresent, there will still be a question as to what the mixture is. (The difficulty here is obscured by Sharvy's exposition. For he defines 'homoeomerous' in a tensed sense of the term; something is only homoeomerous for him at a time. But one naturally construes the term in a tenseless way as picking out a certain sort of object.)

To overcome this difficulty, it might be supposed that the mixture is a temporal segment of the sum, its restriction to that period during which the ingredients are compresent. But then for reasons that are elaborated in Fine (1994a), it can no longer reasonably be maintained that the ingredients are part of the mixture. Thus we are still left with no reasonable conception of what the mixture might be.

We might note that a similar difficulty arises if one thinks of growth as taking place through merging and then identifies the object that has grown with the mereological sum of the object that grew and the object by which it grew. For this sum is a new object, whereas in a genuine case of growth, the object which grew must be the same as the object that has grown (*G&C.* I.5, 321a21, "the thing which grows is preserved and remains"). Thus Aristotle might also have objected to the compresence model of growth at *G&C* I.5, 32115–16, on the grounds that it could not properly account for the continued identity of the object that grows (presumably, at this point in the argument, he was regarding the identity of the grower as a negotiable assumption).

The inadequacy of Sharvy's proposal on this issue arises from his failure to take any account of form. For the form of a mixture for Aristotle is a ratio of elements; and it is because the form is essential to the mixture that the mixture will cease to exist once the given ratio of the elements is no longer maintained. But there is nothing in Sharvy's proposal that enables him to pick out this particular aspect of the mixture as its form. He is therefore unable to satisfy the seventh requirement (Proportionality).

Indeed, on Sharvy's actual analysis, a compresent sum of elements may not even conform to a stable ratio (let alone essentially conform); for different parts of the mixture may contain the same elements, but in different ratios. Thus his formal characterization of homoeomer (D5 on p. 446) must be rejected as unfaithful to Aristotle's intentions. Of course, we might rectify the analysis by requiring that the ratio be constant from one part of the mixture to another. But we still face the problem of why this particular feature of the mixture should be taken to constitute its form.

It would be natural at this juncture to build the form into the very identity of the mixture. But this is not Sharvy's approach. Instead, he boldly asserts "the theory of mixtures is wholly within the pure theory of matter" (p. 456) and accepts complete relativity on the question of form (p. 447). Thus, for him, a mixture is not in itself a homoeomer; it is only a homoeomer with respect to one form, i.e. one possible decomposition of the ingredients, as opposed to another. And of these various decompositions, none is privileged; none is integral to the homoeomer itself.

But this view, whatever its merits, is not Aristotle's. For him, the form of a mixture, or of anything else informed, is intrinsic to the thing itself. There is therefore no relativity in the notion of being homoeomerous. For once we have the thing, we have the form; and once we have the form, we have the respect in which the thing is to be homoeomerous.[6]

The neglect of matter/form distinction is not only responsible for Sharvy's failure to provide an adequate account of the identity of a mixture. It is also responsible for his failure to provide an adequate account of how things are altered in the process of being mixed. For this involves the accommodation of form, something of which he takes no account. What we have in Sharvy's proposal is not an Aristotelian conception of mixture but an essentially modern conception that takes on board one aspect of the Aristotelian conception, the idea that a mixture should be through and through the same. The proposal provides a mereological, not a hylomorphic, conception of the homoeomerous.

## 5. BOGEN AND GILL

I want briefly to discuss the more recent views of Bogen (1995) and Gill (1989). They go one step further than Sharvy in giving due recognition to Aristotle's views on form and potentiality but do not, in my opinion, go far enough.

There are two related strands to Bogen's paper on mixture, one concerning the relationship between a thing and its concurrent matter and the other concerning the analysis of potential existence. His view on the first is that a thing and its concurrent matter are the same; there is no real distinction between them (section viii). Thus he follows Sharvy in adopting a 'shallow' conception of the objects in Aristotle's universe. In the case of elemental matter, this leaves him with a choice: either a thing is the same as its elemental matter; or the elemental matter is antecedent rather than concurrent matter. He opts for the second, from which it follows that a mixture will not contain any of the elements as part of its concurrent matter or as concurrent part in some other way.

This is not the place to consider the general question of whether a thing is identical to its concurrent matter. But let us note that the adoption of the present position makes it exceedingly difficult to see how the second puzzle is to be solved. For this requires that there be a sense in which the elements are currently in the mixture; and if they are not currently part of the mixture, it is hard to see what this sense might reasonably be. We might also note that the position makes it hard to sustain Aristotle's view that the elements in a mixture can be the independent bearers of potentiality.

The other main strand in Bogen's account revolves around Aristotle's claim that the ingredients are potentially present in the mixture that is generated from them. He thinks that Aristotle makes this claim in order to explain why a mixture resembles its ingredients to some extent (section iii). I find it rather odd that Bogen should think this. For the claim that the ingredients potentially exist (at *G&C* I.10, 327b23–27) is made before the facts of resemblance that it is thought to explain are ever mentioned (at 328a23ff). The claim is, in fact, made immediately after the statement of the first puzzle and is presented *as* a solution to that puzzle. Similarly, in the other main context in which he appeals to the potential presence of the ingredients (II.7, 334b), his purpose is to explain how mixture is possible. It therefore seems clear that Aristotle's *primary* motivation for making the claim is to solve the first of the puzzles.

All the same, it does seem to be true that Aristotle thinks of the potential presence of the ingredients in a mixture as explaining their resemblance to the mixture. Now on the account of potential presence that I develop below, the one will indeed explain the other. But on Bogen's account of potential presence (or what he prefers to call 'presence by ability'), I do not see that it will.

For him the primary contraries associated with each element are abilities. The elements will possess these abilities to a maximal degree, while the mixtures formed from them will possess them to an intermediate degree. He then wants to say, "The presence by ability of an element in a compound consists of (nothing more than) the possession by the compound of the relevant non-maximal abilities" (11(b) of section v).[7]

It is unclear whether Bogen intends this as an account of the presence by ability of a particular ingredient—this earth, this water—or of a generic ingredient—Earth or Water. Sometimes he talks the one way, sometimes the other.[8] But, of course, if it is intended as a particularist account, then we should also require that the mixture *acquires* the modified abilities from the ingredients in the appropriate way; for we do not want to say that any water whatever is present by ability in any waterish mixture.

Now what is meant to explain the resemblance between an ingredient and the mixture, on this account, is the fact that the mixture possesses to a different degree the ability possessed by the ingredient. But under either the generic or the particularist reading, this fact at best explains *how* the ingredient resembles the mixture, not *why* it does.

This is clear in the case of the generic account. But in the case of the particularist account, we should distinguish between its present formulation and a stricter formulation according to which the presence by ability of an ingredient consists in the mixture possessing the very same critical features (whatever they might be) as the ingredient itself. The fact that these features were transferred without modification from the ingredients to the mixture might then perhaps be used to explain their resemblance to the mixture. But, under the looser account, the modification of the features as they are transferred from the ingredients to the mixture will stand as much in need of explanation as the original resemblance.

When Bogen introduces Aristotle's purported explanation of the resemblance it is by way of the stricter account (section iii). He later sees that there is a difficulty in saying what the common features might be and therefore resorts to the looser account (section v). It is perhaps the resemblance between the two accounts that enables him to maintain the illusion that the looser account might still be capable of providing the purported explanation.

The proposed account, whether construed strictly or loosely, generically or particularistically, is in any case quite implausible. Presence by ability, as Bogen understands it, is not strictly a form of presence at all. What is present is not this water or even water, but an ability or modified ability of water or Water. A son may acquire the characteristic abilities of this father (and perhaps not even in a modified form). But we do not want to say, except in a metaphorical sense, that the father is in the son; and yet it is exactly in this sense that Bogen takes the ingredients to be present in a mixture.

However, the main objection to the proposed account of potential existence is that it will not serve the purposes for which the notion was introduced. This, as we have explained, is to solve the skeptical puzzle. The skeptic wishes to know how the ingredients can be radically modified in the manner required by mixing and yet still exist. To be told that the mixture acquires the abilities of the ingredients, though in a modified form, does nothing to alleviate his worries. You may call the acquisition a case of potential existence, if you like; but as far as he is concerned, it is no better than complete destruction. The problem is not to *engineer* a sense in which the ingredients are altered but not destroyed (after all, any skeptical problem might be solved by such verbal chicanery), but to find an intuitively satisfying sense in which this is so.

Like Bogen, Gill is also interested in the relationship between a thing and its concurrent matter and with the analysis of potential existence. She follows tradition in taking a thing and its concurrent matter to be different. But instead of taking the matter to be a particular, she takes it to be a property or universal (p. 156). We might identify this property as the property of being earthen, but of course it is not to be understood as the property of containing some particular earth but in some other way that does not already presuppose that there is some particular earth of which the thing in question is composed.

Again, our concern is not with the general question of whether concurrent matter is a universal but only with its bearing on the topic of mixture. Given her view, she can go some way towards solving the second skeptical puzzle. For she can provide a sense in which earth, as opposed to some particular earth, is in a mixture. But this is not enough. For the skeptic is concerned with the question of how a mixture can be a mixture of particular things; and this requires that those very things should in the mixture, not merely their properties.

She can also go some way towards meeting the requirement that the ingredients of a mixture should be capable of having potentialities independently of the mixture itself. For the potentiality of the water in the wine to turn to vinegar can be taken to attach to the universal water rather than to the wine itself. But it might be added that the sense in which the potentiality might be taken to attach to the universal is quite different from the sense in which it attaches to a thing. Gill's own formulations tend to obscure this point. Thus she writes, "the deterioration and destruction of organisms is caused by their own constituents, which tend to move off to their proper places, if given a chance" and "the generic matter retains a potentiality not to be the higher object but to be something simpler instead" (pp. 212–213). But, of course, the sense in which a universal has the potential to move or to be a simple object is very special and quite unlike the sense in which a thing can be said to have such a potential.

What this special sense might be is somewhat unclear. Perhaps the universal is, in some sense, the potentiality itself. Or perhaps in saying that the universal has a certain potentiality one is saying that things to which the universal belongs will have the potentiality in virtue of having the universal belong to them; earthen things, for example, will tend to fall in virtue of being earthen. But whatever the sense might be, it is hard to see how it can be entirely suited to Aristotle's purposes. For he wants to say that it is the water in the wine that is potentially vinegar and actual water that is potentially wine.But if the potentiality to become vinegar properly attaches to the universal water in the first case then why should the potentiality to become wine not properly attach to the universal water in the second case as well? It is hard on the present conception to resist the conclusion that potentialities should either always attach to a thing or to a universal.

Gill also differs from Bogen on the analysis of potential existence. Her view is summarized in the words, "The pre-existing matter survives in a product potentially, in the sense that its essential properties (as well as some nonessential properties) survive to modify the higher construct" (p. 241).[9] The properties will modify the higher construct in the sense of being accidental properties of it (p. 160). Thus for the preexisting matter to survive potentially in the product is for the essential properties of the matter to become accidental properties of the product.

The account, as it stands, is subject to a serious difficulty. For the essential properties of the preexisting materials will not in general be properties of the product at all, let alone accidental properties. Gill writes "the essential properties of the elements—the hot, the cold, the wet, and the dry, and the elemental principles of motion—are actual, though accidental, properties of higher bodies" (p. 241). But this is not strictly true. Fire will be maximally hot; but things made of fire will not be maximally hot, but only hot to some extent (a similar criticism is made by Bogen (1995), section vii).

In so far as there is a transfer of essential properties, it will be in a somewhat attenuated sense of 'essential.' For the property of being hot to some extent is a consequence of an essential property of fire rather than an essential property itself. Gill may, of course, have such an attenuated sense in mind. But even with this understanding, it is not altogether clear that the essential properties of the elements that are possessed by the "higher bodies" will be accidentally possessed by the higher bodies. In supposing that they are Gill may have anhomoeomers principally in mind. Thus in illustration of the point she writes, "it is not the nature of human beings qua human to move toward the centre if unimpeded." But her claim will presumably be false of homoeomers. Thus the tendency to fall will be essential, in the attenuated sense, both to earth and all mixtures containing sufficient earth; and the property of being more hot than cold will be essential both to fire and to all mixtures containing sufficient fire.

In order to obtain a more satisfactory account along these lines, we must suppose that it is not in general the essential properties of the preexisting matter that survive but some modification of those properties, and we should perhaps also allow that the modified properties might be essential to the product. Thus we must move in the direction of the account proposed by Bogen, according to which it is the properties themselves that are modified rather than the manner of their possession. Whether such an amendment would serve Gill's purposes I do not know. But, as we have seen, it will not serve ours.

Despite their differences, the accounts of Bogen and Gill are, in certain fundamental respects, very similar. They both express the same underlying view as to what goes on during the process of mixing; two objects become a single object that resembles them in various respects. They do indeed differ on some questions of detail. But once Gill's account is modified in the way suggested above, the differences on this score become negligible. As long as the phenomena are described in sufficiently basic terms—in the terminology of individuals, their essential and accidental properties, their abilities etc., then both will be more or less agree on what happens in any given case of mixing.[10]

They also agree that a description at this 'phenomenological' level will provide a basis for a reasonable account of mixture, one that will do justice to what Aristotle wants to say about mixture and its distinction from the other kinds of change and their products. Now some of the things that Aristotle wants to say about mixture will not be directly involved in a description at this level. I particularly have in mind his claim that the ingredients are potentially present in the mixture. They therefore maintain that there is an analysis of such notions as potential presence in terms of the notions involved in the phenomenological description and that, given such an analysis, the required claims will then follow from the phenomenological facts.

They do, indeed, differ on how the analysis is to proceed and on what is true once it is made. Thus Bogen wants to locate potential existence in the downgrading of abilities, whereas Gill wants to locate it in the downgrading of essential properties; and Bogen wants to identify the matter of a homoeomer with the homoeomer itself, whereas Gill wants to identify it with a set of properties. But both agree on the strategy of generating an account of mixture from its underlying 'phenomenology.'

It seems to me, however, that an approach of this sort cannot succeed. For it will fail to satisfy the primary requirement on any adequate account of mixture, which is that it satisfy the skeptic. The skeptic can readily agree to the phenomenological facts, whatever they might be taken to be. But this will not induce him to conclude that mixing has taken place or that a mixture has been produced. For he needs to be convinced that the ingredients are genuinely in the mixture.

All that the phenomenologist can appeal to, in this regard, is a resemblance between the ingredients and the mixture. But no resemblance—no matter how striking—will itself ensure inherence. As far as the skeptic is concerned, the phenomenology of mixture will be compatible with a case in which the antecedent materials are destroyed and something new, but very like, is created in its place.

The most that Gill and Bogen can do is to create a facade of having resolved the skeptical doubts. They may so use such terms as 'in' or 'potentially exists' that we can, in a manner of speaking, maintain that the ingredients are potentially present in the mixture. It therefore *looks* as if the skeptical doubts have been removed. But once we strip off the verbal veneer and get down to the fundamental reasons for believing in inherence, we see that they have not been removed. What we have is the semblance of a solution, not its substance.[11]

Gill and Bogen do not themselves discuss the puzzles—Gill because the main emphasis of her book is on the more general Parmenidean problem of how change is possible, Bogen because he views Aristotle's project in *Generation and Corruption* as explanatory rather than as irenic. One can therefore only speculate on what they might say in response to the present criticisms. But if they stick to their views, it seems that they are faced with an awkward choice: they must either deny that Aristotle posed a substantive skeptical problem or that he presented a real solution to it. If we thought that there were no solution to the substantive problem, then this would be a choice that we would in any case be forced to make. But, as I hope to show, there *is* a real solution of this sort to be found in his work.

## III. The Hylomorphic Approach

What we require in order to solve the skeptical puzzles is not a semantic super-structure, constructed over the phenomenological facts, but an ontological sub-structure. The solution to skepticism must come from below, if I may put it that way, rather than from above. Rather than distort the semantics of inherence, we need to have a clearer view of the metaphysics of inherence.

This is to be achieved, it seems to me, by taking Aristotle's hylomoprhic outlook more seriously. It is not sufficient to treat form as merely external to an object, as Sharvy supposes. Nor is it sufficient to treat form merely as an essential feature of an object, as Gill and Bogen suppose. What we must do is recognize the *mereological* aspect of hylomorphism, the fact that a thing is a *compound* of matter and form and that the matter and form may themselves have a mereological structure. It is this, I contend, that will provide the account of mixture with the required ontological underpinning.

From a certain perspective, the problem of determining the identity of a mixture under the hylomorphic approach might appear straightforward. For a mixture, like any other sensible thing, is a compound of matter and form; and so the problem of determining the identity of a mixture simply reduces to the problem of determining its matter and its form. However, the exact determination of the matter and form of the mixture turns out to be far from clear.

One problem, concerning the relationship of the matter of the mixture to the matter of the ingredients, is readily resolved. But the other problem, concerning the relationship of the form of the mixture to the form of the ingredients, is not.[12] We shall consider two main hypotheses concerning this relationship, one (Ascent) placing the form of the mixture on a higher level than that of the ingredients, the other (Leveling) placing it on the same level. Both will initially be seen to suffer from enormous difficulties; and it is only in the next part that leveling will emerge as a viable option.

## 6. THE BASIC FRAMEWORK

According to Aristotle, as I understand him, every sensible thing submits to a hylomorphic analysis; it is somehow composed from matter and form. Thus given any sensible thing x, there will be a form F and some matter m such that x is identical to the compound Fm of F and m. So a man, for example, will be a compound of his body and soul, while a mixture will be a compound of some elemental matter, let us tentatively suppose, and a 'rational' form.

The matter of a compound may itself be a compound. Thus a man's body might be taken to be the compound of his bodily parts with a bodily form, and the elemental matter of a mixture the compound of some prime matter with a rational form. It is such possibilities that permit us to conceive of the hylomorphic structure of world as hierarchical in character.

When the matter m of a compound x = Fm is itself a compound Gn, we may also treat the original object x as the compound Hn of a composite form H = FG and the non-proximate matter n. So we might analyse a man, for example, as the sum of his bodily parts, on the side of matter, and the composite of his soul and the (intrinsic) bodily form, on the side of form. We may call a form *composite* when it has an analysis FG of the sort above and *noncomposite* otherwise.

One might think from reading Aristotle that a form must be monadic or single-pronged, only having application to a single material component. But this may just be a defect of some of his formulations. For it is plausible to suppose that he would have allowed a form to be polyadic or multi-pronged, with application to several material components (see *Met.* VIII.6, 1045a7–10, for example). So, in the case of a man, he would perhaps treat the body m as many, i.e., as consisting of its various bodily parts $m_1$, ... , $m_n$. A man would then be the compound $F(m_1, \ldots , m_n)$ of a polyadic form and the several bodily parts $m_1, \ldots, m_n$ rather than the compound Fm of a monadic form and the single body m.

Aristotle seems willing to admit other means of composition besides the compounding of matter with form. A heap of sand or a mere aggregate do not, for him, properly speaking have any form. But rather than banishing such objects from his ontology, he seems more inclined to treat them as some sort of formless sum or 'heap.' Thus the sand s will be a formless sum $g_1 \cup g_2 \cup \ldots \cup g_n$ of its grains $g_1, g_2, \ldots , g_n$ and, in general, an aggregate will be the sum $c_1 \cup c_2 \cup \ldots \cup c_n$ of its various components $c_1, c_2, \ldots, c_n$.

One might think of summation as a horizontal or flat method of composition, it results in objects of essentially the same level of complexity as the ones to which it applies. Compounding, on the other hand, is a vertical means of composition: it results in objects of an essentially higher level of complexity than the ones to which it applies. Thus the ontology that contains both methods of composition might be compared to something like the ramified theory of types, with its distinction between the horizontally placed orders and the vertically placed types.

If all form is required to be monadic, then it is plausible to suppose that the analysis of any anhomoeomerous substance will eventually require appeal to a formless sum. Consider the case of a man, for example. If his soul is monadic, then either his proximate matter must be taken to be the sum $m_1 \cup m_2 \cup \ldots \cup m_n$ of his various bodily parts or it must itself be taken to have a monadic form. But in the latter case, we may ask of the matter of the body whether it is a formless sum or another monadic compound. Continuing in this way, we must either appeal to a formless sum at some point, or, at the level of the elements (or even of flesh and blood and the like), the matter will be a single heterogeneous aggregate of elements (or of bodily homoeomers) and hence clearly in the nature of a formless sum.

On the other hand, if polyadic forms are allowed, then the appeal to sums in the analysis of anhomoemerous substance can be avoided. For whenever we are tempted to apply a form F to a formless sum $m_1 \cup m_2 \cup \ldots \cup m_k$ of the formed components $m_1, m_2, \ldots, m_k$, we can instead apply a polyadic variant $F'$ of F to the components $m_1, m_2, \ldots, m_k$ themselves. Thus, on this view, the formless sums or heaps will play no role in the formation of compounds. All the same, it will be reasonable to suppose that any sum (with the exception of prime matter) will be a sum of compounds. Thus although sums need play no role in the formation of compounds, compounds will in general play a role in the formation of sums.

Aristotle seems willing to admit yet further means of composition beyond the two already mentioned. For in addition to the substantial compounds, he is prepared to allow accidental compounds, such as "musical Coriscus" (see Lewis (1991)); and, as we have seen, he might also be prepared to allow the composition of forms. But even noncomposite forms (such as the soul or a ratio of elements) may possess a great deal of internal structure; and this suggests that there should be further means by which the forms may be composed.

For the project of understanding Aristotle's whole ontology, it would desirable to have a full inventory of the basic means of composition. However, for our own more limited purposes, we may confine our attention to compounding, summation, and whatever special operations might be involved in explaining the elemental and rational forms.

Given a repertoire of basic means of composition, we may successively decompose any item, first decomposing the item itself according to the means of composition, then decomposing the items that result from this decomposition, and so on. It is natural to suppose that such a process of successive decomposition will eventually terminate in certain basic items. These items will not themselves be decomposable or, at least, will not admit of any significant decomposition into other items.[13]

It is generally agreed that hylomorphic decomposition terminates in something basic for Aristotle, but there are two opposing views as to what it is. The traditional interpretation is that it is prime matter, the matter of the elements, that is basic. But an alternative interpretation, which has recently gained ground, denies that there is any prime matter and takes the elements themselves to be basic. Under such a view, the elements are not themselves compounds of matter and form, although they may possess the analogues of form and matter as strictly conceived.

I myself favor the traditional primalist interpretation; and in what follows, I shall for the most part presuppose that it is correct. However, some (though not all) of what I say will also hold under the more recent elementalist interpretation.

It will be helpful in what follows to be a little more careful in our use of terminology. We shall use the term *item* in the broadest sense to include any item from any category—sensible substances, forms, contraries, or what have you. By the term *object* is meant anything material, i.e. anything that is matter or is composed of matter. Thus it includes prime matter and the sensible substances, but excludes forms and contraries. The term *thing* or *individual* is used more narrowly for compounds of matter and form. Thus it includes mixtures and men but excludes prime matter and heaps. A thing is classified as *homoeomerous* or *anhomoeomerous* according as to the nature of its form, which may then—in a derivative sense—be classified as homoeomerous or anhomoeomerous. The term *body* is used for any object that either is an homoeomerous thing or is the sum of homoeomerous things. It is natural to assume, on Aristotle's behalf, that every object is the sum of one or more anhomeomerous things, homoeomerous things, and parcels of prime matter.[14]

## 7. ELEMENTAL AND HOMOEOMEROUS FORM

After these general remarks on matter and form, let us turn to the more specific topic of the form of the elements and the homoeomers. The present remarks are preliminary; a fuller discussion is given in the ensuing sections.

For Aristotle, there are two primary pairs of contraries (ones to which all others can be reduced): the hot and the cold; and the wet and the dry (*G&C.* II.2, *De An.* II.11, 423b27–29). In between each primary pair of contraries, are the 'intermediates', the various degrees of 'warmth' or of 'dryness' (II.7, 334b8). Thus the countraries represent absolutes or extremes, with the hot being maximally hot, the cold being maximally cold, and similarly for wet and dry.

There are four elements for Aristotle—earth, air, fire and water. The form of each element can be specified as the combination of a contrary from each contrariety. Thus Earth is the combination of cold and dry, air of hot and wet, fire of hot and dry, and water of cold and wet (*G&C*. II.3).

For the purposes of the following discussion, let us distinguish between (i) the four primary contraries—hot, cold, wet and dry (in a generic sense), (ii) the particular instances of a contrary—the hot bodies, say—and (iii) the manifestations of the contrary—the hotness in a hot body,[15] for example. Similar distinctions can be made for the intermediates, the elements and the homoeomers. Thus, in the case of the elements, we need to distinguish between (i) the four (generic) elements, (ii) the elemental bodies, and (iii) the elemental forms. It will usually be clean from the context which of these three items we mean. But occasionally we shall capitalize a term, as in 'Hot' or 'Earth', to indicate that it is (iii), the inherent quality or form, that is in question.

There are different conceptions of the numerical identity of qualities and forms that might be attributed to Aristotle. Under a universalist conception, the Heat in any two hot things and the Fire in any two fiery things will be the same. The form of heat might therefore be identified with the contrary itself. Under an individualist conception, each hot thing will have its own Heat, each fiery thing its own Fire. There are also intermediate conceptions, under which some hot things or some fires may share the quality of Hot or the form of Fire while others do not. For the most part I shall remain neutral on this issue of identity,[16] though sometimes it will be convenient, for purposes of exposition, to adopt the individualist conception.

Within the category of inherent qualities or forms, we shall also need to distinguish between the (primary) contraries, the corresponding, intermediates, the elemental forms, the homoeomerous forms, and forms in general. Let us use the term 'quality' to cover both contraries and intermediates and the term 'homoeomerous' to cover both the forms of homoeomers, properly speaking, and of the elements. We then make use of the following symbols (and variants thereof):

'I'     for inherent intermediates from either contrariety;
'C'     (caloric) for intermediates of hot/cold, with **H** being reserved for the contrary Hot and **C** for the contrary cold;
'D'     (dessication) for intermediates of dry/wet, with **D** being reserved for Dry and **T** for Wet;
'E'     for the elemental forms, with '**E**', '**A**', '**F**' and '**W**' being reserved for the forms of earth, air, fire and water respectively;
'F'     for forms in general; and
'G'
'H'     for the homoeomerous forms.

With any contrary or intermediate may now be associated two magnitudes, one intensive and the other extensive. Suppose that a given object is warm (the case of the other intermediates being similar). Then the intensive magnitude is the *degree* or *power* of its warmth, hot being the maximum degree and cold the minimum. The extensive magnitude is the *quantity* of warmth in the object, a poker having a certain amount and two pokers twice the amount. (It seems clear that Aristotle has such a conception of quantity, as opposed to power, for at *P.A.* II.2, 648b, 19–20, he writes, "Again, of two masses of one and the same substance, the larger is said to have more heat than the smaller"). The two magnitudes together constitute what might be called the resultant character of the warmth.

We can talk of the degree of a contrary or intermediate apart from the object in which it resides. But whether we can talk of the quantity of a contrary or intermediate apart from the object depends upon our conception of its numerical identity. Under an individualist conception and certain intermediate conceptions, we can; but under a universalist conception, we cannot.

Given a homoeomer h whose intermediate quality within a given contrariety is I, we use:

$p(I)$ for the power of I;
$q_h$ for the quantity of I within h; and
$r_h(I)$ for the resultant character $<p(I), q_h(I)>$ of I within h.

It is natural to suppose that the power $p(I)$ can be measured on a scale from 0 to 1, with the 'lower' contrary (cold or wet) receiving the value 0, the 'higher' contrary (hot or dry) receiving the value 1, and the intermediates proper receiving the values in between. Under an individualist conception of the quality, the subscript 'h' in '$q_h$' and '$p_h$' may, of course, be dropped.

The notions of extensive and intensive magnitude also have application to homoeomerous form. Thus, we can talk of the quantity of an homoeomerous form in a homoeomer—so much Water in a tumbler of rum or so much Rum in a cocktail. We may also talk of the *power* or *type* of a homoeomerous form, but the relevant notion of power is multidimensional in contrast to the unidimensional notion of power for a contrary or intermediate.

A simplified measure of the power may be given in terms of the 'mix' of the intermediates from each contrariety. With each homoeomerous form H may be associated a caloric quality $C_H$ and a dessicative quality $D_H$. The *contrarietal* power of the form $p(H)$ of H may then be defined by the combination of the component contrarietal powers:

(1) $p(H) = <p(C_H), p(D_H)>$.

In the case of the elements, the power of their respective forms—Earth, Air, Fire and Water—will be given by the 'principal' vectors $<0,1>$, $<1, 0>$, $<1,1>$ and $<0, 0>$.[17] The combination $r(H) = <p(H), q(H)>$ of the contrarietal power and the quantity of a Homoeomer H may be called its *contrarietal* character (assuming, of course, that the Homoeomer is suitably individual—otherwise reference to an underlying homoeomer must be made).

A more refined measure of the power of a homoeomerous form may also be given. For with each such form may be associated relative proportions of the elements—so much earth to so much air to so much fire to so much water. The *elemental* power p\*(H) of the Homoeomer H might then be taken to be a four-place vector p = <$p_1$, $p_2$, $p_3$, $p_4$> with $p_1$, $p_2$, $p_3$, $p_4 \geq 0$ and $p_1 + p_2 + p_3 + p_4 = 1$. A homoeomer whose form is of type p will contain the elements earth, air, fire and water in the relative proportions $p_1$, $p_2$, $p_3$ and $p_4$. Thus a 'balanced' mixture, containing elements in equal proportion, will have a form of power <1/4, 1/4, 1/4, 1/4>, while the elemental forms will have as their power the principal vectors <1, 0, 0, 0>, <0, 1, 0, 0>, <0, 0, 1, 0>, and <0, 0, 0, 1>. The combination r\*(H) = <p\*(H), q\*(H)> of the elemental power and the quantity of the Homoeomer H might be called its *elemental* character.

It is important to distinguish between a homoeomerous form and its power or type. It is clear that the form is not *identical* to the vector p = <$p_1$, $p_2$, $p_3$, $p_4$>. For it could with equal legitimacy be taken to be the vector p' = <$p_2$, $p_1$, $p_3$, $p_4$> let us say (with the places for earth and air reversed); and it therefore cannot with any legitimacy be taken to be either.[18] Nor need the power or type be an adequate *representation* of the form; for perhaps each homoeomer has its own form or has a form of a certain intrinsic quantity. In taking the form of each homoeomer to be a ratio, Aristotle is perhaps allowing that distinct homoeomorous forms might correspond to the same mathematical ratio.

Nor should we assume that to each two-place vector <$r_1$, $r_2$>, with $0 \leq r_1, r_2 \leq 1$, or to each four-place vector <$p_1$, $p_2$, $p_3$, $p_4$>, with $0 \leq p_1, p_2, p_3, p_4$ and $p_1 + p_2 + p_3 + p_4 = 1$, there is a Homoeomer whose contrarietal or elemental power is that vector. In our preliminary version of Aristotle's theory, this assumption will indeed be made. But as a result of the discussion of the quantum effect, it will need to be revised. It does seem acceptable, however, to let the variables $r_1$ and $r_2$ or $p_1$, $p_2$, $p_3$ and $p_4$ assume irrational values. For in *De Sens.* 439b29–440a5, 442a15–18, he countenances sensible mixtures with irrational proportions, these being ones that 'jar.'

## 8. THE MATTER OF MIXTURE

A satisfactory account of the nature of mixture rests upon the resolution of two general issues. One concerns the ultimate matter of a mixture and will be raised and, to some extent, resolved within the present section. The other concerns the proximate matter of a mixture and will be raised in the following three sections. It is only, however, in the subsequent part that the issue will be finally resolved and a satisfactory account of mixture thereby obtained.

Any homoeomer will have some ultimate matter, some matter that is not itself a compound of matter and form. I adopt the traditional view and take this matter to be prime, although some of the same considerations will apply when the matter is taken to be elemental. Given that two homoeomers mix, what happens to their prime matter? Suppose that the prime matters of the homoeomers, prior to the mixing, are $m_1$ and $m_2$, and that the prime matter of the mixture, once the two homoeomers have been mixed, is m. Then what is the current relationship between m, on the one hand, and $m_1$ and $m_2$, on the other?

We here face what appears to be the analogue, within the hylomorphic framework, of the problem of mixture as conceived by Sharvy; for the quantities or parcels of prime matter are without form and hence are much the same as Sharvy takes the ordinary ingredients to be. There is an important difference, however. For we are under no obligation to suppose that the prime matters of the ingredients mix even though the ingredients themselves do. Indeed, it is plausible to suppose that what happens, at the level of prime matter, under mixing is essentially the same as what happens under growth or under any process in which two things genuinely become one. Thus there is no reason to suppose that what happens should be geared in the direction of one of these processes as opposed to another.

This point is reinforced when we note that the various processes of two things becoming one all involve the participation of form; mixing involves the accommodation of two forms, growth the domination of one form by another, and creation the replacement of the two forms by a new form. Since the prime matter has no form, it cannot properly be said to engage in any of these processes. Thus what goes on in mixing or growing or any other kind of unification must, at the level of prime matter, be fundamentally different from what goes on at the level of the things themselves.

There are perhaps only three plausible positions on the relationship between the three primal parcels m, $m_1$ and $m_2$. One, which we call *Convergence*, is that m is the (temporarily compresent) sum of $m_1$ and $m_2$. Thus the natural assumption to make, from the present position, is that the prime matter of the two ingredients persists during the process of mixing and forms a compresent sum. Another position, which we call *Emergence*, is that m is distinct and, indeed, disjoint from both $m_1$ and $m_2$. Thus in becoming one the prime matter of the ingredients become something completely new. A third *anti-Haecceitist* position, in a way intermediate between the other two, is that the question of identity over time for prime matter does not properly arise. Parcels of prime matter, such as $m_1$, $m_2$ and $m_3$, are not fully fledged objects that can properly be said to be the same or different from one time to the next.

Of these three positions, the first is most implausible. For it conflicts with what one might take to be a fundamental requirement on static analysis, which is that the kind of material constitution a thing enjoys at a given time should simply be a function of how the thing is at that time.

To see how this is so, suppose that a pint of wine with prime matter $m_1$ mixes with a gallon of water with prime matter $m_0$. Then the prime matter of the resulting mixture, under Convergence, will be the sum $m_0 \cup m_1$. Next suppose that this mixture mixes with another pint of wine, with prime matter $m_2$. Then the prime matter of the second mixture will be the sum $(m_0 \cup m_1 \cup m_2)$ of three compresent parcels of matter. Now suppose that two pints of wine with prime matter $n_1$ mix with a gallon of water with prime matter $n_0$. Then the prime matter of this third mixture is $n_0 \cup n_1$. Thus the prime matter of the second mixture will consist of three compresent parcels of matter, the prime matter of the third of only two. But the two mixtures are currently indistinguishable in kind; for prime matter is a mere substratum or 'filler' and there is no difference that can be marked by its being singly or doubly or multiply present at a given time. So what accounts for the difference in the number of compresent matters depends solely upon what happened in the past, upon how the mixtures were formed. But this is what the requirement rules out (and is, in itself, unacceptable).

A similar line of argument applies to the other cases in which several things become one, and also to the cases in which one thing becomes many. But these cases would appear to be the only ones in which we might be tempted to suppose that two parcels of prime matter could become compresent. So even though prime matter has only a potential existence, these cases provide yet another circumstance in which it would appropriate for Aristotle to exclude the possibility of compresence.

I shall not here attempt to adjudicate between the two other positions since the difference between them will not be important for the purposes of static analysis. What matters for these purposes is the exclusion of the first position. For this implies that the prime matter of the mixture cannot be regarded as a compresent sum. Thus even though we will wish to maintain that the ingredients are currently part of the mixture, they cannot be taken to possess their own original matter. The only plausible view, given the coincidence in location, is that their prime matter is the same and the same as that of the mixture.

## 9. TWO HYLOMORPHIC HYPOTHESES

The second general issue is of the utmost importance and concerns the level of mixtures in the hylomorphic hierarchy. As we have noted, any (enmattered) object can be assigned a level. The level of an object without matter will be 0; the level of something with matter of level 0 (and no matter of higher level) will be 1; and so on. Our question then is whether the level, in this sense, of the elements and the mixtures is the same or different.

For the primalists, the elements are of level 1 and so the question is whether the mixtures are like the elements in having prime matter as their (proximate) matter. For the elementalists, it is the elements that are of level 0 and so the question is whether mixtures and elements are alike in lacking a decomposition into matter and form. Under either interpretation, the only reasonable alternative to the view that the levels are the same is that the mixtures are of a higher level than the elements and have the elements as their proximate (or, at least, as their nonproximate) matter. Thus we may also pose the question in the form: are the elements matter for the mixtures?

But in posing the question this way, it is important to understand the term 'matter' in the appropriately strict sense. It may be granted that there is a sense in which the elements compose mixtures and hence a sense in which they are the matter of mixtures. But our question is whether they are the matter of mixtures in the sense that is complementary to form. For m to be the matter of x in this strict sense it is necessary that x be a compound Fm of m with some form F.

Thus our question concerns the manner in which the elements compose the mixture. Do the elements laterally compose the mixtures, thereby providing the mixtures with the same kind of hylomorphic analysis as the elements themselves? Or do the elements vertically compose the mixtures, thereby providing the mixtures with a hylomorphic analysis in which the elements figure as matter?

Call the view that the mixtures are at the same level as the elements 'Hylomorphic Leveling' and the view that they are at a higher level 'Hylomorphic Ascent.' Under each view, a further question arises as to whether the form of the mixtures should be taken to be monadic or polyadic. Under Leveling, it is hard to see how the form could be polyadic. For what are the parcels of prime matter to which it applies? They cannot sensibly be taken to occupy different locations. For on what conceivable basis could the form induce one spatial division of the total underlying matter as opposed to another? Nor can they be taken to occupy the same location; for this would conflict with the conclusions of the previous section. But even if we were to grant that the prime matter of the mixture could be a sum of two compresent matters $m_1$ and $m_2$, it is still not clear that the form could sensibly be taken to apply to them as two rather than as one. For let us suppose than $m_1$ is the prime matter of some earth, that $m_2$ is the prime matter of some air, and that the form is a ratio of earth to air. Then there is no way to 'read off' from the current state of the mixture that $m_1$ corresponds to the earthy and $m_2$ to the airy component. Thus nothing could properly justify the application of the form to $m_1$ and $m_2$ (in that order) rather than to $m_2$ and $m_1$ or to some other division of the matter in which part of $m_1$ is exchanged with a compresent part of $m_2$.

Under Ascent, however, the form can be, and perhaps is most plausibly taken to be, polyadic. For the form is a ratio of elements and, as such, applies most naturally to the four elements taken separately rather than to their sum. One might think of the form as a scale with four arms, one for each of the elements, which somehow manages to keep them in balance.

Of course, if there is only one undifferentiated mass of prime matter in the mixture, as we have supposed, then all of the elements must share that prime matter, whether or not the form is taken to be polyadic. There is not, however, the same difficulty in supposing the elemental matter to be compresent as there was for the prime matter; for, in contrast to the different portions of prime matter, each element will have its own distinctive characteristics and hence may serve to differentiate the total mass of elemental matter into its elemental components.

## 10. DIFFICULTIES WITH ASCENT

Which of the two hypotheses is to be preferred? After surveying the difficulties with each in this and the following section, we shall amount a defence of Leveling in the next part.

The great advantage of Ascent is that it is able to meet requirements (1)–(6) from sections 1–2. For the ingredients are the constitutive matter of the mixture and hence can be said, in the manner of matter, to have potential existence, to be part of the mixture, and to be recoverable and derivable from the mixture. There are difficulties, however, over *how* some of these requirements are to be met and over whether some of the other requirements can be met at all; and to these difficulties we must now turn.

(1) *Mixing Mixtures.* Ascent is subject to a problem over what might be called higher level mixture. Suppose that some earth and water are mixed in the proportions 1 to 1 to obtain the mixture $m_1$, and that some other earth and water are mixed in the proportions 1 to 2 to obtain a less earthy mixture $m_2$. Suppose now that $m_1$ and $m_2$ are mixed in the proportions 1 to 1 to obtain yet a third mixture m. Then $m_1$ and $m_2$ will be of hylomorphic level 2 (given that the elements are of level 1); and m should be of level 3, for it is formed from the mixtures by a physical processes which is of the same sort as that by which the mixtures were formed from elements, and so it should stand in the same hylomorphic relationship to those mixtures as the mixtures stand to the elements.[19]

The possibility of being able to ascend the hylomorphic hierarchy in this way leads to some troubling questions. For suppose that earth and water are mixed in the proportions 2 to 3 to obtain the mixture n. Then n is a mixture of level 2 with the same proportion of earth to water as m above. But the only difference in the formation of m and n is that m is obtained by adding earth in two stages while n is obtained by adding it in one. But it is a matter of common observation (at least in certain cases) that this should make no difference to the physical characteristics of the resulting mixtures; and given that it makes no difference, it is hard to see how the mixtures could differ in the type of their form or hylomorphic analysis.

The case is troublesome for Aristotle quite apart from the physical facts. For he takes the form of a mixture to be a ratio of elements. But the form of the higher level mixture is not a ratio of elements but more like a ratio of ratios (it might be represented by a vector of vectors rather than by a straight vector). Nor can he sensibly take the higher level form to be identical to the corresponding lower level form. For the higher level form will have the mixtures as its matter, whereas the lower level form will have the elements themselves as its matter.

There is a variant of Aristotle's theory according to which there are two fundamentally different ways in which things can mix: one, typified by chemical reaction, results in ascent; the other, typified by dissolving, keeps the mixture at the same level as the ingredients. A view of this sort was proposed by the Stoics (see Sorabji 1988: 79–80) and, if adopted, would remove the difficulties that arise from supposing that all mixing proceeds by ascent. But plausible as the view might be as a development of Aristotle's thought, it is not his own; for his invariable tendency is to draw no distinction between the two kinds of case.

There is perhaps a somewhat different way in which Aristotle might be prepared to countance two fundamentally different kinds of homoeomer, if not mixture, one of which is subject to Ascent and the other not. For as we have seen, he seems willing to distinguish between functional and nonfunctional forms of flesh and blood and the like. But such a distinction, even if it is one that Aristotle is willing to make, will still leave us with a problem. For it will still be true that many, if not all, of the nonfunctional homoeomers will be capable of being obtained from mixing mixtures and not just from mixing elements.

(2) *Intermediacy.* Aristotle believes that the form of a mixture is somehow intermediate between the forms of its ingredients. Thus at *G&C.* I.10, 328a27–30, he describes mixing with the words: "But when the two are more or less equal in strength, then each changes from its own nature in the direction of the dominating one, though it does not become the other but something in between and common to both."

But suppose that the respective forms of some elemental ingredients $e_1$ and $e_2$ are $E_1$ and $E_2$ and that the form of the mixture m that results from them is F. Then given that the form F is of a higher level than $E_1$ and $E_2$, it is hard to see how it can properly be said to be the result of a movement of each of the elemental forms in the direction of the other. For F is a higher level form that applies to the elements, while $E_1$ and $E_2$ are lower level forms that apply directly to prime matter. But how can a form that has the elements as its matter be the result of a compromise between forms that have prime matter as their matter?

Perhaps the best that can be done to achieve the compromise is to compare the forms $E_1$ and $E_2$, not with the noncomposite form F of the mixture, but with the corresponding composite form $G = F(E_1, E_2)$, the form whose application to two (identical!) parcels of prime matter, $m_1$ and $m_2$, results in the mixture $F(E_1m_1, E_2m_2)$. But the difficulty now is to see how a composite form might result from a compromise between two noncomposite forms.

(3) *The Analogy with Growth.* At *G&C.* I.5, 322a10–11, Aristotle asks how that by which something grows affects the growing thing and answers: "Mixed with it, as if one were to pour water into wine, and it (the latter) were able to make what is mixed with it into wine" (cf. *G&C.* I.10, 328a17–33). Here Aristotle seems to conceive of growth as a special case of mixing, as broadly conceived. If we think of mixing as involving reciprocal accommodation of form, then growth represents the degenerate case in which all of the accommodation is done by one of the forms and none is done by the other.

Now it is clear that growth involves no hylomorphic ascent in the supervening form, for the form of the thing which issues from the growth is the same as the form of the thing which grew (*G&C.* I.5, 321a33–321b7). But then how can growth, which involves no ascent, be a special case of a process which does?

It is also difficult to see, under Ascent, how mixing could *underlie* growth. Suppose one thing grows by means of another. We may then ask: what happens to the (proximate) matters of the two things? It seems reasonable to suppose, especially under the hypothesis of Ascent, that the growth of a higher level homoeomer might in certain cases involve the *mixing* of the matters. But given that the associated mixture ascends the hylomorphic hierarchy in such a case, then so does the thing that grows. Thus we should have the bizarre phenomenon of a homoeomer changing its hylomorphic level as it grows over time.

(4) *Compresence.* It might be thought a virtue of the hypothesis of Ascent that it avoids the stark form of compresence required by Sharvy's account. For although the ingredients of a mixture are compresent, they do not actually exist, they only exist potentially, as matter of the mixture. It therefore seems that Aristotle could tolerate compresence of this kind, given that it does not take place in the 'open' but only under the cover of a form.

Certainly, his arguments against the compresence model of location of growth could be taken to be compatible with the compresence of matter within a substance. But the considerations concerning contraries would seem to dictate against such a form of compresence. For if, as we have argued, the elements in a mixture have the same prime matter, we would still have contraries (or opposed forms) simultaneously attaching to the same subject; and even if the elements retain their own prime matter, we would still have contraries simultaneously attaching to the same place.

But if we are at a loss to understand these possibilities as they occur in the open, then how can we have an intelligible idea of what they would be like under the cover of a form?

This is not an argument against the possibility of contraries somehow attaching to the same location or even to the same subject. For this must be possible if mixing is to be possible. The difficulty with Ascent is that it does not enable us to see how it could be possible.

(5) *Constitution.* At various places, Aristotle claims that the elements are the matter of mixtures. For example, in the previously cited passage at *G.A.* I.1, 715a9–11, he writes: "and the material of animals is their parts— of every whole animal the anhomoeomerous parts, of these again the homoeomerous, and of these last the so-called elements of bodies." The passages strongly suggest that the elements are matter for the homoeomers in the strict sense of the term, i.e. in the sense that is complementary to form. For the relationship between a homoeomer and its elements is meant to be the same as the relationship between an animal and its parts; and this latter is certainly the relationship of a thing to its matter. Again, his view that the form of a homoeomer is a ratio of elements strongly suggests that its matter consists of the elements themselves.

It appears to be a strong point in favor of Hylomorphic Ascent that it squares with these passages. For under this interpretation, the elements are, quite straightforwardly, the underlying matter of homoeomerous bodies and the form is quite straightforwardly a ratio of elements. The interpretation might also be taken to receive confirmation from Aristotle's view that the ingredients of a mixture only exist potentially once the mixture is formed (*G&C.* I.10, 327b25–26); for it is characteristic of matter to exist potentially.

The texts, however, are not altogether clear or consistent on these points. At *P.A.* II.1, 646a12–24, he writes, in words reminiscent of the previously cited passage:

There are three cases of composition; and of these three the first in order, as all will allow, is composition out of what some call the elements, such as earth, air, water and fire. Perhaps, however, it would be more accurate to say composition out of the elementary forces [*dynamesis*]; nor indeed out of all of these, as said elsewhere in previous treatises. For wet and dry, hot and cold, form the material of all composite bodies; and all other differences are secondary to these, such differences, that is, as heaviness or lightness, density or rarity, roughness or smoothness, and any other such properties of bodies there may be. The second case of composition is that by which the homoeomerous parts of animals such as bone, flesh, and the like, are constituted out of the primary substances. The third and last is the composition of the anhomoeomerous parts, such as face, hand, and the rest.

But here composition in the later stages from what is clearly matter is compared to composition from the contraries.[20] So he is prepared to compare like with unlike; and it is especially odd, if he believes that the elements are matter of the homoeomerous bodies, that he is prepare to give up this strictly analogous form of composition (from the elements) for one that is not strictly analogous (from the contraries).

Finally, we should mention that in his attempt to say what mixture is at *G&C.* I.10 and II.7, he does not say that the elements constitute the matter of the mixture. It would have been straightforward, within the general hylomorphic framework that he seems to presuppose, to have made this central point clear had he thought it to be true. The fact that he does not make it clear therefore strongly suggests that he did not take it to be true.

## 11. DIFFICULTIES WITH LEVELING

The alternative hypothesis, Leveling, is able to avoid many of the difficulties of Ascent. The first difficulty does not even arise, since any mixture will be on the same level as the things that are mixed. Thus there will be no need to distinguish between a two-stage mixture and the corresponding one-stage mixture.

The second difficulty of how the form of the mixture could be intermediate between those of the ingredients is also not troublesome. For suppose g is a mixture whose form G is of power $<p_1, p_2, p_3, p_4>$ and h a mixture whose form H is of power $<q_1, q_2, q_3, q_4>$. Then, under Leveling, the mixture of g and h will be a mixture whose form is of the mean power $<r_1, r_2, r_3, r_4>$, where $r_i = (p_i + q_i)/2$ for i = 1, 2, 3, 4; and there would appear to be no difficulty in supposing that there was a form G + H, of the same type as G and H, whose power was of this intermediate type.

Nor is there the same trouble in solving the third difficulty, of seeing growth as a degenerate case of mixing broadly conceived; for the mixture and the ingredients are at the same hylomorphic level. But there is another difficulty. For the compromise form G + H, as described above, can only be of the same power as one of the component forms when it is of the same power as them both. This suggests that growth is only possible when the thing which grows and the thing by which it grows are alike in form. But, for Aristotle, this is one of the cases in which growth is considered to be impossible (*G&C.* I.5, 321b35–36); it is only if the two forms are dissimilar that the one can affect the other in the way required by growth. This difficulty, however, is quite general and not at all peculiar to Leveling; and we shall see in our discussion of the quantum effect how it might be resolved.

The fourth difficulty, concerning compresence, does not seem to arise. For under Leveling, a mixture is simply taken to be the "application" of a rational form to some prime matter; and in the mixture, as so conceived, no two things are competing for the same subject or for the same space.

However, Leveling completely flounders over the last difficulty of accounting for the fact that mixtures are composed of the elements. For how can a mixture, with one form, be composed of an element, with a different form? It is not as if the one form occurs "beneath" the other, as with Ascent. The two are on the same level; and given that this is so, the presence of the one form would appear to exclude the presence of the other. The powers of the elemental forms (viz. $<1, 0, 0, 0>$, $<0, 1, 0, 0>$, $<0, 0, 1, 0>$, $<0, 0, 0, 1>$) do indeed provide a basis for the powers of the homoeomerous forms; their powers are all "means" of the elemental powers. But this purely mathematically point goes no way towards explaining how the elements themselves might be parts of the homoeomers.

A related difficulty concerns Aristotle's treatment of the form of a mixture as a ratio of elements. For how can it be a ratio of elements when the matter to which it applies is not elemental? Surely it would be more appropriate to treat it as a ratio of contraries rather than of elements, since it could then be taken to apply to the same kind of matter as the contraries themselves apply to.

We have reached an impasse. Only two hylomorphic hypotheses suggest themselves; and each suffers from enormous difficulties. Ascent results in an unworkable account of mixture for the reasons already given; and Leveling completely flounders over the question of containment. If a satisfactory account of mixture is to be given, then some other angle on the problem must be found.

## IV. In Defence of Leveling

In the next three Sections I shall attempt to provide a near to complete vindication of leveling. In the first, we shall show how a variant of Leveling is able to resolve the difficulties over containment; in the next, we shall show how the peripheral problems concerning mixture might also be solved; and in the final part, we shall deal with the dynamical issues. No other account comes close, as far as I can see, in providing such a satisfactory or comprehensive resolution of the various difficulties.

The problem over the constitution of mixture will be resolved by appeal to two rather different, but related, doctrines. The first is the doctrine of intermediates. It is stated in the next subsection; its consequences for the theory of mixture are then developed; and an attempt is made to guard it against certain metaphysical and epistemological doubts. The second, the doctrine of derived part, is stated and defended in the next to last subsection. It is hoped that the discussion of some of the issues in this part may have a general interest quite apart from their relevance to understanding Aristotle.

### 12. THE DOCTRINE OF INTERMEDIATES

Let us, for simplicity, suppose that there are only two primary contraries, hot and cold. There will therefore be only two elements: the hot (whose form is Hot); and the cold (whose form is Cold). We shall later consider the complications that arise from admitting the other primary contraries, dry and wet.

Suppose some hot is mixed with some cold. We then obtain a mixture, some warm. Its form, Warm, is somehow intermediate between the forms Hot and Cold. But what exactly is the relationship between the three?

One natural view, which seems to be implicit in Bogen's approach, is that there is a sliding scale of different degrees of hot and cold, with no one degree being more basic than the others. There will certainly be qualitative relationships among the different degrees: Warm will be colder than Hot and warmer than Cold. But Warm will not be constituted out of Hold and Cold or, in some other way, reducible to Hot and Cold.

This, however, is not Aristotle's view. His general doctrine on intermediates is announced in the opening lines of *Met.* X.7, 1057a18: "Since contraries admit of an intermediate and in some cases have it, intermediates must be composed out of the contraries."[21] The rest of the chapter is then devoted to an elaborate argument in support of the view.

It is not my intention to discuss this argument in any detail. But we may note that its nub occurs at 1057b22–29. He is there considering a primary pair of contraries, ones not analyzable in terms of others, and raising the question of why the transition from one contrary to the other always take place in the orderly manner that it does through the various intermediates or why, as he puts it, there is a 'change from the contrary to it [the intermediate] sooner than to the other contrary' (1057b23–5). His answer is that it is because the intermediates are 'compounded out of the contraries' (1057b23). Thus the gradual change in quality is explained as a gradual change in quantity—the increase in Warmth, for example, being either an increase in the amount of Hot or a decrease in the amount of Cold.

The reader might be forgiven for thinking that Aristotle's talk of composition was merely a fanciful way of talking of qualitative difference. We mark the qualitative distance of an intermediate from its contraries by saying that it has so much of either contrary. But his subsequent argumentation and language make it quite clear that he is to be taken at his word. The contraries are basic; the intermediates are literally composed of them; and the qualitative difference among the intermediates will simply consist in a quantitative difference in the contraries from which they composed (1057b27–29).

That this is his general view is confirmed by his discussion of particular cases elsewhere. For example, in his discussion of colors at *De Sens.* 3, 439b18–440b25, he takes it for granted that the different colors are combinations[22] of white and black; his only real concern it to determine the nature of the combination (which he takes to be identical, or at least analogous, to mixing). This account is extended to savors: "As the intermediate colours arise from the mixture of white and black, so the intermediate savours arise from the sweet and bitter" (442a13–14). And he seems to hold a similar view of the other sensory qualities: "Our conception of the nature of the odours must be analogous to that of the savours" (442b26).

He also holds an analogous view of motion. Thus at *Phys.* VIII.9, 265a14–16, he writes "every locomotion … is either in a circle or in a line or mixed [*mikte*]; and the two former must be prior to the latter, since they are the elements of which the latter consists" (cf. *De Cae.* I.2, 268b17–20). Indeed, at *De Cae.* I.2, 269a13, he explicitly remarks that 'upward and downward motions are the contraries of one another'; and so motions that are the 'mixtures' of these will exactly conform to the general doctrine of the *Metaphysics*.

The formulations in GC strongly suggest the view that the warm is a combination of the hot and cold. Thus at II.7, 334b9–16, Aristotle writes:

When one [of hot and cold] exists *simpliciter* in actuality, the other exists in potentiality; when, however, it is not completely so, but hot–cold or cold–hot,[23] because in being mixed things destroy each other's excesses, then what will exist is neither their matter nor either of the contraries existing *simpliciter* in actuality, but something intermediate, which, in so far as it is in potentiality more hot than cold or vice versa, is proportionately twice as hot in potentiality as cold, or three times, or in some other similar way.

Here the intermediate is described as hot–cold or cold–hot, thereby suggesting that it is some sort of combination of hot and cold. The Hot and Cold only have a potential existence in the mixture; and when he says that the hot–cold is 'proportionately twice as hot in potentiality as cold,' we may take him to mean that there is twice as great a quantity of the (potentially existing) Hot in the combination as there is of the (potentially existing) Cold, it being these different proportions of Hot to Cold that correspond to the different degrees of warmth.

There are two other pieces of textual evidence from the context that confirm the present interpretation. The first occurs at 334b8, "When one exists simpliciter in actuality, the other exists in potentiality," and is echoed at 334b22, "for the actually hot is cold in potentiality and the actually cold hot in potentiality." This point is meant to explain how something can be of an intermediate degree of warmth. But how can the potential of something that is absolutely hot to be absolutely cold explain its potential to be warm? The difficulty can be resolved if we take the potential in question to be the potential to be cold as well as hot. The other piece of confirmatory evidence occurs at 334b16–17, "It is as result of the contraries, or the elements, having being mixed that the other things will exist." For this suggests that there is a sense in which the contraries might themselves be mixed and hence makes it all the more reasonable to suppose that what he previously had in mind was some sort of combination of the two contraries.

It must be conceded, however, that the statement of the view in *Generation and Corruption* is not as clear or explicit or forthright as the corresponding formulations in the *Metaphysics* and *De Sensu*. The earlier discussion of the accommodation of form at I.10 is certainly compatible with the view that the intermediates are combinations of forms or contraries but does not commit him to such a view; and it is significant in this regard that he feels obliged to return to the topic at II.7 and to explain afresh how mixture is possible. The discussion there is much more detailed than before, and more suggestive of the present interpretation, but still not as definite as the discussion in the other works.[24]

This is odd; and I can only speculate on why it should be so. But given the general uncertainty surrounding the chronology and integrity of Aristotle;s works, the difference is not enough in itself to cast serious doubts on the present interpretation. I suspect that a large part of what may have stood in the way of accepting the present interpretation of Aristotle is not so much the absence of textual corroboration as the difficulty in seeing the position itself as reasonable or even intelligible. It will therefore be worth attempting to show how a view of the sort might reasonably be held.

One major difficulty in the view concerns the possibility of conflict. If Warm is a combination of Hot and Cold, it follows that Hot and Cold, which are parts of Warm, will both attach to a warm body. But how can this be? How can something be both hot and cold? It is presumably a difficulty of this sort that leads Aristotle to say that two contraries cannot both be present in the same subject.

The difficulty is very understandable if we think of hot and cold as occurrent features. How can a sensation of warmth, for example, be simultaneously (and uniformly) both hot and cold? The presence of the one feature seems to be in direct conflict with the presence of the other.

However, it is more faithful to Aristotle's way of thinking to treat the various degrees of hot and cold as (or in terms of) potentialities or powers. The word used for them at *P.A.* II.1, 646a16, is *dynameis*; and this conception is spelt out at *G&C.* II.2, 329b26–33, where he writes: "heat is that which aggregates things that are of the same kind," "cold is that which gathers and aggregates indiscriminately things that are related and things that are not of the same type," "wet is that which is not bounded by any boundary of its own but is easily bounded," and "dry is that which is easily bounded by a boundary of its own, but is hard to bound."

On this view, no *direct* conflict is involved in the presence of opposed contraries. But there may still be an indirect conflict. Suppose, for simplicity, that the potentiality (of) heat is the potentiality to warm a non-hot body that is placed next to it and that the potentiality (of) cold is the potentiality to cool a non-cold body that is placed next to it. Take now a warm body. By supposition, it possesses both the potentiality of heat and of cold. But when another warm body is placed next to it, that body should be both warmed and cooled, it should become *occurrently* warmer and cooler; and this is impossible.

To overcome this difficulty, we should distinguish between the qualified and unqualified presence of a potentiality. A potentiality is said to be *latent* and to have a *qualified* presence in an object if its normal operation is modified by the presence of another potentiality in the object; and otherwise it is said to be *patent* and to have an *unqualified* presence. A potentiality may exist in the presence of other potentialities and yet still be patent as long as its operation is not *modified* by the presence of the other potentialities. The standard way in which the operation of a potentiality is modified is through being constrained; but it may also be enhanced or modified in some way that is not readily classifiable either as a constraint or as an enhancement. Whether a potentiality is patent is, of course, independent of whether the normal conditions for its realization obtain; a body may be patently hot even when it is not warming another body.

The resolution of the indirect conflict between opposed contraries is now at hand. For it is only when heat has an unqualified presence in a body that we can be assured that it will warm a non-hot body that is placed next to it; and it is only when cold has an unqualified presence that we can be assured that an adjacent non-cold body will be cooled. Thus there is no contradiction in supposing that heat and cold are simultaneously present in a body given that their presence is of a qualified sort.

It is in just such a way that Aristotle attempts to soften the conflict between opposed contraries in the previously cited passage at 334b9–16. For hot and cold existing '*simpliciter* in actuality' corresponds to their unqualified presence and their not being completely actual corresponds to their qualified presence. It is also presumably in such a way that he will avoid conflict with his doctrine that contraries cannot simultaneously belong to the same subject. For the doctrine should only be taken to apply to contraries whose presence in the subject is unqualified.

But although the distinction may serve to resolve the logical worries, metaphysical misgivings may remain. For in what can the potentiality of an object consist except in its disposition to behave in a certain way—to cool under certain conditions, to be cooled under certain conditions, and so on. But in that case, what sense can be given to the idea of a *latent* potentiality?

The picture we have of latent potentialities may be illustrated by the case of two people pulling on opposite ends of a rope. On one view, there is only one force acting on the rope; for the two opposed forces cancel one another out, so to speak, and all that remains is the resultant force. But on the view we are considering, the two opposed forces are still acting on the rope, although their combined effect is no different from that of the single resultant force. We might imagine that the two people increase how much they pull by equal amounts. Under the first view, there will be no difference in the forces acting on the rope. But under the second view, there will be a difference, for each of the opposed forces will increase by the same amount, though without any difference in their combined effect.

But how can we make sense of the idea of there being different latent potentialities within an object when there is no difference in behavior to which they correspond? How we answer this question will depend upon whether we construe potentiality claims in an existential or neutral manner. In claiming that an object has the potentiality to warm, we may be committing ourselves to the existence of a *capacity* possessed by the object (the existential construal) or we may merely be saying that the object is *capable* of warming without any commitment as to the existence of a capacity (the neutral construal). The first construal involves reference to an item, the capacity, which serves as a link between the object and its disposition to behave in a certain way. The second involves no such reference; it merely ascribes to the object a certain disposition to behave, without appeal to any intermediary.

Of course, even under the neutral construal, there will be a relatively innocuous sense in which the object may be said to possess a capacity; for it will possess the *property* of being capable of warming; and this property might be identified with the capacity in question. However, under the existential construal, as we intend it here, the capacity is meant to account for the behavior of the object; it is a *source* of change (the "*arche metaboles*" of *Met.* IX.1, 1046a10).

One might be tempted to identify the capacity, as so understood, with those 'categorical' features of the object in virtue of which it behaves in the way that it does. This is a view of the sort advocated by Armstrong (1969). But in the most basic cases of capacity, of which the primary contraries are examples, there are no such categorical features; there is no inner structure of a hot body, for example, in virtue of which it heats. The capacity must therefore be taken to be an entity in its own right—a primitive force or power which is not reducible to a categorical feature of the object possessing the power.

From henceforth, let us use the terms 'behavior,' 'disposition,' and 'capability' in connection with the neutral construal, and the terms 'capacity,' 'power,' and 'force' in connection with the existential construal. We continue to use 'potentiality' (which is meant to correspond to Aristotle's term *dynamis*) ambiguously; and we use the term 'tendency' for a capability or capacity that is readily realized.

The metaphysical misgivings have real point when potentiality claims are understood in a neutral manner. For all that need exist, on such an understanding, is a disposition to behave in a certain way. But then the idea of a latent potentiality, one that need not be manifest in behavior, can get no hold. It is not, after all, as if the object were subject to some kind of shadow behavior.

Perhaps the best that can be done on this approach is to suppose that a warm body possesses the very same disposition as is possessed by a hot body but that it is differently circumstanced. For it will also possess the very same disposition as is possessed by a cold body; and because of this difference in circumstance, it will behave differently from the hot body even though the remaining circumstances are the same. But on such an account, we must understand the common possession of the one disposition in terms of the common possession of the other. There is no independently grounded account of what that common possession might consist in.

Such an account can be given, however, once capacities are recognized. For these can be taken to have an existence that is independent of the dispositions to which they give rise. There is, so to speak, an ontological underpinning for the common possession of a potentiality. Thus the capacities of Hot and Cold will give rise to certain characteristic behavior when they exist on their own, in a patent state, and to certain characteristic behavior when they exist together, in a latent state. But no attempt is made to understand the possession of a capacity as itself a form of disposition.

An analogy with desire may help to make the present conception more vivid. Imagine someone with conflicting desires; she wishes to move to the left and also to the right. We may suppose that these desires leave her 'paralyzed' and hence result in the same behaviour as would obtain had she no desires at all. (For the purposes of illustration, we adopt a simplified view of human psychology.) But still, we recognize a distinction between the cases of conflicting desires and of absent desire. For in the former case, there exist in the agent certain states that would, on their own, lead to certain characteristic behavior; while in the latter case, no such states exist. Indeed, if we identify a desire with a potentiality to act, then we have more than an analogy; for the case of conflicting desires will simply be a special case of conflicting potentialities.

There is no real difficulty, it seems to me, in supposing that Aristotle would endorse the existential conception of potentialities, at least in so far as it is relevant to the case at hand. If warmth genuinely is a combination of hot and cold, then hot and cold must *be* something. We cannot simply adopt a predicative view and take the presence of hot or cold in an object to consist in its being hot or cold. Perhaps a contrary or an intermediate or an homoeomerous form is more than just a 'carrier' of a disposition. But these items will at least be capable of performing the role required of capacities, as it has here been described. (And, as Eric Lewis has pointed doubt to me, the detailed chemical descriptions of *Meteor.* IV seem to presuppose an existential conception of the relevant potentialities.)

Even if the metaphysical misgivings can be laid to rest in some such way, epistemological doubts may still remain. For there is a relatively straightforward test for determining the unqualified presence of a capacity: one may simply observe how the capacity manifests itself in the behavior of the object under a variety of different circumstances. But given that the general link between the presence of a capacity and its manifestations has been severed, no such simple test will work when its presence is qualified. What then can be used in its place?

There are two forms of support that are necessary for a belief in latent capacities to be reasonable and that might even be sufficient in the absence of countervailing considerations. The first is that it be possible to determine the behavior of the object on the basis of the latent capacities that it is taken to possess. There must be a rule for the 'composition' of the capacities, one that will determine the patent capacity (or capability) of the object on the basis of its latent capacities. It is perhaps conceivable that latent capacities might exist and yet have no systematic influence on the behavior of the objects in which they reside. But it is hard to see how we could have good reason to *believe* in such capacities and yet lack any account of their influence.

A rule of composition, if effective, will show how the behavior *might* be explained in terms of latent capacities. But in general there will be many such explanations, many different ways of resolving a given capacity (or capability) into component capacities. If we are to believe in latent capacities, then we must also have some ground for supposing that one of these resolutions is privileged in the sense of corresponding to the latent capacities that are actually present in the object itself. In the absence of such a ground, it would be more reasonable to treat the difference resolutions as different ways of viewing the given capacity, the choice of one over another perhaps being of great mathematical significance in the context of a particular problem but of no special ontological significance.

Now I believe that both of these epistemological challenges to Aristotle's postulation of latent capacities can be met; and in the next three subsections I shall show how this is to be done. Of course, this is not essential for the purposes of defending my interpretation of Aristotle. But it adds considerably to its interest; for it shows that he had an empirically viable theory of mixture, one that would have been defensible had the facts been in its favor.

## 13. RULES OF ADDITION

I state Aristotle's rules for the determination of contrarietal and elemental character. In the interests of neutrality, I have stated the rules without making any commitment to the existence of underlying capacities. It is only later that I show how the rules might also be interpreted as rules for the calculation of the patent capacities of an object on the basis of its latent capacities. I have also not considered the complications that arise from taking into account the 'quantum effect.'

Any homoeomerous body b, for Aristotle, will contain a certain quantity $q_h$ (b) of hotness. When b is completely cold, the quantity will be zero; and when b is completely hot, the quantity will be proportionate to the volume of b and the density of the hotness within that volume. But even when b is of an intermediate temperature, it will still be taken to contain a certain quantity of hotness, though in latent form.

In the same way, b will contain a certain quantity $q_c$ (b) of coldness. And again, when b is completely hot, the quantity will be zero; when b is completely cold, the quantity will be proportionate to the volume of b and the density of the cold; and when b is of an intermediate temperature, it will contain some latent cold (and also some latent heat).

Our preferred interpretation of the equations $q_h$(b) = r and $q_c$(b) = s is by reference to the capacities of being hot and cold. The equations then say that there is so much of the respective capacity in the given body. However, the equations as they stand are compatible with the repudiation of capacities and can simply be given an operational definition in terms of whatever measurements are used to determine their truth.

The basic idea behind Aristotle's theory of temperature is that the temperature, or thermal power, $p_t$(b) of a body should be taken to be the proportion of hot to cold. It is this idea that is expressed in his remark that a mixture "in so far as it is in potentiality more hot than cold or vice versa, is proportionately twice as hot in potentiality as cold, or three times, or in some other similar way" (*G&C.* II.7, 334b15–16). It is, of course, the theory of intermediates as combinations of contraries that enables Aristotle to conceive of temperature in this way.

Let us use $q_t$(b) for the *distributed* thermal quantity of the body b, i.e., for the respective quantities of hot and cold in b:

(1) $q_t$(b) = $<q_h$(b), $q_c$(b)$>$.

And let us use $Q_t$(b) for the corresponding *undistributed* quantity, i.e. the total quantity of hot and cold in b:

(2) $Q_t$(b) = $q_h$(b) + $q_c$(b).

(The first is a vector quantity, the second a scalar quantity.) The temperature of b is then given by:[25]

(3) $p_t$(b) = $q_t$(b)/$Q_t$(b).

Or, to express the equation directly:

(3)′ $p_t$(b) = $<q_h$(b)/q, $q_c$(b)/q$>$, where q = $q_h$(b) + $q_c$(b).

Of course, $p_t$(b) may be represented more simply by the single number $q_h$(b)/($q_h$(b) + $q_c$(b)), since the second component $q_c$(b)/($q_h$(b) + $q_c$(b)) = 1 − $q_h$(b)/($q_h$(b) + $q_c$(b)). This number will lie between 0 and 1 and will be 0 when the body is completely cold, 1 when the body is completely hot, and between 0 and 1 when the body is of an intermediate temperature. If, for example, there are two units of hot in b and one of cold, then its temperature will be 2/3 (or <2/3, 1/3>).

Equation (3) is remarkable in that it defines an intensive magnitude, temperature, in terms of extensive magnitudes, quantities of heat and cold. It is this reduction of the qualitative to the quantitative that I take to be the hallmark of Aristotle's approach. The interesting applications of (3) are, of course, to the cases in which b is of an intermediate temperature. In this case, hot and cold will correspond, for Aristotle, to latent capacities within the body. Thus (3) will provide a method for determining the manifest temperature of the body on the basis of its latent capacities towards hot and cold.

It should be noted that equation (3) will also have application to *aggregates* of bodies. But in that case it will yield a *mean* temperature, since there is no reason to suppose that the temperature of the aggregate will be uniform throughout its parts. The equation will also have application to objects that are not bodies at all (in the sense of subsection 6). Indeed, underlying any non-bodily object will be a body; and the temperature of the non-bodily object will be the same as that of its underlying body.

Given the thermal power and quantity of a body, we may define the resultant thermal character $r_t(b)$ as the vector:

(4) $r_t(b) = <p_t(b), Q_t(b)>$.

But, of course, $r_t(b)$ may be directly determined on the basis of the quantities $q_h(b)$ and $q_c(b)$; and, conversely, $q_h(b)$ and $q_c(b)$ can be determined on the basis of $r_t(b)$, since $q_h(b) = p_h(b).Q_t(b)$ and $q_c(b) = p_c(b).Q_t(b)$.

The rules governing dessication are exactly analogous. Let $q_d(b)$ be the quantity of dryness in b, $q_w(b)$ the quantity of wetness, and $p_s(b)$ its degree of dessication. Then, as counterparts to (1), (2) and (3), we have:

(5) $q_s(b) = <q_d(b), q_w(b)>$;

(6) $Q_s(b) = q_d(b) + q_w(b)$; and

(7) $p_s(b) = q_s(b)/Q_s(b)$.

Thus, in the characteristic application of (7) for Aristotle, the manifest degree of dessication of a body will be determined on the basis of its latent capacities towards dryness and wetness.

In the statement of the above rules, the body b has not been credited with any internal complexity. But it is possible to extend the rules in a natural way to bodies that are explicitly taken to be mixtures. To this end, we shall need a notation for the mixture of two or more bodies. Let us use "$b_1 + b_2 + ... + b_n$" for the mixture of n disjoint bodies $b_1$, $b_2$, ...

$b_n$ so that 'a + b', in particular, will represent the mixture of the two bodies a and b.

This operation of mixture is implicitly taken to be relative to a given time. Thus the bodies $b_1$, $b_2$, ..., $b_n$ are taken to exist at that time (if only potentially) and $b_1 + b_2 + ... b_n$' is taken to represent the mixture of those bodies $b_1$, $b_2$, ..., $b_n$ at that time. Aristotle may plausibly be taken to hold the view that if two (or more) bodies form a mixture at different times, then the mixtures that they form are one and the same. In this case, we can give an absolute meaning to the notation '$b_1 + b_2 + ... + b_n$'.

Under either the relative or absolute interpretation of '+' the mixture of the given bodies may not exist and hence the notation '$b_1 + b_2 + ...$ $b_n$' may not be defined; for the bodies may be incapable of being mixed, and, even if they are capable of being mixed, they may not have been mixed at the given time or ever mixed at all. Because of this possibility, the present interpretations lead to certain inelegances of formulation. We cannot, for example, assume that (a + b) + c = a + (b + c) even if the left hand side is defined, for c may be the same kind of homoeomer as b and hence be incapable of being mixed with c; and this means that many of the usual rules of calculation must be abandoned.

In order to avoid these inelegances, we may take a + b to be the aggregate of a and b if the mixture does not exist. Or, to be more accurate, we should take a + b to result from mixing in so far as this is possible and otherwise to result from aggregation.[26] Suppose, for example, that a is of the form $a_1 + a_2$ and b is of the form $b_1 + b_2$, and that $a_1$ mixes with $b_1$ but that no part of $a_2$ mixes with any part of $b_2$. Then 'a + b' may be used to represent the result of aggregating the mixture of $a_1$ and $b_1$ with $a_2$ and $b_2$; and similarly for the more general notation '$b_1 + b_2 + ... + b_n$'. The result in such cases may be called a *pseudo*-mixture. This interpretation requires, of course, that '+' be taken relative to a time; for even if the mixture of given bodies does not vary over time, their pseudo-mixture will.

It will turn out to be more convenient to state the rules for mixture using the broader interpretation of '+'. Associatively of binary '+' will then hold and '$b_1 + b_2 + ... + b_n$' can be defined in the obvious way as '$((...b_1 + b_2) + ...) + b_n)$.' The various notions of magnitude can be taken to determine a mean in application to the resulting pseudo-mixtures. Many of the equations that would only hold with qualification under the narrower interpretation will then hold without qualification under the broader interpretation. Thus despite the huge metaphysical gulf between mixtures and aggregates, they are subject to analogous principles and are best treated together for the purposes of systematic exposition.

The basic principle governing the quantity of a mixture (or pseudo-mixture) is additivity. Thus in the case of thermal quantity, the principle takes the form:

(8) $q_h(a + b) = q_h(a) + q_h(b)$;

(8)' $q_c(a + b) = q_c(a) + q_c(b)$.

The quantity of hot (or of cold) in a mixture of two disjoint ingredients is equal to the sum of the quantities of hot (or of cold) in those ingredients. More general principles, such as:

(8)'' $q_h(b_1 + b_2 + \ldots + b_n) = q_h(b_1) + q_h(b_2) + \ldots + q_h(b_n)$,

can then be derived in the obvious way using the fact that $b_1 + b_2 + \ldots + b_n = ((\ldots(b_1 + b_2) + \ldots) + b_n)$.

In these equations, a and b represent the *concurrent* ingredients (or components) of the mixture a + b. It is natural to assume that the antecedent and succeedent ingredients are the same as the concurrent ingredients and also that the quantities of (internal) hot or cold in them remain the same over time. In that case, the equations can be used to determine the quantity of hot or cold in a mixture on the basis of the quantity of hot or cold in the ingredients at any preceding or succeeding time. But even if the quantities of hot or cold in the ingredients change under mixing or separation, or even if the ingredients themselves change, it will still presumably be true that the quantity of hot or cold in the concurrent ingredients will sum to the quantity of hot or cold in the mixture itself.

In the special case in which '+' represents aggregation, the equations may be used to determine the quantity of hot (or cold) in a body b on the basis of the hot (or cold) in its component homoeomers. We must assume that any body b is an aggregate $b_1 + b_2 + \ldots + b_n$ of finitely many disjoint homoeomers $b_1 + b_2 + \ldots + b_n$ and then apply an equation such as (8)'' above. Similar reductions can also be carried out (under the same assumption) for the other notions of magnitude.

From (3), (8) and (8)' can be derived the rule for the determination of the temperature of a mixture on the basis of the temperature of its ingredients:

(9) $p_t (a + b) = [p_t(a) . Q_t(a) + p_t(b) . Q_t(b)]/(Q_t(a) + Q_t(b))$.

A mixture's temperature is the sum of the temperatures of its ingredients as weighted by their relative quantity. So if, for example, a is hot and of one unit while b is quarter warm and of two units, a + b will be of temperature $(1.1 + (1/4) . 2)/3 = 1/2$.

In analogy to (8), we may assume the additivity of dessicative quantity with respect to mixture:

(10) $q_d(a + b) = q_d(a) + q_d(b)$;

(10)' $q_w(a + b) = q_w(a) + q_w(b)$.

In analogy to (9), we may then obtain:

(11) $p_s(a + b) = [p_s(a) \cdot Q_s(a) + p_s(b) \cdot Q_s(b)]/(Q_s(a) + Q_s(b))$.

The dessicative and thermal powers of a body may be combined into a single contrarietal power $p_{s,t}(b)$:

(12) $p_{s,t}(b) = <p_s(b), p_t(b)>$.

Given the complementary status of the contrarieties hot/cold and dry/wet, it is natural to assume that the quantity of intrinsic hot and cold in a body is equal to the quantity of intrinsic dry and wet (an assumption that will later be justified on the basis of more fundamental principles):

(13) $Q_s(b) = Q_t(b)$.

Let us use $Q(b)$ for this single quantity. Then we may derive a principle for the combined contrarietal power, analogous to principles (9) and (11) for the two component powers:

(14) $p_{s,t}(a + b) = [p_{s,t}(a) \cdot Q(a) + p_{s,t}(b) \cdot Q(b)]/(Q(a) + Q(b))$.

The principles for the determination of elemental character may be developed and derived in the same way as the principles for contrarietal character. For just as a body may contain certain (possibly latent) quantities of hot and cold or of dry and wet, so it may contain certain (possibly latent) quantities of the elements, earth, air, fire and water; and just as a thermal or dessicative quality may be regarded as a proportion of contraries, a homoeomerous form may be regarded as a proportion of elements. The homoeomerous forms are, if I may put it this way, the intermediates between the elemental forms.

Let us use $q_1(b)$, $q_2(b)$, $q_3(b)$ and $q_4(b)$, respectively, for the quantity of earth, air, fire or water in the body b; and let us use $p_e(b)$ for the elemental power or 'form' of b. The distributed and undistributed elemental quantities $q_e(b)$ and $Q_e(b)$ may be defined by:

(15) $q_e(b) = <q_1(b), q_2(b), q_3(b), q_4(b)>$; and

(16) $Q_e(b) = q_1(b) + q_2(b) + q_3(b) + q_4(b)$.

The elemental power is then given by:

(17) $p_e(b) = q_e(b)/Q_e(b)$.

Or, to express the equation directly:

(17)' $p_e(b) = <q_1(b)/q, q_2(b)/q, q_3(b)/q, q_4(b)/q>$,
where $q = q_1(b) + q_2(b) + q_3(b) + q_4(b)$.

Thus just as thermal quality is given by the relative proportion of the primary contraries hot and cold, elemental quality is given by the relative proportion of the elements. (And, as before, the last component $q_4(b)/q$ of the vector may be dropped since it is identical to $1 - (q_1(b)/q + q_2(b)/q + q_3(b)/q)$.)

It is again natural to assume that the measures $q_i(x)$ of elemental quantities are additive:

(18) $q_i(a + b) = q_i(a) + q_i(b)$ for $i = 1, 2, 3$, and 4.

We may then derive the fundamental rule for determining the elemental quality of a mixture, in analogy to (9), (11) and (14):

(19) $p_e(a + b) = [p_e(a) . Q_e(a) + p_e(b). Q_e(b)]/(Q_e(a) + Q_e(b))$.

It is clear that the quantities of the elements and of the contraries should be connected. Since air and fire are the elements that are hot, we should have:

(20) $q_h(b) = q_2(b) + q_3(b)$;

and since earth and water are the cold elements, we should have:

(20)' $q_c(b) = q_1(b) + q_4(b)$.

Similarly, since earth and fire are the dry elements, we should have:

(21) $q_d(b) = q_1(b) + q_3(b)$;

and, since air and water are the wet elements, we should have:

(21)' $q_w(b) = q_2(b) + q_4(b)$.

From these equations, we can derive the identity of the thermal, dessicative and elemental quantities:

(22) $Q_t(b) = Q_s(b) = Q_e(b)$.

We can also straightforwardly determine the contrarietal power $p_c(b) =$

<$p_t$, $p_s$> of a body in terms of its elemental power $p_e(b) = <p_1, p_2, p_3, p_4>$. For:

(23) $p_t = p_2 + p_3$; and

(23)′ $p_s = p_1 + p_3$.

It should be noted that if b is an elemental body $e_i$ of type i, for i = 1, 2, 3, 4, then $q_j(e_i) = 0$ for $j \neq 1$; and so from (2), (20)′, (21), and (21)′ follows:

(24) $q_c(e_1) = q_d(e_1) = q_e(e_1)$,

$q_h(e_2) = q_w(e_2) = q_e(e_2)$,

$q_h(e_3) = q_d(e_3) = q_e(e_3)$,

$q_c(e_4) = q_w(e_4) = q_e(e_4)$.

The quantity of the element will be identical to the quantity of each of the two component contraries.

The above theory leaves open the question of how the various magnitudes are to be defined and measured. This is a problem of which Aristotle is to some extent aware but to which he provides no systematic answer. It will therefore be worth considering, if only to show that an systematic answer is indeed available to him.

Equation (3) shows that thermal power can be defined in terms of thermal quantity, i.e. of hot and cold; and, similarly, equation (7) shows that dessicative power can be defined in terms of dessicative quantity, i.e. of dry and cold. Equations (20), (20)′, (21) and (21)′ show that thermal and dessicative quantity can be defined in terms of elemental quantity, i.e. of earth, air, fire and water. It therefore suffices, in order to define all of the other magnitudes, to define the elemental quantities of homoeomerous body.

Now Aristotle seems to believe that any homoeomerous body can be separated out into its elemental ingredients (*G&C.* I.10, 327b26–7). Given that the succedent elemental ingredients are of the same quantity of the concurrent elemental ingredients, we can measure the quantity of an element in a body by measuring the quantity of the element that can be extracted from it.[27] It therefore suffices to determine the quantities of the elemental bodies, i.e., to determine $q(e) = q_i(e)$ when e itself is the i-th element.

Now Aristotle also believes in elemental transformation; any one element can be transformed through one or more steps into any other (*G&C.* II.4). It is natural to assume that quantity is preserved under the most basic forms of elemental transformation. For one contrary will remain the same; and as long as the quantity of that contrary also remains the same, then so will the quantity of the element. Thus when an elemental body e is transformed into another elemental body e' by a series of transformations, we will have q(e) = q(e'). And given that this is so, it will suffice to determine a quantitative measure for just one of the elements.

Perhaps water is the most suitable for this purpose, on account of its combination of malleability and stability. What we essentially need to do is to say when one body of water is of the same quantity as another body of water. A natural test of equiquantity is in terms of volume: the quantities are the same when the volumes are the same. But in applying this test we need to be sensitive to the conditions under which the volume is measured; for the volume may vary even though the quantity remains the same (*Phys.* IV.9, 217a26–217b15). The conditions of measurement must be such as to guarantee that a given quantity of water will be incapable of changing its volume as long as those conditions remain the same. But what they might reasonably be taken to be can only be determined on the basis of the physical theory itself.

There may be other, more direct, ways within the context of Aristotelian science by which the various magnitudes might be measured. For example, following the lead of Aristotle (*G&C.* II.6, 333a24–25), we might measure the quantity of cold in a body by means of its power to cool a given quantity of fire. (Bogen's own (1995) proposal along these lines is not really adequate for Aristotle's purposes since it does not yield a quantitative measure and, as we shall later see, both proposals fail to distinguish between internal and external heat.) But the previous method has the advantage of being relatively clear-cut and of resting almost entirely upon fundamental assumptions of Aristotelian science.

It is also an advantage of the present method that it provides a natural means of *coordinating* the measurement of the different magnitudes. Given a certain quantity of one element, on what grounds can one say that there is the same quantity of another element? And given a certain quantity of one contrary, on what grounds can one say that there is the same quantity of another contrary, either from within the same contrariety or from within a different contrariety? The foundations of Aristotelian science presuppose positive answers to these questions; for his assumptions that the form of a mixture is a ratio of elements does not really make sense without some coordination in the units of measurements for the different elements. The development of Aristotelian science also presupposes a positive answer. Thus the chemical theory of *Meteor.* IV requires cross-elemental comparisons of quantity, as when he writes "If a body contains more water than earth, fire only thickens it; if it contains more earth, fire solidifies it;' and the explanation of jarring sensible in terms of irrational ratios (*De Sens.* 3, 439b29–440a15, 440b20, 442a15–17) requires exact coordination within a contrariety.[28]

However, as Aristotle is himself aware (*G&C.* II.6, 333a16–33, *Phys.* VII.4, 248b13ff), the relevant notions of coordination or comparison cannot simply be taken for granted, nor it is clear how they are to be understood. We cannot, for example, simply say that a quantity of water is the same as a given quantity of air when their volume is the same, even under similar conditions, since that is to presuppose that their density is the same and so already to presuppose a measure of quantity. But, as we have seen, a very satisfactory account can be given in terms of elemental transformation. This is the account that Aristotle himself appears to favor; and, indeed, for reasons that are not entirely clear to me, he seems to hold the stronger view that it is *only* through elemental transformation that the required coordination can be achieved (*G&C.* II.6, 33a30–34).

Given such a coordination, the measure of the quantity of the elements will be unique up to a positive multiplicative factor. For there is a natural 0; and so all that remains is to fix the unit quantity of one of the elements (taking for granted certain natural continuity assumptions). The measure of the other quantities will likewise be unique up to a positive multiplicative factor. The measure of the 'powers,' by contrast, will be unique, since they are a matter of proportion and hence indifferent to any change of unit.[29] This means, in particular, that there will be an absolute mean between any pair of contraries, an absolute midpoint between hot and cold or between dry and wet (and, conversely, given an absolute mean, the measurement of the two contraries can be coordinated, since their quantities will be the same when their combination results in the absolute mean).

### 14. THE REALITY OF LATENT CAPACITIES

We have seen how Aristotle is in a position to give rules for the determination of an object's contrarietal and elemental attributes. We must now ask what reason there might be for interpreting these rules in realist terms, by reference to underlying capacities, rather than in instrumentalist or operational terms. The reality of the latent capacities is considered in the present subsection and the reality of the patent capacities in the next. We focus attention on the case of thermal character, since the case of dessicative and elemental character are entirely analogous.

Any homoeomer b for Aristotle will have a certain thermal character $<p, q>$ constituted by its thermal power p and its thermal quantity q. He thinks of its thermal character as resulting from the latent hotness and coldness in the body. The latent hotness will have a character $<p_1, q_1>$, where $p_1 = 1$ and $q_1$ is the quantity of hotness, and the latent coldness will have a character $<p_2, q_2>$, where $p_2 = 0$ and $q_2$ is the quantity of coldness. The general equation for determining the thermal character $<p, q>$ of b is:

(25) (i)   $p = (p_1q_1 + p_2q_2)/(q_1 + q_2)$;

　　(ii)  $q = q_1 + q_2$.

But in the present case, $p_1 = 1$ and $p_2 = 0$; and so $p = q_1/(q_1 + q_2)$.

We see that the thermal character rests ultimately on the quantities $q_1$ and $q_2$. But what is meant by saying that there is a given quantity of hot or cold in a body? How are we to interpret the identities $q_h(b) = q_1$ and $q_c(b) = q_2$? Aristotle, I have suggested, adopts a realist interpretation. There are, for him, capacities H and C of hot and cold in the body and it is how much of each of these capacities that is in the body that determines its quantity of hot and of cold. Let us use $q_b(H)$ for the quantity of H in b and $q_b(C)$ for the quantity of C in b (on a suitably individualist conception of the contraries, the subscript "b" may be dropped). Then the quantities of hot and cold are determined by means of the identities:

(26) $q_h(b) = q_b(H)$ and $q_c(b) = q_b(C)$.

Thus, 'hot' and 'cold' have been moved up from a purely predicative to a nominal role.

One might, however, adopt a radically different point of view, one that is instrumentalist rather than realist in character. Under this alternative, the vectors $<p_1, q_1>$ and $<p_2, q_2>$ would merely represent one mathematical decomposition of the vector $<p, q>$ out of many. Any other decomposition that conforms to the equations (25) (i)–(ii) (and for which $0 \leq p_1, p_2 \leq 1$ and $q_1, q_2 \geq 0$) would be equally legitimate; and there would be no reason to suppose that one, as opposed to any another, was ontolgically privileged. Supposed, for example, that $<p, q>$ is the vector $<1/2, 2>$ of a body containing two units of warmth. Aristotle's favored decomposition is into equal portions of hot and cold, as represented by the vectors $<1, 1>$ and $<0, 1>$. But one might equally well think of the thermal character as being constituted out of portions of the somewhat hot and the somewhat cold, as represented by the vectors $<2/3, 1>$ and $<1/3, 1>$ or $<3/4, 2/3>$ and $<3/8, 4/3>$ or one of innumerable other combinations.

It might even be allowed that each decomposition $<p_1, q_2>$ and $<p_2, q_2>$ of the vector $<p, q>$ should correspond to thermal capacities, endowed with appropriate power and quantity. But from the present point of view, these capacities would be mere fictions, a way of rounding out the theory to suit mathematical convenience, perhaps, but not corresponding to anything in reality.

In the face of this alternative, Aristotle should at least provide a basis for supposing that his favored decomposition is privileged. If we consider the analogous problem of two people pulling on a rope (within the framework of Newtonian mechanics), we see that there is such a basis;

for the preferred decomposition of the resultant force is the one that corresponds to the two forces that each person separately applies to the rope. There is, that is to say, an *external* basis for favoring the decomposition, one not lying in the character of the resultant force itself but in the situation in which it is realized.

In the case of mixture, however, no such basis would appear to be available. For the only external factor that might conceivably be relevant is the formation of the mixture from its ingredients. But let us suppose that a mixture is formed from one unit of earth and two of water and that another mixture is formed from one unit of water and a mixture of one unit of each of earth and water. Then if formation were relevant to the decomposition into capacities, the two mixtures should have different decompositions. But once the two mixtures have been formed, there will be found to be no physical differences between them, nor will the manner of formation make any difference to how they affect other things or are themselves affected. Their decomposition into capacities should therefore be the same.

So if there is a privileged decomposition, it should be possible to discern it from the mixture itself; the decomposition into $<p_1, q_1>$ and $<p_2, q_2>$ should be determinable from $<p, q>$ alone. For Aristotle, though, there *is* such a decomposition; for $p_1 = 1$, $p_2, = 0$, $q_1 = pq$, and $q_2 = (1 - p)q$. Any quantity of warmth resolves into the proportionate quantities of Hot and Cold.

What makes this remarkable circumstance possible is the fact that hot and cold are extrema or absolutes; there is nothing hotter than Hot and nothing colder than Cold. This means that any intermediate temperature can be regarded as a fixed proportion of Hot and Cold and hence that any quantity of intermediate temperature can be regarded as a fixed quantity of Hot and Cold.

Without such extrema, a unique and uniform resolution of this sort would not be possible. For only two temperatures could be chosen as the basis for the others (since otherwise the resolution would not be unique); and given only two temperatures in the basis (or, indeed, any finite number), one could not then obtain a temperature higher than them all or one lower than them all. Thus his view that all intermediates are combinations depends essentially on his view that they 'stand between opposites of some kind' (*Met.* X.7, 1057a30).

The existence of extrema confers a certain objective status on the proposed decomposition, but it does not enjoin a realist construal of that decomposition. One might stick with the instrumental interpretation; or one might adopt an operational account, according to which the quantities of hot or cold in a body would correspond to independent capabilities of the body that were somehow correlated with its temperature. But what makes the realist construal especially plausible, it seems to me, is that it makes possible an explanation of how a mixture *acquires* the capabilities that it does. Given that a mixture has been formed from ingredients with certain capabilities, we wish to know what accounts for the capabilities of the mixture.

Now we might just take it as a brute fact that the capabilities of the mixture are related in a certain way with the capabilities of the ingredients from which it is formed. But by positing capacities, it is possible to provide an explanation of *how* the mixture acquires the capabilities that it has. For certain capacities will 'carry' the capabilities of the ingredients. These will then be transformed to the mixture and, upon being transferred, will interact in such a way as to produce the characteristic capabilities of the mixture.

It is partly the possibility of providing an explanation of this sort, one can surmise, that might have made the reality of latent capacities seem so plausible to Aristotle.

### 15. THE REALITY OF PATENT CAPACITIES

Let us grant that latent capacities may be present within a mixture. Aristotle wants to go one step further and maintain that the latent capacities will combine to form an intermediate capacity, that the latent capacities of Hot and Cold, for example, will combine to form a capacity of Warmth. There is no need to take this further step, however. For we could suppose that there are only contraries, but no intermediates. Contraries could combine in the sense of existing with other contraries— hot with cold, for example. But there would be no patent capacity of which both are parts.

On such a eliminativist view, each of the basic underlying capacities would be associated with a *broad ranging* capability, one that would cover the behavior of the object not only in situations in which the capacity had an unqualified presence but also in those in which its presence was qualified by that of another basic capacity. In the absence of such a broad range, no basis could be found for the behavior of the object in situations in which the presence of the capacity was qualified. However, under a suitable assignment of broad ranging capabilities, a basis for the behavior could be taken to reside either in just one of the capacities (perhaps the 'dominant' one) or independently in both (in which case we would have a form of over-determination). It should be noted that such a broad ranging capability could not even be specified without making reference to the other capacities. Thus an ontology of capacities would be built into the very content of the capability.

Although this is a possibly view, it is not Aristotle's. For he explicitly takes the intermediate to be a combination of the contraries. Similarly, it is not just the latent elemental capacities that he takes to be present in a mixture but also their combination. For each homoeomer is a compound of matter and form; and the form here will presumably be constituted by each of the latent elemental capacities.

It might conceivably be argued that just as I have allowed the matter to be many, one might likewise allow the form to be many. Thus not only could the soul inform the body *qua* plurality of its parts, but the body could be informed by the soul *qua* plurality of *its* parts. But such a view does not fit well with the way Aristotle talks of form or with the unifying role ascribed to it in books Z and H of the *Metaphysics*. Nor is it easy to make sense of the view on its own terms. We can sensibly talk of a function applying to a single argument or to several arguments, but we cannot sensibly talk of several functions applying to a single argument, unless this is a way of referring to the several applications of the different functions to the given argument. In the same way, it is hard to see how a form as many could have application to some matter without giving rise to many compounds.

Given that two contrary capacities combine to form an intermediate or that two elemental forms combine to form a homoeomerous form, how do they combine? What is the nature of the resulting combination? One view is that it is some sort of 'logical construct' from the two components. On such a view, the presence of the combination will simply amount to the presence of the two component capacities and the capability associated with the combined capacity will simply be the conjunction of the capabilities associated with the two component capacities. Thus the view will not differ significantly from the eliminativist position above; for the presence and operation of the combined capacity will merely consist in the presence and operation of the component capacities.

There is, however, a significant alternative to the eliminativist position, one in which the combined capacity plays an independent though intermediate role in the determination of the object's behavior. Under this alternative, each capacity will be associated with a narrow ranging capability, one that only relates to the behavior of the object in situations in which the capacity has an unqualified presence. Thus in those situations in which each of two contrary capacities is present, the capacities will not be directly able, through their associated capabilities, to determine the behavior of the body. They will, however, be indirectly able to determine the behavior. For they will constitute a combined capacity; associated with this capacity will be a narrow ranging capability; and it is through this that the behavior of the body can then be determined.

On this view, a capacity may operate, or exercise its power, in two fundamentally different ways. On the one hand, it may operate without constraint and thereby provide the basis for a capability in the normal way. On the other hand, it may operate under constraint and thereby contribute to the operation of another capacity. What would otherwise be the normal operation of each of two capacities is subject to modification by the other; and the result is the normal operation of a third capacity of which both are part.

In contrast to the previous view, the combined capacity cannot simply be regarded as an 'idle' construct from the component capacities that plays no independent role in the determination of behavior. Nor can its presence simply be taken to consist in the compresence of the components. For in order for this 'active' combination to exist the component capacities must somehow engage or lock on to one another. It may be phsycially impossible for two contrary capacities to be compressent without engaging in this way. But still there is something more to the existence of the combination than the mere compresence of the components.

The relative status of actual (or unqualified) existence and potential (or qualified) existence is quite different under the two views. Under the reductive view, the basic notion of existence should be taken to be the broad one of potential-or-actual existence. For a capacity to exist actually is then for it to exist, in this broad sense, on its own. Under the realist view, the basic notion is more plausibly taken to be that of actual existence. For a capacity to exist potentially is then for it to be a part of a combined capacity that actually exists.

Of the two views, it seems plausible that Aristotle's holds the second, at least in relation to homoeomerous form. For if a homoeomerous form were merely a logical construct from the elemental forms, then a homoeomer would lack any genuine unity. Given that the homoeomerous form consisted in the various component elemental forms, the homoeomerous body would merely consist in the corresponding elemental bodies. It is these elemental bodies that should be taken to be more truly substantial; and the homoeomer itself should be regarded as some kind of 'heap.' Thus we would have a variant of Sharvy's view, but with the flat mereological conception of a component body replaced with a more sophisticated hylomorphic conception.

We might also note that the second view is more in conformity with Aristotle's general line on the definitional priority of the actual to the potential (*Met.* IX.8, 1049b13–17) and that it seems to make the compresence of conflicting capacities more palatable. If the presence of warmth in a body simply consisted in the compresence of hot and cold, then we would appear to have a straightforward case of two contraries in the same subject. However, if the contraries do not themselves directly attach to the subject but only attach in so far as they belong to a combination, then it is not so clear that their joint attachment is of a sort that should be considered objectionable.

All the same, two difficulties need to be resolved before a view of this sort can properly be maintained. The first concerns density. It seems reasonable to suppose that a quality or form may not be uniformly dense within a given homoeomer. Some part of a body of air might have been 'stretched,' for example, so that there is less hot and wet there per unit volume than elsewhere in the body. Suppose now that this body of air is mixed with a uniformly dense body of water in such a way that the density distribution of each element is preserved within the mixture. Then the resulting 'mixture' will not be homoeomerous, for where the air is rarefied there will a smaller proportion of Hot to Cold than elsewhere.

This means that the combination of Hot and Cold or of Earth and Air, as it is found in the 'mixture,' will not, properly speaking, be an intermediate; for its temperature or thermal power will vary from one location to another. We will have something closer to an aggregate of intermediates, rather than an intermediate itself. The question then arises as to exactly what we should take the operation of combining on qualities and forms to be in such cases. What combines? And what results from the combining?

One response is to insist that the qualities and form that combine should be uniformly dense. The results of combining them will then also be uniformly dense; and so the difficulties are avoided.

Such a response is naturally taken to be part of the broader view that *all* qualities and forms should be uniformly dense, and not just those that 'mix.' Thus what one might have taken to be the qualities or forms, under an individualist or universalist conception, must now be differentiated with respect to density; each of the originally envisaged qualities or forms must give way to its uniformly dense portions. In the same way, there will be a change in the conception of an individual homoeomer; for it must be like its form in being uniformly dense. Thus what we normally take to be an individual homoeomer will normally be an aggregate of such homoeomers.

Another response, at the other extreme, is to suppose that what combines are aggregates of the qualities or forms. The result of such a combining will then be another aggregate of qualities or forms. But however convenient such a conception of combination might be from a mathematical point of view, it is hard to take seriously from a metaphysical point of view. For surely the most basic physical operations, such as mixing or growing, must take place at the level of qualities or forms themselves, not at the level of their aggregates.

The only reasonable way to allow the qualities and forms to be non-uniformly dense is to allow the combining of them to result in many intermediate qualities or forms rather than a single quality or form. The original qualities or forms, when combined, will 'fracture' into the different combinations.[30] The single Hot and Cold under a strictly universalist conception, for example, will combine to produce a medley of different Warmths. But it should be noted that, under this view, the same quality or form may be a part of many different combinations and hence may not be wholly located within a particular combination of which it is a part. The view does not therefore sit well with an individualist conception of qualities or forms.

The second difficulty arises from the case in which the qualities or forms to be combined contain a common contrary or elemental form (though the difficulty is not peculiar to those who would posit a *combined* quality or form). Let us suppose, to fix our ideas, that a mixture of water and earth is mixed with some earth to produce an earthier mixture of water and earth. The original mixture will have a form $H = W + E$ and the earth a distinct form $E'$ (the difficulty I am considering will not even arise under a suitably universalist conception of form). The form of the resulting mixture will therefore be $H' = W + E + E'$; and so under our conception of the operation of combining, the forms $E$ and $E'$ will both be part of the resulting combination $H'$ and hence will both have a real, though latent, presence within the mixture itself.

But this is impossible. It makes no sense to suppose that two coincident forms of earth might both be present within a given body; for there is nothing in the mixture that could correspond to such a division. Let us suppose that some water with form $W^*$ was mixed with some earth with form $E^*$ in the same proportions as in $H$. Then the resulting mixture would possess a single indivisible form of earth and yet would be physically indistinguishable in kind from the original mixture. There could therefore be no basis, in terms of the current constitution of the mixtures, for assigning compresent forms of earth to one but not to other.

We have here the analogue, at the level of form, of the previous problem at III.8 concerning prime matter. In both cases, the undifferentiated character of the items prevents them from converging in any meaningful sense.

It follows that the operation '+' of combination on forms and qualities cannot meaningfully be applied to forms, such as $W + E$ and $E'$ above, that contain distinct elemental components of a common kind. One might for mathematical purposes represent the form $H$ of the resulting mixture as $W + E + E'$; its character could then be calculated from the character of the components in the usual way. But the decomposition into component forms, in this case, would be a mere fiction; it would correspond to no real division within the resultant form itself.

It likewise follows (again assuming an individualist conception of form) that the forms of the antecedent ingredients may not always be present within the mixture; for when the ingredients have a common kind of element, their forms will possess a common kind of elemental component. There will still exist decompositions of the resulting form; but none will correspond to the forms of the ingredients.

16. THE DOCTRINE OF DERIVED PART

Ascent places the form of the elements within a mixture; for the mixture contains the elemental bodies as constituent matter and these then possess the elemental forms. We have now seen how this is also possible under Leveling. For we need no longer think of a mixture as possessing an undifferentiated form; this form will itself contain the elemental forms as parts.

Such a conclusion may be of succour to those, such as Bogen and Gill, who take the presence of an elemental body in a mixture to consist in the 'survival' of some of its features. For instead of having to concede that it is only a watered-down version of the features that survive, they can maintain that it is the features themselves. We can revert to the original model proposed by Gill (1989), under which the very same features survive though under a different mode of predication, but instead of the switch being from essential to accidental, it is now from actual to potential.

However, the presence of the elemental forms does not provide us with what *we* are after. For we want the elemental bodies themselves to be present in the mixture—and not merely in the quixotic sense that their forms are present but in a manner that is robust enough to satisfy the skeptic. Consider a mixture of earth and fire. Using E for the form of the earth and F for the form of the fire, the form of the mixture will be $E + F$. If m is the prime matter of the mixture, then the mixture itself will be the compound $(E + F)m$. Thus the forms E and F will both be part of the mixture. But what we require is that the bodies Em and Fm should be part.

How can this be maintained? How can the transition from the presence of the elemental forms to the presence of the corresponding elemental bodies be made? Before examining this question, it will help to consider some analogous cases from entirely unrelated domains. One case is familiar from the philosophy of language and perhaps occurs, in its most explicit form, in the work of Frege. Consider the proposition that Socrates is wise and Socrates is Greek (a similar point holds in regard to the *sentence* 'Socrates is wise and Socrates is Greek'). Then the most natural way to analyze this proposition is as the conjunction $P + Q$ of two propositions P and Q, where the first proposition P is the predication Ws of the property of being wise to Socrates (or to a component corresponding to Socrates) while the second propositions Q is the predication Gs of the property of being Greek to Socrates (or to the corresponding component).

But we may also take this proposition to be the result of predicatively applying the conjunctive property of being a wise Greek to Socrates. This complex property may itself be seen to be the result of appropriately conjoining the two component properties. Using W and G for the component properties and $(W + G)$ for their conjunction, we may represent the possibility of analyzing the given proposition in these two ways by means of the identity:

(1) $(W + G)s = Ws + Gs$.

(For Frege, the possibility of such alternative forms of analysis was significant for showing how logical inference could be fruitful.)

It is plausible to suppose, especially under a structural conception of propositions, that each of these analyses will correspond to a different way of decomposing the given proposition into parts. For each of the predicative propositions Ws, Gs and $(W + S)s$ will be constituted from

its subject and predicate components; and each of the conjunctive items
(P + Q) and (G + W) will be constituted out of its conjunctive components.
Thus the analyses, as a whole, will correspond to two different
decompositions of the propositions into parts.

Another very different case, though closer to home for us, derives from
Aristotle's discussion of Hermes and the half line in the *Metaphysics*. At
V.7, 1017b8, he claims that 'Hermes is [potentially] in the stone and the
half of the line is [potentially] in the line.' But what does this mean?

A weak reading is that the potential presence of x in y consists in its
being possible for x to come from y; and this reading might be taken to
be supported by his remark at *Met*. IX.6, 1048a32–33, that "potentially,
for instance, a statue of Hermes is in the block of wood and the half-line
is in the whole, because it might be separated out" (cf. *De Sens*. 6,
446a6–7), "So the foot-length too exists potentially in the two-foot length,
but actually only when it has been separated from the whole"). But such
a reading is much too weak, since it would permit one to say that one
element was potentially in another out of which it had come; and this, I
take it, is not a relevant case of one thing being potentially in another.
Nor is the reading really supported by the remark. For in order for one
thing to be separated out from another, it is not sufficient for the one to
come from the other; it must already be in the other. Indeed, it is for this
reason that we would not want to say, in the case of elemental
transformation, that the one element had been separated out from the
other.

It seems to me that, in these passages, Aristotle is not trying to explain
a sense in which one thing is present in another. Rather, he is already
presupposing that there is a sense in which the one thing is present in
another and then attempting to explain what makes the presence
potential. (Further considerations in favor of this alternative reading are
given in the next section.) But this then leaves open the question of what
would lead us to say, in the first place, that the one thing was in another.

To avoid needless complications, let us suppose that we are dealing
with a block of butter rather than with a stone or a line. The whole block,
on Aristotle's view, will be composed of two half-blocks. Neither half-
block actually exists, since that would require it to exist in separation
from the other. But each still is in some sense in the block. Our question
is to say what that sense is.

The whole butter, we may suppose, is a compound Bm of the buttery
form B and some underlying matter m. This matter is the juxtaposition
$m_1 + m_2$ of the parcels of matter $m_1$ and $m_2$ corresponding to the two
half-blocks; and so the butter itself is of the form $B(m_1 + m_2)$. But we
may also regard the butter as the juxtaposition of the two half-blocks.
Thus, just as in the case of the conjunctive proposition, we may suppose
that the block of butter is subject to the following identity:

(2) $B(m_1 + m_2) = Bm_1 + Bm_2$,

and we may take this identity to represent two alternative ways of decomposing the block of butter into parts. (We should note that this example requires that the form B be suitably universal. If the form were tied to a particular spatial extent, then it could not be attached both to $m_1$ and to $m_2$.)

I now wish to maintain that an analogous account can be given for mixtures. For as well as seeing a mixture as a compound of some matter and a 'mixed' form, we may also see it as a 'mix' of simple compounds. The homoeomer $(E + F)$ m above, for example, will be subject to the identity:

(3) $(E + F)m = Em + Fm$;

and this identity will then represent two different decompositions of the homoeomer into parts, one containing the complex form $(E + F)$ as a part and the other containing the two elements Em and Fm as parts.

I do not wish to maintain that Aristotle explicitly sanctions the transition from the one form of decomposition to the other. But it is what his position on mixture seems to require; it is implicit in what he says in the account of Hermes and the line; and, given how natural the transition is, it is not surprising that it should be made without explicit comment.

We should guard against some misunderstandings. Principle (3) is an identity, not a biconditional, and its constituent expressions, 'Em' and the like, are terms denoting compounds, not sentences expressing predications. Thus (3) does not say that m has E and F if it has E-and-F, but that the mix of the compounds of E and F with m is the compound of the mix of E and F with m. Of course, this true identity will be connected to a true biconditional; for the right 'object', Em + Fm, will exist potentially (or actually) iff the left 'object', $(E + F)m$, exists potentially (or actually). Moreover, there will be a sense of predication for which it is true that a compound Fn will exist potentially (or actually) iff n is potentially (or actually) F. However, we should not suppose that Em + Fm actually (or potentially) exists if Em and Fm actually (or potentially) exist. Thus the biconditional concerning predication to which the identity corresponds will not, under the most natural construal, even be true.

There are some obvious differences between the different cases. In (1), the operations of 'product' and 'summation' are interpreted as predication and conjunction respectively; in (2), the 'product' is interpreted as hylomorphic compounding and the 'sum' is interpreted as juxtaposition; and in (3), the 'product' is again interpreted as compounding while the 'sum' is interpreted as the operation of mixing. Or again: in (2), as opposed to (1) and (3), the 'subject' is distributed over the 'predicate' rather than the 'predicate' over the 'subject.' But despite these differences, the underlying form of the account remains the same: the operations are subject to a distributive law, whose left and right hand sides determine different decompositions of the same item.

It is natural, though perhaps not necessary, to regard one of the two alternative decompositions as basic, i.e. as representing the most basic way in which the item is formed from its parts. Whether it is the decomposition on the left or the right varies from case to case. In the first case, it is the 'right-hand' decomposition of the proposition into propositional conjuncts that is most naturally regarded as basic; while in the second and third cases, it is the 'left-hand' decomposition of the body into matter and form.

Each of these decompositions will involve certain applications of the operations of summation and product; and again, it is natural to regard the applications that are involved in the basic decomposition of the item as basic. Thus, in the propositional case, it is the application of conjunction to propositions (rather than to properties) and the application of predication to simple properties (rather than to complex properties) that is basic; in the case of the butter, it is the application of 'juxtaposition' to the matter (rather than to the bodies) that is basic; and in the case of mixtures, it is the application of the mixing operation to the forms (rather than to the bodies) that is basic.

One could imagine someone believing that the existence of the one form of decomposition somehow served to exclude the other. The application of the basic operations of 'summation' and of 'product' would be confined to the basic cases and the extension to the cases required by the alternative forms of decomposition would not be permitted. But a much more plausible view is that the existence of the one form of decomposition, far from excluding the existence of the other, actually provides a basis for it. It is because we can see the proposition or body as being composed in the one way that we are in a position to see it as being composed in the other. We might concede that one of the decompositions is basic and the other derivative; but each is equally legitimate.

If I am asked under what conditions one form of decomposition might serve as a basis for another, then I can provide no general answer. It merely seems evident, in certain cases, that alternative forms of decomposition exist and that one might serve to ground another. This is not to say that there are no constraints on what the permissible forms of decomposition might be; the intuition that the parts are somehow present in the whole must be preserved; and the purely formal properties of part-whole and of composition must be respected.

However, there seem to be no special difficulties in regarding the elements as part of a mixture and, indeed, there are some strong reasons for so regarding them. For given that the component forms $E$ and $F$ have a presence within the mixture $(E + F)m$, it seems reasonable to suppose that their embodiments also have a presence within a mixture. But the embodiment of either form must be in the matter m; for there is no alternative matter in which either can be embodied. This means that some sort of compound for each of the forms with m must be present within the mixture.

Let us use E[m] and F[m] for these 'compounds' and let us call them *quasi-elements*. Then these quasi-elements are certainly part of the mixture. The only question that remains is whether the operation E[m] of 'quasi-compounding' is the same as the operation E(m) of compounding; for if the two operations are the same, then E[m] will be an element. Now I can imagine a view according to which the quasi-compound E[m] and the compound E(m) are distinct. It would be required that for E(m) to have any sort of presence the form E must be directly attached to the underlying matter m, and not indirectly as in the homoeomer (E + F)m. But such a view would not rule out the possibility of another sort of compound whose presence did not require that the form be directly attached to the matter; a looser, or less direct, form of attachment would be allowed. Under such a looser conception, it could then be maintained that the operation of compounding applied both internally, within a mixture, and externally.

We should note some ramifications of the present account. First, it renders plausible the idea that the basic notion of mixture is of the forms or contraries, rather than the bodies. We understand the mixture (Em + Fm) of Em and Fm as the result of applying the mixture (E + F) of the forms E and F to the matter m. Aristotle suggests such a view in his account of mixture in terms of the interaction of the contraries at *G&C*. II.7, 334b8–30; and he suggests a similar view on growth at *G&C*. I.5, 321b17–34 and on interaction generally at *G&C*. I.7, 324a4–11.

It also renders plausible the idea that the elemental parts Em and Fm are, in a certain sense, posterior to the mixture (E + F)m. For their status as parts is to be understood by deriving them from the whole rather than by deriving the whole from them; they are to be obtained by analysis from the whole rather than the whole by synthesis from them. However, this is not to deny that there is an independent way of understanding what the elements are, not qua parts, but as objects in their right; and, indeed, there is. In the same sort of way, it might be supposed that (E + F) is posterior, as part, to the mixture (E + F)m (not that it is altogether clear that this is Aristotle's view) even though there is an independent account of what it is in terms of the prior parts E and F.

The derived parts Em and Fm of the mixture (E + F)m have the further property of being *distributed*. Normally, something is taken be a part when it can be composed with other objects to form the whole. But there is another, less direct, way in which an object x may be part of another y. For the part x may itself be composed of other parts, and it may be possible to obtain the whole y by replacing one or more of the parts of x with wholes to which they belong. It is in this sense, for example, that the string ac may be said to be a part of the string abcd; for abcd may be obtained from ac by replacing a with ab and c with cd.[31]

The Aristotelian cases above are undistributed with respect to the derived means of composition but distributed with respect to the primary means. Thus the homoeoemer $(E + F)m$ may be obtained from the element $Em$ by replacing the formal part $E$ with $(E + F)$. Similarly, the block of butter $B(m_1 + m_2)$ may be obtained from the half-block $Bm_1$ by replacing the material part $m_1$ with $(m_1 + m_2)$.

Finally, we should note that the present account critically depends upon submitting the homoeomers to a hylomorphic analysis. If it was thought that there merely existed the homoeomer b and the form or form analogue $E + F$, but no matter m complementary to the form, then it is hard to see how an account of the sort we have proposed could plausibly be maintained; for it would then be impossible to discern any analogue to the components $Em$ or $Fm$ within the body b. This constitutes an argument, albeit a very indirect one, in favor of the primalist as opposed to the elementalist position, since elementalism, when combined with Leveling, is unable to provide an adequate account of the constitution of mixture.

## 17. SOLUTION TO THE PUZZLES

We shall show how the puzzles might be solved and how some other requirements and desiderata might be met under the proposed version of Leveling.

We begin with the requirements associated with the second puzzle ((3)–(5) of Section 1). Uniformity is unproblematic. It follows from the doctrines of intermediates and derived part that a mixture will be composed of elements (and also of certain mixtures of elements); and so Containment will also be satisfied. Indeed, not only will the mixture be composed of elements, it will be exhaustively constituted by the elements. The mixture $(E + F)m$, for example, will be constituted by the elements $Em$ and $Fm$.

There might be thought to be room for a certain form of skepticism here; for the skeptic might insist that it is only the matter m, the form $(E + F)$, and the component forms $E$ and $F$ that can properly be said to be a part of the mixture $(E + F)m$. But such a form of skepticism is of quite a different order in regard to the present account than it was in regard to the accounts of Gill and Bogen. Skepticism in the previous cases rested upon an insistence that the notion of parts be used in an ordinary intuitive sense; skepticism in the present case rests upon an insistence that the notion of part *not* be so used. It rests upon the demand that the notion of part be confined to the most basic cases and that it not be applied to the derivative cases. But such a demand, far from being in conformity with our ordinary understanding of part, is at odds with that understanding.

Not only does the present account meet our central challenge of showing how Leveling might be reconciled with Containment, it also shows how certain related difficulties can be removed. The first concerns Aristotle's vacillation over the question of constitution. We noted, in connection with the apparent success of Ascent in dealing with Containment, that Aristotle displayed some hesitation in treating the elements as the constituent matter of a mixture. He does not provide a straightforward account of mixing or of mixture in terms of the previously understood hylomorphic notions, as should be possible under Ascent. But the reason is now clear; there is no such account. The relationship of element to mixture is not exactly that of matter to compound of matter and form, nor can it be understood without invoking a completely new form or composition among the contraries or forms.

Aristotle also vacillates over whether to compose a mixture from the elements or from the contraries. But we now have an explanation for this. For neither is strictly matter and yet each has a right to be considered as the analogue of matter, the contraries being favored by virtue of being that from which the mixture is primarily composed and the elements being favored by virtue of being more akin to the kind of thing that is normally taken to be matter. Nor should we be worried by the fact that Aristotle is prepared to describe the elements as the matter of other things; for the term 'matter' is one which Aristotle tends to stretch to the limits of its useful employment.

A second difficulty concerns Compresence. I previously expressed some reservations as to how under Ascent, two elements, as the constituent matter of a mixture, could be compresent (subsection 10(4)). For how could their potential existence, their being subject to a supervening form, render possible what would be impossible if they were actually to exist, i.e. not be subject to a supervening form? This suggests that our proposed ban on compresence (in the context of the discussion of Sharvy) is not strong enough; the mere fact that two objects potentially exist (at least in the sense of constituent matter) is not enough to render their compresence palatable.

In the present case, however, we can appeal to something much stronger than this notion of potential existence to justify compresence. For at the most basic level of analysis, under Leveling, we do not have a decomposition of the mixture into the elements at all. We merely have the combined form $(E + F)$, say, superimposed upon some matter m. The elements Em and Fm merely have a derivative status. They can be discerned within the mixture by means of structural realignment; but at the most basic level they are not there. In these circumstances, there seems to be no real bar towards their being compresent.

We can also remove one of the difficulties involved in supposing that the form of a mixture is a ratio of elements (a further difficulty is discussed in the next section). How, one might wonder, can the form of a mixture be a ratio of elements when the matter of the mixture is not elemental? The answer is that the form is a certain combination of elemental forms. It can therefore in a clear sense be said to be ratio of elements even though it applies to the same sort of matter as the elemental forms themselves.

We turn to requirements associated with the first puzzle ((1) and (2) of Section 1). The elements of a mixture will not actually exist since they do not enjoy a separate existence. It is perhaps necessary for something to enjoy a separate existence that it not be part of a prior whole (cf. *Met.* IX.6, 1048a32–24). If that is so, then it is clear that the elements in a mixture do not enjoy a separate existence, since they are part of the mixture which is prior. But even without the priority of the mixture, it can still be maintained that the ingredients exist in an altered form; for the power of one will be checked by the power of the other.

The elements of a mixture will potentially exist since they enjoy an unseparated existence. It is perhaps sufficient for something to enjoy an unseparated existence that it be a part of a prior whole. It will then be the same condition that serves to establish the non-actual and the potential existence of the elements. But again, it seems independently plausible that the elements have some sort of existence; and if it is not actual, then it must be potential.

I turn finally to the Latency requirement. Under the present account, it is evident that ingredients will have capacities independently of the mixture to which they belong. For each such ingredient will be endowed with a certain characteristic form and associated with that form will be range of capacities. In some cases, the corresponding capabilities will transfer directly to the mixture. Smoke, for example, will tend to rise because the fire in the smoke tends to rise. In other cases, the capabilities will be modified in their transfer to the mixture. Thus the tendency of the fire in smoke to rise fast will be checked by the tendency of the earth in the smoke to fall. But, in either case, the underlying capacities in the ingredients will provide some sort of basis for determining the capabilities of the mixture.

As I have mentioned, it is plausible to suppose that among the capacities possessed by the elements in a mixture will be the tendency actually to exist, i.e., to exist in 'unmixed' isolation from other elements. Such a capacity in the ingredients will result in a tendency for the mixture to be inherently unstable, i.e. to disintegrate into its component elements. Thus the tendency towards disintegration in the mixture will derive from the tendency towards isolation in its ingredients, rather than the other way round. (The tendency of each element to find its natural place will also contribute towards the instability of the mixture.[32])

This sense in which the ingredients exist in potentiality is very strong; they themselves will have the tendency to exist. The sense is also very strange; for the bodies that have this tendency will not themselves actually exist. They must, of course, exist potentially in the sense explained above.

But this sense of potential existence is very weak and falls far short of the sense that is now in question.

To appreciate the full force of the present proposal, it may be helpful to compare it with some of its more obvious rivals. In saying that a given ingredient has the potential to exist we are not merely saying that there is some possible future in which it does exist. For this is compatible with its spontaneously springing into existence at some future date. We want to say, by contrast, that the potential existence of the ingredients already resides in the mixture.

Nor are we merely saying that there is the potentiality for something in the mixture, distinct from the ingredient itself, to become the ingredient. This is a way in which one *might* construe the claim about Hermes having a potential existence in the stone or the half-block of butter having a potential existence in the full block; for there is some stone in the stone and a potentiality for that stone to become Hermes and there is some butter in the block and the potentiality for that butter to become a block of butter.

But this interpretation will not serve Aristotle's purposes. For in order to satisfy the skeptic he wants the ingredients themselves to be in the mixture, not some surrogates for the ingredients. Not is it even clear, in contrast to the case of Hermes or of the butter, what the surrogates in the mixture could plausibly be taken to be.

Aristotle must therefore at least be saying that there is a potentiality for the ingredients themselves to become existent or actual. But even this relatively strong interpretation should be taken in a relatively strong way. One is not merely saying that there is a possible future in which the nonactual ingredient becomes actual. One is also saying that this possibility has its basis in the ingredient itself; it is because of some capacity or tendency in the ingredient that it is possible for it to become actual.

In this respect, there is a clear difference between the case of mixture and the cases of Hermes or of the butter. For even if one admits that Hermes is already in the stone or that the half blocks are already in the full block, one does not want to allow that Hermes, as it is in the stone, or that the half-blocks, as they are in the full block, possess a tendency to become actual.

To many philosophers, the present suggestion for understanding the potential existence of the ingredients might appear barely intelligible. For it appears to involve the absurd idea that it is possible for something nonexistent to become existent; and it appears to involve the additional absurdity that this possibility might be grounded in the capacity of the nonexistent. But it is important that the relevant notion of potentiality be properly understood. It would indeed be absurd to suppose that a merely possible child of a childless couple might possess the capacity to exist or that a person, once he is dead, might possess the capacity to become alive. But the objects that we take to possess such a capacity are not mere possibilia or mere 'have-been's; they will have a more substantive form of existence as derived parts. This means that their forms will have a 'living' or active presence within the mixture, they will be attached to some matter and in such a way as to influence its behavior; and to the extent that the forms have a real and active presence within the mixture, we may also take the ingredients to have such a presence. Thus it is because the ingredients have the weak form of potential existence in their status as derived parts that they are able to sustain the stronger form of potential existence.

## V. Peripheral Problems

We shall show how the problems of Underdetermination and of the Quantum Effect may be solved on the basis of Leveling. These problems are not peculiar to Leveling, they arise under any approach; and the essentials of the present solutions may also have application to some of the other approaches.

### 18. ELEMENTAL UNDERDETERMINATION

Suppose that a mixture consists of the same amounts of hot, cold, wet and dry. Then the proportions of the elements in the mixture is vastly undetermined. It could consist, for example, of two units of earth (which is cold and dry) and two units of air (which is hot and wet) or two units of fire (which is hot and dry) and two units of water (which is cold and wet) or one unit of each element, and so on through infinitely many alternatives. And the same is true of any other mixture.

This is not in itself objectionable. But it is given the view that the contrarietal power of a body, its proportion of hot to cold and of dry to wet, should determine its elemental power, its proportion of the elements. And this is something that Aristotle appears to hold. Thus at *P.A.* II.1, 646a19–21, he writes: "and all other differences are secondary to these (the primary contrarieties], such differences, that is, as heaviness or lightness, density or rarity, roughness or smoothness, and any other such properties of bodies as there may be"; and at *G&C.* II.3, 330a23–4, he writes, "Manifestly, then, all of the other differentiae are reducible to these four primary ones." Now presumably mixtures with different proportions of the elements will have different physical characteristics. But how can this be, given that the proportions of the primary contraries are the same?

Quite apart from Aristotle's explicit remarks in favor of supervenience, it is hard to see, given his other views, how the doctrine could reasonably be denied—at least in application to elemental constitution. Consider, for example, a mixture of a unit of earth and of air and a mixture of a unit of fire and of water. Each mixture contains a unit amount of each of the primary contraries, hot, cold, dry and wet. But given that the elements are constituted out of these contraries, in what could the difference between the two mixtures then consist?

There are two solutions to this problem that should be mentioned if only to be dismissed. The first is that not all ratios of elements need correspond to a homoeomerous form and that it is therefore possible that, of all the ratios of elements that correspond to a given ratio of contraries, only one will correspond to a homoeomerous form. It might be supposed that every element should be present to some degree within any homoeomer, so that within any ratio $<p_1, p_2, p_3, p_4>$ of the elements each of the values $p_i$, i = 1, ... , 4, must be positive (cf. *G&C.* II.8); and we shall later have our own reasons for restricting the values of the proportions $p_1, ... , p_4$. But the indeterminacy in the elemental ratios is so vast that it is hard to believe that any reasonable restriction on the legitimate ratios could completely eliminate it. There would appear to be nothing to prevent a mixture from consisting of elements in the proportions <1, 1, 0, 0,> and <0, 0, 1, 1> or in the proportions <1, 1, 1, 1> and <1/2, 1/2, 3/2, 3/2> (should it be required that every component value be positive).

In the second place, it might be thought that the same kind of mixture could be associated with different ratios of elements. Perhaps the ratio is really rough rather than exact, and so exact ratios that are in the same range will correspond to the same rough ratio and hence to the same homoeomerous form. I myself am not inclined to follow this path. But even if some slack between the elemental ratio and the form is allowed, it is again hard to see how it could be sufficient to resolve the indeterminacy. Surely, the mixture that consists of equal proportions of earth and air must be different from that which consists in equal proportions of fire and water. Indeed, if the two were the same, it is hard to see on what basis Aristotle could take the form of a mixture to be a ratio of elements rather than a ratio of contraries.

The solution to the problem must lie, I believe, in a more fundamental examination of the relationship between the two contraries that make up a given element. Consider fire. Its form is given by the pair of contraries hot and dry. But how do the two contraries combine? What is the nature of the resulting combination? We have here the analogue of the earlier question of how hot combines with cold in a warm body or dry with wet in a moist body. But whereas before the combination was of contraries from the same contrariety, it is now of contraries from complementary contrarieties.

As before, there are two main lines of solution. On the one hand, one might treat the form of fire as a mere conjunction of the contraries hot and dry. On this view, all that is involved in the presence of the form is the presence of the two contraries, and all that is involved in the operation of the formal capacity is the operation of the component capacities.

However, in contrast to the previous intra-contrarietal case, the presence of each contrary can now be taken to be of the normal unqualified sort and the operation of each capacity can be taken to have its normal narrow range. Thus no extension need be made to the normal notions of existence or of capability.

On the other hand, it might be supposed that the contraries combine to produce an elemental form with a certain degree of independence from the contraries. Its presence will not simply consist in the presence of the hot and dry and its operation will, or need, not simply consist in the independent operation of the hot and dry. Each component will indeed operate in the way that it would independently of the presence of the other contrary; but the two may also *co*operate and thereby produce behavior that is not simply the product of their independent behavior.

Of these two views, the first completely fails to solve the problem of undetermination. The presence of equal quantities of earth and air in a mixture will simply consist in the presence of equal quantities of the four contraries; and likewise for a mixture of fire and water. Thus no difference in the proportion of elements can emerge without a corresponding difference in the proportion of contraries.

The second view, by contrast, completely succeeds in solving the problem. For in a mixture the contraries are no longer 'freely floating' in a mixture but will be linked or bonded in certain characteristic ways. Thus, in a mixture of earth and air, the contrary cold will be linked with dry and the contrary hot with wet while, in a mixture of fire and water, the contrary hot will be linked with dry and cold with wet. The contraries are the same but the links are different; and because of the difference in the links, there will be a difference in the nature of the bodies.

Under the first view, two elements will mix through their contraries mixing. Thus if we represent the respective forms of earth, air, fire and water by CD, HW, HD and CW, then we should represent the form of the mixture of earth and air by $(C + H) (D + W)$, and the form of the mixture of fire and water by $(H + C) (D + W)$. Since the order of the components in the sums is of no account, the two mixtures will be of the same form.

Under the second view, two elements will mix through their elemental form mixing. The homoeomerous form will be a combination of the elemental forms in much the same way that an intermediate has been taken to be a combination of contraries. We should therefore represent the form of the first mixture by $CD + HW$ and the form of the second by $HD + CW$. It is then clear that the forms of the two mixtures cannot be the same, since the links between the complementary contraries are different.

Despite their common contrarietal character, the difference between the two mixtures is considerable. For in order to obtain the one from the other, the internal links between the complementary contraries must first be broken and then realigned. This will require not just dissolution of the first mixture and the reconstitution of the second but some form of elemental transformation as well.

Of the two views, it is the second that seems closer to how Aristotle thinks of the elements and of the way they behave. He talks of the contraries being 'yoked' within an elemental form (*G&C.* II.3, 330a30), thereby suggesting that the two somehow work together as a unit or team. He also takes pairs of complementary contraries to constitute a unitary elemental form. But whereas this makes good sense under the realist view, it would be more appropriate, under the reductive view, to regard the contraries themselves as the forms. The four elements would then be the hot, the cold, the dry and the wet and an elemental body, as standardly conceived, would be a 'heap' of elementary bodies of this more rudimentary sort.[33] Furthermore, it is only the realist position that squares with Aristotle's account of the form of a mixture as a ratio. Why, it might be wondered, should Aristotle treat the form of a mixture as a ratio of elements rather than of contraries? Under the reductive position, the form should be treated as a ratio of *contraries*; for it is only with considerable indirection and overdetermination that it could also be treated as a ratio of elements. Under the realist position, by contrast, the form should be treated as a ratio of elements; for it is only with considerable indirection and underdetermination that it could also be treated as a ratio of contraries.

We should also note that several of Aristotle's more specific beliefs about mixing would make no sense under the reductive view. Aristotle believes that things of the same kind cannot mix (*G&C.* I.7, 324a19–23). But suppose that earth (which is cold and dry) is mixed with fire (which is hot and dry). Then under the reductive view, this would seem to require the merging of Cold with Hot and also of Dry with Dry. But if Dry can merge with Dry when Cold merges with Hot and, similarly, if Hot can merge with Hot when Dry merges with Wet, it is hard to see why it should not be simultaneously possible for Hot to merge with Hot and Dry with Dry. Or again, Aristotle seems to believe that if earth is mixed with air, then we can extract the earth and air but not the other elements. But under the reductive view, the mixture of earth and air is simply a combination of equal quantities of the four contraries and so it should be possible to extract each of the elements and even each of the different homoeomers.

All the same, there appears to be textual evidence that tells against attributing the realist position to Aristotle. One piece of evidence, the remarks at 646a19–21 and 330a23–4 on the reducibility of a body's features to the primary contraries, has already been mentioned. But we are now in a position to see how the truth of these remarks might be maintained while the strict doctrine of supervenience is denied. For their truth only requires that there should be some account of what the features of a body are in terms of the primary contraries; and, as the realist position makes clear, the existence of such an account is compatible with there being a difference in the features without any corresponding difference in the contraries.

Some further troubling evidence emerges from the discussion of intermediates in the *Metaphysics*. Aristotle defines a contrariety with the words, "Since things which differ from one another more or less, there is also a greatest difference, and this I call contrariety" (1055a3–5). The subsequent discussion makes clear that he thinks of a contrariety as linear or mono-dimensional rather than as partial or multi-dimensional. Thus at 1055a19–21 he writes; "it is clear that one thing cannot have more than one contrary (for neither can there be anything more extreme than two extremes, nor can there be more than two extremes for the one interval)." But homoeomerous form seems to present a case of a two-dimensional contrariety with four extrema—Earth, Air, Fire and Water.

In response to this point, it should be acknowledged that Aristotle has a natural but unduly narrow conception of what a contrariety might be. Aristotle himself comes close to conceding this when he writes at *De Cae.* II.3, 286a29, "each element stands in a contrary relation to every other."[34] In his discussion of contraries at I.6 of *Metaphysics*, he is able to avoid the postulation of multi-dimensional contrarieties by considering only the cases in which the contrariety is primitive or is derived from another contrariety by relativization to a fixed genus. But had the considered cases in which a contrariety is derived from several other contrarieties by means of, what we would now call, their cartesian product, he would have had no difficulty in admitting the broader conception.

In any case, we should note that the present point tells equally against the reductivist. For he must also admit that the four pairs of complementary contraries represent the extrema of a two-dimensional contrariety. If the point favors anyone, it is the eliminativist, whose position we have already found reason to reject.

Perhaps the most disturbing evidence arises from the discussion of the formation of homoeomers at *G&C*. II.7. Aristotle there seems to be open to the view that elements will mix through the mixing or accommodation of the contraries, hot with cold and dry with wet. Thus at 334b17–18, he writes: "it is as a result of the contraries, or the elements, having been mixed that the other things will exist" and later, at 334b24–30 he writes, "but flesh and bones and suchlike come from these <elements>, the hot becoming cold and the cold hot ... Similarly dry and wet and suchlike produce flesh and bone and the rest in the middle range."

But under the present interpretation, this cannot be right. For the result of mixing earth with air will then be a mixture of the form (C + D) (D + W) and the result of mixing fire with water will be a mixture of the form (H + C)(D +W); and so these two forms will be the same. It may not even be correct to regard the intermediate temperature or degree of dryness as *part* of the form of the resulting mixture. For the form in the first case, let us say, will be HD + CW and the linkage of H to D and of C to W will then prevent (H + C) from being a part. It might be supposed that a distributive law holds, with CD + HW = (C + H) (D + W); and this might then be used to justify the claim that (C + H) is a part of CD + HW. But such a law cannot possibly be correct, since it leads to the identification of CD + HW with HD + CW. Thus if the homoeomerous form is composed of intermediates it must be in a sense that is compatible with its not being completely constituted by the intermediates.

Given the weight of the evidence in the other direction, I am inclined to think that what Aristotle allows in this passage is not, by his own lights, strictly speaking correct and that it involves either an oversight or a deliberate oversimplication on his part. He is attempting to explain the formation of the homoeomers. He raises the question in two rather different ways, "how is something to come from both, e.g. from cold and hold or from fire and earth" (334b3), one relating to the formation from the contraries and the other to the formation from the elements. He answers the question in its first form (334b8–17). But in summary of his answer, he takes himself to have answered the question in both forms, "It is as a result of the contraries, or the elements, have being mixed that the other things will exist" (334b17–18). This suggests that the answer he gives for the one case should apply in the other. But the only sensible way in which it can apply is if mixing takes place through the mixing of elemental forms; for to say that it takes place through the mixing of elemental bodies is not to say anything analogous or to explain how mixing is possible.

Now Aristotle may have been prepared to allow that these two answers were compatible. In this case he was guilty of an oversight for the reasons that have already been given. On the other hand, he might have been unwilling to admit that the two answers were compatible. In that case, he was presumably engaged in a deliberate oversimplification. Strictly speaking, mixing results from the mixing of elemental forms but, for purposes of simplicity, it is presented as resulting from the mixing of the contraries.

It is perfectly conceivable, to my mind, that Aristotle took these two approaches to mixing to be compatible and even to be equivalent. This is a natural assumption to make and there is no direct evidence that he was aware of the difficulties to which it gives rise. However, it seems clear that had these difficulties been presented to him, he would have given up the idea that mixing proceeds through the mixing of contraries. For this idea is incidental to the main lines of his thought, and it is only by giving it up that they can be sustained.

If this interpretation of Aristotle is correct, then we should attribute to him a belief in two sorts of 'bond' within a homoeomerous form. On the one hand, there is the bond which holds together complementary contraries within a given elemental form. On the other hand, there is the bond which holds together the elemental forms within a given homoeomerous form. The first bond has been represented, in our notation, by a 'product', the second by a 'sum.'

The two bonds must be taken to be distinct; for otherwise the forms HD + CW and CD + HW will collapse to the same form CDHW. Aristotle perhaps gives implicit recognition to the distinction between the two when he eliminates the pairing of hot with cold or of dry with wet in the combinatorial reckoning of the elements at *G&C.* II.3, 30–35. For given his account of the intermediates, there is a way in which hot can combine with cold; and so the way that a contrary combines with an opposed contrary must be different from the way in which it combines with a complementary contrary.

In any case, the view that the two bonds are distinct is in itself very reasonable. The intra-elemental bond is one of cooperation between two complementary capacities. Indeed, on Aristotle's view, one of the two capacities—the hot or day—will play an active or dominant role in the cooperative endeavor, while the other capacity—the wet or cold—will play a passive or subordinate role (*Meteor.* IV.1, 378b12–13, *G&C.* II.2, 329b24–26).[35] The extra-elemental bond, by contrast, is one of accommodation between two competing capacities. Each destroys the 'excesses' of the other.

It is irresistible, at this point, to think in terms of the analogy with the classical model of a molecule. The contraries correspond to the subatomic particles; an elemental form, such as HD, corresponds to an atom, and the bond between its contraries to the bond between the subatomic particles in an atom; while an homoeomerous form, such as HD + CW, corresponds to a molecule; and the bond between the elemental forms to the bond between the atoms within a molecule. For all his hostility to atomism, Aristotle's own view is not so different, in its general structure, from contemporary atomic theory.[36]

## 19. THE QUANTUM EFFECT

At *G&C.* I.10, 328a26–27, Aristotle remarks that "a drop of wine is not mixed with ten thousand pitchersful of water, for its form dissolves and it changes into the totality of the water." Likewise, at I.5, 322a,32–34, he talks of 'water in increasing quantities continually mixed with wine, which ends up by making it watery, and indeed water;' and, at II.7, 334b21–29, he requires that the contraries should be broadly equal for mixing to occur.

These passages suggest that there is a definite threshold that must be crossed before an elemental body can combine with another body (elemental or not) to form a mixture. The proportion of the one to the other must be sufficiently great.

He takes a similar kind of threshold to exist in the case of motion; for a certain amount of power is required for one thing to move another (*Phys.* VII.5, 250a7–25).[37] But, in contrast to the dynamical case, Aristotle seems to have held a somewhat stronger thesis in the case of mixture. Let us suppose that we add enough wine to water to form the faintest possible mixture of wine and water. And let us now ask what happens when we add a little more wine. Does the faint mixture merely grow? Or do we obtain a slightly less faint mixture? Is there just a single threshold that needs to be crossed to reach a mixture or a series of thresholds?

Aristotle seems to believe in a series. For the discussion at I.10, 328a26–27 is meant to be completely general. The illustration of wine and water is prefaced by the remark: 'But amongst things which are capable of acting and of being affected, those things which can easily be divided when many of them are juxtaposed to few or large ones to small, then indeed they do not give rise to mixing, but to growth on the part of that which is dominant; for the other changes into the dominant one.' Thus it is entirely incidental to the illustration that wine is added to an element, such as water, rather than to another mixture. The passage therefore suggests that there is a general 'discrepancy threshold' that must be crossed before mixing can take place; the successive mixtures must not merely be unlike, they must be *sufficiently* unlike.

We might talk here of a 'quantum effect', since the formation of a mixture will in general require the quantum leap from one homoeomerous state to another. Given that the 'quanta' cannot be indefinitely small, there will only be a finite number of different kinds of homoeomerous form. We will therefore have something closely analogous to the finite partitioning of the sensible qualities in book 6 of *De Sensu* (which is unsurprising given that the sensible are themselves taken to be mixtures).

But how can Aristotle have believed in a threshold, even an initial threshold, in the case of mixture? For suppose that a miniscule amount of wine is added to water. The result, according to him, is water. Suppose now that another miniscule amount of wine is added. The result is again water. By continuing in this way, one may add an enormous amount of wine and still obtain water. But surely this is not something Aristotle could have believed. He must have known that it makes no difference to the result whether the wine is added in one go or a bit at a time. Indeed, his talk at 322a, 32–34 of "water in increasing quantities continually mixed with wine" suggests as much.[38]

In order to overcome the problem, it must be supposed that the water which results from adding wine to water is physically distinguishable from the original water. But how can this be, given that they are both water? The water to which the wine has been added must somehow 'remember' that the wine has been added.[39] But in what can the 'remembering' consist?

The solution to this problem lies, I believe, in Aristotle's distinction between internal and external heat. This is explained at *P.A.* II.2, 648b35–649a9:

In some of the bodies which are called hot the heat is derived from without, while in others it belongs to the bodies themselves; and it makes a most important difference whether the heat has the former or the latter origin. For one of them comes close to being hot accidentally and not in its own right—as if, finding that some man in a fever was a musician, one were to say that musicians are hotter than healthy men. Of that which is hot *per see* and that which is hot *per accidents*, the former is the slower to cool, while not rarely the latter is the hotter to touch.

A similar distinction for wet and dry is drawn at II.3, 649b10–35; and the two distinctions are ones of which Aristotle makes extensive use in his account of physical and biological phenomena (eg. at *P.A.* II.3, *Meteor.* IV.5, *Meteor.* IV.11, and *G&C.* II.2, 330a15–23.)[40]

Consider again the case in which a small amount of wine is added to some water. Then what I would like to suggest is that the contraries which were internal to the wine become external to the water. If, for example, the wine contained some internal heat, heat that was constitutive of its form, then this will become external heat of the water, heat that is no longer constitutive of the form. The water will, in this sense, have become 'ionized.' Thus we need no longer maintain that the water before and after the addition are physically indistinguishable; for although their formal or internal features will be the same, their accidental or external features will differ.[41]

Not only may internal features in this way become external; external features may also become internal. For as wine is added to water, there will come a point when a faint mixture is obtained. At this point, the externalized features of the wine become internal. The pressure on them builds up, as it were, and pushes them inwards. The process of externalization will then resume until the next critical point is reached; and so until ever more heavily ionized forms of wine are obtained.

Such a position is strange; and it is tempting to regard it as some sort of aberration from the main lines of his thought. Would it not have been more natural for Aristotle, and more in line with common observation, to have supposed that the mixtures form a continuous range becoming ever fainter in one direction and ever stronger in the other?

Such a view would perhaps have been preferable had Aristotle's concern been solely with mixing. But he wished to fit mixing into a general account of the different kinds of change; and given his views on growth, it is hard to see how this could be done except in the way that he actually adopts. As already remarked, Aristotle takes growth to be a limiting case of mixing in which the mutual accommodation of form is replaced by the domination of one form by the other. But then what will determine whether the addition of one thing to another will result in growth or mixing? The obvious answer is the one that Aristotle provides: if the one form swamps or dominates the other, there will be growth; and otherwise there will be mixing. Thus it is essentially by postulating a discrepancy threshold that the unity of growth and mixing is achieved.

The existence of quanta has important ramifications for the theory of mixture and change, though it is not clear to what extent Aristotle had thought them through. In the first place, the existence of quanta will imply the existence of discontinuities; for as the wine is added to the water there will be a discontinuous change from one mixture to another. Aristotle seems to believe that changes of this sort should be continuous (*Phys.* VI.6, 237a17–b3, b9–21). But as Sorabji (1976: 80) suggests in an analogous case, it may be the underlying change in the proportions of the ingredients that is meant to be continuous. Thus the underlying changes (the 'endogeneous variables') will be continuous even though the induced changes (the 'exegeneous variables') are not.

In regard to the process of mixing itself, there is the question as to which features can be externally attached to a body and the nature of the attachment. It is clear from what Aristotle says that the contraries can be external. But can the elemental forms also be external (though not, of course, *as* forms)? If not, then it is hard to see how the build-up of contraries, when wine is added to water, would result in the internalization of the homeomerous form of wine rather than of some homoeomerous form whose contrarietal constitution was the same as that of the wine. But if the elemental forms can be external, then they must somehow be disassociated from the internalized forms. Both the external and the internal form will somehow be present in the body and yet because of the weakness of the external attachment they will not 'engage.'[42]

There is also a question as to how the resultant form of mixture should be determined. Consider again the question of what happens when one thing is mixed up with another—some earth, let us say, with some water. Before we could have said that the result would be a mixture whose form was the given ratio of earth to water. But now we must be more careful. Whether the two things can mix will no longer depend upon their purely formal features. For the presence of an external contrary or elemental form may facilitate a mixing that would otherwise not be possible. When one adds the critical drop of wine to the water that turns it into a faint mixture, it is because of the external presence of the form of the wine that had previously been added. If the same drop had been added to untreated water, the result would have been more water.

But even when mixing occurs, the ratio may not be that of the ingredients. For some of the internal features of one of the ingredients may be 'precipitated out.' Suppose one adds a little more wine than is necessary to form a faint mixture of wine and water. Then the ratio of wine to water in the form will be slightly less than the ratio of the wine to water in the ingredients, since the form of some of the wine will acquire a merely external presence.

The formal development of such a view involves some complications. Let us first make the simplifying assumption that the only two elements are earth and water. We use r, $0 \leq r \leq 1$, to represent the fact that the (internal or external) Earth and the (internal or external) Water are in the proportion of r to 1 − r. We now divide the interval [0, 1] into finite number of subintervals or 'bands'; and from within each band we select a 'critical' point. The points corresponds to the permitted internal ratios of Earth to Water; and the band to which a point belongs represents the range within which the overall ratios of Earth or Water may vary while the internal ratio remains the same. It would be a substantive empirical question within Aristotelian science what these bands were like and how they related to their critical points.

Let us suppose that a homoeomer contains a given overall ratio of Earth to Water. There are then two additional hypothesis that should be made. The first is that the internal ratio of the homoeomer is given by the critical point of the band to which the overall ratio belongs; the internal ratio is chosen from the 'neighbourhood' of the overall ratio. The second is that either all of the Earth or all of Water is internalized; as much Earth or Water as possible is used in forming the internal ratio.

Suppose now that we mix together given quantities of earth and water. We can then determine the overall ratio r of Earth to Water in the result. From the first hypothesis, we can determine the internal ratio r* of Earth to Water; and from the second, we can determine the internal and external quantities of Earth and Water. If r = r*, the result is an 'ideal' mixture in which there is no excess of Earth or Water; if r < r*, there is an excess of Water though not of Earth; and if r* < r, there is an excess of Earth though not of Water.

The general theory is complicated by the fact that there are four elements and that the contraries can be externalized independently of a complementary 'mate.' The 'bands' must therefore be three-dimensional; and it must be allowed that water, for example, can contain external coldness that is not matched by any corresponding wetness or dryness. The extension to three dimensions creates no special problems, though the possible existence of unattached contraries gives rise to questions as to how and when they will mate.

## VI. The Dynamics of Mixing

I turn finally to the process of mixing, the process whereby two or more ingredients become a mixture. I first address the general topic of change; I then take up the question of how mixing, as opposed to mixture, is possible; and I finally consider the question of how the ingredients may be tracked in and out of a mixture. The discussion is brief and speculative, being based more on what Aristotle's point of view demands than on direct corroboration from the text.

## 20. CHANGE

Before considering Aristotle's particular vies on mixing, it will be helpful to set them within a more general framework. This framework is presupposed by a great deal of what he says concerning change but is not discussed as such.[43] I feel that, quite apart from its relevance to Aristotle, the framework may have a more general relevance in understanding the concept of change.

Any change involves an initial object or objects (those that change) and some terminal object or objects (those that result from the change). We may say that a change is one–zero, zero–one, one–one, many–one, one–many, or many–many according to whether there is one initial but no terminal object, one terminal but no initial object, one initial and one terminal object, many initial objects and one terminal object, one initial object and many terminal objects, or many initial and many terminal objects.[44] When there is no terminal object, the initial object must turn into nothing, there is destruction *an nihilum*; when there is no initial object, the terminal object must come from nothing, there is creation *ab nihilo*. It is clear from Aristotle's stand against Parmenides that he does not believe in these possibilities, though they may still be allowed as part of the general framework.

A change may be taken to concern any one of its objects, initial or terminal. When the object is initial but not terminal, the change is said to be a *destruction* of the object; and when the object is terminal but not initial, the change is said to be a creation of the subject. Changes of this sort, in which the object is either not terminal or not initial, are called *substantial*[45]. By contrast, a change in which the object is both initial and terminal is said to be *accidental*. A change that has one status with respect to one of its objects may, of course, have a different status with respect to another of its objects.

The simplest kind of accidental change is the one in which there are no other initial or terminal objects. If there are additional initial objects but no additional terminal objects, we have a case of a growth. The additional initial objects accede to the given object. If there are additional terminal but no additional initial objects, we have a case of diminution. The additional terminal objects secede from the given object. And if there are both additional initial and additional terminal objects, then we have a cross between growth and diminution. Of course, these are somewhat technical senses of 'growth' and 'diminution.' An object that grows in this sense may actually become smaller and an object that diminishes may become larger (cf. Aristotle's remarks on nutrition at *G&C.* I.5, 322a20–29).

There is a clear sense in which one change may be reducible to others. The reduction may be either temporal or mereological or a combination of the two. Suppose that a cold metal bar becomes hot over a period of time. Then we may reduce this change to a sequence of two changes in which the bar first goes from being cold to being warm and then goes from being warm to being hot; or we may reduce it to the simultaneous change from cold to hot in the two halves of the bar; or we may reduce it to two sequential changes in each of the two halves (see *Phys.* V. 4).

I doubt that there are any irreducible many–many changes for Aristotle; all are reducible to changes that are not many–many. Suppose that something hot warms something cold. Then we might regard this as the single two–two change in which the hot and cold things become two warm things. But we can also see it as the two one–one changes in which the hot and cold thing each become warm. Likewise, if two things mix and then separate, we might regard this as a single two–two change from the antecedent to the succeedent ingredients. But we can also see it as the sequence of two changes, in which the two things first become one and the one then becomes two.

It is also unclear to me whether Aristotle would admit any irreducible many–one or one–many changes in which the many was more than two. The mixing of three things, for example, might be reduced to a sequence of two mixings in which first two of the things are mixed and the resulting mixture is then mixed with the third. Be that as it may, there will be little difference for the purposes of general theory between polyadic changes in which there are two initial or terminal objects and those in which there are more than two. So no great loss in generality is incurred in confining our attention to the one–one, two–one, and one–two cases.

Moreover, the one–two changes may be regarded as the result of reversing time's arrow in the two–one changes; and so, to the extent that this is possible, we may further limit our attention to the one–one and two–one cases. These are, in fact, the cases to which Aristotle seems to devote most attention; and the previous considerations can be seen as providing some kind of justification for this apparent bias.

Given Aristotle's anti-atomistic stand, it is natural to suppose that changes involving bodies will, like the bodies themselves, be indefinitely divisible—though the divisions in this case can be either temporal or mereological. Consider a two–one change that is from bodies x and y into the body z and that occurs over a certain period of time. Then the change will be reducible to changes over indefinitely small periods of times and to changes involving indefinitely small parts of x, y and z. Thus given any part z' and z, no matter how small, there will be a one–one subchange of a part of x to z', or a one–one subchange of a part of y to z', or a two–one subchange of parts of x and y to z'; and similarly for the cases in which we are given a part of x or a part of y.

Some two–one changes will be reducible in this way entirely to one–one changes. If, for example, one block is placed upon another to produce a 'tower,' then the change may be regarded as a simultaneous change in the location of the two things considered separately. In many cases, the reduction will be much more complicated than this, each of the two things will perhaps fragment into very small pieces; these pieces may come together in various ways, only to be fragmented further; and so on. But the general principle remains the same.

The view that all two–one or one–two changes are reducible to one–one changes is very attractive. It is the denial that two things ever truly become one or that one thing truly becomes two. What *looks* like a case of a genuine fusion turns out on, closer inspection, to be a complex form of intermingling; and what looks like a case of genuine fission turns out to be complex form of disassociation. But attractive as the view may be, it is not Aristotle's. For it leads to aggregative models of growth and mixing and dissolution; and these are models that Aristotle adamantly rejects.

But even when a two–one change is not reducible to one–one changes, it may still be reducible in a significant sense to restricted class of two–one changes or to a combination of such changes and one–one changes. An aggregate of earth and air, for example, may change, with an aggregate of fire and water, into an aggregate of a mixture of earth and fire and a mixture of air and water. This two–one change is therefore reducible to two more basic one–two changes; and presumably most observable two–one changes will be reducible to more basic changes in such a way.

This therefore raises the question of finding a class of basic changes to which all others are reducible.[46] The whole matter calls for a very thorough discussion, but let me merely make some observations that are specially relevant to the case of two–one changes and to mixings in particular.

(1) It is plausible to suppose that the objects involved in any basic change between bodies will be homoeomerous. Indeed, without this assumption, it is hard to see how the static view of bodies as decomposed into homoeomers could be reconciled with a reasonable dynamic view of their formation.

Given this assumption, the basic changes among bodies can be classified according to the type of their homoemerous form. In the one–one case, the change will be accidental when the homoeomerous form of the initial and terminal object are the same and otherwise it will be substantial. In the many–one case, the change will be a growth when the homoeomerous form of the terminal object is the same as that of one of the initial objects and otherwise it will be a mixing. It is these facts that explain the underlying topology of Aristotle's discussion of change among bodies in *Generation and Corruption*.

It should be noted that this classification of mixtures is peculiar to the case of homoemerous bodies. When Socrates drank the hemlock, there was a two–one change from Socrates and the hemlock to Socrates' corpse. The corpse is of a different form than Socrates or the hemlock, but it is not a mixture of Socrates and the hemlock. Two homoeomers, however, can only become a third through mixing.

(2) The basic bodies, the homoeomers, are through and through the same. It seems reasonable to assume that the basic changes are in a similar way through and through the same. Consider, for example, a mixing that changes x and y into z. Then according to this assumption, for any part x′ of x there will be a mixing included in the given mixing which changes x′ and part of y into a part z′ of z; similarly for any part y′ of y or for any part z′ of z, and for the other kinds of change.

Such an assumption seems to be demanded by the divisibility of the homoeomers. For what intelligible conception can we have of change among homoeomers that does not rest upon changes among their parts? And what intelligible conception can we have of a change among the parts that is not at bottom uniform? Thus the hypothesis of uniformity or through-and-through-ness runs very deep. It is not merely the basic bodies that must be through and through the same but also the basic changes that those bodies undergo (cf. *G&C.* I.8, 326b31–34).

(3) Consider a basic change from x and y into z. There should then be no subchange of y into something other than y or from something other than x into x (and similarly for the many–one and the one–one cases). For if there were a subchange from y into something other than y, we could obtain a more basic form of change by 'stopping' the given change at the point at which y changes into something else; and similarly for the other case.

A somewhat stronger assumption, in the case of a basic two–one change, is that its basic subchanges should either be of the same type as the given change or else be accidental changes (principally movements). Thus, in conformity with this assumption, a basic mixing might be taken to consist in the movements of the parts of the bodies to be mixed and the mixings of these parts when they come into contact (and, of course, these component mixings would themselves submit to a similar analysis).

21. THE POSSIBILITY OF MIXING

I want to now to consider the question of how mixing, or irreducible two–one changes in general, might be possible. My emphasis is on the dynamic rather than the static aspect of the question. Thus even if it is granted that there is a possible state of two bodies being through and through mixed, it might be wondered how two bodies, which formerly were separate, could ever get to be in such a state. For one might think that all that they can do is to break up into a finite number of small pieces, join up with other small pieces, break up again, and so on (as in the brick-to-wall model of *G&C.* II.7, 334a26–30). No matter how complex this process might be or how long it might endure, it is hard to see how it could result in anything better than a 'mosaic' of pieces from the different bodies.

We have here the dynamic version of the second puzzle. But Aristotle's response to the puzzle is no clearer as a solution to the dynamic version than it is as a solution to the static version. He says that things mix through interacting with one another. But he cannot simply be claiming that when two mixable items are placed side by side they will mix. For interaction requires contact (*G&C.* I.6, 322b26–323a13); and when two items are placed side by side, they will only have contact at the boundary. It therefore needs to be made clear how the parts of the bodies beyond the boundary are capable of interacting.

Aristotle does consider the general question of how things are capable of affecting one another (*G&C.* I. 7–9) and, in response to the present difficulty, seems to suggest that the affectation of something through and through is made possible by its being divisible through and through. As he writes at I.9, 327a7–14:

> If the extended thing were not everywhere divisible but there were such a thing as an indivisible body or surface, it would not be everywhere capable of being affected, but nor would anything be continuous. If, however, this is false and every body is divisible, it makes no difference whether it is divided into parts which are in contact or is divisible. For if it can be segregated along the lines of contact, as some say, even though it is not yet in a divided state, it will be in a divided state.

But it is unclear *how* the one might render the other possible. How might the bodies divide so as to affect one another through and through?

In considering this question, it is essential to appreciate the metaphysical standpoint from which it is being raised.[47] Suppose that a body B moves from the location P to the location Q during a given time-period T. There are then two ways in which we might imagine giving a more detailed account of what happens. One is in terms of descriptions of the same sort but making ever finer reference to the body, the location, and the time. Thus for any part of the body and subperiod of the time, one would say from and to where the body moved. The other account is in terms of an ontology of material particles, instants of time, and points in space. We would say of each particle of the body where it was at any given instant within the period. Thus the account in terms of motions would be eliminated in favour of an account in terms of exact locations.

Now from one metaphysical standpoint, the description in terms of exact location would be the more basic and the descriptions in terms of motions approximations to it. However, from Aristotle's standpoint, it is the descriptions in terms of motion that are the more basic; the description in terms of location is, at best, a convenient fiction. The former descriptions do indeed provide ever finer approximations. But there is no truth of a fundamentally different sort to which they approximate. There is no more to reality, as it were, than is embodied in the approximations themselves.

This means that if we are to give an adequate description of reality from an Aristotelian standpoint, we need do no more than provide a satisfactory account of these approximations. We do not also need to ask what sort of atomistic reality might lie behind them. Indeed, in certain cases the approximations that we provide might be incompatible with there being a single underlying reality or with there being an underlying reality at all. But from an Aristotelian standpoint, this is no reason for rejecting the successive approximations as an adequate account of how things are.

From this perspective, the requirement that action takes place at a point of contact merely dictates that in each of the approximations it is only bodies that are in contact that can be taken to affect or act on one another. This means that the question as to how the bodies affect one another will never go away; for we can always ask how the interiors of the bodies affect one another, given that only their surfaces are in contact. But although the question can never go away, it can always be answered. We can always provide a more fine-grained account of the action in terms of the division of the bodies into finer and finer parts.

With this in mind, let us now consider how mixing might take place. One possible account that might be provided on Aristotle's behalf is that the bodies mix through a form of interpenetration. Suppose, for simplicity, that the one body is hot and the other cold; and imagine that each body is a unit cube. One cube is placed on top of the other and they then mix. It will *look* as if the body on top is being pushed through the body underneath and as if the common part of each thereby changes from being hot or cold to being warm. But we will wish to model the process in terms of the confluence of the Hot and the Cold.

Using an obvious notation, we may model the basic act of mixing by means of the following diagram:

$$
\begin{matrix}
C \\
H
\end{matrix}
\quad \rightarrow \quad
CH
$$

A more fine-grained description is then given by the following sequence of actions:

$$
\begin{matrix}
C_1 \\
C_2 \\
H_1 \\
H_2
\end{matrix}
\quad \rightarrow \quad
\begin{matrix}
C_1 \\
C_2H_1 \\
H_2
\end{matrix}
\quad \rightarrow \quad
\begin{matrix}
C_1H_1 \\
C_2H_2
\end{matrix}
$$

Similarly, one of the actions at the next level of description will be given by:

$$
\begin{matrix}
C_{11} \\
C_{12} \\
C_{21}H_{11} \\
C_{22}H_{12} \\
H_{12} \\
H_{11}
\end{matrix}
\quad \rightarrow \quad
\begin{matrix}
C_{11} \\
C_{12}H_{11} \\
C_{21}H_{12} \\
C_{22}H_{12} \\
H_{11}
\end{matrix}
$$

Continuing in this way, as fine-grained a description as one might wish can be given of the underlying mechanism, appealing at each stage only to action at the point of contact. Of course, in the case as described, the volume of the mixture would be the same as each of the ingredients. But if we imagined that the cubes expanded as they coalesced, we could obtain a model in which the volume of the mixture was the combined volume of the two ingredients.

There are, however, at least two reasons why Aristotle might wish to reject this model, simple and elegant as it is. The first is that it requires that the ingredients from within a mixture be capable of mixing with items outside the mixture. Consider the middle portion $C_2H_1$ in the second diagram above. The latent Cold $C_2$ combines with the patent Hot $H_2$ below to form the lower Warmth $C_2H_2$, while the latent Hot $H_1$ combines with the patent Cold $C_1$ above to form the Warmth $C_1H_1$. Similarly, when two mixtures are in contact, as with $C_{22}H_{12}$ and $C_{21}H_{11}$ in the third diagram, the latent Hot from the one below will combine with the latent Cold from the one above. However, there is no evidence, as far as I know, that Aristotle would have accepted such possibilities. Indeed, his strictures against like mixing with like seem to rule out the possibility of an exchange of ingredients between two mixtures of the same type.

A related difficulty concerns the instability of the mixture as it is being formed. One naturally supposes that the mixture that results from a given process of mixing is gradually formed; first one part of the resulting mixture is formed, then another part, and so on until each part of the ingredients has been mixed. But this is not true under the model proposed above. For while the process is going on, the Hot and Cold in any part of the mixture will detach themselves by rising or falling and hence no part of the mixture will remain numerically the same from one moment to the next. It is only when there is no further unattached Hot or Cold that the process will come to an end; and the mixture that then results will be disjoint from any of the mixtures that will previously have been formed.

There is, however, another type of model which is better suited to Aristotle's purposes. Instead of imaging that the hot drifts up and the cold drifts down, we now imagine that, as the warm mixture is formed. It is pushed to one side and then rises to the top. The underlying mechanism may be depicted as follows:

$$
\begin{array}{c}
C_1 \\
C_2 \\
H_1 \\
H_2
\end{array}
\quad \rightarrow \quad
\begin{array}{c}
C_1 \\
C_2H_1 \\
H_2
\end{array}
\quad \rightarrow \quad
\begin{array}{c}
C_2H_1 \\
C_1 \\
H_2
\end{array}
$$

Of course, various details need to be spelled out: how much of the Cold combines with how much of the Hot in a given period; how does the mixture move once it is formed; and how are its movements synchronized with the mixing? But the general principles should be clear.

This model involves a more complicated kinetics than the first, but it avoids the difficulties over latency and instability; there is no 'interpenetration,' or 'movement' of one thing through another. It is therefore clear that a satisfactory solution to the dynamical puzzle is at least available to Aristotle, even if it not clear exactly what form it would take.

## 22. TRACKING

I want finally to consider the question of recoverability and the related question of derivability. Can Aristotle maintain, as is required by a full solution to the exegetical problems, that the ingredients from which a mixture is formed are the same as those from which it is currently composed and also the same as those into which it separates?

This issue raises the general problem of identity over time: when is a thing at a given location at one time also at a given location at another time? A plausible answer (with some support from the text) is in terms of continuity: the thing will be at the second location at the other time if its form traces out a continuous path that begins with the one location and terminates in the other. It might also be maintained, though with somewhat less plausibility and support from the text,[48] that continuity under a form is a *necessary* condition for the thing to be at a given location at the other time.

In applying this criterion to the questions of recoverability and derivability, we need to ask whether the form of an antecedent ingredient can be traced forward and whether the form of a succeedent ingredient can be traced back to the location of the mixture. But even if we ignore the general problems that might arise in applying the criterion, there are some special problems that arise from applying it in the present case.

One problem is to understand how it could ever be possible to track homoeomerous bodies with disjoint locations at an initial time to the same location at a later time. Given that two bodies cannot be at the same location at the same time, the two disjoint bodies must surely remain disjoint. But it has to be remembered that as one tracks the bodies, they may not remain actual; and there is then no bar to their becoming coincident. Moreover, the dynamic models described above provide a more or less concrete picture of how the bodies might become coincident.

Another problem is to understand how a body (an ingredient) could be tracked to the location of a body (the mixture) with a different nature. For given that the form is no longer present at the location of the mixture, we do not even have a putative application of the criterion. So if the body is still to be tracked, it must be under the aegis of a different form. But how can this be? For even if we do not require continuity under a form, we should surely still require the stability of the form.

However, this is not how Aristotle conceives the situation. For him, the object is not simply warm or intermediate in nature between earth and air; it is, in a certain sense, both hot and cold, both earthen and airy. The way the ingredient is hot or earthen, is of course, quite different from the way the mixture is hot or earthen; the contrary or form has an unqualified presence in the ingredients, whereas it has a qualified presence in the mixture. But this difference in the manner of presence should make no difference to the possibility or legitimacy of tracking the body by means of its form. We should imagine an observer who is blind to the presence of cold or of air. All she sees, when she looks at the mixture, is something hot or something earthen (though something that may be more or less densely hot or earthen). For her, the difficulty that we have been envisaging would simply not arise.

This picture, however, cannot be extended across the board. For in case the antecedent ingredients are mixtures with a common element, their forms will not even enjoy a qualified presence within the resulting mixture. Suppose, for example, that a unit of equal proportions of earth and air is mixed with a unit mixture of equal proportions of air and fire. Then, as we have argued in Section IV.15, there is no sense to be given to the claim that the form of either the ingredients is present in the resulting mixture. In such cases, therefore, Aristotle must give up the idea that the ingredients can be tracked through to the mixture or he must resort to the questionable idea that the object might be tracked under a variation in form.

A further problem concerns prime matter. What happens to the prime matter of the ingredients as they enter into the mixture? We have already argued (Section III.8) that the prime matter of the ingredients, once they have entered the mixture, must be the same and that there are only two reasonable views on its relationship to the original prime matter: either the Haecceitist option, under which it is wholly distinct from the original prime matter; or the anti-Haecceitist option, under which the question of its identity to the original prime matter does not properly arise. In neither case can it be maintained that the prime matter remains the same during the process of mixing.

We might note that a similar consequence holds in the case of growth. For suppose that one homoeomerous body grows by means of another. Then what happens to the prime matter of the grower and the growee? Again, the only reasonable view is that it does not remain the same. One might think that, in this case, one could take the prime matter of the grower to remain the same while the prime matter of the growee becomes something different. The prime matter of the one will grow, as it were, by means of the prime matter of the other. But there is, in fact, no good reason to prefer the grower to the growee in this regard. For there is an equally strong presumption in favour of the prime matter of the growee enduring across a substantial change as there is in favor of the prime matter of the grower enduring through an accidental change.

These results might be thought to be odd, at least if regarded from an Haecceitist perspective. For how can the matter of some stuff—of some water or some earth, let us say—fail to remain the same? But the oddity here has more to do with the Aristotelian conception of a homoeomerous body than with the tracking criterion. We naturally think of material bodies as being materially rigid. But that is because we think of the bodies as being identical to their matter. There is therefore no possibility of independent variation in the matter. For Aristotle, though, the homoeomerous bodies are hylomorphic entities, consisting both of matter and form. They can be tracked across time by means of their form; and so this leaves open the possibility, in principle, that the matter might vary while the thing itself remains the same.

However, the way such a possibility might be realized is very different in the case of homoeomers than in the case of anhomoeomers. For the (non-prime) matter of anhomoeomers can be identified in terms of its own inherent form; and a change in the matter can therefore be identified in terms of a change in the form. But the matter of a homoeomer is exclusively prime and hence lacking in inherent form. Some other way of accounting for its identity over time must therefore be found.

The obvious way is in terms of the things of which it is the matter. Any prime matter is the proximate matter of some thing (or divides into the proximate matter of various things). The prime matter may therefore be tracked in terms of the thing or things of which it is the prime matter.

Since the things are tracked in terms of form, the prime matter may also be tracked, more directly, in terms of form. But this form is not the inherent form of the prime matter, since it does not have any, but its supervening form, i.e. the form of the things of which it is the proximate matter. In contrast to particular 'things,' the tracking is in terms of supervenient rather than inherent form.

But how is the tracking in terms of the supervening forms or things to be achieved? If all change were one–one or reducible to one–one change, the tracking could be done in the obvious way. For we could take prime matter to be what endures through all change, accidental or substantial; it would endure through any change in which the thing remained the same and through any change from one thing to another. The first kind of change corresponds to the continuation of a form, the second to its displacement. Thus an alternative formulation of the criterion, in terms of form, is that the prime matter should be taken to be the same through the continuation and displacement of form.

Since homoeomers have only prime matter, the criterion will imply their material rigidity.Thus despite the possibility in principle of material variation, the peculiarities in the criterion of identity for prime matter and in the hylomorphic structure of homoeomers will ensure that the possibility is never realized.

The situation is very different if there are many–one or one–many or many–many changes that are not reducible to one–one changes. For when applied in the obvious way to such a change, the criterion will lead to the intolerable conclusion that there are two or more distinct parcels of prime matter at the very same location. The criterion must therefore somehow be modified.

The obvious and, in a way, minimal modification is to confine the application of the original criterion to the case of one–one changes. In the case of an irreducible many–one change, the prime matter of the things that fuse cannot be taken to continue beyond the point of fusion; and in the case of an irreducible one–many change, the prime matter of the thing that divides cannot be taken to continue beyond the point of fission. Any encroachment on the career of a thing will be taken to bring the career of its prime matter to an end.

The modified criterion may also be stated in terms of form. For there are four kinds of irreducible many–many change for Aristotle: mixing, growth, separation, and diminution. Each kind of change corresponds to its own distinctive kind of transaction among the forms. Thus mixture corresponds to the case in which two forms accommodate themselves to one another, and growth to the case in which one form dominates another. We must then insist that the criterion apply exclusively to the continuation and displacement of form, properly so-called, and not to any of the other kinds of transaction.

The modified criterion, as stated in terms of things, is not 'local' in character. For one cannot tell, simply by tracking a thing, whether or not there has been an encroachment on its career. It is possible, however, that when stated in terms of form, the criterion will have a local character. For there may be a 'internal' mark of the difference between the accommodation of a form and its displacement or the continuation of a form and its domination, and similarly for the other cases. The relevant notions of continuation and displacement can then be understood in terms of the presence of this internal mark rather than in terms of the absence of a countervailing change.

The upshot of our discussion is that it is in cases of irreducibly many–one and one–many changes, and only in these cases, that Aristotle is required to maintain that the prime matter of a homoeomer will not remain the same. I have argued for this conclusion basically in terms of what his position demands. How it might be reconciled with the traditional account of prime matter as the substratum of all change is not something that I shall consider. But it is worth noting that the interpretation receives support from the discussion of growth at *G&C*. I.5. He is there discussing the question of how growth is possible and seems to be adamant in his opposition to the view that the matter of the thing that grows might also grow. Thus at *G&C*. I.5, 321b21–2, he asserts that "The thesis that every single part grows and that in growth something accedes to the growing object is a possible one in terms of the form, but in terms of the matter it is not;' and later, at 321b33–4, he maintains: "So there is way in which every part of the flesh grows and a way in which it does not; for there is an accession to every part in terms of form, but not in terms of matter." I am even inclined to interpret the passage at 321b23–27 in this way. He there writes:

> We should think of it as though someone were measuring out water in the same measure: that which comes to be is all the time different. This is how the matter of flesh grows: an addition is not made to each and every part, but some flows away and some comes in new.

One might think that he is here envisaging a many–many process in which there is both accession and secession. But it is odd that in trying to explain growth he should bring in the complication of a parallel process of secession. The matter "flows away," I suggest, in the sense of being supplanted. Where the old matter was there is new matter; but there is nowhere the old matter goes.

The final problem is the analogue for things of the previous problem concerning prime matter. Let us suppose, pace Aristotle, that two bodies of water could mix. Then both bodies could be tracked to the total location of the composite. The tracking criterion would therefore demand that two bodies of water be at that location. But common sense and Aristotelian metaphysics demands that there be only one; no sense can be given, either intuitively or within Aristotelian metaphysics, to the claim that there are two or more bodies of water throughout a given location.

Indeed, what goes for the original water also goes for its parts. For if one part had a location within the composite water then every part should have a location within the composite, and so we would again be stuck with the intolerable conclusion that the two original bodies of water had the same location within the composite. Since no part of the original water can be part of the composite without being located within the composite, it follows that the composite must be totally new, having no part in common with any of the original water.

Aristotle rejected the possibility that water could mix with water on the grounds that like cannot affect like. But it is interesting to note that even if he had allowed like to affect like, he still should not have allowed water to mix with water; for no part of the original water could sensibly be taken to be present within the composite water. What *might* have been regarded as a case of water mixing with water should have been taken to be a case of the waters combining to produce a completely new body of water, in exact analogy to the previous case of prime matter.

The present case is not a difficulty for Aristotle, since he does not believe it to be possible. But there is a closely related case that is a difficulty. For even though water cannot mix with water, it can still mix with a mixture that contains water. But the water that is mixed and the water that is in the mixture to be mixed can then both be tracked to the location of the resulting mixture. Thus the tracking criterion will again require that the two waters should occupy the same location within the mixture.

A similar possibility arises from separation. Suppose part of the water is extracted from a mixture, not totally from some part but partly from the total. From each part of the mixture some water is 'squeezed out' and some left in. Again, the tracking criterion—now applied backwards—will require that the extracted water and the remaining water should occupy the same location in the mixture from which both have been derived.

The tracking criterion will therefore break down in these cases and for much the same reasons as before. But the cases will also suffer from further difficulties over identity. Not only will it be impossible to maintain that any part of the succeedent or antecedent water is the same as any part of the concurrent water, it will also be impossible to maintain, in such cases, that any part of the antecedent water is the same as any part of the succeedent water. Suppose, for example, that some water is mixed with some earth and that half the quantity of water that has been added is then extracted from throughout the resulting mixture. Then it makes no sense to say that the extracted half is the same as any given half of the original water; for nothing could count as extracting one half of the original water as opposed to any other half.

Such a view might be thought odd. It is conceded that if all of the water is extracted in one go, then there is no difficulty in supposing that the antecedent, the concurrent and the succeedent water are all the same. But then what is the difficulty in supposing that the original water is extracted in two stages, by first extracting one half and then the other?

One naturally, but illicitly, assumes in these cases that the original materials are being reassembled. But this conception already presupposes that some of the original material has been extracted;, and, as we have seen, there is no reasonable basis upon which it can be maintained that the material extracted is one part of the original material as opposed to any other part. Once even the smallest amount of water has been extracted from throughout the given mixture (but leaving some left throughout), the whole of the original water will have been destroyed. Thus the idea that the tracking of a body might be interrupted by the formation of a mixture should be given up; one can only track a body in and out of a mixture by tracking it *through* the mixture.

If the above considerations are correct, they will prevent Aristotle from maintaining the tracking criterion in its unqualified form. But, more significantly, they will require him to give up the general doctrine that the ingredients from which a mixture derives or into which it separates are always present in the mixture. The doctrine can be maintained for the elemental ingredients, and even for some homoeomerous ingredients, but not for ingredients with a common element. The process of mixing will indeed result in a mixture in these cases, but of its concurrent, not of its antecedent or succeedent, ingredients. This is perhaps a small concession to the skeptic, but it is one that Aristotle is obliged to make.[49]

# NOTES

[1] I have taken some liberties in formulating the puzzles but in such a way, I hope, as to preserve their point. In stating the first puzzle, Aristotle deals with the possible states of both ingredients; but it suffices for the purpose of his argument to deal with the possible states of either one of the ingredients. In stating the second puzzle, Aristotle also objects to the first model on the grounds that mixing would then be 'relative to perception'. I suspect, however, that the reference to perception is incidental to his point. What he is here endorsing is a form of 'anti-sizism', whereby something's being a case of mixing or of mixture should be indifferent to considerations of size (a similar anti-sizist sentiment, relating to divisibility, is expressed at G&C. I.8, 326a25–29).

The translations are loosely based on those in Williams (1982) and Barnes (1984), the deviations being uncontroversial, I think. I am very grateful to Gavin Lawrence for assistance with the Greek texts.

[2] There are other difficulties in giving a rigorous account of Aristotle's idea that the parts of a mixture should be alike. For it is not completely clear what is meant either by 'part' or by 'alike.' These difficulties are by no means trivial. However, for present purposes, we may ignore them and work with a more intuitive notion of uniformity.

[3] The reasoning rests upon certain assumptions, such as that any part of the location of an object is the location of part of the object, that I have not bothered to spell out. It is in fact possible to develop a formal framework within which this argument and many other considerations of this paper can be made more precise and systematic. But this is not something I shall do here.

[4] See the 'Theorem' on p. 450. His formulation of the theorem presupposes that mixtures are mereological sums. But by following the proof mentioned above in footnote 3, we can dispense with this assumption, and also with assumption that space possess a Euclidean metric.

[5] P. 450. He also cites G&C. I.5, 320b8–13 as positive evidence that Aristotle would endorse compresence. But Aristotle is here distancing himself from the conclusion that infinitely many matters might be compresent, not embracing it.

[6] Thus Sharvy's example of the stuff in my pocket being homeomerous (pp. 443–4) would give Aristotle no difficulty, though there are some other difficulties in providing a correct formal definition of homoeomer that are not so easily remedied.

[7] The interpretation is somewhat similar to the one proposed by Joachim (1992): 179–80.

[8] Some other complications should be noted. (1) If air (which is hot and wet) is mixed with fire (which is hot and dry), then the result will presumably be maximally hot. Thus the potential presence of the element does not require the non-maximal presence of both of its contraries. (2) When one of the ingredients is itself a mixture, one of the intermediate abilities of the ingredient should be present to a different degree (rather than simply to a non-maximal degree) in a resulting mixture. (3) We should provide a general account of when one thing x is present by ability in another y. This requires that we specify an appropriate range of abilities for x. These presumably should be taken to be its *characteristic* abilities, those that are constitutive of the kind of thing it is.

Taking all these complications into account, the general account of the presence by ability of one thing in another should perhaps be that all of the characteristic abilities of the one are present to no greater degree in the other and some are present to a lesser degree.

[9] I think that the parenthetical remark is meant to suggest that some nonessential properties *may* survive, not that their survival is *necessary* for the potential survival of the matter. Earlier she writes, "the preexisting matter is preserved in the product in the sense

that many of the properties that identified the preexisting material as a definite stuff survive in the product" (p. 157). This suggests that only some of the essential properties of the preexisting matter need survive. But I suspect that she really has the stronger requirement in mind.

[10] This seems to be Bogen's own understanding as expressed in footnote 22 of his paper.

[11] I would be tempted to subject Gill's solution of the Parmenidean problem of why change is not sheer replacement to a similar criticism. For again, at the fundamental level of description, all we have on her account is a certain resemblance between a given object and the object it becomes.

[12] This issue was a focus of debate in medieval times: see Maier (1982): 142, who writes, "The real question, which sums up the whole problem, is whether the elemental forms are preserved in the *mixtum* and, if so, how. It is thus understandable that this question, posed in the form *utrum substantiales elementorum maneant in mixto*, became one of the most discussed topics of fourteenth-century natural philosophy." I have not attempted to relate my own discussion of this question to the medieval discussion, despite many points of contact.

[13] If compounding is the only method of composition for Aristotle, then the basic items may be taken to be basic in the strict sense of not being further decomposable. But if summing is also allowed, then it might be maintained that each basic item is a homoeomer that admits of arbitrary decomposition through summation into parts of the same kind. However, such a decomposition should not be treated as 'significant', i.e., as resulting in something more basic.

There are many other issues that should be considered in developing a systematic account of the structure of Aristotle's ontology. A small start is made in Fine (1992); the distinction between a strict and weak form of decomposition is developed in Fine (1995a); and the general study of constructional ontologies is pursued in Fine (1991).

[14] Which is not to say that he would countenance every such sum. The proposition can in fact be derived from the weaker assumption that any object must contain an object from one of the three categories along with assumptions of a more general nature.

[15] We shall later need to distinguish between hotness as a formal and as an accidental feature of a body. Here it is only the formal feature that is in question.

[16] In particular, I remain neutral on how the hylomorphic puzzles presented in Fine (1994b) are to solved.

[17] Thinking of the components of the vectors as coordinates in two-dimensional space, we obtain an elemental "square." It is amusing to note that the square of opposition in syllogistic logic can be regarded in a similar way. Corresponding to the two pairs of contraries are the two pairs of contrasts: particular/universal; affirmative/negative. The propositional forms (A, E, I, and O) then correspond to the elemental forms. There are, in general, strong bipolar tendencies in Aristotle's thought.

[18] Aristotle, in *Met.* I.9, 991b14–20, is perhaps getting at a related point.

[19] In presenting these and other examples, I have often supposed that a mixture may be of some of the elements, and not of the others. But this is for purposes of simplicity only. Nothing of significance would be lost if we went along with Aristotle's contention that "All of the mixed bodies, which are around the place of the middle body [the Earth], are composed of all the simple bodies" (*G&C.* II. 334b31).

[20] Peck (1961: 30–1, 106) takes *dynameis* here to be the pre-Aristotelian technical term for the elements. But the reference seems clearly to be to Aristotle's own theory of the primary contraries; and this makes better sense both of the reference to his own previous work and of his claim that the other differences and properties are dependent upon them.

[21] Where the English has 'composed out of', the Greek has '*ek*'. This is the only interpretation of '*ek*' that the rest of the passsage will bear and its correctness is confirmed by his later referring to intermediates at 1057b27–28 as compounds (*syntheton*). The doctrine is also stated at *Phys.* I.5l, 188b21–26).

[22] I use the term 'combination' in preference to 'compound' to avoid confusion with hylomorphic compounding.

[23] The Greek text has the simple juxtapositions "hot cold" and "cold hot". Williams (1982) adds the qualification "as it were" and, in a similar spirit, Joachim (1922) translates the juxtapositions as 'a hot which (for a hot) is cold and cold which (for a cold) is hot.' But if I am correct in my interpretation, these attempts to tone down the contrast are misguided. I might also note that a literal rendering of the clause preceding the cited passage is "there is more and less hot and cold" (rather than Williams' "things can be more or less hot and cold")—again, in line with the proposed quantitative interpretation.

[24] For this reason, I find it hard to believe that the reference at De Sens. 3, 440b3–4, to "the work on mixture, where we dealt with this subject universally concerning everything" (or, later at 440b14, to "our work on mixture" in which it is explained "how such a mixture is possible") is to the extant version of Generation and Corruption.

[25] I adopt the usual rules for the addition and scalar multiplication of vectors. Thus $<r_1, \ldots, r_n> + <s_1, \ldots, s_n> = <r_1 + s_1, \ldots, r_n + s_n>$ and $k. <r_1, \ldots, r_n> = <k.r_1, \ldots, k.r_n>$.

[26] Alternatively, if we were prepared to countenance the aggregate of bodies that had only a potential existence, we could state the rules entirely for aggregates and then have a rule for transferring the measure of a magnitude from an aggregate to the corresponding mixture.

[27] It may be practically impossible to extract the elements in a pure form (G&C. II.8). To the extent that the extracted elements are impure, the measure will be approximate. However, the quantity of the pure quantity might still be operationally defined, in this case, as the limit of the successive approximations.

[28] Sorabji (1972) has suggested that in some of these passages Aristotle has in mind the distinction between complicated and uncomplicated ratios. But even if this is so, a strict form of coordination will still be required.

[29] Even without coordination, the permissible variation in the measure of the powers will be constrained. Suppose that p is the measure of thermal power. Then any other permissible measure must be of the form $p/(p + k(1-p))$ for some positive constant k.

[30] From a more purely formal point of view, we suppose either that the operation of compounding is multi-valued or that there are different ways of compounding the same qualities or forms, each corresponding to a given proportion of each component.

[31] It is not clear to me, though, that anything that might be taken to be a part in this way should be taken to be a part.

[32] Gill (1989): 166–7, and Freudenthal (1995): 1.1.2, have both argued for the inherent instability of substances, though Bogen (1995): vii, has cast doubt on some of the textual evidence. Gill also attributes this instability to the elemental matter.
How exactly the details of such a position are to worked out is far from clear. Is the tendency towards actualization to be subsumed under a more general tendency, such as the tendency of an element to find its natural place? And how do such tendencies in the different elements combine?

[33] Met. VII. 16, 1040b7–9 is puzzling in this regard: "for none of them [earth, fire and air included] is one, but they are like a heap, until they are worked up, and some kind of unity comes to be out of them." But perhaps his point is not that these things literally are heaps but their lack of unity in comparison with whole living things make them somewhat akin to heaps.

[34] Though it should be pointed out that, at G&C II.3, 331a1–3, he adopts a stricter conception of contrary and only allows water to be contrary to fire and earth to air.

[35] The passive and active roles of the primary contraries are emphasized by E. Lewis (1995) in his introduction to his translation of Alexander's commentary on Meteor. IV. It might even be suggested that the bond between complementary contraries within an elemental form is essentially the same as the bond between form and matter within a substance, with the active contrary playing the role of form and the passive contrary the role of matter. Thus just as an ordinary substance is the hylomorphic compound F(m) of a form F with some matter m, an elemental form is itself a hylomorphic compound A(P)

of an active contrary A (hot or cold) with a passive contrary (Wet or Dry). On such a view, it is not only the proximate matter of a substance that may admit of further hylomorphic analysis, but also the proximate form.

[36] The problem of underdetermination is also discussed in Bogen (1995). However, he differs from me in thinking that "indeterminacy is the price Aristotle must pay for treating chemical compounds as perfectly homogeneous stuffs rather than aggregates" (section ix).

[37] This and related passages are discussed by Hussey 1991: 219–20.

[38] Moreover, as *Phys.* IV.6, 213b5–12 makes clear, he was familiar with slippery slope arguments of this sort.

[39] This way of putting the point was suggested by Yiannis Moschovakis.

[40] See Lewis (1994): 262–5, for further discussion of this distinction and Freudenthal (1995) for an extended discussion of the role of heat in Aristotle's account of the material world.

[41] Curiously, the process of externalization I here posit to explain mixture manqué is the very process to which Gill (1989) appeals in explaining the survival of matter in substantial change.

[42] In the obscure passage on the pipe (*G&C.* I.5, 322a29–35), Aristotle suggests that when wine has been swamped with so much water as to result in water, "the form (of what I take to be the wine) will nevertheless persist." Perhaps what he has in mind is that it will still be present externally as an accident rather that internally as a form. He may have something similar in mind in the case of tin and bronze (I.10, 328b6–14); the tin merely leaves its mark without itself being mixed.

[43] A detailed account of Aristotle's views on change is given in chapter III of Waterlow (1982).

[44] There is an obvious resemblance here to the sequent calculus of Gentzen. The resemblance is more than suggestive.

[45] This is a broad and somewhat non-standard notion of substantial change that includes the cases of both growth and mixing. Growth is not substantial through and through, though, since it involves an accidental change in the object that grows; and mixing is not substantial through and through since it involves an accidental change in the ingredients (or their elemental components). Thus both involve a coincident subchange that is at the same hylomorphic level as the original change but yet not substantial.

[46] A similar issue arises in the context of Husserl's theory of dependent part (see Fine (1956): section V).

[47] See White (1992) for a general discussion of Aristotle's views on the metaphysics of the continuum.

[48] It is perhaps the felt need for continuity that leads Aristotle to refrain from saying that, in an elemental transformation from fire and back to fire, the two fires are numerically the same (*G&C.* II.11, 338a16–17).

[49] The present paper was written while I was a visiting fellow at All Souls College, Oxford. It is very loosely based upon a transcript of a talk that I gave at a conference on Aristotle's conception of matter held at USC in December of 1993. The talk was also presented at the British Association for the Philosophy of Science meeting at LSE in December of 1994, at a Philosophy of Science Workshop at LSE in January of 1995, at a colloquium at UCLA in April of 1995, and at a discussion group at Oxford in May of 1995. I should like to thank All Souls for its support and the participants at the various talks for their comments. I am especially grateful to Rob Bolton, James Bogen, Nancy Cartwright, John Carriero, David Charles, Alan Code, Mary Louise Gill, Richard Jennings, Eric Lewis, Frank Lewis, and Richard Sorabjei.

## REFERENCES

Armstrong, D. 1969. "Dispositions and Causes", *Analysis* 30, 23–6
Barnes, J. 1985. *The Complete Works of Aristotle.* New Jersey. Princeton.

182       KIT FINE

Bogaard, P.A. 1979. "Heaps or Wholes", 19–21, *Isis* 70: 11–29.
Bogen, J. 1992. "Change and Contrariety in Aristotle", *Nous* XXXVII, No. 1.
Bogen, J. "Fire in the Belly: Aristotelian Elements, Organisms, and Chemical Compounds", this volume.
Cartwright, N. 1989. *Nature's Capacities and Their Measurement*. Oxford: Clarendon Press.
Charles, D. 1994. *Unity, Identity and Explanation in Aristotle's Metaphysics* (ed. with M. L. Gill and T. Scaltsas). Oxford: Clarendon Press.
Clark, S. R. L. 1975, *Aristotle's Man*. Oxford: Clarendon Press.
Fine, K. 1991. "The Study of Ontology," *Nous* 25, 263–94.
Fine, K. 1992 "Aristotle on Matter", *Mind*, 101, 401, 35–57.
Fine, K. 1994a. "Compounds and Aggregates", *Nous*, 28(2), 137–58.
Fine, K. 1994b. "A Puzzle Concerning Matter and Form". in Charles (1994) pp. 13–40.
Fine, K. 1995. "Ontological Dependence", *Proceedings of the Aristotelian Society*, 269–90
Fine, K. 1995b. "Husserl on Part-Whole." In *The Cambridge Compansion to Husserl* (ed. B Smith), Cambridge: Cambridge University Press, Cambridge.
Freudenthal, G. 1995. *Aristotle's Science of Matter: Heat and Pneuma in the Account of Substance, Form, and Soul* Oxford: Clarendon Press.
Gill, M. 1989. *Aristotle on Substance: The Paradox of Unity*. New Jersy: Princeton University Press.
Joachim, H.H. 1992. *Aristotle on Coming-to-be and Passing-away*. Oxford: Clarendon Press.
Joachim, H.H. 1904 "Aristotle's Conception of Chemical Combination," *Journal of Philology*, 29, 179–81
Hussey, E. 1991. *Aristotle's Mathematical Physics: A Reconstruction*" In Judson (1991)
Judson, L. (ed.) *Aristotle's Physis: A Collection of Essays*. Oxford: Clarendon Press.
Lewis, E. 1995. Translation of and Introduction to Alexander of Aphrodisias's Commentary on Meteor. IV. (forthcoming).
Lewis, F. 1991. *Substance and Predication*. Cambridge: Cambridge University Press.
Lewis, F. 1994. "Aristotle on the Relation Between a Thing and Its Matter", In Charles (1994).
Peck, A. L. 1961. *Parts of Animals*, translation and commentary, Cambridge: Harvard.
Maier, A. 1982. *On the Threshold of Exact Science*. Philadelphia: University of Pennsylvania Press.
Mourelatos, A. 1984. "Aristotle's Rationalist Account of Qualitative Interaction", *Phronesis*, 1–16.
Sharvy, R. 1983. "Aristotle on Mixtures", *Journal of Philosophy*, LXXX, no. 8, 139–457.
Sorabji, R. 1972. "Aristotle, Mathematics and Colour", *Classical Quarterly* 22, 293–308.
Sorabji, R. 1976, "Aristotle On the Instant of Change," *Proceedings of the Aristotelian Society*, sup. vol. 50, 69–89.
Sorabji, R. 1988. *Matter, Space, and Motion: Theories in Antiquity and Their Sequel*, London.
Waterlow, S. 1982. *Nature, Change and Agency in Aristotle's Physics*. Oxford: Clarendon Press.
White, M. J. 1992. *The Continuous and the Discrete: Ancient Physical Theories from a Contemporary Perspective*. Oxford: Clarendon Press.
Williams, G.F.G. 1982. *Aristotle's 'De Generations et Corruptione'*. Oxford: Clarendon Press.

# FIRE IN THE BELLY: ARISTOTELIAN ELEMENTS, ORGANISMS, AND CHEMICAL COMPOUNDS

BY

JAMES BOGEN

## I. Some Levels of Hylomorphic Analysis

It is a commonplace that Aristotle believes living organisms are subject to hylomorphic analysis into various levels of form and matter. Thus Thelonius' highest level matter is body, and his highest level form is soul. His body can be analyzed into lower level matter (limbs and organs) and a lower level form. The non-uniform parts which are matter on the second level can themselves be analyzed into third level matter and form. Their matter is flesh and the other uniform parts.

At the lowest level of analysis, 4, the matter consists of the primary elements, Earth, Air, Fire and Water, and the form is a ratio of some sort. I do not know whether Aristotle thought the elements were the matter of the uniform parts, or of intermediate stuffs which are themselves their matter. For simplicity, assume the former.

The matter at each of the first three levels is a *concurrent constituent* of Thelonius by which I mean these matters are present in Thelonius while he is alive.[1] In addition to being concurrent constituents, the matters on the first three levels are actually present in Thelonius, and the duration of their actual existence is exactly—or in the case of level 3 almost exactly—the same as the duration of Thelonius' actual existence. Thelonius comes to be as his body and its parts come to be. When he perishes, his body and its non-uniform parts perish too. Despite its resemblance to a living body, Aristotle thinks the body of even the most

183

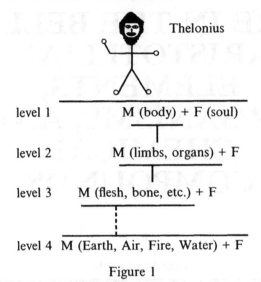

Figure 1

recently deceased organism is a body in name only. Despite their resemblance to the non uniform parts of a living organism, the non-uniform parts of a corpse are fingers, eyes, etc. in name only (*Met.* Theta, 10, 1035b/22ff, *Meteor.* IV, 12.389b/30ff, *G.A.* II, 1, 734b/25ff). Flesh, bone and the other uniform parts which constitute the matter of level 3 are actually present in Thelonius throughout his lifetime, but Aristotle does not appear to think they are exactly contemporaneous with him. They come to be before the limbs and organs whose matter they are, are fully formed (*P.A.* II, i, 646a/25ff).[2] And although he sometimes talks as though the matter of a corpse is flesh in name only (*G.A.* II, i, 734b/25ff), he also says that Calias perishes into flesh and bone just as a clay statue perishes into clay, a bronze sphere into bronze (*Met.* Z, 1035A/31ff). Since the bronze which survives the sphere is synonymous with the bronze the sphere was made of, this suggests that when Thelonius dies his flesh could survive him at least for a short time.[3,4]

The picture changes below level 3. With regard to (4) if Earth, Air, Fire, and Water are present in Thelonius at all, this is because they are ingredients of his flesh (or of other uniform stuffs which are the ingredients of his flesh). But if flesh is composed directly out of the four elements, it is a chemical compound—my term for '*migma*' (which is often translated 'mixture'). Aristotle proposes (at *G&C.* 327b/1–34) that Earth, Air, Fire and Water are not unqualifiedly destroyed in the generation of the chemical compounds (*migmata*) which come out of them. However he does not think they are fully or actually present (present *energeiai*) in the compound. Instead, they are present potentially or with regard to a power or ability (present *dunamei*). Whatever that means, it is different both from actual survival as well as from unqualified destruction of the ingredients of a compound (*G&C.* 327b/24–27). Since Earth, Air, Fire, and Water are present in Thelonius only in virtue of the fact that they are ingredients of flesh (or of its ingredients) while Thelonius' flesh, his body parts, and his body enjoy actual existence as long as Thelonius lives, it follows that even if the elements are concurrent constituents of Thelonius, they are not present in him in the same full blooded way as the matters of levels 1, 2, and 3 (Figure 1). Furthermore, the elements out of which Thelonius' flesh was generated do not actually exist at anything like the same time as Thelonius. Some unproblematic connections between the elements and Thelonius' flesh are illustrated in Figure 2.

The four elements are actually present from $t_1$ until they contribute to the generation of the food involved in the production of the semen and katamenia from which Thelonius arose, and of the nutrients which sustained him during and after gestation. We find actual Earth, Air, Fire and Water after $t_d$ when Thelonius dies if he is allowed to decompose completely. This makes it natural to ask:

(1) whether the elements which existed at $t_1$ are the same as those which exist at any time after $t_d$ if Thelonius decomposed completely.

and

(2) whether the elements which existed at $t_1$ are present in Thelonius during his lifetime, even though they are not fully actual during his lifetime.

A negative answer to (2) means they are not concurrent constituents of Thelonius, even though bits of Earth, Air, Fire, and Water constitute his most distal matter.

## II. The Concurrence Thesis

Mary Louise Gill and Frank Lewis both think Aristotle subscribed to what I will call the Concurrence Thesis (CS), according to which all

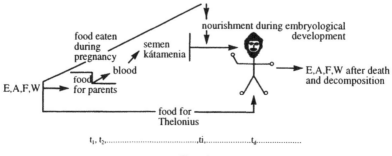

Figure 2

matters below level 3 are concurrent constituents of living organisms. Gill believes Aristotle's commitment to CS for the case of Earth, Air, Fire, and Water enabled him to comply with the Parmenidean Constraint (PC), according to which nothing can come to be out of, or pass away into, what is unqualifiedly not. On her account he made PC safe for coming to be, passing away, and change.

> ... by insisting that coming to be ... involves continuity ... [Aristotle] thus avoids the charge that, when change takes place, the preexisting entity simply perishes into nothing and is replaced by a product that emerges out of nothing. Since some part of the preexisting entity survives in the outcome, change is not sheer replacement.[5]

(Gill (1989): p 7 (1991); 109, etc.). By contrast, I think (Section III) that although Aristotle subscribed to PC, it was not one of his reasons for denying that the production of a chemical compound unqualified destroys its ingredients.

Lewis appeals to a Concurrence Thesis for katamenia as well as the four elements in support of his view that organisms are not identical to their proximate matter (Lewis (1994): pp. 257ff). Ignoring details, suppose each item with proximate matter is identical to its proximate matter. Where x is any item with proximate matter, and $M(x)$ is proximate matter, we can write this supposition as follows:

(3) $x = M(x)$

Call this the Identity Thesis. But if $M(x)$ itself has proximate matter, then by substitution,

(4) $x = M(x) = M(M(x))$,

and so on, if $M(M(x))$ itself has proximate matter. Thus by the Identity Thesis (3) if Thelonius' proximate matter is his body, Thelonius = his body. If Thelonius' flesh (bone, etc.) is the proximate matter of his body, then by 2 Thelonius = his flesh, etc. By the same argument, if katamenia is the proximate matter of Thelonius' flesh, and blood from Thelonius' mother is the proximate matter of the katamenia. Thelonius is identical to blood from his mother (Lewis (1994): pp. 759ff). Repetitions of this argument will get us from the Identity Thesis (1) to the conclusion that Thelonius is identical to the Earth, Air, Fire and Water his mother's blood came from.[6] Lewis thinks the implausibility of such conclusions argues that not everything is identical to its proximate matter.

I see no implausibility in identifying Thelonius with his body, with all of its parts, or even with the flesh and bone which are their matter. If (as Lewis assumes) for every x on every level of hylomorphic analysis, values of $M(x)$ must be concurrent constituents of x, and if no matter below level 3 is a concurrent constituent of Thelonius,[7] the argument just sketched exposes no implausibility in identifying Thelonius with his proximate matter. I will postpone the question of how Lewis' argument fares for the lower levels of matter to Section VIII.

## III. Chemical compounds and the Parmenidean Constraint

PC requires that what a chemical compound comes out of must be something that is. 'to ex hou', Aristotle's term for what a thing comes to be out of, often refers to the material something is made out of—the bronze shaped into a statue or the wood shaped and assembled into a box or a bed.[8] These examples satisfy PC, e.g. since the statue comes to be out of pre-existing bronze which survives its generation. In elemental change, by contrast, one stuff comes out of something which is utterly destroyed in the process. For example, if some Water (whose essential features are coldness and wetness) is generated out of some Fire (which is essentially hot and dry) the Fire is utterly destroyed; no Fire is to be found in the Water generated from it.[9] But Water does not come out of nothing in this processes. Because it comes to be out of Fire, its generation does not violate PC. And even though the Fire is destroyed, it does not violate PC by perishing into what is nothing at all.

Some commentators have thought that elemental change requires utterly bare matter which underlies first the element which is destroyed and then the element which emerges from it. But it is hard to see how Aristotle could have accepted the notion of bare matter that this would require, and Gill shows us how to avoid ascribing it to him. For example Fire is hot, dry stuff. When it turns into Air it loses its dryness and becomes hot wet stuff. In this process dryness and wetness are predicated not of bare matter, but of a hot subject. When the Air is generated, the Fire does not change into what is unqualifiedly not, i.e., into what lacks every item in every category. Its destruction is a loss of the dryness which was essential to it which turns it into Air.[10] If the Air generated from the Fire is swamped by Water, it will turn into cold wet stuff which lacks every single feature which is essential to Fire. By this time, there is no Fire. But since the Fire has turned into Water, neither it nor the Air initially generated from it has perished into what is nothing whatsoever; PC remains unviolated.

What Aristotle's account of elemental change shows is that PC can be satisfied by the coming to be of something out of what does not survive the generative processes. It follows that although Aristotle accepted PC (e.g., at *Phys.* 1,8), this constraint is not what requires him to say the ingredients of a compound are present potentially or by ability (dynamei) in the compound generated from them. Instead, his motivation is to be found in the following considerations. They are dubious, but they are empirical, natural scientific claims.

(5) If wine and drinking Water are mixed in the right proportions, the result is a liquid which is neither Water nor Wine. But if this liquid had been generated by a process like elemental change which completely destroys one of the ingredients, it would be wine (if the Water had been destroyed) or Water (if the wine had been destroyed) instead of a new stuff. (328a/23ff)

By parity of reasoning, if two elements combine to produce a new stuff which differs from both of them, neither element should have been completely destroyed in the process.

(6) If tin and copper are combined the product (bronze) is a new metal which differs from both tin and copper even though it resembles them to various extents. (328b/10ff). For example the color of bronze resembles the color of copper. Similarly, a chemical compound like flesh will resemble the elements it comes out of in some respects even though it is not the same stuff as any of those elements. (*G&C.* 334a/15–22 cp. 334b/8ff).

Aristotle thinks these resemblances, together with such features as a compound's solidity, its ability to hold together instead of crumbling apart, etc. are best explained as due to the influence of features (temperature, dryness, etc.) which belong to its ingredients.

Where PC requires chemical compounds to be generated from what is and prohibits its ingredients from perishing into what is not, (5) and (6) argue a different point—that the ingredients or their causal capacities must endure in some sense to explain the features which are characteristic of the compounds they give rise to.

## IV. Chemical compounding does not destroy the elements, but it does not actually preserve them either

Aristotle assumes that if the four elements survived the production of a new stuff in such a way as to be fully and actually present in it, the new stuff would have to be an aggregate rather than a uniform product. In an aggregate, different little bits of each ingredient are actually present in different spatial locations within the stuff. Aristotle compares such aggregates to a wall made of bits of stone and mortar. These mixtures result from a process of mixing or connecting (*synthesis*) which Aristotle contrasts with *mixis*, the process which produces chemical compounds. ('*Mixis*' is often translated as 'mixing'. I will use 'compounding' instead.) By contrast, uniform stuffs cannot be divided into heterogeneous parts; for example, if the division of the bit of flesh were repeated indefinitely, Aristotle thinks, the results of every division would still be a bit of flesh.[11] (*G&C.* II, 7, 334a/27ff)

Why are these the only alternatives? Why couldn't Earth, Air, Fire and Water all be fully present at every place within a batch of uniform stuff? Aristotle neither considers nor argues against any such possibility explicitly, but he has at least two reasons to reject it. First, in order for the elements to be actually present in every spatial part of a bit of uniform stuff, they would have to occupy exactly the same place at the same time. Thus every bit of the place filled by a body of uniform stuff would have to be occupied by a body of Earth, another body of Water, another of Air, and another of Fire. The principles of Aristotelian chemistry set out in *G&C.* II, *Meteor.* IV, etc. provide no mechanism by which two or more elements simultaneously fill the same place without destroying or changing one another. More importantly, Aristotle did not think a single place could be entirely filled by two or more different bodies.[12,13] For these reasons, Aristotle's only alternatives are to say that chemical compounds are uniform stuffs in which their ingredients are not fully or actually present, or that compounds are aggregates and their ingredients are actually present at different spatial locations within them. Aristotle rejects the latter alternative because he thinks that

(7) When chemical compounds decay, they behave in ways that would be impossible for aggregates. For example, if a bit of flesh decayed as far as possible, any one of the elements it was generated from could come to be out of any spatially distinct portion, no matter how small (334a/30ff). If flesh were an aggregate, its ingredients would occupy different places, and on decomposition, only the ingredient occupying a given place could come out of that place (334a/30ff).

This means, as Lewis emphasizes, that the components of a compound are not distributed over different spatial locations within the compound.[14] But if two or more bodies cannot occupy the same place, and if all of a compound's components are present in the same way, none of them can actually be present in the compound.

## V. *"Potential presence" and presence "by ability"*

How must the ingredients of a chemical compound be present in order to account for (5), (6), and (7)? Aristotle typically discusses the interaction of elements to produce a compound as depending upon the contraries (cold and hot, moist and dry) which are essential to the elements.[15] Under the simplifying assumption that flesh comes to be out of Fire and Earth, and that heat is the only essential feature of Fire, and cold, of Earth,[16] Aristotle suggests flesh is generated when Earth and Air are changed so that their heat is cooled and their cold is heated. The result is an intermediate temperature falling somewhere between the heat and the cold the interaction began with (*G&C.* 334b/24ff). Intermediate temperatures are hot and cold *dynamei* (334b/14). It should follow that the compounds which have the intermediate temperatures are also hot and cold *dynamei*.[17] In saying this Aristotle can not mean just that flesh is potentially hot in the sense that it can be made hotter until it turns into Fire which is maximally hot. His own account of elementary change requires the hot elements to be potentially cold in just this sense.[18] But Aristotle introduces the notion of being hot (cold etc.) *dynamei* for an entirely different purpose at 334b/14. Here the idea is to show how chemical compounding differs from elemental change, and how the heat, moisture, cold, and dryness which are essential to compounds differ from the features of Earth, Air, Fire, and Water he appeals to in explaining elemental change. Aristotle uses the term '*dynamei*' again to characterize the intermediate temperatures of compounds as ratios. He says what has an intermediate temperature may be twice, three times, etc. as hot *dynamei* as it is cold. To visualize such ratios, imagine trying to write down values of $\frac{h_x}{c_x}$ where x is a compound, $h_x$ is a measure of its heat, and $c_x$ is a measure of its cold. Similarly, we could try to write down values of $\frac{w_x}{d_x}$ to obtain ratios of x's wetness (w) to its dryness (d) (*G&C.* 334b/15). '*Dynamis*' is Aristotle's term for ability. It applies to abilities to act and to bring about change, to suffer change by being acted upon, and to resist change.[19] I think it is natural to understand values of $h_x$ as abilities of the same kind that Fire and Air have by virtue of their heat, and $c_x$ as abilities of the same kind that Earth and Water have by virtue of their cold—and so on for $m_x$ and $d_x$. Accordingly, I will call values of $\frac{h_x}{c_x}$ (and their counterparts for wetness and dryness) 'ability ratios.' I will say something in the near future about how these ratios might be interpreted and about what would be involved in writing down values of them. But first—in hopes of motivating a consideration of these gory details—here is what I think ability ratios have to do with the presence *dynamei* of elements in the compounds generated from them.

Aristotle contrasts the possession of heat and cold by flesh with the complete and unqualified (*haplos ... entelecheia*) possession of heat by Fire and of cold by Earth (*G&C,* 334b/10–14).

I suppose Aristotle is committed to the principle that

(8) Any bit of stuff which possesses the essential features of Earth (or Air or Fire and Water) in exactly the same way as Earth (or Air, etc.) actually is Earth (or Air, etc.). And anything (an aggregate, for example) which contains a spatial part which possesses the essential features of Earth, etc. in exactly the same way as Earth, etc., contains actual Earth (or Air, or Fire or Water).

To be hot or cold or moist or dry is to have certain abilities. For example, to have heat is to have the ability to warm other things, to rarefy them, and to segregate parts of one sort from parts of another. To possess cold is to have the ability to cool, to condense, and to make heterogeneous bits of stuff cohere. To be moist is among other things to have the ability to be congealed by heat. And so on.[20] To possess heat and dryness in just the same way as Fire and Air should mean having the ability to do, suffer, and withstand just what Fire and Air can do, suffer, etc., by virtue of their heat. To possess moisture in just the same way as Water and Air should mean to have the ability to do suffer, and withstand just what Water and Air can do, by virtue of their moisture. And so on. If this is correct, we should be able to understand the heat of a compound in terms of its abilities to do, to suffer, and to resist the same sort of things Fire and Air can do, suffer, and resist by virtue of their heat—and similarly for a compound's coldness, wetness and dryness.[21] The next step is to identify the presence of Earth, Air, Fire and Water in a compound with the compound's possession of the same kinds of abilities which are essential to uncompounded elements.[22]

I emphasize that the heat and dryness of flesh should be understood as the flesh's having the same *sorts* of abilities as Fire. But they cannot be the same in every respect. If there were no difference whatever between them, then by (8) flesh would be (or contain) actual Fire. The heat of flesh should be identified with the ability to warm, but to warm less, to rarefy, but to rarefy less, to resist cooling, but to resist it less than the corresponding abilities of Fire and Air.[23] This would mean that

(9)  To possess heat fully and completely *haplos ... entelecheiai* is to have maximal abilities to heat, to rarefy, etc., and similarly for cold, moisture, and dryness. To possess the features which are essential to any element in the same way as the element is to have the relevant maximal abilities.

(10)  To possess heat *dunamei* (by ability) is to have *non-maximal* abilities of the same kinds as the abilities (to heat, to rarefy, etc.) which are characteristic of heat—and similarly for moisture, etc.[24]

Now if we understand values of $h_x$, $c_x$, $w_x$, and $d_x$ to be measures of the relevant non-maximal abilities, a compound's ability ratios will characterize it in terms of comparisons e.g., between its abilities to do, suffer, etc. what hot things can do, etc., and its abilities to do, etc. what cold things can do, etc. I think Aristotle's view is that

(11) (a)  Fire, Earth, Air, and Water are present in a chemical compound only by ability (*dynamei*), i.e. in virtue of the possession by the compound of intermediate abilities of the same kinds of the maximal abilities which are peculiar to the heat of Fire and Air, the cold of Earth and Water, the dryness of Fire and Earth, and the wetness of Air and Water;

(b) The presence by ability of an element in a compound consists of (nothing more than) the possession by the compound of the relevant non-maximal abilities.[25]

If this is correct, the ability ratios of hot to cold and wet to dry, etc. are measures of intermediate abilities that constitute the presence of the elements in the compound. But what kind of metric would this involve? It would be nice if the values of $h_x$, $c_x$ etc., were additive measures of distance from a fixed point—like degrees on a Celsius or Kelvin scale.[26] But Aristotle's theory provides no basis for additive measures of the abilities which are characteristic of heat, cold, wetness and dryness. However it may allow for non-additive measures like the following. Take uniformly sized samples of some stuff, x, and put them in contact for a fixed amount of time with uniformly sized comparison samples of other stuffs, $cp_1$, $cp_2$, ...[27] Aristotelian chemistry guarantees that some of the cps should exhibit observable results of warming as the heat from x changes such features as their hardness and softness.[28] And Aristotle says that in order to settle questions about which of two stuffs (e.g., blood or bile) is the hotter (*P.A.* II, 2, 648a/32) and to find out whether things are said to be hot in one or different ways (648b/12)—i.e., in virtue of the same or different methods of measurement—we must

...determine the work (*ergon*) of something which is hotter, or if there are many [different works] how many'. [648/b12ff]

Melting or burning something would be examples of what Aristotle means by 'works' (648b/18ff).[29] The number of different comparison samples which burn, melt, or exhibit the results of other sorts of work, might be used to assign a value to $h_x$. The length of time it takes to make a given cp exhibit such signs might also be used for this purpose. The number of cps which exhibit observable signs of cooling, or the time it takes to make cp exhibit signs of cooling might be used to assign a value to $c_x$. Thus we could write $\frac{1}{2}$ as a value of $\frac{h_x}{c_x}$ if three of the cps showed signs of warming for every two which showed signs of cooling. Alternatively the number of cps which warm x or the time takes for a given cp to warm it might provide an inverse measure of $h_x$. In short, Aristotelian science might have some resources for use in interpreting ability ratios.[30]

## VI. How presence with respect to ability may explain what Aristotle took to be three basic facts about compounds

How is it that (first fact) compounds differ from the products of elemental change? We saw (in Section III) that the features which are essential to compounds made of Earth, Air, Water, and Fire are of the same kinds as features which are essential to their ingredients. No compound is maximally hot or cold, but each compound is hot (i.e., has the ability to heat, etc.) and cold (i.e., has the ability to cool, etc.) to some intermediate degree. The same holds for wetness and dryness. Every type of ability which belonged to the elemental ingredients of a compound is represented in the compound by a weaker ability of the same type in the compound. In elemental change, on the other hand, one or more essential abilities are destroyed altogether. Thus the result of an elemental change involving Earth and Fire is either Earth which is maximally cold and has no ability to heat, or Fire, which is maximally hot and has no ability to cool.

The presence in a compound of counterparts of the abilities of its ingredients would explain not only why (second fact) compounds resemble their ingredients to some extent (6), but also (third fact) why they differ from them with respect to their characteristic features (5). For example, because a maximal ability to heat is essential to Fire, and an intermediate ability to heat will belong to every compound in which Fire is present by ability, resemblances are to be expected. But the intermediate abilities of the compound will not enable it to produce exactly the same effects as the maximal abilities of Fire, and will enable it to produce other effects which Fire is too hot to produce.

## VII. Explaining what Aristotle thinks is a fourth fact: natural deterioration and decomposition

Aristotle thought elements must be present by ability in a compound because any one of the elements can come out of any spatial part of a compound when it decomposes (see (7) = *G&C.* 334a/30ff).

May Louise Gill thinks Aristotle explains natural deterioration (ending, e.g., in the emergence of Water and the other elements from rotting flesh) as the result of the exercise of the abilities of Earth, Air, Fire and Water which were present in the organism while it lived and which remain in the flesh after the organism dies until its deterioration is completed. In support of this she glosses Aristotle's claim that 'natural things are destroyed by the same things out of which they are constituted' (*De Cae.* 283b/21–22) as implying that

... the deterioration and destruction of organisms is caused by their own constituents which tend to move off to their proper places, if given a chance ... given the behavior of the elemental constituents ... no external destroyer is needed to bring about its destruction. Instead, composites are always on the verge of annihilation on account of their own lower material properties, and the project of remaining the same and avoiding decay ... demands considerable exertion. (Gill, 1989: 213)

As I read him Aristotle can give no such explanation. If the intermediate abilities (to heat, to cool, etc.) of flesh differ specifically from the maximal abilities of the elements, nothing in human flesh can produce the very same effects as the exercises of the elemental abilities. In particular, the intermediate abilities which constitute the heat in flesh should be unable to heat flesh above its natural temperature, let alone to reduce it to Fire. And if there is any regular correlation between heat, cold, moisture and dryness of compounds and their natural places, the intermediate abilities which belong to flesh will be incapable of natural motion to the natural places of any of the elements.[31]

When Aristotle says natural things are destroyed by the same things out of which they were constituted I believe he means external rather than internal things of the same kinds (e.g. hot, cold, wet, and dry stuffs) rather than the very (token as well as type identical) bits of Earth, Air, etc. out of which natural thing are generated. Because flesh is not an aggregate, it contains no actual Fire, Earth, Water, or Air. But it would take something with the maximal abilities of these elements to decompose bits of flesh into stuff which is as hot as Fire, or as cold as Earth, as wet as Water, etc. By (8) above, only fully actual Fire, Earth, etc. have those abilities. Thus nothing to be found in flesh can account for its decomposition into Earth, Air, Water, and Fire. The cause must lie outside of flesh, and this is just what Aristotle says. Putrescence—the final stage of natural decay—is due to the agency of external things (*allotrias*) rather than the ingredients out of which the decaying compounds were produced (*Meteor.* 379a/16ff). More generally natural destruction and decay (including the effects of age) 379a/2–3) occur when the moisture and dryness held in the proper ratio by a body's (intermediate degree of) heat is disrupted by external heat (*allotrias thermotetos*) (379a/17).[32] In virtue of its being moist, a thing cannot retain any definite spatial form. Because cold is required to hold unlike factors together (*G&C* 329b/28ff), flesh should be expected to lose its integrity if it becomes too warm. The change in temperature should alter the moist–dry ability ratio in such a way as to make the compound behave more like wetter stuffs which cannot maintain their own limits, and less like dryer stuffs which can. Beyond this the mechanism for decomposition is quite unclear.[33] An Aristotelian chemist might say liquid stuff comes out of decaying flesh when the warming process changes its moist-dry ability ratio to give it an ability—call it $A_L$—to behave more like a liquid than a solid. This would agree with Gill insofar as it represents decomposition as resulting from a compound's exercise of one of its own abilities. But if Water and Air are both maximally wet, there is no way to identify $A_L$ with the moisture of either one of these elements. And if Air is less moist than Water, it should still be wetter than any compound. In either case $A_L$ will not correspond to the abilities or the degree(s) of moisture of Air or of Water.

This doesn't tell us what role a compound's intermediate temperature and degree of moisture plays in its natural deterioration, and I do not know any texts which indicate that Aristotle had a story to tell about it. What it does tell is is why a compound does not deteriorate in the same way as an aggregate—why any one of the elements can come out of any bit of a compound, no matter how small. This would not be the case if compounds were aggregates composed of spatially discrete bits of Earth, Air, Water and Fire.

## VIII. Fire in the Belly

Section I of this paper gave some reasons to think that an organism (Thelonius) is not related to the matter on the lowest levels of hylomorphic analysis (see Figure 1) in the same way as the matter on the upper three levels. One reason was that the matter on the lowest-level—the Earth, Air, Fire and Water which went into the production of the reproductive materials from which Thelonius was generated, and the food which nourished him, existed before Thelonius was conceived (Figure 2). Another was that unlike the upper level matters—the flesh, the body parts, etc.—the elements occur in Thelonius only by ability. This raised two questions. One question was whether any of the elements the reproductive materials and the food were generated from are concurrent constituents of Thelonius, present in him throughout his life. If what I have said so far is correct, the answer is that they are present only by ability.

The second question was this: If Thelonius decomposed completely after his death, were the bits of Fire, etc. he decomposed into identical to any of the bits of Fire, etc. which existed before he was conceived. To illustrate what is at issue here consider the difference between the following chemical manipulations: (a) pour a little distilled water into some oil, stir well, and then let the water separate out, and (b) decompose some water by electrolysis, and then combine the resulting hydrogen with some oxygen from another source to produce some more water. Any two bits of Fire exhibit the similarity illustrated by (b). But what about the stronger similarity illustrated by (a)? My interpretation of Aristotle's chemical theory favors a negative answer. If Fire existed in Thelonius' flesh (and hence in his organs and bodies) only by ability, neither he nor his body contained any stuff of the same nature as any bit of Fire which existed either before or after his lifetime. The bits of Fire which turned into hamburgers which nourished Thelonius' mother did not survive the generation of the hamburgers, let alone the production of the katamenia Thelonius was conceived from (except by ability). If bits of Fire were generated out of Thelonius' flesh when he decomposed, they came to be after Thelonius ceased to be. On my interpretation no bits of Fire existed in Thelonius' body during his lifetime fullbloodedly enough to be identified with any of the Fire into which he decomposed. The negative answers to these questions suggest a way to deal with a problem posed by Mary Louise Gill. As we saw in Section II above, Gill understood PC as requiring some sort of material continuant which exists before any given organism comes to be and continues to exist throughout its conception, development, decline and eventual demise. And she proposed that the material continuant that persists through generation and passing away could be identified with the elements that the relevant reproductive stuffs and nutriments were generated from. But then it is hard to see how an individual like Thelonius can have the sort of unity at a time that full fledged substance-hood would seem to require. The problem is that at any given time during his career, Thelonius is one sort of thing (a human being) and his lowest level matter (including the parcel[34] of Fire in his body) is another. The definition of Thelonius' form and the definition of Fire are conceptually independent from one another. On Gill's assumptions about how Aristotle complied with PC, the parcel of Fire which Gill supposes is concurrent with Thelonius existed long before Thelonius came to be, and will continue to exist long after he ceases to be. Given the Fire's conceptual and existential independence of Thelonius, why isn't Thelonius two independently definable unities, a human being or a human soul connected somehow to a parcel of Fire?[35] I think the answer to this question is that although Thelonius contained abilities which are generically similar to the abilities Fire has by nature, his body contains nothing whatever which conforms to the definition of what it is to be Fire—let alone a parcel of Fire which existed both before Thelonius came to be and after he perished.

What about Lewis's argument (Section II) against the identification of a substance with its matter? If an individual like Thelonius is identical to its concurrent matter on any level, it is identical to its concurrent matter on every level. Lewis thinks this allows us to deduce absurdities from the claim that individual substances are identical to their matters. But we saw that there is no absurdity in identifying. Thelonius with his matter on the first three levels illustrated in Figure 1, Section II. Thelonius was identical to his body (level 1), his body parts (level 2), and his flesh and bone (level 3). It would be absurd to identify him with the Earth, Air, Water, and Fire on level 4 but these are not concurrent with Thelonius and the identity thesis identifies an individual only with its concurrent matter. It would be absurd to identify Thelonius with the blood which gave rise to the reproductive materials he emerged from (Figure 2), but the blood is not concurrent with him either. The status of the reproductive materials is less clear. If they perished during Thelonius' embryological development they are not concurrent matter for Thelonius, and the identity thesis does not require us to identify him with them. If the semen, the katamenia, or the fertilized katamenia survive—if the embryological process is their development into a neonate rather than their destruction and replacement by a neonate[36]—the identification of Thelonius with this matter seems no worse than the identification of the mature Thelonius with the neonate or the fetus he used to be. Thus my interpretation supports the identity thesis against Lewis' argument.

## IX. The Indeterminacy of Aristotelian compositional analysis

Marie Boas identifies the problem of understanding exactly what happens '... when two substances combine to produce a third ...' as '... the most perplexing of all the chemical problems associated with an understanding of chemical composition' faced by 17th century chemists and the Aristotelians and Paracelsians who preceded them.

[A]s long as chemists ... spoke and wrote in terms of the 'sulphureous', 'watery,' 'saline,' 'spirituous' 'earthy', 'oily', or 'mercureous' *parts* of substances, rather than in terms of real chemical entities, there was no way of describing the course of the reaction so as to convey useful information ... (Boas, 1958: 159)

The terms 'sulphureous', 'saline', and 'mercurious' along with the more Aristotelian sounding terms 'watery' and 'earthy,' referred to powers which were thought to be characteristic of different elements such as sulfur and mercury. Boas suggests chemical compositions would have been easier to understand if the Aristotelians and Paracelsians had thought of compounds as aggregates containing actual corpuscles or atoms of different stuffs which bore the relevant powers so that a chemist who

... spoke of the 'sulphureous' part of a substance ... truly meant the part containing the substance sulfur, not the part imagined to share the attributes of the element sulfur. (ibid)

But as long as the 'sulphureous part', the 'watery part' etc. were not thought of as discrete and distinguishable chemical entities such statements as that

... it was the 'saline' part of oil of vitriol (sulfuric acid] which reacted with copper to produce vitriol [copper sulfate] [could] contain ... no very precise information, and even less information would be conveyed if one tried to identify the part of the metal which entered into the compound. (ibid)

The Aristotelian and Paracelsian conceptions of the parts, the powers, and their ontological states were ill defined and amorphous—too murky to allow them to tell an intelligible story of how the parts and powers could enter into the production of a compound, inhere in the product, and be separated out by further reactions.

I believe the seeds of such difficulties can be found in Aristotle's own program for a compositional analysis of the natures of chemical compounds, their production, and their decomposition, which would not require him to treat them as aggregates of distinct atoms or corpuscles. To see why, consider an Aristotelian compound, S, whose temperature, T, is a hot-cold ability ratio, $\frac{h_s}{c_s}$ of one to two. Its degree of moisture, M, is a wet–dry ability ratio, $\frac{w_s}{d_s}$ of one to one.

If chemical compounds are perfectly homogeneous, S has exactly the same temperature and degree of moisture in every spatial subpart, no matter how small[37] (Figure 3a). That is to say that the abilities which constitute its temperature and moisture are uniformly distributed throughout every bit of the stuff. But this means that there is no non-arbitrary, uniquely correct answer to the question which elements are present (i.e., present by ability) in the compound. If the compound were analyzed as composed of two pairs of abilities, $<w_s\text{-}h_s>$ and $<d_s\text{-}c_s>$, then, as shown in Figure 3b, it would contain two elements, Air and Earth. If its proper analysis featured four paris ($<w_s\text{-}c_s>$, $<w_s\text{-}h_s>$, $<d_s\text{-}c_s>$, $<d_s\text{-}h_s>$) as shown in Figure 3c, it would contain not just two, but all four elements. Still other pairings would analyze it as containing three element combinations. Yet another would pair $w_s$ with both $h_s$ and $w_s$, limiting its components to Fire and Water. Because S is M and T all over and all of its abilities are to be found everywhere within it, its structure (such as it is) favors no one of these analyses over any other. For example there is no unique structural relation between $w_s$ and $h_s$ to make their pairing any more natural than the pairing of has with $d_s$. Thus compositional indeterminancy is the price Aristotle must pay for treating chemical compounds as perfectly homogeneous stuffs rather than aggregates.[38,39] I believe that no principled compositional analysis of chemical compounds is possible unless the compounds are treated as aggregates. I speculate that the difficulties Boas reported (above) can be understood as generated by unhappy conceptions of the components of chemical aggregates.

## I.  Addendum

Kit Fine's remarkably rich paper on Aristotelian compounds (this volume) shows how Aristotle might try to make it plausible that there can be genuine examples of thoroughly homoeomerous compounds (my term) or mixtures (Fine's term)[40] whose distinct components really exist

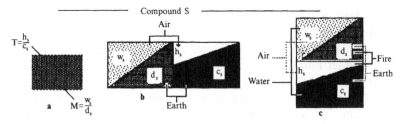

Figure 3

within them. For textual reasons I lack space to discuss, it is unclear to me whether Aristotle views the status of the components his chemistry uses to analyze compounds as realistically as Fine supposes. But even if he did, I do not think anti-atomist theories like Aristotle's have the resources to make it plausible both that mixtures are homoeomerous in the sense that Aristotle thinks they are, and also that they contain distinct components as Fine interprets him as thinking. That is why I did not try to tell a realist story about the components of Aristotelian homoeomers. I wanted instead to consider Aristotelian chemistry as an example of some general difficulties with compositional analysis.

In this addendum I will sketch some examples (involving the compositional analysis of motion) of why it's worth looking into the possibility of theories which meet Fine's conditions for an Aristotelian account of mixtures (§1).[41] I will argue that Fine's proposal for such a theory requires a notion of amount or density which is unavailable to Aristotelian chemistry. But even if this argument succeeds, I think it leaves open the possibility of treating the components of motions in something like the way Fine thinks Aristotle should treat the components of chemical compounds. I think these issues are of some interest in connection with the history and philosophy of science, even though my discussion of them will not address the textual question of whether Aristotle is the kind of realist Fine thinks he is.

## II. Compounds, aggregates, and homoeomerities

Chemists explain facts about both aggregates like unpurified tap water, and compounds like chemically pure water, by appeal to facts about their components. Some characteristic properties of tap water where I come from are explained by features of the spatially distinct bits of undissolved mineral and organic material it contains. Some characteristic features of pure water are explained by appeal to features of the oxygen and hydrogen it contains. But despite this similarity in explanatory strategies, the differences between aggregates and compounds is so important that we want a chemical theory to account for it.

Atomists believe compounds are collections of small, spatially distinct bodies with distinctive causal abilities. For a present-day atomist these bodies are molecules whose causal abilities are due to the natures and arrangements of their atomic components and the particles which belong to them. Ancient atomists like Leucippus and Democritus think the basic components of things are indivisible, impenetrable atoms separated by empty spaces. What Aristotle treats as a chief alternative to his own theory of compounds (G&C II.7) is due to Empedocles. Empedocles differs from the ancient atomists in holding that the basic components of compounds are spatially contiguous and (I think) divisible (McKirahan (1994); 265).

But as long as he believes the components are really present in the compound and that they do not occupy the same places within it, what I have to say about atomistic theories will apply to Empedocles as well.

Modern atomists think the difference between aggregates and compounds lies in differences between the sorts of bonds which connect their basic components and between the resulting structures. They draw a sharp distinction between chemical and other sorts of connections. This enables them to distinguish chemical reactions which break the bonds between the atomic components of a compound from processes of physical division which separate out the components of an aggregate but are incapable of breaking chemical bonds. For example physical division can divide a parcel of dry concrete mix into parcels of sand, gravel, lye, and cement, but the physical division of a parcel of lye separates out smaller and smaller bits of lye without dividing it into its elemental components. An atomist with a clear enough idea of the difference between physical division and chemical reaction[42] can say that compounds are homoeomers in the sense of meeting the following weak requirement:

(1) *Atomist Homoeomerity*: Every sub volume into which a volume of a compound can be physically divided contains the same components in the same proportion as the original, undivided volume.

So conceived, compounds are not homoeomers in the sense of meeting the stronger requirement:

(2) *Aristotelian Homoeomerity:* Every sub volume (no matter how small) of any amount of a compound contains the same components in the same proportion as the original amount.

Aristotelian homoeomerity requires more than atomist homoeomerity, but just how much more depends upon what it is for different sub volumes of stuff to belong to a larger undivided volume of that stuff. Lacking a clear account of this in Aristotle,[43] let us suppose that the sub volumes of any given amount of stuff are parts into which it can be divided by a well defined method of division—leaving open the question of just what methods of division Aristotle would countenance. This means that the number and size of the sub volumes of any given volume of stuff will be relative to the method of division, and the number of times it can be applied. Given this, Aristotelian homoeomerity is stronger than atomist homoeomerity because, as Aristotle believed,

(A3) *Divisibility:* any volume can be divided an unlimited number of times into unlimitedly small sub-volumes.

Even an atomist who thinks no compound can be physically divided into bits of different stuffs will maintain that the different components of a compound occupy different places. Accordingly, he will subscribe to

(A4) *Component Realism:* the components in a compound enjoy a existence which is every bit as full blooded as that of the components in an aggregate.

According to (A4) even if the bonds which bind the components of a compound together resist physical division, and even if the bound components interact with one another and with other things in different ways than do the components of an aggregate, the components of a compound are real causal factors fully present in the compound. Thus atomists can appeal to the components of a compound—no less than to those of an aggregate—to explain facts about its nature and behaviour.

Fine's interpretation of Aristotle raises the question whether the components of compounds and aggregates can enjoy a similar ontological and explanatory status in a non-atomistic world where compounds are Aristotelian homoeomers satisfying conditions (A2) and (A3).

## III. Fine's Account of Aristotelian Compounds

Suppose $M$ is a compound obtained by mixing two parts Fire to one part Water. For simplicity suppose $M$ contains no Earth or Air, and ignore the fact that Fire is dry as well as hot, and that Water is wet as well as cold. As I read him, Aristotle would say $M$ has an intermediate temperature (this means, e.g. that it can warm and rarefy certain things, cool and congeal certain others—but not as much and not as many as could pure Fire or pure Water) because it was made out of two parts Fire and one part Water. But as I read him Aristotle does not subscribe to Component Realism; he does not believe the ingredients that were combined to form the compound are really to be found within the compound. Instead, $M$ is an Aristotelian homoeomer because it consists, as it were, of just one component. The chemical principles which explain its temperature govern the interactions of Fire and Water which produce $M$, rather than interactions of Fire and Water contained within the compound after its production from Fire and Water.

By contrast, Fine's Aristotle is a component realist (A4) who thinks the temperature of $M$ is due to the interaction of Fire and Water which literally exist within the compound (§12).[44] Ignoring details, this requires the matter in every bit of $M$ to be extremely hot, extremely cold, and of an intermediate temperature all over. Or, what amounts to the same thing, there is Fire and Water, and the heat of Fire and the cold of Water in every place which contains any of the mixture.[45] Impossible as that might sound Fine shows that it does not involve a contradiction or impossibility of the same kind as a real number which is both even and odd, a figure which is both a triangle and a square, or a note sung by Michael Bolton which is both sharp and flat.[46] To be extremely hot, for Aristotle, is to have an ability (Fine's term is 'capacity') whose untrammeled exercise would produce certain effects. To be extremely cold is to have an ability whose untrammeled exercise would produce the opposite effects. There is no contradiction or impossibility in something being extremely hot and extremely cold all over in this sense as long as the relevant abilities cannot be exercised to produce mutually exclusive effects in the same object at the same time (§12). Fine's idea is that the components of a compound exercise their opposed capacities together in such a way as to "mutually check" each other's excesses and produce single, intermediate effects (§12). Thus when $M$ acts on another thing, instead of producing (as would be impossible) mutually exclusive effects, it produces compatible effects (e.g., a single degree of warmth along with a single degrees of dryness) which fall somewhere in between what would have been produced by pure Fire or pure Water acting alone. The intermediate temperature of a bit of $M$ is the resultant intermediate ability to warm, rarefy, etc. produced by the interaction of the Fire and Water contained in $M$. So conceived, the compresence of extreme heat, extreme cold, and intermediate warmth does not involve impossibilities like the sharp flat tone, the triangular square, or the odd even number (§12).

## IV. Some examples of the compositional analysis of motions

You do not have to reject atomism, subscribe to a five-element periodic table, or commit yourself to any other obsolete detail of Aristotelian chemistry to be intrigued by the idea of an Aristotelian homoeomer with real, distinct, causally efficacious components. Fine gives several reasons for this. In this section I will illustrate another.

Compositional analysis is widely applied to items whose components are not believed to enjoy anything analogous to the status molecules, atoms, or particles in a chemical compound, or ingredients in an aggregate. The kinetic theory of gases and Newton's moon test of the law of universal gravitation are examples. In the first of these, the momentum of a gas molecule moving around in a closed container is analyzed in terms of components which are described as if they made distinct contributions to the ability of the molecule to exert a force on the side of the container. In the second example, the orbital motion of a moon or planet is analyzed in terms of component motions described as if they were different enough from one another to require different explanations. It is certainly far from obvious just how these descriptions should be understood. But they do seem to treat velocities as causally distinct constituents of motions. These motions bear considerably more interesting analogies to the homoeomerous stuffs of Aristotelian chemistry than to aggregates, or to compounds as understood by atomists. And as Fine observes, Aristotle himself thought that non-circular motions which are directed neither straight up nor straight down are like compounds with circular and rectilinear upward and downward motions as their components (see, e.g., *De Cae.* 1.2). The application to motions of a story like Fine's would show how descriptions of their components might be taken realistically and at face value.

KINETIC THEORY OF GASES

Why is the pressure of an enclosed gas roughly proportional to its temperature (for temperatures within a limited range)? The kinetic theory's answer[47] supposes (a) that the gas is a collection of molecules bouncing around from wall to wall in the container, (b) that the temperature of the gas is a function of the mean kinetic energy of its molecules, and (c) that pressure is a function of the force exerted on the walls by the molecules striking it. The force exerted by each molecule depends on the rate at which its momentum (the product of its velocity and its mass) changes at impact. The kinetic energy of a moving object varies with its momentum; it is one half of the product of the mass of the body and the square of its velocity. A leading idea of the kinetic theory is that as temperature—hence mean kinetic energy, hence momentum— increases, so do the number of collisions and the magnitude of force (hence pressure) exerted at each collision. Similarly, decreases in temperature— in mean kinetic energy, hence momentum—will produce decreases in pressure.

This story is told with the help of compositional analysis. For example (Figure A1) consider a molecule, $b$, which moves downward in a container from one wall, $W_1$, collides with another wall, $W_2$ at $o$, and rebounds towards a third wall, $W_3$.

For simplicity, assume that $b$'s mass and speed are constant, and that $b$ is perfectly elastic and never wastes energy by spinning in place, vibrating, etc. The magnitude of the force this molecule exerts on $W_2$ depends upon the rate at which its momentum changes when it collides with that wall. Since, as we are assuming, $b$'s mass does not change, any change in $b$'s momentum must be due to change in velocity. Since, as we are assuming, it hits the wall and leaves the wall at the same speed, its change of velocity must be due to change of direction.[48] As $b$ bounces off the wall, it continues to move in the same direction along the $y$ axis. Before collision it was moving downwards from the top of the container. After collision, it continues to move downwards. The same goes for motion along the $z$ axis. To get to $o$ from where it started, $b$ moved toward the front of the container. After collision it continues to do so. Thus $b$'s change in velocity (hence momentum) is due to the reversal of its motion along the $x$ axis. $b$'s velocity is analyzed in terms of three components—

one for each axis—only one of which is relevant to the force exerted on $W_2$. The other components are considered in other connections. For example, the angle of rebound will vary (in part) with the $b$'s motion toward $o$ along the $y$ and $z$ axis. And other collisions will involve changes along the other axes. Thus different components of the motions of gas molecules play different roles in explaining what goes on in the container.[49]

Needless to say, a molecule's motion, velocity, and momentum do not involve spatially distinct, individual massive items moving in three different directions at three different speeds. In this respect they are much more like Aristotelian homoeomers than aggregates. So how does the analysis of such quantities into components help a scientist understand the relation between the pressure and temperature of a real gas in a real container?

An instrumentalist answer is that all Figure A1 illustrates is a model, and that both it and more realistic models (incorporating density, imperfect elasticity, more complex molecular structures, more complex motions, etc.) are imaginary systems[50] which facilitate the calculations and derivations the theorist needs to make in order to deal with real systems. In order to apply the explanatory and predictive principles at his disposal, the kinetic theorist needs a model which includes distinct velocity components. But this is no reason to think the real motions of real objects actually contain distinct components, let alone components which correspond to those which constitute the imaginary motions of the imaginary molecules in the model. Clearly, instrumentalists do not have to worry about how distinct components can be contained in the real world items the model is used to explain.[51]

But instrumentalists have worries of their own. It is not obvious how explanations of real world motions can be obtained from the study of imaginary motions analyzed into imaginary components, or why predictions grounded in the analysis of imaginary systems approximate as well as they sometimes do to accurate descriptions of real systems. I

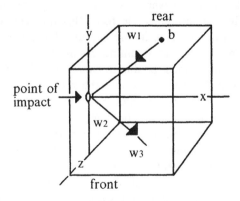

Figure A1

do not think this is an insurmountable problem for an instrumentalist, but for a Finean realist, it is not a problem at all. If the components of motions could be treated in something like the manner Fine thinks Aristotle intended, it would be easy to see how compositional analysis contributes to successful prediction and explanation.

## NEWTON'S MOON TEST

Here is a description of how the earth orbits the sun from a popular survey of physics ideas.

> The Earth is continually accelerating towards the Sun, but this motion is continually offset by the tangential motion, so it gets no closer ... (Ridley, 1995; 84).

Ridley's talk of an accelerating component motion "offsetting" a tangential component is reminiscent of Aristotle's talk of opposed ingredients checking each other's excesses to produce intermediate temperatures, degree of dryness, etc. (Aristotle, *G&C.* 334b/9–16). The following from Newton can be read in a similar way.

> ... the Moon gravitates towards the earth, and by the force of gravity is drawn continually away from rectilinear motion, and retained in its orbit (Newton 1962; 407).

Figure A2 illustrates Newton's description of the motion of the moon.

The earth $e$, follows a Keplerian path, $Ke$, around the sun, $s$, while its moon, $m$, orbits the earth along a Keplerian path, $Km$, of its own. Newton treats the moon's motion at each instant as if it consisted of a tangential component, $C_1$ directed away from the earth and a second, accelerating component $C_a$ directed toward the earth. $C_a$ is due to an attractive force identical—Newton will argue—to the force which attracts mundane objects falling at the surface of the earth. $C_1$ is explained by an entirely different factor, the moon's inertia.[52] The motions of the earth, the other planets, and their moons will be treated the same way.

To argue for an instance of *Universal Gravitation*—the law that every body attracts and is attracted to every other body by the same gravitational force—Newton calculates what would happen without inertial motion if the moon fell to earth under the exclusive influence of the attractive force which accounts for $C_a$. By his calculation, the moon's motion at the surface of the earth would resemble that of any mundane object in free fall at the same place. Newton concludes from this that the attractive force which holds the moon in its orbit is none other than the force which makes things fall at the surface of the earth.[53] What is the status of $C_a$ (the 'gravitation [of the moon] toward the earth') and $C_1$, the 'rectilinear motion' the moon is 'continually drawn away from'? For an instrumentalist, these are useful fictions employed by Newton in calculations which somehow helped legitimize the use of the law of

Universal Gravitation in predicting and explaining various observational data. But if forces are real pieces of ontological furniture, $C_a$ and $C_1$ may deserve a more realistic treatment—not just because Newtonian mechanics provides a principled analysis of elliptical motions into distinct, measurable components, but also because $C_a$ and $C_1$ are explained as due to entirely different factors. One of them, the attractive force that accounts for $C_a$ is a full fledged cause. The other resembles a cause sufficiently for Newton to have called it a force (see Note 52 above). It is natural to think that an effect should have the same ontological status as its cause. So why shouldn't someone who believes causes are real think the same of $C_a$ and $C_1$?[54]

Newton's argument may provide a further reason to be a realist about the components of a motion. His calculation of the acceleration the moon would have in free fall requires the use of Kepler's laws. What has fascinated philosophers about Newton's argument (at least since Duhem) is that although Newton submits that calculation as evidence for Universal Gravitation, Universal Gravitation is incompatible with Kepler's laws for systems (the solar system, for one) containing more than two orbiting bodies whose relative distances and positions change as they move. For example, if Kepler's first law applied to the moon, its orbit would be a smooth ellipse. But, as Figure A2 may suggest, the distances between the moon, the earth, and the sun change as the moon travels around the earth and the earth travels around the sun. Since the influence of gravity varies inversely with the square of the distance between the attracting and the attracted body, it follows by Universal Gravitation (without even considering the attractive influences of the other planets and moons) that as their relative positions change, the moon will be pulled out of $K_m$ toward the sun, and then back toward the earth. Such departures from a Keplerian orbit are called perturbations. Newton's theory predicts them for the orbits of all of the planets and their moons. They were calculated from observational data and made known to Newton by Flamsteed, the Royal Astronomer![55] How can Newton use Kepler's law that the orbits of the planets are smooth ellipses to make the calculations he needs to argue for a principle whose truth would guarantee the falsity of that very law?[56]

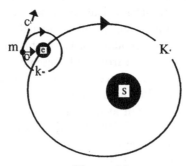

Figure A2

Perhaps Newton's argument is no good, but that is a hard position to maintain without embracing general skepticism with regard to science. For if Newton's argument is bad, so are depressingly many of the arguments scientists use to support theoretical claims they rely on and have the most confidence in.[57] It's more plausible that Newton's argument differs from deductive arguments, and inductive arguments (as philosophers often portray them) in not requiring true premises.[58] But an intriguing alternative is available to a realist who thinks the components of motions are real items which are present in the motions they compose. Suppose (as I think Newton did) that there could be a principled analysis of the orbits of planets and moons into elliptical and perturbing components.[59] Then an analog of Component Realism (A4) could make Universal Gravitation safe for Kepler's laws. The idea would be that Kepler's laws are true after all—not true of the actual composed, perturbed motions of planets and moons, but true, nevertheless, of their elliptical components.[60]

## V. Troubles with chemical compounds, and a pious hope

Back to Fine. How can we interpret the claim that a compound is composed of Fire and Water if we assume Aristotelian Homoeomerity (A2), Divisibility (A3) and Component Realism (A4)? According to Fine's proposal (which I think is the best version of anti-atomism these assumptions could hope for) Fire and Water fill every volume of $M$ (regardless of size) so that the volume of Fire in any given volume of $M$ is identical to the volume of Water. Thus in order for a volume to contain more Fire than Water, we need a quantity (like density) which can vary independently of volume. As I understand Fine, his idea is that the Water in $M$ is spread more "thinly' than the Fire, or that the Fire in $M$ is twice as "dense" as the water (§13). But what can that mean?

Obviously, it cannot mean that each parcel of the mixture contains two spatially discrete little bits of Fire for each discrete bit of Water. That way lies atomism.

It had better not mean that the intensive, volume independent, magnitude of the heat Fine calls a thermal power (§7) of the Fire in the compound is greater than the thermal power of the cold of the Water in the compound. In order for that to explain the differences between the compositions and the behaviors of $M$ and a 1 Fire/2 Water mixture, $M'$, the Fire in $M$ would have to have a more intense heat than the fire in $M'$, and the Water in $M'$ would have to have a more intense cold than the Water in $M$. Fine is right to say that Aristotle supposes that every instance of Fire always has the same intensive degree of heat, and that every bit of Water has the same intensive degree of cold.[61]

That the Fire in our mixture is twice as dense as the Water had better not mean that every volume of $M$ contains two sub volumes of Fire for every (equally large) sub-volume of Water. Aristotelian homoeomerity requires there to be Water in every sub-volume which contains Fire, and Fire (twice as much of it) in every sub-volume which contains Water.[62]

Density is standardly understood as mass per volume, but I do not think that this will help. For the ancients (and for Leibniz, among others) mass is what keeps two bodies from occupying the same place.[63] But the Fire in $M$ is supposed to be in every place where the Water is. In mechanics, inertial mass is '... the characteristic of a body that relates the force on the body to the resulting acceleration' (change in speed or direction).[64] Accordingly, the greater a thing's inertial mass, the harder it will be to start it moving, stop its motion, speed it up, slow it down, or change its direction. Gravitational mass is the characteristic of a body that determines the magnitude of the changes it can bring about in the motion of another body of given inertial mass at a given distance. The analog of gravitational mass for Aristotelian chemistry would be the characteristic which determines the magnitude of the changes in temperature, degree of dryness or wetness, (and features like rarity which Aristotle uses these to explain) a bit of stuff can produce in something else. In Aristotelian chemistry, the analog of inertial mass should be a characteristic which determines the magnitude of a bit of stuff's ability to resist changes in temperature, and in degree of dryness or wetness (and the other features Aristotle uses these to explain), under the influence of other things. As Aristotle understands temperature and degree of dryness and wetness, these features reduce to abilities to bring about and to suffer warmings, coolings, dryings, moistenings, etc. Thus, all things equal, the more "massive" a bit of stuff is, the more heating, cooling, etc. it can do, and the more it takes to reduce the amount of heating, cooling, etc. it can do.

If mass is understood in this way, the notion of density as mass per volume will involve the same drawbacks as the notion (rejected above) that density can be explained in terms of magnitude of thermal and dessicative power. Suppose we have one container filled with $M$ and another filled with M'. By Aristotelian homoeomerity, the first container must hold exactly the same volume of Fire as the second. If the Fire in the first container has twice the "mass" of the Fire in the second, and "mass" is understood in terms of the magnitudes of abilities to produce, resist, and suffer changes, the thermal and dessicative abilities of the Fire in our first container differ quantitatively from the thermal and dessicative abilities of the Fire in our second container. As noted above, this is a decidedly non-Aristotelian result because in Aristotelian science, the kind which any given bit of stuff belongs to is determined by the magnitudes of just those abilities. The trouble with the account of density under consideration is that it requires "mass" to be defined and measured by the factors by which stuffs are classified—e.g., the magnitudes of thermal and dessicative abilities which determine, e.g. whether the hot component of $M'$ is Fire or some other kind of stuff, and whether the cold component of $M$ is Water. Thus it is hard to see how the conception of density under consideration can allow different masses for equal volumes of the same stuff.[65]

This need not be a problem for atomist chemistry. An ancient atomist can classify stuffs according to peculiarities of the shapes or sizes of their atoms. Given a classification of ingredients in terms of the shapes or sizes of their atoms, together with the principle that two atoms cannot occupy the same place, the ratio, e.g., of Fire to Water can be understood as the ratio of atoms of the one kind to atoms to the other per unit volume. And the explanatory strategies of an ancient atomist require no notion of mass which cannot be reduced to sizes and numbers of atoms. In modern chemistry, the notion of mass connects in various ways to notions and measurements of such crucial factors as differences between atoms of different elements, the number of atoms of different elements in a molecule, the structure of the molecules they belong to, and the number of molecules in a given volume. But these connections are not such as to make mass, its measurement, and calculations involving mass, indistinguishable from the other factors, their measurement, and the calculations they figure in. By contrast, I do not think Aristotelian chemistry has the resources to distinguish the determination of a stuff's mass from a determination of what kind of stuff it is. And to repeat, if what it is to be Fire, Water or any other element cannot be distinguished from what it is for the Fire or Water in a given volume to have certain mass, then either (a) containers filled with equal volumes of different stuffs cannot not contain equal volumes of Fire, or (b) equal volumes of Fire can have different heats and drynesses. The former alternative is unacceptable on Fine's reading of Aristotle. The second is unacceptable on his or any other plausible interpretation. In Aristotelian chemistry the natures, the components of a compound, and the ratio of their magnitudes are theoretically indispensable quantities which must be differentiated clearly enough from one another to allow them to play different explanatory roles.

I do not know any alternative understandings of how equal volumes of an Aristotelian homoeomer can contain different amounts of the same component which fare better than the ones we have just looked at. Thus I think it was a good idea for chemists to give up trying to develop anti-atomist accounts of chemical compounds incorporating conditions like (A2), (A3) and (A4).

But if it is as hard as I think to accommodate Fine's account to Aristotelian chemistry, it is not at all clear whether it would be equally difficult to treat motions in something like way Fine treats Aristotelian homoeomers. Without a realist account of the compositional analysis of motions as detailed and well worked out as the one Fine supplies for the case of chemical compounds, there is no way to tell just what (A2), (A3) and (A4) would amount to in connection with motions. Thus I do not think skepticism about the compositional analysis of Aristotelian chemical homoeomers is enough all by itself to show that a realist stance is hopeless with regard to the components of motions involved in the kinetic theory of gasses, Newton's moon test, and with related examples of compositional analysis[66].

Pitzer College

## NOTES

[1] Not *all* of Thelonius' body, bodily parts, or flesh needs to exist as long as Thelonius does; he may lose a thumb, go on a diet, have an appendix removed. I will ignore such details; their resolution (or its impossibility) would have no effect on the main claims of this paper.

[2] Presumably, formless batches of flesh and bone are not produced in the early stages of development and later shaped into body parts in the way that clay is mixed before it is formed into pots. The idea may be, e.g. that although the embryology of the hand is not a matter of the production of flesh which is later formed into a hand, there is a actual flesh in the immature, developing hand in the early stages of development before the hand becomes fully formed.

[3] For this sense of 'synonymous' see *Catg.* 1, 1a, 5ff. The example of the circle is complicated by the fact that its segments are not actual semicircles until the circle is destroyed. I will mention a related problem in Section VII below. The clay example is philologically difficult. As far as I know, clay statues were fired at high enough temperatures to prevent them from deteriorating into stuff from which which a new item could be made in the same way as the original statue. The philological question is whether the dust and grit into which a statue might crumble would be called clay.

[4] I do not know how to reconcile this with *G.A.* 743b/25ff. But it is consistent with a related text. At *Meteor.* IV, 12, 390a/14ff, Aristotle says that like the eyes, the fingers and the tongue, flesh is defined by its work (*ergon*) and that what cannot do the work flesh does is flesh in name only. Aristotle says the same thing about fire (390a/16), bronze and other non-living stuffs (390a/18). Each is what it is in virtue of its natural and characteristic abilities (*dunamei*) to act or to suffer (*poiein e paschein*) (390a/18–19). I assume that what has the relevant abilities can do the required work. The bronze or fire into which some things perish are full fledged bronze and fire because they retain their essential abilities and therefore are capable of doing the relevant sorts of work. Although Thelonius' eyes and fingers lose their essential abilities when he dies and therefore cease to be eyes and fingers, it does not follow that his flesh cannot keep its essential abilities. It cannot remain non-homonymous flesh for long because its abilities and work depend upon its retaining a certain temperature which was maintained by the functioning of the living body. But there is no reason why it should not maintain its vital temperature and, hence, its essential abilities for a short time.

[5] Gill (1989), p. 7.

[6] If I have read Lewis's discussion of chemical compounds and their ingredients correctly (§7) he thinks that Earth, Air, Fire, and Water are concurrent constituents of Thelonius: Lewis (1994): 272–5.

[7] Lewis entertains a related possibility, but I think he inclines to reject it in (1994) §8.

[8] *Phys.* B1, 193a/10–29 for example. At *Phy.* B3, 194b/23–26, it looks as though '*To ex hou*' and '*hyle*' can be used interchangeably in connection with these examples.

[9] In discussing elemental change I rely on Gill's definitive account; Gill (1989): 68ff.

[10] Gill (1989): 68 ff.

[11] Despite its anachronism, it may be helpful to think of atmospheric air—free oxygen, nitrogen, ozone, carbon dioxide, and other gases along with particles of free carbon and other things I would rather not think about—as an example of an aggregate in contrast to carbon dioxide, which is more like a compound. I do not think Aristotle makes the same kind of distinction we can make between solutions like salt water and compounds like water, or between solutions and aggregates.

[12] For example, there is no reason why an object moving through a medium (e.g., a stone falling through a body of air or water) should meet resistance, or why it should have to part the medium in order to pass through it (as Aristotle supposes in *Phys.* IV, 8, 215a/28–23) if the body could occupy exactly the same places as bits of the medium along its path, without moving the medium out of the way. And at *Phys.* 209a/4–7, and *De An.* 409b/3, he rejects theories (that the place occupied by a body is itself a body and that the soul is a body distributed throughout the body of an organism) on the grounds that they would require two bodies to occupy the same place.

[13] I take it that this rules out Bogaard's idea that the fire in Thelonius' flesh is an item which possesses the ability to do and to suffer exactly the same things as uncompounded Fire. Ignoring subtleties he interprets its "potentiality" in terms of limitations on the exercise of these abilities imposed by the Earth, Air, and Water which are also present in the compound. By exercising their abilities (to the extent that they are able—limited as each one is by the activity of the others) they either prevent the Fire from doing all it could if it were not kept from exercising its abilities fully, or they exert influences which somehow balance out the activity of the Fire. Thus the elements in a compound interact in such a way as to "screen" each other off "from our view" (Bogaard (1979): 19, 21). I do not know how this suggestion can be developed without violating the principle that two or more bodies cannot occupy the same place.

[14] cf. Lewis (1994) §7

[15] See, e.g., *G&C.* 334b/3ff, 335a/1ff, *Meteor.* IV, 1, IV, 6.

[16] In fact Aristotle thinks that the production of all chemical compounds including flesh involves all four elements, the wetness of Water and Air and the dryness of Earth, the heat of Air, and the cold of Water as well as the temperatures of Earth and Fire (*G&C.* II, 8). For a related simplification see *G&C.* 331b/1–5).

[17] And similarly for moist and dry if we drop the simplifying assumption.

[18] *G&C.* II, 4, e.g., 324b/8–9, 332a/1.

[19] *Met.* theta 1, delta 12, Bogen and McGuire (1986–88). In most cases I use 'ability' rather than forms of 'potential' to translate '*dunamis*'.

[20] *G&C.* II, 2, *Meteor.* IV.

[21] This interpretation accords with E. S. Forster's Loeb translation of 334b/14ff.

[22] I think this agrees in spirit with Gill's idea that one thing might be present in something generated from it in the sense that 'its essential properties ... survive' (Gill (1989); 241). And if I understand her correctly, we both believe the presence of the relevant properties is a matter of similarities between the characteristic abilities (*dunamei*) of what the product is generated out of and the characteristic abilities of the generated item. But (Section VII) I think we hold different views about the nature of the resemblances, and the conclusions that can be drawn from them.

[23] In DCI/11 Aristotle says abilities are defined and distinguished from one another not just in terms of what their exercise accomplishes, but also in terms of maxima and minima. For example, we distinguish the ability to lift a maximum of one hundred talents or walk a maximum of one hundred stades from the ability to lift more or walk farther (281a/7–27). I think the heat abilities of Fire should be distinguished from those of flesh in the same way.

[24] To see how potential heat differs from heat by ability, suppose (what I believe is Aristotle' view) that Water is just as cold as Earth, Air is just as hot as Fire, that Fire and Earth have the same degree of dryness, and that Air is just as moist as Water. Then, since what is cold by ability has an intermediate degree of cold, while Water and Earth are

maximally cold, neither Water nor Earth are cold by ability. Nor are they hot by ability, since that would require them to have an intermediate degree of heat. However, both Earth and Water are potentially hot, which is just to say that they can be turned into Fire and Air which are maximally hot. Alternatively, if Earth is colder than Water, Earth will be potentially hot but not hot by ability. In general, where F is any member of a pair of contraries, every thing which is F by ability is potentially F, but not everything which is potentially F will be F by ability.

[25] As will be expected from Note 24, where $e_1$ is any element you choose, whatever contains $e_1$ by ability will be potentially $e_1$, but not everything which is potentially $e_1$ contains $e_1$ by ability. For example, since Earth is not moist and not hot to any degree and Air is hot and moist, Earth does not contain Air by ability, even though Earth is potentially (can be turned into) Air.

[26] Intermediate temperatures might fall between the heat of Fire and the Cold of Earth (Bogen, 1992) but this does not tell us how to measure them or guarantee a common scale of measurements for them or the additivity of any measures of them (on one or two scales) we might be able to devise.

[27] We need uniformly sized samples because Aristotle thinks that the larger of two bits of the same stuff is hotter (or cooler as the case may be) then the smaller (*P.A.* II, 648b/19–20).

[28] Aristotle says that what is absolutely hard is not compressed by anything and what is absolutely soft is compressed by everything. Intermediate degrees of hardness and softnesses can be determined *pros ti*, e.g. by comparing them to the flesh of a finger. This suggests the possibility of something like a Mohs scale for these quantities (*Meteor.* IV/4 382a/10–20).

[29] He also suggests that the hotter of the two things should be able to cause keener sensations when touched, although he admits that this test may be unreliable. And he says that the hotter a thing is, the more heat it can impart to something else, but this test assumes an independent measure of the amount of heat which is imparted (648/b13ff).

[30] Though Aristotelian, the scheme is not ideal. For example, it would assign the same value to a stuff which heated 300 cps and cooled 200 as to a stuff which heated only three and cooled only two.

[31] There is a correlation for the elements. Unless Fire is hotter than Air, Air is less moist than Water, etc., natural place must correlate with combinations of essential features so that what is maximally hot and dry will have a different natural place than what is maximally hot and wet. I cannot find any indication in Aristotle that there is a causal connection (as opposed to a regular correlation) between temperature, etc. and natural place. One would expect compounds to have natural places, the earthier ones being closer to the center of the earth, the fiery ones being closer to the place of fire, etc. There is some evidence for this in Aristotle's discussion of exhalations. For this see Lee's notes on *Meteor.* I, 3, Lee, (1962) 26–7, and *Meteor.* 335a/32ff.

[32] In this passage Aristotle is considering putefraction. But since putrefaction is the final stage of natural destruction (379a/7) I suppose the same holds for earlier stages in the process. It is suggestive that the deterioration of bodily and mental functions in ageing is due to changes in the body which Aristotle compares to both disease and to drunkenness (*De An.* I, 4, 408b/230–25). Drunkenness is clearly initiated by the abilities of adult beverages rather than abilities belonging to the distal matter of bodily parts. Ancient Greek medicine thinks the same holds for many though probably not all cases of diseases.

[33] *Meteor.* IV/379a/15ff is particularly difficult. In the space of just a few lines it seems to say not only that external heat causes the process (379a/17) but that a thing's *loss* of heat makes it decay (379a/19–20) without explaining how these mechanisms go together.

[34] I am indebted to G. E. M. Anscombe for telling me about this felicitous term.

[35] Cf Gill, p. 6ff.

[36] For an account of how this could have been Aristotle's view, see Code (1987): 56–8.

[37] Assume that nothing is heating it on one side and cooling it on the other, or doing anything else to give different parts of it different temperatures or degrees of moisture.

[38] Kit Fine (this volume) coined the apt term 'the problem of underdetermination' for this sort of problem. Unlike myself he believes it might be possible to solve it without treating compounds as aggregates. See addendum below.

[39] Notice that the indeterminacy is not relieved by considering what elements were combined to produce the compound. Suppose S was generated from bits of all four elements. The fact that S was generated in this way leaves no mark on the structure of the compound. Its structure (the perfectly uniform compresence in every subpart of $h_s$, $c_s$, $w_s$, and $d_s$). is compatible with analyses into two and three components as well as with the analysis of S into four elements, and Aristotle provides no chemical reason why S should have as many (let alone exactly the same) components as it had ingredients.

[40] I will use these terms interchangeably. Notice that I use 'compound' for chemical compounds as opposed to aggregates, not for Fine's form-matter composites.

[41] All citations in this style give section numbers in Fine (this volume).

[42] It is unlikely that Empedocles and the ancient atomists could draw (or conceptualize the importance of) a distinction between chemical change and physical division. Lacking such a distinction, it is not surprising that as Aristotle claims, Empedocles had trouble explaining how compounds differ from aggregates. Aristotle insists that the process by which a volume of some compound is divided into smaller volumes (e.g., by cutting it up) is decisively different from the process by which compounded elements are separated out, and he says a little about what processes chemically decompose compounds. But he cannot say much about the difference between physical division and chemical reactions except that one produces smaller portions of the same stuff, while the other produces portions of different stuffs. I speculate that Aristotle's anti atomism is what kept him from developing an account of a chemical bond. I speculate that their failure to attribute enough structure to their basic bits and particles to ground a clear idea of chemical bonding explains why Empedocles and the ancient atomists did not get a better idea of the difference between physical division and chemical reaction. I am indebted to Tad Beckman for discussion of the importance of that difference.

[43] Although Aristotle thinks any continuous magnitude can be divided unlimitedly, the sub volumes into which it can be divided are not actually, but only potentially, present in it (*Phys.* III). To say what he would think it is for a sub volume to be contained within a larger volume would require an account of the relevant notions of potentiality and actuality which I do not know how to provide.

[44] On Fine's preferred interpretation, the components of an elemental mixture (or their capacities) are identical to the ingredients (or their capacities) that went into the mixture (§12). He says roughly the same thing about compounds whose components are themselves compounds.

[45] Fine says the Fire, the Water, the extreme heat, and the extreme cold are in a compound 'latently' (§ 14), but as I understand this, it will not affect my discussion.

[46] Typically they are flat.

[47] For details, see Jeans (1940): 1–50.

[48] Recall that speed is distance per time regardless of direction, while velocity is distance in a single direction per time. Thus the velocity of a car travelling around a circular course would change constantly even if the car maintained a constant speed.

[49] These components belong to the idealized motion of an idealized molecule. In principle, the real motion of a real body would be analyzed in something like the same way.

[50] More realistic treatments (e.g. Gierre 1990): 78ff.) characterize them as abstract objects which bear certain resemblances to real systems they are used to explain.

[51] This is analogous to Sellarsian readings of Aristotle (as I understand them) which treat a substance as identical to its matter. Instead of treating Aristotelian metaphysics as a colorful way way to describe how "we" talk about things, Sellars' idea (as I understand it) would be that what Fine calls form-matter compounds are actually models used to study real bodies whose forms and matters are not really distinct items joined together to constitute the bodies (see Sellars (1957) and (1967).

⁵² Newton actually calls inertia a force (*materiae vis insita, vis insita*), thereby committing what Howard Stein (1990) calls '... the notorious crime of the freshman physics student' (p. 211). Whatever Newton meant by this, it is clear that whatever does explain $C_1$ is not the attractive force which explains $C_a$.

⁵³ For Newton's argument for Universal Gravitation, see Newton (1962b): 398–422. For a clear, simplified version of the moon test, see Born (1965): 60–7. For discussion see the citations in Note 56 below.

⁵⁴ Lacking a satisfactory interpretation of what Newton says about inertia (Note 52) I will not try to guess what a realist might be tempted say about $C_1$. It is what is left of a bit of the moon's motion after we abstract $C_a$ away from it. Maybe that argues that it was really present in that motion. But it will be enough for my purposes if what I have said suggests how $C_a$ might look like a real component of the moon's motion.

⁵⁵ They are acknowledged at Newton (1962a) Prop. LXV. Theorem XXV, pp. 171ff, Newton (1962b) Prop., Prob. VI, pp. 440ff.

⁵⁶ By violating Kepler's orbital law, the perturbations also guarantee violations of Kepler's areas and harmonic laws as well. For sophisticated, detailed discussions of the difficulties raised by Newton's employment of Kepler's law see Duhem (1991): 190–5; Glymour (1980): 203–26; Laymon (1983).

⁵⁷ Just one reason for saying this is that premises typically employed in theory testing are too highly simplified and idealized to qualify as true descriptions of real systems. This is unavoidable in many cases because the calculations required to test the theoretical claim of interest against the available empirical evidence could not be carried out without considerable simplification and idealization. Thus in using false premises to argue for his theory Newton is far from alone. For another example of an important theoretical claim confirmed by arguments employing premises which are incompatible with it, see Laymon (1988).

⁵⁸ See Laymon (1985): 150 ff.

⁵⁹ Each elliptical component will itself be treated as having a component (like $C_a$) directed toward the centre of the orbit, and a tangential component (like $C_1$). If we thought of this on analogy to the elemental ingredients of Aristotelian mixtures, the perturbed orbit would be analogous to a mixture, some of whose ingredients are themselves mixtures composed of elemental ingredients.

⁶⁰ William Harper suggested this as a possibility in discussion some time ago; I do not know what he would say about it now: (cf. Harper (1991).

⁶¹ It would be impossible to analyze compounds into ratios of elements non-arbitrarily without the supposition that the thermal and dessicative powers of the elements are constant (p. 99ff.)

⁶² I am indebted to Sandy Grabiner for telling me about a theorem in measure theory (The Hahn Decomposition Theorem) which shows that if the distribution of intrinsic temperature throughout a volume of our mixture is such that some sub-volumes are lower, and others, higher than the ambient temperature and if a volume of mixture can be modeled as a set of sub-volumes which meet certain conditions, at least one part of a volume of $M$ must contain just one of its components. This is congenial to Fine's argument (§15) that the Air, or the qualities of the Air, in a compound cannot be unevenly stretched through the compound. For details see Royden (1988): 81ff.

⁶³ Jammer (1961): 23–4, 77ff.

⁶⁴ Halliday, *et al.* (1993): 101.

⁶⁵ Although modern mechanics has its troubles explaining just what mass is, it does not have this particular trouble. The mechanical equations which involve mass are completely insensitive to the chemical classification of the bodies whose motions they are applied to. Thus mechanics has no interest in the question how to distinguish determinations of mass from determinations of what kind of stuff has the mass.

⁶⁶ I am indebted to the organizers (Rob Bolton and Frank Lewis) and participants of the 1992 USC-Rutgers conference on Aristotelian metaphysics at which I delivered the original

version of this paper, and to Kit Fine for extremely helpful discussion of the original paper and of the addendum which I wrote in response to his paper. I am also indebted to Henry Mendell and to Charles Young who helped with various parts of this paper, and to Frank Lewis for editorial help. Unlike Fine who seems to have disagreed with some of what I said about his views, they are fully responsible for any mistakes in this paper.

## REFERENCES

Boas, M. 1958. *Robert Boyle and 17th Century Chemistry*. Cambridge: Cambridge University Press.

Bogaard, P.A. 1979. Heaps or Wholes: Aristotle's Explanation of Compound Bodies', *ISIS*, 70, #251.

Bogen, J. 1992. 'Change and Contrariety in Aristotle', *Nous*, xxxvii, 1.

Bogen, J. and McGuire, J.E. 1986–7. 'Aristotle's Great Clock', *Philosophy Research Archives*, vol. XII.

Born, M. 1965. *Einstein's Theory of Relativity*. New York: Dover.

Code, A. 1987. 'Soul as Efficient Cause in Aristotle's Embryology', *Philosophical Topics*, XV, no. 2, Fall.

Duhem, P. 1982. *The Aim and Structure of Physical Theory*. Princeton: Princeton University Press.

Fine, K. 'Problems of Mixture', this volume.

Forster, E.S. 1965. *Aristotle on Sophistical Refutations: On Coming-to-be and Passing Away*. Trans. Forster (with *On the Cosmos*, trans. D Furley), Cambridge: Harvard University Press.

Giere, R.N. 1990. *Explaining Science*. Chicago: University of Chicago Press.

Gill, M.L. 1989. *Aristotle on Substance The Paradox of Unity* Princeton: Princeton University Press.

Glymour, C. 1980. *Theory and Evidence* Princeton: Princeton University Press.

Halliday et al. 1993. *Fundamentals of Physics* 4th edn, expanded. New York: Wiley.

Harper, W. 1991. 'Newton's Classic Deductions from Phenomena', in Fine, A.

Forbes, M., Wessels, L., eds. PSA 1990, Vol. Two, East Lansing: Philsophy of Science Assocation.

Jammer, M. 1961. *Concepts of Mass*. Cambridge: Harvard University Press.

Jeans, J. 1940. *An Introduction to the Kinetic Theory of Gases.* New York: Macmillan.

Laymon, R. 1983. 'Newton's Demonstration of Universal Gravitation and Philsophical Theories of Confirmation', in J. Earman, ed., *Testing Scientific Theories*, Minnesota Studies in the Philosophy of Science, vol, X, Minneapolis, University of Minnesoata Press.

——— 1985. 'Idealizations and the Testing of Theories by Experimentation', in Achinstein, P. and Hannaway, O., eds. *Observation, Experiment and Hypothesis in Modern Physical Science*. Cambridge: MIT Press.

——— 1988. 'The Michelson-Morely Experiment and the Appraisal of Theories', in Donovan, A., Laudan L. and Laudan, R., eds., *Scrutinizing Science*, Baltimore: Johns Hopkins University Press.

Lee, H.D.P. ed., tranls. 1962. *Aristotle, Meterology*. Cambridge: Harvard University Press.

Lewis, F. 1994. 'Aristotle on the Relation Between a Thing and Its Matter,' in Scaltsas, T., Charles, D., and Gill, M.L., eds, *Unity, Identity and Explanation in Aristotle's Metaphysics*. Oxford: Oxford University Press.

McKirahan, R.D. 1994. *Philosophy Before Socrates*, Indianopolis: Hackett.

Newton, I. 1962a. *Principia*, vol. I, *The Motion of Bodies*, tr. Motte, Cajori. Berkeley: University of California Press.

——— 1962b, *Principia*, vol II. *The System of the World*, tr. Motte, Cajori. Berkeley: University of California Press.

Ridley, B.K. 1995. *Time, Space, and Things.* Cambridge: Cambridge University Press.

Royden, H.L. 1988. *Real Analysis*, 3rd edn. New York: Macmillan.

Sellars, W. 1957. 'Substance and Form in Aristotle', *Journal of Philosophy*, 54: 688–99.

——— 1967. 'Aristotle's Metaphysics: An Interpretation', in W. Sellars, *Philosophical Perspectives*, Springfield: Charles C. Thomas.

Stein, H. 1991. 'From the Phenomena of Motions to the Forces of Nature": Hypothesis or Deduction?' in Fine A., Forbes, M. and Wessels, L. eds., *PSA 1990, Vol. Two*, East Lansing: Philosophy of Science Assocation.

# POTENTIALITY IN ARISTOTLE'S SCIENCE AND METAPHYSICS

BY

ALAN CODE

## I. Fine's Interpretation of the Solution to a Puzzle about Mixture

At the beginning of his discussion of mixing and mixture, in *De Generatione et Corruptione* I.10, Aristotle lists the questions to be discussed concerning this topic. We need to find out both what mixing is, and what a mixture itself is, and in what way mixtures fit into our ontology. Additionally, we need to inquire if there *is* such a thing as mixing at all, or if it is false to say that such a process takes place. The last of these questions is the first he addresses.

It is addressed by presenting the following puzzle about the very possibility of mixing. Suppose that two things have been mixed. If they still exist and have not been altered, it follows that they are no more mixed than they were before. On the other hand, if either one or both of the original items has been destroyed and and no longer exists, it also follows that the two things have not been mixed. If only one of the two still exists, then the two items are not in the same kind of state, and hence cannot be mixed. If neither of them still exists, then once again, they cannot be mixed (for they need to be present if the mixture is a mixture of *them*). Thus, on the assumption that they have been mixed, it would follow both that the items mixed no longer exist and that they do still exist. This of course is impossible, and hence mixing itself is impossible.

If there is such a thing as the mixing of two items, as opposed to the generation of one thing and the perishing of others, obviously mixing must be different from generation and perishing. For instance, consider a chemical process involving both earth and fire.[1] If the earth were destroyed and became fire, this would be a generation of more fire out of the earth, and a destruction of the earth. It would be the passing away of the earth, not a mixture of the earth with the fire. Hence in order to solve his puzzle Aristotle needs to show how to make a clear distinction between mixing on the one hand, and generation and perishing on the other. This in turn will help us get clear on the nature and definition of mixture. His purpose in considering the puzzle is not to refute somebody who denies the possibility of mixing, but rather to use it to test any proffered definition of mixing and mixture. It is a condition of adequacy on the definition of mixing that mixing can be distinguished from generation and perishing, and hence that this puzzle can be solved.

His own solution is to distinguish actual from potential existence, and to claim that when two items are mixed, although they do not *actually* exist in the mixture, they do exist in potentiality.[2] Regardless of how this distinction is understood, it must at least give us a sense in which the elements themselves are potentially present in a mixture. It is tempting to take an element's potential existence in a mixture as no more than the existence of some potentiality possessed by the mixture. For instance, perhaps Aristotle means that for earth or fire to be potentially present in a mixture is for the mixture to have the potentiality to become or to be earth or fire. If so, then the potential existence of the elements consists in the fact that some physical process can undo the mixing, and the mixture can be physically decomposed into fire or earth. Alternatively, the potential presence of the elements may be thought to consist in some potentiality of the mixture that is derived from some kind of interaction of the potentialities of the elements contained in it. In that case, the potential existence of the elements consists in the fact that the mixture has either the potentialities of the original elements of which it is a mixture, or some similar potentialities that result from the combination of the potentialities of the original elements. On either kind of view, since we are taking the presence of the elements to consist in the possession of a potentiality, the definition of the potentiality in question cannot itself require the elements to be present in some more robust sense. In particular, the claim that the original elements have not been destroyed cannot be a defining condition for the possession of P, at least if possession of P is supposed to explain the sense in which those elements still exist. On pain of circularity, Aristotle's definition of the relevant potentiality cannot have as part of its content that the elements have not been destroyed if he is going to go on to use the notion of potential existence to explain the difference between mixing on the one hand, and generation and destruction on the other.

However, any interpretation according to which the potential existence of the elements in a mixture consists in the mixture itself having some potentiality will fail to satisfy Aristotle's condition of adequacy for a solution to the puzzle: it will fail to distinguish mixing from the passing away of two or more items and the generation of something new. Suppose that we start with two substances, some fire and some earth, and end up with something X that is not actually fire or earth. How do we distinguish cases in which X is a new substance from cases in which it is a mixture of substances? Since the four elements are subject to mutual transformations, it is possible to start with fire and earth and end up with air. The air is not a mixture of the fire and earth, but rather a new substance the generation of which was the passing away and destruction of the fire and earth. What kind of case is supposed to contrast with this? Under what conditions is the new item X is a mixture of substances rather than a new substance? What the kind of interpretation we are now considering attempts is a specification of some candidate potentiality P such that for the fire and earth to exist potentially in X just is for X to possess P. However, on this kind of deflationary construal of potential existence, the claim that the original elements now enjoy 'potential existence' cannot (if it is to be deflationary) entail the more robust claim that the original elements have not been destroyed. However, if the original elements have been destroyed in the process resulting in X, then we are not considering a case in which the elements have been mixed. Thus we are not able to appeal to the possession of P to explain the difference between mixing and substantial change.

What this shows is that Aristotle cannot both (i) explain what it is for the elements to exist potentially in terms of the existence of a potentiality possessed by the mixture, and (ii) use the notion of the potential existence of the elements to explain how the process of mixing differs from generation and passing away. However, Aristotle does accept (ii), and so in consistency cannot also accept (i).

Professor Kit Fine develops an account of mixture that avoids this unwelcome consequence. On his view, the potential existence of the elements in the mixture does not get reduced to the possession by the mixture of some potentiality. Instead it is due to the fact that the form of the mixture is a ratio of the elements that enter into the mixture. Putting it crudely, since this form is a ratio of elements, *the form cannot be instantiated except* when the elements are present in the prescribed ratio. Of course, if the elements are present in the prescribed ratio, then they are present. However, for them *actually* to exist, each of the elements must be separate from the others, but when they are present in the mixture, the fire and the earth do not each have their own matter. Rather the matter for each is the matter of the mixture, and hence they do not exist separately when in the mixture.

Although nothing in Fine's analysis turns on his choice of the defining properties for elements, it does require that there are defining properties. In his presentation he attributes to Aristotle the view that the basic defining properties of the four elements are two pairs of contraries: the hot and the cold, and the wet and the dry. The substantial form of fire is a bonding of 'hot/dry', and that of earth is 'cold/dry'. On Fine's view, *prime matter* is the material substratum for the four elements. (I will consider below the question whether his analysis can dispense with this assumption.) Earth, for instance, is a compound of prime matter, and its substantial form is a bonding of the cold and dry. If some earth is heated up in such a way that the prime matter loses the substantial form 'cold/dry' and acquires the substantial form 'hot/dry', this is the destruction of the earth and the generation of fire. It is not the mixing of earth with fire. However, it is also possible without destroying either of the two things, to mix something hot with something cold in such a way as to get something that has some intermediate degree of heat. This is what happens in mixing. Hot and cold are extremes, and intermediate degrees of heat are compounds of these extremes. A mixture of fire and earth possesses a form that is derived from, and in certain ways similar to, the defining properties of these elements. This form is a ratio of the two elements fire and earth, and the intermediate degree of heat possessed by the mixture will depend upon the particular ratio of these elements.

There are indefinitely many possible intermediaries between hot and cold, and likewise between wet and dry. Warmth (of some degree) is not itself a basic elementary power, but is rather a compound or combination of elementary powers that results from the mixture of elements in a certain ratio. Although Fine discusses the generalization of the notion that the form of a mixture is always a ratio of elements (the rationality of form for mixtures), for purposes of explaining the central idea of his analysis, it is convenient to make the simplifying assumption that the ratio is always one to one. On this assumption, the form of fire just is $hd$ and the form of earth just is $cd$. Earth is prime matter that is cold and dry ($e = cd/m$) and fire is prime matter that is hot and dry ($f = hd/m$). The result of *mixing* fire and earth will be a compound having as its material substratum prime matter, and having as its form fire and earth in a ratio of one to one ($f + e$). The compound ($(f + e)/m$) is some prime matter m having the form $f + e$. This form is a ratio of the elements fire and earth.

If for fire to exist is for some prime matter to possess $hd$, and for earth to exist is for some prime matter to possess $cd$, then for a (one to one) mixture of fire and earth to exist is for some prime matter to be simultaneously characterized by both $hd$ and $cd$. However, the mixture itself cannot have all of the elemental properties of earth and fire, for the simple reason that hot and cold are contraries, and Aristotle thinks that the principle of non-contradiction rules out the possibility that the same substratum could be characterized simultaneously by contraries. The form of the mixture is a ratio of the two elements, and hence the mixture itself possesses some intermediate degree of heat defined as a combination of the extreme contraries. The key to Fine's solution to the problem about mixture is that in his theory the compound $(hd) + (cd)/m$ is identical with $hd/m + cd/m$, where the $m$ is the same prime matter throughout the equation.

Consequently, there are two alternative ways of decomposing or analyzing the mixture. On either the material substratum is the same prime matter, but on one the mixture is analyzed as the prime matter that has this complex form $hd + cd$, and on the other it is analyzed as the sum of this prime matter informed by $hd$ plus this prime matter informed by $cd$. This mixture itself does not have all of the potentialities of the original two elements, but does have a potentiality that is derivative from those elemental potentialities. The elements are parts of the mixture due to the fact that the form ($hd + cd$) is a ratio of fire and earth, and the mixture is a genuine mixture of *elements*.[3]

The mixture itself is identical with the sum $(hd)/m + (cd)/m$, where $(hd)/m$ just is some fire and $(cd)/m$ just is some earth. Of course the fire and earth are not *actually* present. If they were actually present, then they would each have their own matter. We could represent their actual presence by $(hd)/m$ and $(cd)/m'$, where $m$ and $m'$ are different. If the matter is different for each element, they are discrete parts of the whole—one part that is the earth, another that is the fire. However, if they are two separately existing elements, then they are not mixed.

Nonetheless, even though the elements are not actually present in the mixture, since fire just is the substantial form of fire ($hd$) predicated of some prime matter, and since earth just is the substantial form of earth ($cd$) predicated of some prime matter, the conditions for being fire and the conditions for being earth are satisfied in these two parts of the complex entity that is the mixture. Hence although they do not have their own matter and hence do not actually exist, there is a sense in which the fire and the earth are present as parts of the mixture.

The equation "$(hd + cd)/m = hd/m + cd/m$" is not meant to capture a dynamic picture according to which the mixture $(hd + cd)/m$ is the result of a physical process by means of which $hd/m$ is combined with $cd/m$. Prior to the act of mixing, the fire and the earth are separate from each other, each in different locations, and each having its own prime matter. Prior to the mixing the fire is $hd/m1$ and the earth is $cd/m2$, where $m1$ is not identical with $m2$. The form of the mixture is not a new *substantial* form, and the mixing of the fire and earth is not the coming to be of a new substance. For the four elements, their passing away is always the generation of something else. However, in the case of *mixing*, fire and earth are not destroyed, but must still exist in the mixture.

Consequently, since they have not been destroyed, this fire ($hd/m1$) and this earth ($cd/m2$) are present in the mixture $(hd + cd)m$. If the persistence of substances requires sameness of prime matter, then since $(hd + cd)/m$ is the same as the fire ($hd/m$) + the earth ($cd/m$), it follows that $m$, the matter of the mixture, is the same as both $m1$ and $m2$. To see this all we need to do is observe that given that the original fire ($h/m1$) is identical with the fire ($h/m$) that is in the mixture, and the original earth ($c/m2$) is identical with the earth ($c/m$) that is in the mixture, it follows that $m1$ is identical with $m$, and that $m2$ is identical with $m$, and consequently that $m1 = m2$. Nonetheless, prior to the mixing, $m1$ and $m2$ are distinct. I will not here explore the problem, or its ramifications for Fine's interpretation, except to note that it points to the fact that prime matter (if such there be) has no identity independently of the compound of which it is the matter. This tells against the idea that prime matter is a principle of identity. Rather, the identity of prime matter is derivative, and needs to be relativized to the identity of the compound of which it is the matter. Since prime matter has no characteristic by virtue of which its identity can be traced through time, its identity must be determined compositionally by reference to the whole of which it is the matter.

Suppose now that the mixture is physically resolved into its ingredients, and some fire $hd/m3$ and earth $cd/m4$ are recovered. Although Fine claims that his general analysis does not require that the fire and earth that are recovered are identical with the fire and earth that originally went into the mixture (what he calls 'strict recoverability') he argues that this is in fact the case for Aristotle. If so, then on the assumption that sameness of substance requires sameness of matter, $m1 = m3$ and $m2 = m4$.

To Fine's arguments can be added the observation that given that mixing is different from generation and passing away, the original fire and earth were never destroyed. By the same token, the reclaimed fire and earth were not generated. However, material compounds cannot just pop into existence without a process of generation, and so the reclaimed fire and earth must be the same as the original fire and earth.

## II. Does Fine's Analysis Solve the Problem?

Fine's analysis is designed to allow us to distinguish cases in which some fire and earth have been replaced by something new that does not have them as in some sense parts, from cases in which they have been mixed but not destroyed. If on Fine's analysis the sense in which the elements are present in the mixture is given by the formula $(hd) + (cd)/m = hd/m + cd/m$ one might reasonably object as follows:

> The expressions "$(hd) + (cd)/m$" and "$hd/m + cd/m$" represent alternative decompositions of the mixture. The only sense that his analysis attaches to the claim that the elements are present in the mixture is that the latter expression can be used to refer to it. However, or so the objector would have it, this is just a notational variant for "$(hd) + (cd)/m$," and as such makes the presence of the elements amount to no more than the fact that some matter possesses the complex form $(hd) + (cd)$. If so, his analysis fails to give us a non-Pickwickian sense in which the elements are present in the mixture.

This objection may be elaborated more fully. In the notation there is an expression "$hd/m$" that in a stand–alone context refers to some element. However, in his analysis it is embedded in the expression "$hd/m + cd/m$."

No reason has yet been given for thinking that in this context "*hd/m*" refers, much less refers to an element. After all, the expression "*(hd + cd)/m*" is used to refer to a compound in which the form *hd + cd* is predicted of *m*. Although Fine says that the form *hd + cd* is a ratio of the elements fire and earth, it (or so the objector would have it) is really just a ratio of elemental potentialities. Calling it a 'ratio of elements' does not make it one. The fact that this kind of 'ratio of elements' is predicated of some matter requires only that the matter has the form (*hd + cd*), not that some elements are present. When *hd + cd* is predicated of the matter all that actually exists is the result of the mixture, namely (*hd + cd*)/*m*. As yet we have been given no reason to suppose that use of the expression "*(hd + cd)/m*" involves a commitment to the presence of the elements in the mixture. Moreover, the referent of the expression "*hd/m + cd*" is identical with the referent of "*(hd + cd)/m*." The use of the former expression has no ontological commitments over and above the ontological commitments of the latter, and so the former need not be interpreted as attributing to some matter either the substantial form of fire or the form of earth. Hence it need not be construed in a way that requires the presence of elements. Given that the referent of "*hd/m + cd/m*" is identical with that of "*(hd + cd)/m*", and that the ontological commitments involved in the use of the two expressions cannot be different, Fine's analysis has not revealed any meaningful sense in which fire and earth are present in the mixture. In effect, this objection is attempting to tell a deflationary story according to which "*hd/m*" as it occurs in the expression "*hd/m + cd/m*" has no referent at all, and this latter expression is treated as no more than a notional variant of "*(hd + cd)/m*."

In order to meet this objection, Fine needs to insist that despite the fact that the mixture is susceptible of alternative decompositions, the one expressed by "*hd/m + cd/m*" is privileged in the sense that its structure represents the way the ontological primitives are related to Aristotle's theory. Be seeing how he is able to meet this objection we can appreciate the importance for his analysis of the idea that the elemental potentialities are genuine and primitive forces in nature.

The four elements themselves are ontologically basic, and at the present level of analysis their substantial forms are the most basic physical powers.[4] The decomposition "*hd/m + cd/m*" is privileged because it shows how to decompose the mixture into prime matter and the potentialities of the most basic physical bodies. The decomposition expressed by "*(hd + cd)/m*" is not in *this way* privileged because the expression "*(hd + cd)*" does not pick out one of the ontologically basic forces in nature. The potentiality that it refers to is a combination of elementary potentialities, and as such is derived from them. If the form of the X that results from some physical transformation of elements was not in this way derivative, but in fact was a new primitive, then the form of X would be a substantial form, X would be a new substance, and the change in question would not be mixing but instead would be generation.

This is what happens in the case of living things. The form is a new primitive, and the acquisition of that form is generation. For living things, the form is the soul, where the soul is not a potentiality derived by means of combinations of the potentialities of elementary matter. The point of having substantial form account for generation is that the substantial form, for example the substantial form of a horse, is not derived from the basic primitive powers of the matter. For mixtures, the forms are derivative in this way, and that is why mixtures are not substances. For a living thing, however, its generation is in principle different from mixture because the form or soul is not defined simply in terms of some kind of vector summation of some elemental forces. Souls are substantial forms, and as such are new primitive powers.

For the purposes of Fine's analysis of mixture itself it is not important what the primitive forces are, but if he is to avoid the kind of objection sketched in this section it is crucial at this level of analysis that the substantial forms of the elements either are, or have as necessary concomitants, primitive forces. Although I do not claim that this in fact correctly represents Aristotle's considered view, the following intuitive picture should help to make clear the kind of commitment his analysis requires in order to treat certain decompositions as privileged. The sublunary sphere contains the four natural places of the four elements. Fire has the potentiality to go to and occupy the natural place at the periphery. Think of its substantial form as the natural potentiality that is responsible for it moving to that place and for it staying in that place when it gets there. This nature or potentiality may be thought of as a bonding of heat and dryness. (Here perhaps we might think of dryness as responsible for motion to an extreme, and heat as responsible for motion away from a center.) Likewise, earth by nature occupies the center of the universe, and is characterized by coldness and dryness.

The substantial forms of the elements are taken as basic. These themselves are analyzed as being or entailing bondings of hot, cold, wet and dry, and each substantial form may be decomposed into two component potentialities. The forms of mixtures are themselves defined not as ratios of these potentialities, but rather as ratios of bondings of these potentialities. Hence they are in effect ratios of the elements. As a consequence, although it is true to say that the mixture is the substantial form $(f + e)$, or $(hd + cd)$, predicated of $m$, there is a still more basic level of decomposition in terms of the most basic primitive explanatory powers in the physics. This is the composition represented by "$f/m + e/m$" (or, alternatively, "$hd/m + cd/m$"). This view about the primitive nature of substantial forms explains why one decomposition is privileged, and in a sense that requires that according to the theory the elements are present in the mixture.

Of course this does not show that they are *actually* present, and of course it should not. Although the elements are present in the mixture they are not active. On pain of violation of the principle of non-contradiction, the theory cannot treat the behaviour of the mixture as the behavior of something having the potentialities of earth and the potentialities of fire. The powers and potentialities of the mixture are, however, derivative from elemental potentialities not merely in some computational sense that would be acceptable to the instrumentalist, but in the sense that in order for them to exist at all the elemental potentialities must be there in a certain combination. Their ontological status is that they are combinations of such potentialities, and this requires that they cannot exist without the potentialities of which they are combinations. Since the elemental potentialities cannot exist without the elements, this in turn requires the presence of the elements in mixtures in order for the mixture to have the form and the potentialities it does.

## III. Prime Matter

It is crucial for Fine's view that neither the potentialities of the basic elements, nor their combinations, are given an instrumentalist construal in his account of the forms of mixtures. In this Section I consider whether his use of prime matter is also crucial to his analysis and his solution to the puzzle. If the elements are compounds, it will be difficult to free Fine's analysis from this commitment. Furthermore, if the analysis is to explain the potential existence of the elements, it requires the mixture to have the same matter as the elements (when in the mixture), and so requires the elements to be compounds.

To see these points, consider once again the mixing of fire and earth. The analysis of mixture should tell us what the form of the mixture is, and in Fine's analysis it does so in terms of some kind of operation on the forms of the elements that serve as ingredients of the mixture. The form will be $f + e$ (or $hd + cd$). What about the matter? His analysis requires that the elements themselves are subject to hylomorphic analysis, and that when in the mixture the elements have the same matter as each other. (Thus in the expression "$hd/m + cd/m$", it is important that the "$m$" picks out the same matter in both of its occurrences.)

Without the identity "$(hd + cd)/m = hd/m + cd/m$" his account does not give us the elements themselves as present in the mixture. All we would have is the decomposition expressed by "$(hd + cd)/m$." That gives us merely some complex form predicated of some matter, but does not allow us to say that the elements are present in the mixture. The identity statement needed to capture this further idea requires that the elements themselves are compounds. So, whether or not the matter for the elements is *prime* matter, the analysis which allows Fine to explain how the elements are present in the mixture is incompatible with any view according to which the elements themselves are not compounds.

What then is at stake in treating the substratum of the elements not just as matter, but as *prime* matter? Traditionally it has been thought that in *Metaphysics* Z3 Aristotle introduced the notion of prime matter by reference to the notion of predication. The (alleged) need to distinguish subject from what is predicated of the subject was said to require that there is some subject, the being of which cannot be captured by any predicable—a subject that has whatever determinations it does have accidentally.

The mathematically structure of Fine's analysis does not by itself commit Aristotle to this notion of prime matter. However, it is also a part of the traditional view that Aristotle's account of the mutual transformations requires a *persisting* matter for the elements so that whenever one element is transformed into another there is a persisting substratum. On this view, the basic elemental potentialities are predicated of prime matter, thus giving us a way to treat the elements themselves as compounds.

Fine's analysis is neutral on the question as to whether there is a persisting substratum for elemental change, and if so, what it is. However, if we add the premise that the elements never exist in an unmixed state, and that all bodies contain all four elements,[5] his analysis does require a common matter for the elements. This is due to the fact that regardless of whether when unmixed the elements have prime matter as their substratum, when mixed the material substratum of each has to be the same as the material substratum for the mixture. Thus any attempt to provide different kinds of material substrata for the elements *as they occur in mixtures* will fail if Fine's analysis is accepted. Fine's analysis will not be able to avoid commitment to prime matter as traditionally conceived unless the material substratum that the elements have in common when in mixtures is not the same as the persisting material substratum for their transformations.

Given that the persisting substratum for change is the substratum that comes to possess the form of the mixture, it follows that the material substratum for elemental transformation has to be the same as their material substratum when present in a mixture. This material substratum, however, cannot be identified with the elements or any combination of the elements for the simple reason that *all* of the elements are analyzed in terms of it. Furthermore, it cannot be something that is or is necessarily characterized by a defining potentiality of the elements, or any combination of them, for no matter which potentiality (or potentialities) one chooses for this role, there will be some element that has as a defining property a potentiality that is logically incompatible with that. The common substratum that the elements share when in a mixture has none of the defining properties of the elements as its essential nature, and hence is prime matter as traditionally conceived. Thus, although the mathematical structure of Fine's account does not make use of the fact that it treats the matter of the elements as prime matter, this feature of his presentation cannot be detached from the rest of the theory without giving up claims that Aristotle wants to make.

It is clear that Fine's analysis (i.e., the analysis in terms of levelling) cannot avoid commitment to prime matter by denying that the four elements are hylomorphic compounds, and it is hard to see how the analysis can be used as an interpretation of Aristotle if their substratum is not prime matter. If the type of analysis he offers is the best or only way to solve the puzzle about mixture, this gives us good reason to attribute a doctrine of prime matter to Aristotle.

## IV. Persistence of Matter in Substantial Change

So far we have been considering Aristotle's claim that when mixed together the elements exist potentially. He also uses the notion of potential existence in his account of substantial change, and holds that the matter from which a substance is generated exists potentially in the substance. In some sense the matter is a part of the substance. Like elements potentially existing in mixtures, it has potential though not actual existence when the substance exists.

Can this potential existence of the matter be accounted for in terms of the possession by the substance of some potentiality derived from that matter? This concluding Section looks briefly at the way in which Professor Gill provides an account of this sort of the potential existence of matter in substantial compounds.[6] It will be argued that her account is subject to the same kind of difficulty we found above for attempts to characterize the potential existence of the elements in mixtures in terms of potentialities of the mixtures.[7]

For Aristotle the three elements of change are form, privation, and a persisting substratum. In the case of the generation of a perceptible substance the persisting substratum is matter, and the substance itself is a compound of matter and substantial form. Aristotle avoids the charge that they are generated out of nothing by insisting that they come to be from matter that exists prior to the generation of the new substance that it becomes. If the preexisting matter persists and still exists as the same substance even when it is the matter of the new substance, then the new substance is merely an accidental compound. The result of the change is simply that individual matter having some new form as an accidental property. Such a product is an accidental unity in the way that a pale man is. It is a unity of a substance and accidental attribute. However, a substance itself is not an accidental unity of substance and attribute, but instead is an intrinsic unity. If we try to avoid this consequence by denying that the matter persists as a constituent of the substance that comes to be, we are no longer able to distinguish substantial change from sheer replacement.

Aristotle is able to solve the problem in this way. Prior to the coming to be of an F, the matter is potentially but not actually an F. What makes it the case that the change is the generation of an actual F out of a potential F is the fact that the matter persists as a constituent of the compound substance that is generated. However, the matter is potentially, but not actually present in the new substance. The potential presence of the matter must be robust enough to secure the continuity of the change, but without threatening the intrinsic unity of the compound.

On Gill's view Aristotle can vindicate the composite substance's status as a genuine unity by distinguishing its functional matter from the matter from which it was generated, and showing that neither the functional matter nor the original matter are related to the form in such a way as to entail that material composites are accidental unities. The functional matter is defined by reference to its capacity to function, and hence by reference to the form of the substance. It does not have a nature of its own distinct from that of the form, and so the fact that living things have functional matter does not make them accidental unities. This, however, is not the matter from which they came to be. That matter is something that has a nature of its own prior to becoming the composite. Although prior to the change it makes sense to refer to that matter as an individual, it simply cannot be the case that it survives as an individual after the new substance has come into being. No individual substance is composed of individuals. Once the composite exists, the matter survives not as a separately existing substance with a nature of its own, but rather as a universal possessed by the composite. For the matter to exist in potentiality after the coming to be of the new substance is for that substance to have the potentialities of the original matter. The preexisting matter had defining powers or potentialities, which prior to the change were possessed essentially by the matter itself. After the change they are accidental properties of a new substratum, namely, the new substance. As such, the matter is in fact a universal property that, although possessed by the composite, is not part of the nature of the composite. The nature of the composite substance is definable by reference to its form alone, and the composite itself is not an accidental composite of some original matter and form. On this view, then, the persistence of the original matter consists in the possession by the substance of a kind of universal property.[8]

Earlier we considered attempts to explain the potential existence of the elements in mixtures as consisting in the possession by the mixture itself of some potentiality derived from the potentialities of the elements. It was argued that these kinds of accounts all fail in that they do not enable one to distinguish mixing from generation and corruption. Aristotle needs to be able to distinguish genuine coming to be from sheer replacement if he is to answer the Parmenidean successfully. However, if the potential existence of matter in a compound simply consists in the fact that the compound possess some potentiality, or set of potentialities, then the claim that the matter has this kind of 'potential existence' does not rule out the possibility that the original matter was destroyed, and this new compound just popped into existence. The claim that the new object has a set of powers that are a lot like the defining powers of the old thing is compatible both with the view that the old thing has become this new substance and the view that the matter was destroyed and this new thing has replaced it. Consequently, any attempt to explain the continuity of substantial change by reference to some set of powers or potentialities of the product will fail. In order to reply successfully to the Parmenidean, one needs to provide an account of potential existence of matter that can be used to distinguish generation from sheer replacement.[9]

The Ohio State University

## NOTES

[1] Aristotle's view (see II.3 and II.8) is that the elements never occur in a pure unmixed form, and that all mixed bodies contain all four of the elements. Among other things, this helps to explain why in *Met.* Z16 Aristotle says that the elements exist only as potentialities. In the real world, they occur only in mixtures. However, since the analysis of mixture is independent of these claims I will not try to take them into consideration here.

[2] They exist in a certain mode, *dunamei*. For the purposes of this paper, this will be translated either as "potentiality" or "in potentiality". The nominative *dunamis* will be translated as "a potentiality." These translations should be thought of as stand-ins for the Greek, and not as involving a particular view about the important issues concerning how the notion of a physical power is connected with his notion of potentiality.

[3] Strictly speaking, in this representation the ratio is a ratio of the substantial forms of fire and earth. However, those substantial forms cannot be instantiated in the given ratio unless fire and earth are present in that ratio. The formula can be rewritten directly as involving a ratio of elements as follows: $(f + e)/m = f/m + e/m$. In either case, the elements themselves must be present in the mixture.

[4] Although Fine is treating the forms as bondings of pairs of powers, all that is in fact necessary is that the substantial form has such pairs as a necessary concomitant.

[5] See Note 1 above.

[6] Mary Louise Gill, *Aristotle on Substance: The Paradox of Unity* (Princeton: 1989).

[7] Her interpretation involves an additional interpretive difficulty. The usual view is that 1049a27–29 distinguishes two ways of being a substratum—either as being a *tode ti* (in the way that an individual substance is), or as not being a *tode ti* (in the way that matter is); see Z13 1038b5–6. Her reading (see previous Note) requires us to take 1049a27–29 as *distinguishing* the universal from the substratum (and doing so by virtue of the fact that one of the pair is *tode ti*, and the other is not). However, in the following lines the proximate matter is the substratum of which form is predicable, and if the substratum is to be distinguished from the universal, then the proximate matter cannot be the universal.

[8] In support of this, she takes the manuscript reading to *to katholou* (universal) at 1049a28 rather than the widely accepted emendation of Apelt, *to kath' hou* (that 'of which' something is predicated)—see her footnote 22.

⁹ This paper is a slightly revised version of comments delivered on an earlier and shorter version of Professor Fine's paper (this volume) at the December 1992 Los Angeles Area Colloquium in Ancient Philosophy. I would like to thank the audience and Professor Fine for helpful discussion.

# SCIENCE AND THE SCIENCE OF SUBSTANCE IN ARISTOTLE'S METAPHYSICS Z

BY

ROBERT BOLTON

If it is the business of the *same* science to study substance and also the attributes of substance, then the science of substance must be *a particular demonstrative science.*

*Metaphysics* B.2 997a30–31

## I. Scientific Method in Aristotle's Metaphysics[1]

In the early stages of the development of his own metaphysical science in *Met.* Γ. Aristotle considers various views about scientific method that differ sharply from his own. For instance, he considers the view of those who insist that everything in a science, including even the axioms such as the principle of non-contradiction, must be *demonstrated.* He comments on those who require this as follows:

This they do through lack of education, since not to know of what things one must look for a demonstration, and of what things one must not, shows lack of education. It is impossible for there to be a demonstration of absolutely everything since this would go on to infinity so that, on this proposal, no demonstration would be possible. (4 1006a6–9)

Just what *kind* of education it is that is lacking for those who disagree with Aristotle on this point of method he does not here explicitly say. But his argument in correction of their view clearly draws on material that is more fully developed in the *Posterior Analytics* (I.3 72b5ff). Shortly earlier in Γ.3, moreover, Aristotle comments quite generally on those who would challenge him "about truth and the procedure (*tropon*) which it is necessary to use to grasp it." Such challenges are only raised, he says,

231

"because of a lack of education in the *Analytics*. For they [those who raise such questions] should know about those things [in the *Analytics*] already when they come [to the study at hand] and not need to inquire into them while they are listening" (3 1005b2–5).[2]

Here Aristotle indicates rather plainly that the questions about method or the procedures for reaching truth which are relevant for his current inquiry in the *Metaphysics* are systematically dealt with in the *Analytics*. Needless to say, this message has not been widely received by Aristotle's recent interpreters who have been nearly unanimous in supposing that the method of the *Metaphysics* has little or nothing to do with procedures of inquiry recommended in the *Analytics*. Rather, it is Aristotle's *dialectical* method, either as developed in the *Topics* or as amended in the *Metaphysics* itself, which is now standardly supposed to govern his inquiry.

There are, I believe, two main pillars of support for this currently popular view; one based on the analysis of Aristotle's discussion in *Met.* Γ.4 where he produces a dialectical refutation of an opponent who denies the principle of non-contradiction, the other based on the analysis of *Met.* Z and its background in B. In this discussion I wish to concentrate on the latter.[3] It will be useful to begin, however, with a problem concerning Aristotle's view of the autonomy of the sciences that comes up chiefly in Γ.1–2, since it has often been supposed that Aristotle's treatment of this problem shows by itself that he has given up the picture of science, and thus of scientific inquiry, that he develops in the *Analytics*. The core of this problem concerns the relation between metaphysics and natural science.

## II. The Autonomy of the Sciences in Aristotle

It is widely held both by students of Aristotle's natural science and of his metaphysics that, for Aristotle, these two subjects are intimately connected. Thus, we are often told by students of Aristotle's biology that to properly understand what Aristotle says in his biological works, such as the *Generation of Animals*, we need to understand the detailed metaphysical doctrines which he relies on there, doctrines which are primarily displayed in *Met.* Z–H where Aristotle tells us what is most fundamental about substances, particularly the paradigmatic perceptible substances that the biologist studies. Conversely, we are also often told by students of Aristotle's metaphysics that to understand his mature doctrine of substance we need to understand the details of his biology, particularly his discussions of animal generation and development, since it is there that we see his basic metaphysical concepts such as form and matter most actively at work.

An initial difficulty for these standard assumptions derives from Aristotle's customary claims about the nature of any science, biology included. As he tells us in *An. Po.* I.10:

Each demonstrative science restricts its concern to three things: the entities whose existence it posits which fix the *kind* (*genos*) whose *proper attributes* it is its job to study; also the so-called *common axioms* which are a primary basis for demonstrations; and thirdly the [proper] attributes [of the *genos*]. (76b11–16)

According to this passage the domain of concern of each science is quite precisely fixed by the special *kind* or genus with which the science deals and the *proper* (*kath' hauta*) attributes of that kind (see also I.7 75a38–b2, I.28). Even the *so-called* common axioms (such as the principle of non-contradiction) are the concern of a given science only insofar as they are restricted to the kind with which it deals. Thus, Aristotle says, these principles are not strictly common principles but only "common by analogy." The restricted version of each common axiom actually employed by a given science is as special to that science as its other special principles are (76a37–40). The special versions of the common axioms that are employed by a given science, like all its first principles, are reached by induction starting from the special data that require explanation in that science. Induction from these specific data will not support principles, whether so-called common axioms or other principles, whose extent of coverage goes beyond the things to which these data pertain (I.9, II.19 100b3–5, cf. I.18). Given this, the biologist, for instance, must be concerned *only* with what has *uniquely* to do with a certain kind, living things, and with the *proper* attributes of living things, i.e. their attributes *as* living things. It is unnecessary, and even improper, for the biologist *as such* to introduce material from outside this domain. This means that the biologist does not *need* to rely on strictly metaphysical results or principles in order to do biology. More strongly it means that the biologist *should not* attempt to bring into play in biology strictly metaphysical results or principles since such results or principles do not directly and *uniquely* concern the kind with which the biologist deals. The biologist's proofs must depend *only* on principles unique to the special kind with which he deals (I.7 75b17–18). Simply put, the *autonomy* of the individual sciences, as Aristotle conceives it, requires the biologist or other natural scientist to proceed without interference or input from metaphysics. Aristotle's insistence on this is, of course, fundamental to his opposition to Plato. For Plato, the individual sciences are not autonomous. Their fundamental principles do require support from general metaphysics, which Plato connects closely with the study of the Good (*Republic* VI 510–511e, 508a–509b). This Aristotle rejects.

Some will wish to resist attributing the doctrine of the *Analytics*, concerning the autonomy of biology and other sciences, to Aristotle in his *Metaphysics*, on the ground that the conception of science found in the *Analytics* is modified by Aristotle in the *Metaphysics*. However, on the main point in question here, at least, it seems clear that the doctrine of the *Metaphysics* is no different from that of the *Analytics*. At the beginning of *Met.* Γ Aristotle says of the special (non-universal) sciences that they do not concern themselves with any universal study of what is *qua* being but rather they each simply "cut off a part of *what is* and study what happens to *this*" (1003a23–25). Aristotle repeats this point in E.1 where he says, in words that echo the *Analytics*, that all the special sciences "circumscribe some particular being and kind (*genos*) and occupy themselves with this, and *not at all* (*ouchi*) with what is simply or *qua* being" (1035b7–10). He also repeats in Γ.3 the doctrine of the *Analytics* that even the common axioms are used by the biologist, or other special scientist, "only so far as the genus extends with which their demonstrations are concerned" (1005a26–27). These axioms themselves extend more broadly and cover all that is *qua* being. That is, they cover what is any of the ways in which things are, i.e. *as* substances, *as* qualities, etc. Since every genus studied by any special science *is*, in one of these ways in which things *are*, this makes it appropriate, from the metaphysical point of view, that the special sciences should use the common axioms (1005a23–25). But the knowledge that the common axioms hold specifically of the genus that the biologist studies, namely living things, not *qua* being but *qua* living things, is not supplied to the biologist by the metaphysician, since this specifically restricted version of the principle is the special province of the biologist alone. The biologist as such makes no use of, i.e. takes no stand on, any more general version of the axioms, e.g. as applied to what is *qua* being, which is the only version that could be supplied by the metaphysician (1005a22–29). Equally, the metaphysician takes no stand on the axioms as applied to what is *qua* living thing but only as applied to what is *qua* being, i.e. *qua* substance, *qua* quantity, etc. (1005a23–29).

Aristotle does allow, in the *Analytics*, that material from one science can be applied in a science subordinate to it, as principles from geometry are applied in optics (*An. Po.* I.7 75b14–17, cf. I.9). But this is only possible where the subordinate science does, in part, share the *same genus* with the higher science, as optics for instance does study *lines* of a certain sort or sub-species and so *does* make use of their properties *qua* lines in its proofs (I.7 75b7–10, 9 76a8–15). Biology also shares, in part, the genus of natural science in general, namely naturally changing things, so it can make use of principles that apply to naturally changing things *as such*. But biology does not share the same genus, even in part, with metaphysics. Aristotle does not, and could not, say that optics concerns itself "not at all" with geometry, i.e. with the principles of lines *qua* lines; nor could he say that biology concerns itself not at all with natural science, i.e. with the principles of naturally changing things *qua* naturally changing things. But he does insist in *Metaphysics* E.1 that the special sciences concern themselves "not at all" with the principles of what is *qua* being. The special sciences are, thus, not subordinate to the study of what is *qua* being in the way in which optics is subordinate to geometry, or biology is subordinate to natural science. In general, then, it seems clear that in the *Metaphysics* as well as in the *Analytics* Aristotle is quite firm on the point that the biologist can and should quite work successfully without any need for input from the study of what is *qua* being or metaphysics. (Biologists with whom I have discussed this point find this result unsurprising).

Nevertheless, it might still be argued that the reverse does not hold, that the metaphysician should still pay attention to the work of the natural scientist, specifically the biologist, since the objects of the biologist's study, plants and animals, are, in some sense, paradigms of substances. Furthermore, even if biology is an autonomous science it can be argued that metaphysics is not, since metaphysics is not a science of the sort described in the *Posterior Analytics*, with some particular kind or genus for its province. Thus, it is open to metaphysics, if not incumbent on it, to make use of material from the special sciences, particularly those which study substances such as biology.

The first question to ask in considering the merits of these claims is whether it is in fact the case, as is often supposed, that the science (*episteme*) of metaphysics which Aristotle begins to develop in *Metaphysics* Γ must be a *science* in a quite different sense from the one which Aristotle has in mind in the *Analytics*. Many have argued that it must be different since it is the doctrine of the *Analytics* both that every science restricts its concern to its own proper kind or genus and also that *being* is *not* a kind or genus (II.7 92b13; cf. *Met.* B.3 998b22, *S.E.* 11 172a13–14). So, it has seemed, the *Analytics* rules out *any* general science of being. If Aristotle then introduces a general science of being in the *Metaphysics*, so it is argued, he must have changed his requirements for a science. The first objection to this is that the general science of being which Aristotle introduces in the *Metaphysics* is not one which requires that *being* is a kind or genus. In the *Metaphysics* Aristotle continues to maintain his doctrine of categories, on which there are many different ways of being not subsumable under any generic real kind *being* (see Z.1 1028a10ff). So the *Metaphysics* does not reject the doctrine of the *Analytics* that being is not a genus and that there is, thus, no science that has *being* for its subject genus. But still, it will be argued, the doctrine of categories also rules it out that there is *any* real kind, whether being or any other genus, which fixes the domain of the general study of what is *qua* being since the study of what is *qua* being is simply the study of what is *qua* substance, what is *qua* quantity, etc., and not the study of anything more generic. So on this ground at least, the science of what is *qua* being, i.e. metaphysics, cannot satisfy the requirements for a science prescribed by the *Analytics*.

But this too seems not to be accurate. It is true, of course, as we have seen, that in Γ.1 (and in E.1) Aristotle contrasts metaphysics with those special sciences which deal *only* with some particular genus or part of being and *not at all* with what is *qua* being universally, and insists that metaphysics somehow does deal universally with what is *qua* being. But in Γ.2 he goes on to explain how it can do this, in view of the doctrine of the categories, and still constitute a single science. His well known answer is, in brief, that the science of metaphysics is unified by the fact that its strict and primary object of study is substance and, thus, the principles and causes of substance (1003b16–19; cf. Z.1 1028b2–7, Λ.1 1069a18–19). This study of substance *includes* the study of all the other things that are *qua* being, such as, for instance, the things in the other categories as such, just because their own irreducible kind of being as members of those other categories is derivative on the being of substance. There is a reference to substance in the definition or account of the mode of being of things in the other categories as such (1003b5–16; cf. Z.1 1028a35–36, θ.1 1045b27ff). However, substance *is* a real kind or genus (*De An.* II.1 412a6). In fact, Aristotle immediately follows up his defense of the unity of metaphysics in Γ.2 with the following remark:

Of each kind (*genos*) there is both one mode of perception and one science, for instance the one science of grammar investigates all the articulate sounds. Therefore, it *is* the work of a science which *is one in its kind (genos)* to investigate all the forms of what is *qua* being, and the forms of those forms. (1003b19–22)

Here Aristotle presumes that he is entitled to conclude from his account and defense of the unity of metaphysics that the study of what is *qua* being, which he has just identified with the study of substance, *does* study one kind or genus just as grammar does when it studies articulate sound as genus, and this genus which he has in mind for metaphysics can only be substance.[4] As he says in the lines immediately prior to those just quoted above:

In every case, a *science* deals strictly with its *primary* object (*proton*), that on which the other things depend, and in virtue of which they are called as they are. Since this is *substance*, it is of substances that the [first] philosopher must grasp the principles and causes. (1003b16–19)

It is this doctrine which leads Aristotle to immediately argue that metaphysics is one in its *genus*. In so arguing he is drawing on his doctrine in the *Posterior Analytics* that the genus, and the items that constitute the genus, *are* what is *primary* (*prota*) in any science (I.10 75a32, I.28).

This same presumption, that metaphysics concerns a single genus, is evident in many other passages as well. For instance in Γ.3, after he argues that the science of substance also studies the common axioms (1005a19–21), Aristotle draws the following conclusion:

It is clear, then, that it is the work of the philosopher, that is, the one who investigates the nature of all substance, also to inquire into the principles of syllogisms. Indeed, it is proper that the one who knows each kind (*genos*) best must be able to discuss the firmest principles of his subject, so that the one who investigates the things which are *qua* being must be able to discuss the firmest principles of all things [*qua* being] and this is the philosopher. (1005b5–11; cf. 1005a25–29)

Here new complications are introduced which would require a good deal of discussion to fully sort out. But also, once again, Aristotle is clearly taking it that the metaphysician or (first) philosopher, as the one who studies the nature of all substance (and thereby everything else *qua* being), does study a single kind or *genos*. In Γ.1–2 Aristotle emphasizes that the study of what is *qua* being is primarily the study of "a single particular nature" namely substance (1003a27, 34, b5ff). In E.1 he equates the study of "a single particular nature" with the study of "a particular genus" (*ti genos*, 1026a24–25). Also, in Γ.2, Aristotle argues that the various forms of unity correspond to the various modes of being so that the investigation of the former as well as the latter belongs to the same science, a science that is the same "in its genus" (1003b35).

Consider finally now, in this connection, the passage in *Met*. B.2, where Aristotle lists among the problems or *aporiai* requiring resolution in his inquiry the following:

Does our study concern substances alone or does it also concern the attributes of substances? I mean, to illustrate, if the solid should be a particular sort of substance or if lines and planes should be, would it be the business of the *same* science or of a *different* science to know these things [e.g. the solid] and also to know the attributes *in each such kind* (*genos*), the attributes that the mathematical sciences are concerned with in their proofs? If it is the business of the *same* science to study substance and also the attributes of substance then *the science of substance must be a particular demonstrative science* though, it is held, no demonstration of *what* substance *is* will be possible in this case. (997a25–32)

Here Aristotle asks whether metaphysics or the "science of substance" should be understood as a particular demonstrative science like, e.g., solid geometry, where the scope of the science is strictly delimited by the *genos*, i.e. the solid or the three-dimensional, and its proper attributes. He argues that just as in the geometrical case, metaphysics must be such a particular demonstrative science *if* there is one single science that studies both substance, understood here as a *genos* on a par with the solid, and also the attributes of substance. The direct *answer* to the question as to whether there is such a single science that studies substance and its proper attributes comes, of course, at the conclusion of Γ.2:

The same theoretical science *will* study not only substances but also their attributes, both those already mentioned and also, prior and posterior, genus and species, whole and part and other things of this sort. (1005a15–18)[5]

Here Aristotle indicates that the "science of substance" does satisfy the requirement which in B.2 he said would be sufficient to make it "a particular demonstrative science" like solid geometry. He achieves this result by, in effect, construing everything else that the science is to study besides the *genos* substance as a proper attribute of substance.

This procedure for delimiting and unifying a science, however, is exactly the procedure used in the *Analytics*. For instance, the *genus* studied by arithmetic, Aristotle says in *An. Po.* I.10 is the unit or numbers (I.10 76a34f, b2f; cf. I.1 71a15). But, as Aristotle indicates, arithmetic does not simply study numbers, it also studies such things as the odd and the even, squaring and cubing, addition and subtraction, etc. These other things are studied by the same science as studies numbers, even though these other things are not all numbers or types of numbers, just because these other things are *proper (kath' hauta)* attributes of numbers (76b3–11). It is the doctrine of *An. Po.* I.10, as we have seen, that the domain of a science is fixed not simply by its *genus*, but by the genus *and* its proper attributes (76b11). The latter come into the domain of the same science as the *genus* by virtue of the fact that they are *proper (kath' hauta)* attributes *of* the genus. But this is exactly how Aristotle unifies the study of what is *qua* being in *Met.* Γ, as we have seen from the conclusion of Γ.2. In E.1 Aristotle distinguishes metaphysics from the *special* sciences because the latter study "a particular genus *but not at all* ... what is *qua* being" (1025b8–10). Metaphysics is to be distinguished from them not because it does not study any particular genus (which Aristotle never says) but because it *also* studies universally what is *qua* being, *given* the genus (and attributes) that it does study. To study what is *qua* being is to study what is in all the different ways in which things *are* and the proper attributes of each of these things (Γ.1. 1003a22). That is it is to study what is *qua* substance, what is *qua* quantity, what is *qua* quality, etc., and the proper attributes of these modes of being. But, Aristotle says, this is just to study the genus substance *and* its proper dependencies or proper attributes (Γ.2 1003b5–10, 1005a13–18).[6] Writers sometimes seem to suppose that for Aristotle the study of what is *qua* being is the general study of what is *qua* existing thing, i.e. the study of what belongs to any existing thing as an existing thing. This is a serious error. For Aristotle there are many distinct ways in which things exist and these are not subsumable under any more general kind, existing thing. One can only study what is *qua* substance, what is *qua* quality, what is *qua* quantity, etc. Nevertheless, the study of these different kinds or genera of things is unified because the study of all these things is the study of the *genus* substance and *its* proper attributes.

It has become standard to suppose that the science of metaphysics is unified by Aristotle in *Met.* Γ.1–2 by a device called "focal meaning," a device presumed not to be found in the *Analytics*.[7] Focal meaning, however, is supposed to serve to unify the study of, for instance, substance *and* quantity, just because the real *definition* of the mode of being of a quantity will include some reference to substance. That is, to be a quantity is, by definition, to be a quantification *of a substance* (Γ.2 1003b5ff; cf. Z.1 1028a18ff). This, in Aristotle's view, is sufficient to bring the study of quantity into the scope of the one science of substance. However, the type of definitional connection employed to secure this result is, as we can now see, the one already recognized and employed for the same purpose in the *Analytics*. One of the ways in which one thing can be a proper (*kath' hauto*) attribute of another, according to *An. Po.* I.4, is by having in its definition a mention of that other thing (73a37–38). For instance, number, the genus of arithmetic, has such things as the odd and the even, and squaring and cubing, for its proper (*kath' hauta*) attributes just because the definition of odd and even, and squaring and cubing, includes a reference to number. (73a40) The even, for instance, is by definition a *number* divisible by two. In general, moreover, the reason why the proper attributes of a given genus are *its* proper (*kath' hauta*) attributes and not those of some other genus and, thus, the reason why they are treated by the science which studies *that* genus and not another, is just that the definition of those attributes includes a reference to that genus (see, for examples, *An. Po.* I.10, 76b3–11, cf. *Met.* Γ.2 1004b10–13). Thus, the very same device used in the *Analytics* to secure the assignment of the study of a certain *collection* of attributes to a single science, namely by virtue of their being *proper* attributes, in the sense described at 73a37–38, of the same subject genus, is just the device by which Aristotle assigns the study of quantity, quality, etc. to the same science as the science of substance in *Met.* Γ. So the underlying unifying device which operates in the case of so-called focal meaning is *not* a new device, introduced in Γ but absent from the *Analytics*, but rather the same device as is used to give unity to a science such as arithmetic in the *Analytics*. This is quite explicit in *Met.* Z.5 where Aristotle introduces the notion of a proper attribute on which we have been focusing in the *Analytics* and indicates that the way in which the attribute odd cannot be defined apart from its genus number is the same as the way in which quality, for instance, cannot be defined apart from substance (1030b18–28, 1031a1–4).

Those who have discussed focal meaning have typically supposed that it involves an interconnection among different senses or uses of the same word or expression, and one might wonder whether this comes into play in the case of say, arithmetic. Whether it does or not is not important for the present discussion. What is important for present purposes is that the underlying device that unifies any science according to the *Analytics*, namely that there is a primary subject genus which is referred to in the real definition of the other objects studied by the science, is the same as that used to unify the science of what is *qua* being in *Met.* Γ. Whether the appropriate *words* are in use to justify the application of the non-Aristotelian term 'focal meaning', is, from this point of view unimportant. As Aristotle says in *Categories* 7: "It may sometimes be necessary to create a word if no word is in force where by rights there should be one" (7a5–7).

However, it is of interest in this connection that Aristotle does claim in Γ.2 (1003b16) that *every* science "deals strictly with its primary object, that on which the other things [studied by the science] depend, *and in virtue of which they are called as they are.*" This claim is obviously meant to apply to arithmetic, say, as much as to metaphysics and it seems to indicate that Aristotle believes that there is in fact some single word or expression in use that is applicable to numbers in a primary way and to the other things that arithmetic studies in a secondary way, just as in the case of "what is" (*to on*). The expression which he has in mind for arithmetic is, presumably, *to arithmetikon*, i.e. arithmetical. This applies to numbers in a primary way and, e.g. to squaring and cubing in a derivative way.[8] It is easy to see how to extend this example to "create" a single word to cover all the objects of any science, both primary and derivative, in case there should not be one in use. The *Analytics* does not interest itself in this, nor does it say anything against it. But, in any case, the claim that in any science the things other than the primary items which constitute the subject genus are "called as they are" by virtue of the subject genus, in the crucial sense that there is a reference to the subject genus in the proper real definition of the others, is the clear doctrine of the *Analytics*.[9]

These results are sufficient to show that in the *Metaphysics* Aristotle has not in the least given up the requirement of the *Analytics* that every science is concerned with some distinct kind or genus. On the contrary, he seems to be doing everything he can in Γ to meet the requirements of his *aporia* in B.2 so as to guarantee that despite certain appearances to the contrary, generated in particular by the doctrine of categories, the study of what is *qua* being, as the study of the real kind or genus substance *and* its proper attributes, does strictly satisfy this requirement for a science in the *Analytics*.[10] If this is so then just as the biologist who studies his own proper kind, living things, and their proper attributes and principles *as such*, can and should proceed without any need for expertise in metaphysics, so the metaphysician, who studies his own proper kind, substances, and their proper attributes and principles *as such*, can and should proceed without any need for special expertise in biology. (Metaphysicians with whom I have discussed this point find this result unsurprising.)

## III. The Science of Substance in Metaphysics Z: Starting Points

A natural response to the conclusion which we have come to at this point would, I think, be this. Even if this conclusion is somehow essentially correct, still it requires qualification in light of the following fact. In *Met.* Z–H where Aristotle engages directly in the study of substance, a great deal of his inquiry is concerned, as he himself often says, with the investigation of "perceptible substances," the paradigms of which are living things. It would seem that his study of, so to speak, the ontological structure of these living things, for instance in Z. 7–9, does and must draw on important facts about these things *as* biological or at least natural objects, and that, in turn, his analysis of their ontological principles must help reveal to the biologist or the natural scientist the principles and causes of these objects which interest him (cf., e.g. Z.11 1037a10–17).

The short and quick response to this understandable, and standard, view is just that the metaphysician is interested in perceptible substances and their causes and principles only *qua being*, i.e. *qua* substances, while, as Aristotle indicates in E.1, the biologist is "not at all" interested in them and their principles *qua* being or *qua* substances but only *qua* living things (1025b9). As Aristotle says in Γ.2: "These things [studied by metaphysics] are proper (*kath' hauta*) attributes of what is *qua* being and not of what is *qua* numbers or *qua* lines or *qua* fire," or, one might add, *qua* living things (1004b5ff. Aristotle's fullest statement of this important doctrine is in *Met.* M.3 1077b17ff). To see properly what this quick answer comes to it would be necessary to study in full the details of what Aristotle actually does in *Met.* Z–H where he does investigate perceptible living substances *qua being* and not *qua* living things. While this is hardly possible here I do want to try to make a reasonable start in that direction in order to at least illustrate the significance of the rather general and abstract results to which we have come thus far and to give some indication of the approach to the understanding of *Met.* Z which these results suggest. This approach is quite different from that followed in the recent literature. Since, however, there is space here only to indicate the bare outlines of the new approach and of the arguments which favor it, detailed discussion of the alternatives must be postponed to another occasion (see Bibliographical Note).

The upshot of our discussion so far is that we have good reason to suppose from *Met.* Γ and its background in B that Aristotle takes pains to see to it that his study of substance is "a particular demonstrative science," *as science is described in the Analytics.* If this is so then we would expect Aristotle to follow in the *Metaphysics* the procedures of inquiry which he recommends in the *Analytics*, particularly in Book II, and repeats elsewhere for all such sciences. Generally speaking, as his summary of these procedures, in the opening chapter of the *Physics* for instance, makes clear, scientific inquiry starts from what is most familiar or best known *to us* about some subject and proceeds to find what is best known absolutely or *by nature* in the form of principles and causes which *explain* what is previously best known to us (184a16ff). The previously known data, as described by Aristotle, give us the "knowledge *that*" of which the principles, when discovered, give us the "knowledge *why*." Our ultimate knowledge *why* comes chiefly in the form of *definitions* which tell us *what* our object of study essentially is (*An. Po.* II.1–2, 8, 17). As the *Physics* in particular makes clear, explanation of the previously known data by reference to basic definitions may involve clarification of, and thus some qualification of, those data, but, at least as so qualified, the job of the principles is to *explain* the previously known initial phenomena (184a21–26). So we need to investigate whether these procedures of *inquiry* of the *Analytics* and *Physics* are, for Aristotle, the ones followed in the study of substance in *Metaphysics* Z itself. But it is worth pointing out in advance that already in *Metaphysics* A.1 Aristotle's general description of science and of the procedures by which it is acquired, a description which he clearly takes to cover metaphysics as well as, say, medicine, is in full conformity with the discussion in the *Analytics*. (At 981b25 he refers us to his discussion in *Ethics* VI.3 for further details on what he means by a science and how it is learned, and there, 1139b32–33, he refers us for still further details to the *Analytics*.) How, then, is this reflected in Z?

That Aristotle intends quite generally in Z to be inquiring into the *causes* and *principles* of substances as such is clear from the summary of the contents of Z at the very beginning of H.1 where he says that he has throughout Z been doing just this (1042a4–6). That he intends his procedure in Z to involve moving from what is most familiar or best known to us about substances to what is best known absolutely is clear from the fact that he says at the end of Z.3 (1029b3–12) that this is just what he is doing.[11] That Aristotle intends his procedure to move us from knowledge *that* to knowledge *why*, is clear, for instance, from Z.17 where he describes his aims in just these terms (1041a10ff). He also indicates there that this knowledge *why* will provide us with the definitional knowledge of *what* his object of inquiry, namely substance, *is* (a6ff).

These general descriptions of *scientific* method in Z introduce the procedures of the *Analytics*. How do they help to shed light on what Aristotle is doing in Z? Consider first Z.1–2. There Aristotle, as a preliminary to pursuing the definitional question: What *is* substance?, sets out some initial phenomena about substances or, if you will, basic realities. In particular he says that the basic realities, the things that *are* primarily and without any qualification (1028a30–31) are not such things as walking and sitting and being healthy, since these things do not exist on their own separate from some *more* basic reality or substance. Rather the basic self-subsistent realities are the particular substances (*he ousia kai to kath' hekaston*), e.g. the particular human beings, the subjects that do the walking and the sitting. They are the things which are "implied in the predicates" 'that which is walking,' etc (1028a20–29, cf. *An. Po.* I. 22 83a10: "When I say 'that is which is cultured is white,' I mean that *the man* who is accidentally cultured is white"). So, Aristotle concludes, "it is because of *this* [particular] *substance* that each of those things [walking, being healthy, etc.] *is*, so that this substance will be what is primarily, not what is in a qualified way but what is without qualification" (1028a29–30).

It is important to keep in mind that in Z.1 Aristotle explicitly says that individual substances *of this sort*, particular things that walk and sit, as determinate, self-subsistent basic subjects (a22–27), are the things which *are primarily without qualification*, i.e. are primary substances. (Cf. *Catg.* 5 2b38: "It is because the primary substances are subjects for everything else [i.e. for the secondary substances and the items in the other categories] that they are said to be substances most strictly.")

Aristotle also says, however, in Z.1 that a basic reality, or what is primarily (1028a14), among those items that are *predicated* of things, items which we find in the various different categories, is what we mention when we answer the question *what* some particular self-subsistent thing or "this" *is*, rather than what we mention when we indicate what some "this" is *like*, or how much of it there is, just because the former does indicate "what some *this* is" (a17). (Cf. *An. Po.* I.22 83a24: "Predicates which indicate substance either indicate, with respect to that of which they are predicated, something which *just is* that thing [e.g. a man] or something which *just is* that sort of thing [e.g. an animal].")[12]

It has been common to suppose that in saying these things in Z.1, *before* he goes on to consider the question: What is substance?, Aristotle has already introduced some sort of potentially intolerable ambiguity or inconsistency into his doctrine of substance, by introducing two apparently incompatible marks or criteria for substance—namely (1) being a *particular* self-subsistent individual of the sort that walks or sits, and (2) being *what* such a thing *is*, that is some sort of universal or essence. According to some interpreters this ambiguity is never resolved, at least not explicitly, since Aristotle later says without any correction both that primary substances, i.e. "the things which we say are substances most of all," are particular individuals (Z.7 1032a19, 8 1034a4), and that primary substances are forms (Z.11 1037a28–29). According to most interpreters, however, this ambiguity *is* explicitly resolved when Aristotle determines what it is that does the best job of measuring up to these two criteria. This turns out to be a form, since a form is a very good case of *what* something is and at least a plausible candidate for being a particular individual or "this". However, this resolution is achieved only at the cost of rejecting the idea that particular individuals which walk and sit, such as Socrates, are primary self-subsistent realities, and so at the cost of rejecting what is said about substance in the *Categories*.

## IV. Explanada in Z.1 and in the Categories

Now one might have reservations right away about whether this last story, which is accepted by most interpreters, could be correct on at least two grounds. First, one might doubt whether a form (either a species form or a so-called particular or individual form) could at all be a particular self-subsistent thing *as Aristotle understands that notion in Z.1* since it is unclear how, for Aristotle, any such form could exist on its own as a separate and independent thing that walks or sits. Secondly, one might also doubt whether such a form is at all a good candidate for being *what* some perceptible substance, say a particular horse, *is*, since Aristotle quite regularly emphasizes that a proper definition of *what* some natural biological object such as a horse *is* must take account not only of its form but also of its matter (see, e.g., *Met.* E.1, *De An.* I.1, and further, below).

   But, putting these questions aside for the moment, what seems in any case clear is that if Aristotle is proceeding in Z.1 as he normally does in *scientific* inquiry, as understood in the *Analytics*, it is a mistake to think that when he says the two things which he does say about substance in Z.1 he is doing anything like setting up (potentially competing) marks or criteria for substances by which to judge the merits of various candidates mentioned in answer to the question that he goes on to investigate: What is substance? Consider, for example, what Aristotle would accept as a starting point for inquiry about his favorite scientific paradigm, lunar eclipses, *before* asking: What is an eclipse? As he indicates in *An. Po.* II.1–2 and 8, we might start inquiry into *what* an eclipse *is* by previously knowing *that* an eclipse is a "certain loss of light by the moon" or *that* an eclipse is "a failure of the full moon to cast shadows when the sky is obviously clear" (93a23, a36ff). Given this information, this specification of what is initially best known to us about eclipses, we ask *what* an eclipse *is* (89b34, 93a16ff). But these two different facts are not marks or criteria by which to judge the credentials of various proposed *instances* of eclipses. Rather these are facts of which we are looking for an *explanation*, facts of which a proper answer to the question: What is an eclipse?, will give us an explanation. Consider the proper ultimate answer to the question: What is an eclipse? According to Aristotle the answer is: An eclipse is an interposition of the earth between the sun and moon. This is the ultimate cause or "middle term" which is, for Aristotle, just *what* an eclipse *is* (*An. Po.*II.2 90a1ff, II.8 93b7). But the question: Is this interposition a good candidate for *being an instance* of a loss of light by the moon or for *being an instance* of a failure to cast shadows on the moon's part?, is unintelligible. This kind of event—the earth's coming in between sun and moon—is not even the right sort of thing to be an *instance of* a failure of the moon to cast shadows. What it is, however, is a very good candidate for being what *explains* instances of the failure of the moon to cast shadows and also for being what *explains* instances of a certain loss of light by the moon. As such it is *what* an eclipse *is* as Aristotle understands that notion.

   Let us consider now how to apply this to Aristotle's discussion in Z. In Z.1, I suggest, we are presented with what is initially best known to us about the basic realities. The primary basic realities without qualification, namely the particular individuals such as the things that walk and sit, are the determinate self-subsistent subjects of which the other things, such as colors and sizes, are only attributes. This, surely *is* something that is most apparent *to us*, about basic realities. But also, according to Aristotle, the basic realities or substances include those cases of *"what something is* which indicate a substance" because such things really show us *what a particular substance* or primary reality or "this" is. (Aristotle gives, as an example of what some "this" is, *man*, 1028a17, cf. *Top* I.9 103b27ff.) What does this second claim mean? How might it also plausibly be supposed to be something best known to us about basic realities? To begin with, it is not at all clear that when Aristotle speaks of "what something is" in Z.1 he has in mind what he is often supposed to have in mind, namely something like an abstract universal or form or essence. He does use this expression for such things, of course, later in Z. But here the expression is specifically used to pick out entities in the first category; and at least in the *Categories* itself, where he does use this expression in describing entities in the first category, he clearly uses it not for forms or essences but for the *species* and *genera* of the basic particulars, i.e. the real tribes and races into which they fall.

After the primary substances their species and genera are quite reasonably the only things *said* to be (secondary) substances, since they alone *of the things which are predicated* [of a primary substance] reveal the primary substance. For if one is to say of a particular man *what* he *is*, one will properly give the species or the genus ... So these are the only other things that are reasonably *said* to be substances. (5 2b29–37)

The language which Aristotle uses here, and the point which he makes is, quite clearly, very close indeed to what we find in Z.1. By "what something is" in such a discussion, however, where the first category is in question, Aristotle means, for instance, a species and not a form or an essence or, indeed, any kind of abstract universal. A species is constituted (in part, but only in part) by its members and their concrete matter, and is not an essence or an abstract universal (*P.A.* I.3 643a24, *Met.* Δ.28 1024a29ff, Z.8 1033b24f, 10 1035b27f). A species for Aristotle is something that occupies a certain ecological niche in the concrete natural world (*History of Animals* I.1 487a10ff). This is not true of the abstract objects that we normally call universals. Thus a species, say the self-perpetuating race of kangaroo, can be said to thrive in Australia. But abstract universals are not self-perpetuating and they are not the sorts of things that thrive in Australia. (They are mainly nominalists out there, or so it is said). Also, for Aristotle a universal, at least in one sense, is the sort of thing that can be wholly present in and wholly common to more than one thing at the same time. Thus, it can be wholly present in more than one place at the same time (Z.13 1038b11f, 16 1040b25–27; cf. B.6 1003a7–9). It is simply a "such like" (*toionde*, 1039a2). A species does not have this character. The race of kangaroo, for instance, is not a "such like" wholly present in any particular kangaroo.

A species is, of course, according to the *Categories, said of* many things, namely its members (5 3a9ff). Thus, as something that is in some sense *predicable of many things*, a species is a *katholou* or universal in that general sense (*De Int.* 7 17a39f). But this does not make a species a universal in the sense that Aristotle has in mind in, for instance, Z.13 and Z.16. There a universal is simply a "such like," something of which a standard example is the common form or essence of human beings or, as we might put it, *humanity* (1038b8–23). Humanity is a "such like." It is strictly common to many individuals, so it can be wholly in each of its instances and thus be wholly present in more than one place, e.g. in Socrates and in Callias, at the same time (1040b25–27). The human *species* on the other hand is not the same thing or the same sort of thing as humanity. It is not simply a "such like" that is wholly present in Socrates, or wholly in more than one place at the same time, anymore than a family, say, is a "such like" wholly present in each of its spatially discontinuous members. Rather, the human species is a concrete substance *of* a certain sort (*Cat.* 5 3b20–21). In the *Categories*, Aristotle distinguishes two kinds of universals, i.e. things that are predicated of many things. There is the universal that is *simply* a "such like," for instance a qualification of a certain sort, such as *white color*. But there is also the type of universal, for instance the human species or the genus of the animals, that is not simply a "such like," of this qualitative sort or any other sort, but rather is a "*substance* which *has* a certain qualification" (3b16–21). A differentia by contrast, which Aristotle describes in the *Metaphysics* as comparable to a form, is only a *poion* or a sort of qualification, i.e. a "such like," and in this way quite different from a species or a genus (*Top.* IV.2 122b15f, 6 128a20ff; *Met.* H.2). This does not mean, of course, that a species is just a set of particulars. Rather it is, among other things, a set of particulars with a certain actual concrete ancestry and so similar to a family which is also not simply a set of particulars (see Δ.28 1024a29ff, Z.8 1033b29ff.).

So, for future reference, it is worth noting that, according to the *Categories*, no universal, in the sense of a mere "such like," is a substance— neither a primary substance nor a secondary substance. Moreover, the point which Aristotle introduces in the passage from *Cat.* 5 2b29f is introduced as what is *said*, not said just by some people, or by this person or that, but simply said. That is, he does seem to take this to be the sort of thing that is commonly agreed to or best known to us, and quite plausibly so. What it comes to would seem to be this. In addition to the individual *particular* human beings, buffalo, trees, etc., which we all *take* to constitute, as self-subsistent subjects, the basic realities, there are also the species and genera that these things belong to, namely such things as the human race, the race of horses, the self-perpetuating herds of buffalo, forests of evergreens, etc., which we all also take to be part of the basic furniture of the world. Our reason for this is just that these species and genera with their own special concrete ecological niches fundamentally determine *what* the *particular* basic realities are and could not fail to be without ceasing to be: (Cf. *Top.* IV.5 125b37: "It is impossible for a thing to remain still the same thing if it should completely change its species; the same animal, for instance, cannot be a man at one time and not at another.") That is, reality just would not be what it fundamentally is, *as we ordinarily understand it*, if it did not contain both the basic particular individuals and the actual concrete races and tribes, so to speak, that mark these individuals off from each other and make them what they are. So another fact about basic reality which seems as obvious as anything, to us at least, is that *what* the basic particular things are, their concrete species or kinds, as the things which demarcate them into their basic real self-perpetuating groups, are primary realities by contrast with the qualities, quantities etc., which the particulars also possess.

When Aristotle introduces the claim in Z.1, that "what a thing is" is *primary* (1028a14), he says that it is "primary *among these things*," i.e., among the kinds determined by the ways in which things are said to be as marked out by the modes of prediction (a13). As his subsequent discussion and examples show, Aristotle means that the "whats" which signify and demarcate substances are primary by comparison with the things or "whats" that demarcate items in the other categories. He does not say that they are primary by comparison with the particular individuals (1028a27), since these individuals do not constitute by themselves one of the groups of things which *are predicated in different ways* as marked out by the categories. So what Aristotle says here does not conflict with his later claim in Z.1 that what is primarily "without qualification" is the particular individual substance (1028a25–31). The doctrine that species are basic realities, i.e. substances, is, of course, one that Aristotle takes for granted elsewhere, e.g. in his biological works (see *P.A.* I.4 644a23–25).

The upshot of this is that Z.1 presents us with two facts about primary reality which are indeed most familiar to us. First, the particular individuals of the sort that walk and sit are the basic self-subsistent subjects and as such are the primary realities *without qualification*. Second, the species and genera of these particular individual substances, i.e. their races and tribes, rather than their qualities, etc., are what indicate *what* those individuals really *are*, and must be to be those individuals, and as such are primary realities not without qualification but only by comparison with the qualities, etc. Now these facts are not only rather obvious facts, to us at least, they are also, rather obviously, not inconsistent. They introduce no intolerable or potentially intolerable ambiguity or inconsistency into Aristotle's doctrine of substance. In fact, they summarize, quite succinctly, the consistent doctrine of substance of the *Categories*. It is, moreover, quite reasonable that they should do this since it is clearly the aim of the *Categories*, as any reader can easily verify, to say what substance or basic reality is from the point of view of what "is said" (*legetai*) and what "is held" (*dokei*) and what "appears so most of all" (*malista phainetai*), that is from the point of view of what is most familiar to us, which, as we have seen, is just where Aristotle takes himself to be staring in Z (see, e.g., *Cat.* 5 2a11–12, b15–17, 24–31). What is most familiar "to us," for Aristotle, can, of course, include the predominant views of well-known experts as well as what is commonly supposed but it seems clear that the views in question here are common ones. (The views in question would, of course, have been denied by most experts in Aristotle's day—a matter to which we will return below). The subsequent task of Z should then be, if Aristotle is following his usual scientific procedure, to *explain* or give the *cause* of these facts which are most familiar to us, not to replace them. To do this he should *go on* to explore the question: What is substance?, just as he indicates he will at the end of Z.1. But he should explore this question in the way in which it should be explored in scientific inquiry. In this case the answer to the question will *explain* the things that are best known to us about substances by giving their *causes*. If this is what Aristotle does then, of course, what he does will go beyond the *Categories*, as we go beyond our initial understanding and account of an eclipse as a certain loss of light by the moon when we explain why the moon loses its light, but it will hardly be inconsistent with the *Categories*.[13]

It is, of course, possible that the facts about basic reality, as laid out in the *Categories* and in Z.1, e.g., that particular animals are basic realities and basic self-subsistent subjects, might turn out not to be explicable or only to be explicable with some important qualification added (cf. Z.2 1028b13–15). Similarly, it might turn out that the apparent loss of light by the moon is not, or is not without significant qualification, an explicable natural phenomenon but only some accidental occurrence, or a non-accidental occurrence which is best understood not as a *loss* of light by the moon at all (but only, e.g., as a turning of the bright half of the moon away from us: see *An.Po.* II.8 93b5–6). In either case our initial presumptions will not turn out to constitute knowledge, at least not without some clarification. But if our initial presumptions are explicable, then they were correct and the process of explanation alone can validate their correctness as items of *scientific knowledge* without qualification.

Some will want to resist the thought that Aristotle is starting in Z with the doctrine of substance of the *Categories* as something given which he wants to try to explain. This might seem to beg the question against certain of his materialist opponents who think, e.g., that atoms are the basic self-subsistent subjects not such things as the individual human beings that walk and sit, and also against his Platonist opponents who think that it is their own Forms which indicate *what* the particular perceptible substances *are*, not the species and genera of those particulars. (See *Met.* A.3 983b8ff, 4 985b4ff, 988b4–5; Z.13 1039a8–11: this shows clearly that the material in the *Categories* and in Z.1 is not accepted by Aristotle's main philosophical opponents even if it is commonly accepted and true.) But Aristotle's approach does not so beg the question. If he is successful he will have *explained why* the things he and we take as given about basic reality are so, in proper scientific form, and this is to say that he will have a given a demonstration and proof of them. In this case he will not have simply assumed that his opponents are wrong he will have proved that they are wrong.

## V. Some Questions for this Approach

It remains to be seen whether the whole of Z can be reasonably interpreted as an explanatory project along these lines. But before taking up that topic it will be useful, I think, to consider several natural objections to the proposal that Aristotle does not mean in Z to be replacing the doctrine of substance of the *Categories* but only to be explaining its main constituents. The first objection is that in the rest of Z, after Chapters 1 and 2, Aristotle is clearly attempting to *answer* the question raised at the end of Z.1, namely: What is substance? He considers various proposed answers to this definitional question, such as substratum, essence and universal. Thus, one might argue, he cannot be presupposing that the answer to the question of what we mean by a substance, or what it is that belongs to the first category, is already settled since this is just what he is investigating. This objection, however, is based on a misunderstanding of Aristotle's scientific method. It is like objecting that if we are engaged in investigating *what* a lunar eclipse *is*, we cannot be presupposing that we know what we mean by a lunar eclipse or that we know what (at least some of) the lunar eclipses are. But clearly we can know what we mean by a lunar eclipse–namely a certain loss of light by the moon—and we certainly can know what things are most obviously lunar eclipses when we inquire *what* an eclipse *is*. When Aristotle takes himself, in a scientific context, to be inquiring *what* something *is*, he *always* presupposes that we know *that* the thing in question is. This involves knowing what we mean by the name and also acquaintance with paradigm cases of the thing in question (*An. Po.* II.1–2, 8–10).

Aristotle does speak of the various answers to the question *what is substance* as providing proposals for how substance is to be *defined* (Z.4 1029b–1). In scientific inquiry, however, on Aristotle's standard view, there are various different *kinds* of definitions which come into play (*An. Po.* II.10). There are initial definitions which, among other things, may specify what the name of the thing signifies by mentioning features of the thing with which we are normally initially acquainted. Possession of this kind of definition is prior to any inquiry into what a thing essentially is, according to Aristotle, so this cannot be the kind of definition Aristotle is after in considering these proposals in Z. The other kinds of definition, however, are just those that provide or lead us to a fundamental account on the basis of which we can explain the initial features (*An.Po.* II.10). So that should be what Aristotle takes the proposed candidates mentioned in Z.3 to supply.

A second, more straightforward, objection is simply that Aristotle seems plainly, in Z.7 and 11, to identify *primary* substance with form or essence in some sense. It is hard to see how this can be compatible with the doctrine of the *Categories*, or even the doctrine of Z.1, that particular individuals of the sort that walk and sit are the primary realities without qualification. But here again it is important to remember Aristotle's views on scientific method. In the *Categories* the term 'primary substance' is introduced as an abbreviated form for the longer expression "that which is strictly, primarily and most of all *said to be* a substance" (5 2a11–12). That is, a primary substance there is what is most of all a substance from the point of view of what is said or what is most familiar to us about basic realities, i.e. that they are the self-subsistent basic subjects. However, in scientific contexts, Aristotle customarily distinguishes what is prior or primary *to us* and what is prior or primary without qualification or by nature (*An. Po.* I.2, *Phys.* I.1). In general, moreover, as Aristotle says in *Met.* Δ.11:

Things are said to be prior and posterior, given that there is in each kind something which is primary (*proton*) and a principle, because they are nearer *to* some such principle, which is defined *either* without qualification and by nature, *or* in relation to some thing or some place, *or* according to some people. (1018b9–12)

So primary substance according to what is first "to some people," e.g. *to us*, will not be the same thing as primary substance "without qualification and by nature." Since, as Aristotle himself indicates at the end of Z.3 (1029b7ff), what he is interested in finding in Z is substance which is primary without qualification, i.e. by nature, by contrast with what is primary to us, while in the *Categories*, he is clearly interested in substance which is primary to us, there is no reason why the candidates should be in competition or be the same. Rather, to answer the question what is a substance primarily, not to us but by nature, will be to give a principle which accounts for what a substance is primarily to us.

A third objection to the approach suggested here will be based on material in *Met.* B and its treatment in Z. In B, as we have noted, Aristotle lists a number of problems or *aporiai* for resolution, problems which are generated in part, as he says, by conflicts among the opinions of others (995b2–4). Since Aristotle's method for the resolution of such problems is dialectic, some would argue, we should expect his methodology in the rest of the *Metaphysics* where he offers resolutions of these problems to be dialectical and not to follow the pattern of inquiry described in *An.Po.*

II. The trouble with this objection is that it is based on a false assumption, namely that Aristotle's method for the resolution of *problems* or *aporiai* is dialectic. There are, of course, dialectical problems that require resolution by dialectical means, as Aristotle makes clear in *Top.* I.11. But not all problems are dialectical. In *An. Po.* II.14–18 Aristotle also discusses how to formulate and resolve *problems*, not dialectical problems but problems of a scientific nature (98a1ff). Examples of such problems are: Why are certain plants deciduous?; or Why does the moon suffer eclipse, or loss of light? (II.15 98b32ff, 98b19ff). Such scientific problems, like dialectical problems, can also be generated by differences of opinion (see, e.g., *G.A.* II.7–8, 746b13ff., cf. *An.Po.* II.8 93a36ff.). But these problems are resolved not by dialectical discussion and reasoning but by finding the appropriate cause or middle term through which the effect in question, such as loss of light by the moon or recurrent loss of leaves by certain plants, can be not only deduced but *explained* (98a24ff). This way of resolving problems, in Aristotle's view, is not dialectical or *kata doxan* but scientific or *kat' aletheian* (*An. Pr.* I.30 46a3–10). That is, what matters is not whether the premises of the reasoning which resolves the problem are as *endoxa* or accredited as possible, which is the only standard for dialectical argument, as Aristotle says in *Posterior Analytics* I.19. What matters is whether the conclusion is inferred through a true explanatory middle term, which, he says, is not a standard for dialectical but for scientific argument (81b18–23). So if Aristotle is attempting in *Met.* Z to resolve problems and disputes by finding genuine causes which explain certain results, as we have already seen he is, then the problems with which he is dealing are not being treated as dialectical problems but rather as scientific problems.

This result can be inferred directly from the fact that Aristotle characterizes his inquiry in Z generally as an attempt to answer the question: What is substance? As Aristotle makes clear in the *Topics* and *De Interpretatione*, a question or problem of the form: What is X?, is not a dialectical question or problem.

It is agreed that not every general premise [or question] is a dialectical premise [or question]. For instance, "What is man?" is not ; and "In how many ways is what is good so-called?" is not. For a dialectical premise [or question] is one to which it is possible to *answer* "yes" or "no" and in the cases mentioned this is not possible. (*Top.* VIII.2 158a14–17, cf.I.10, 104a8, *De Int.* 11 20b26–30)

This point is one to which Aristotle returns in *Met.* Z itself. In Z.17 he notes that it is easy to misunderstand the nature of the inquiry when one raises a question of the form: What is X?, "because [in such a case] the object of inquiry is expressed simply and not by specifying [the object by saying] that 'these things are this'" (1041b1–2). That is, as Aristotle goes on to explain, whenever we inquire *what* something *is* we must already know *that* it is, where our knowledge *that* it is takes the form of knowledge of some fact such that to find the true explanation for that fact is just to find the answer to the question *what* the thing is (b4–5). For instance, Aristotle says, to properly inquire "what is thunder?" is to ask "why one thing belongs to another" or, more specifically, "why noise occurs in the clouds" (a23–26). So an inquiry as to *what something is* is *always* a *causal inquiry* (1041 a27–28, b7). Since a dialectical inquiry is not a causal inquiry or search for the true middle term which explains some connection, as Aristotle points out explicitly in *An. Po.* I.19, the inquiry into *what something is*, e.g., what substance is, cannot be a dialectical inquiry. As Alexander says in his commentary on the *Topics*: "All dialectical problems are reducible to the inquiry to determine *that* something is the case, or to determine *whether* something is the case—that is to two of the four types of inquiry of which Aristotle spoke at the beginning of the second book of the *Posterior Analytics*. For problems concerning *why* something is the case, or *what* something *is*, are not dialectical problems" (*in Top.* 63.15–19).[14]

On this way of understanding Aristotle's project it has, arguably, a good deal more philosophical credibility than on the usual approach. On the usual approach, if one may briefly summarize it without excessive travesty, Aristotle's objective is to find a candidate for substance, or basic reality, that satisfies certain so-called criteria, such as being a basic subject and being an essence or what something is. But why should we accept these things as criteria for being a basic reality in the first place? We are usually told that the former criterion for being a basic reality is the one accepted by Aristotle's materialist predecessors, the latter the one accepted by the Platonists. So Aristotle wants a candidate that will be agreed to by both of the main philosophical traditions of his day, or that will at least conform as much as possible to their different views. But that agreement or conformity would only be of interest if the two criteria are initially compelling in themselves. What, for instance, is initially compelling about the suggestion that a basic reality is an essence? Some would reply that it is because essences are the primary knowables. But, even assuming that this is so, why should we suppose that the primary realities are the primary knowables? Not simply because this is Plato's view, surely. And not because this is known *a priori*, surely. Aristotle himself denies this, of course, in the *Categories*, so it would be quite peculiar for him to simply presume in the *Metaphysics* that it is true. The claim that Aristotle's objective in *Met.* Z is to answer his question: What is substance? in a way that conforms as much as possible to the views of his most important predecessors, is based normally on the assumption that his method of procedure in *Met.* Z is dialectic, and this is always his objective in dialectic. But we have just found good reason to doubt that his method of procedure in *Met.* Z is dialectic.[15]

On the alternative suggested here our starting point is not the arcane views of certain philosophers, or any *a priori* certainties, but rather what we are initially presented with in experience. Experience presents us with the fact that particular natural living organisms such as particular plants and animals are self-subsistent realities, basic independent items in the furniture of the world, if anything is (Z.7 1032a18–19, 1 1028a20–31). It also presents us with the fact that the tribes and races to which these particulars belong, such as the human race and the tribe of the trees, are more fundamental in reality than the colors, sizes, etc. of these particulars since they are more fundamental in determining what these particulars are (1028a13–20). Similarly, initial experience indicates to us that the moon is subject to eclipse and that broad-leaved plants are deciduous. In all these cases it is the origination of these facts in our experience that gives them their initial warrant. Equally, in all these cases, our subsequent task as scientists is to clarify if necessary, to explain, and, thereby, to validate these facts of experience. This procedure is as intelligible and credible in the one case as it is in the others. In *E.N.* VI.8 Aristotle claims that both in natural science and in metaphysics (*sophia*) the principles are reached in the same way, starting from the data of experience (1142a19). (For the nature of *sophia* see VI.7 1141a 12–20, a33–b3, cf. *Met.* A.2 982a8–10, 21–25, 983a5–11.)

This does not mean, of course, that there is no room for dialectical investigation in a scientific inquiry concerning *what* something *is*. Dialectic has a role to play in such a scientific inquiry in, for instance, examining and criticizing the proposals of others on definitions as well as other matters, just as Aristotle says it should in *Top* I.2 (101a34–b4). There are many obvious examples of this in Z as we shall see in some detail below, particularly in the analysis of the arguments of Z.13. Nevertheless, the ultimate objective of the inquiry cannot be reached by dialectic since dialectic cannot answer *or even ask* the strictly causal question: What is substance?[16]

## *VI. Substance as Substratum: Z.3*

Let us turn now to see whether it is an appropriate explanatory or causal principle that Aristotle is concerned to find in Z. In Z.3, as we have noted, Aristotle lists several possible answers to the scientific question: What is substance?, namely substratum, essence, universal and genus. However, he describes these things not as candidates for substances but, at 1028b35, as candidates for "the substance *of* each thing," that is, presumably, of each thing which is a substance, particularly the most familiar cases which he has just listed in Z.1–2 (cf. Z.6 1031a18, 13 1038b10, M.1 1076a8). Later, in Z.13, Aristotle makes it clear that he was earlier interested in substratum in Z.3 as a *cause*, and, thus, as providing the kind of answer to the question: What is substance?, or the kind of definition of substance, which gives a cause. He says later in Z.13, referring back to Z.3

(1028b33ff), that of the various things that are said to be what substance is he has already considered two, the essence and the substratum; so he will now go on, he says, to consider the universal, since "the universal is *also* held to be a cause," along with the essence and the substratum (1038b1–8). In fact, of course, no reader of *Met.* A, Γ or E could doubt that Aristotle's whole inquiry is a causal inquiry, particularly a causal inquiry concerning substances (see, especially, Γ.2 1003b16–19, cf. the summary of Z in H.1 1042a3–6). Aristotle opens *Met.* Λ as follows: "The subject of our inquiry is substance, for we are seeking the principles and causes of substances" (1069a18–19). If so, then in looking for the "substance *of* each thing" Aristotle will not be trying to answer the question: What is a substance according to us? He has already answered that question in the *Categories*, and in Z.1–2 (cf. M.10 1086b16–20). He will rather be looking for something which *explains* the facts which he has brought forward in answer to that question. If this is so, then it will be important to keep it in mind that, just as with his uses of, for instance, the term 'eclipse' in *An.Po.* II.1–2 and 8–10, when Aristotle uses the term 'substance' in Z he can be referring to either of two things, the substance which is primary to us, or the "substance of" these things, which is primary by nature and a cause of the features which the substances which are primary to us have *as such*. In *Met.* Δ.8, Aristotle himself distinguishes these two uses of the term 'substance': (1) to denote the basic self-subsistent subjects, and (2) to denote the "substance of" these things and the "cause of" their mode of being (1017b13–16, 21–26, cf. Z.11 1037a25–26). In Δ.18 the "substance of" a thing is said to be "that by virtue of which" it is what it is, and a *cause* in that sense (1022a14–16, 19ff).

A main candidate for the "substance of" each substance, Aristotle says in Z.3, has been the substratum or underlying subject (*hupokeimenon*). So he proceeds to consider this (1028b36ff). On the reading required by Δ.8 and 18, this means that the substratum, as the "substance of" each substance, is a main candidate for *explaining* certain facts including the fact that the primary realities, such as particular human beings, are self-subsistent subjects. That is, one might reasonably try to explain why Socrates (as a primary reality) is a self-subsistent subject for walking, sitting, etc. on the ground that Socrates has an underlying substratum and having this *explains why* he is a self-subsistent subject of this sort. This view, as Aristotle indicates, might amount to the view that having a form or shape (*morphe*) as substratum explains why Socrates is a basic subject, or that having a combination of form and matter as substratum explains why Socrates is a basic subject. But most commonly and naturally, he says, it takes the form of the identification of substratum with matter. That is, it takes the form of the view that what *makes* Socrates a determinate self-subsistent subject is the fact that he or his features belong to some ultimate underlying matter (1029a1ff).

This is certainly a view worth discussion from Aristotle's perspective. Matter, for him, obviously is a cause of various things; that is, the fact that something is composed of a certain matter does explain various facts about it (*De An.* I.1 403a29ff); and one might suppose that *everything* that is explicable about a thing can and should be explained by reference to its matter. At least, or so Aristotle claims in *Met.* A.3, many of his predecessors did suppose just this, i.e. that matter as underlying subject is the only *cause*, and that the matter of a thing, as the persisting substance of a thing, should be invoked to explain *everything* that is explicable about the thing including the fact, should it be a fact, that it is a self-subsistent subject. In A.3 Aristotle directly connects the view he considers in Z.3, that matter is the only cause by being the substance of each thing in the sense of the underlying substratum of each thing, with their view, and this itself indicates that he is thinking of this view in Z.3 as the view that matter is the *cause* of the substantiality of (e.g., of the self-subsistence of) substances (see 983b6ff, a29–30). In *Phys.* II.1 Aristotle refers again to this type of view: "It is held by some that the nature and the *substance of* natural things is [nothing but] the primary constituent present in them, something which is *in itself unformed*, for instance in a bed the wood and in a statue the bronze ... And if the particular kinds of material [such as bronze] are in turn related to something else [such as water] in the same way ... this will be the nature and the *substance of* these things ... This they say is in every case the substance [of each thing] while all the other things [present in them] are just attributes, states and dispositions of them" (193a9–26). Here it is quite explicit that underlying matter is regarded as the *substance of* an independently existing thing, though not itself an informed or independently existing thing.

Thus, it might be argued, as Aristotle indicates in Z.3 (1029a10ff), that matter, as that which is not *in itself* either a particular thing or of any definite quality or quantity, etc., but rather that of which *all* these things are (directly or indirectly) predicated, seems to be the only single persisting thing possessed by a particular substance such as Socrates that could make him a single self-subsistent subject *with* all these features. "When everything else is stripped off it seems that nothing but matter persists ... For the other things are predicated of the [particular] substance [e.g. Socrates], but the [particular] substance itself is predicated of the matter" (1029a11–12, 23–24). Since Socrates is predicated *of* his underlying matter, that would seem to suggest that we can explain his substantiality or self-subsistence in "bottom up" fashion by appeal to his underlying matter. However, as Aristotle argues, this proposal is unsatisfactory because existence on his own as a "this," a particular thing that walks and sits, is crucial to Socrates being a substance in the ordinary sense, i.e. to his being a determinate self-subsistent subject (1029a22–28). The fact that Socrates has underlying matter cannot by itself account for why *he* is a particular thing who exists on his own who can do such things as walking and sitting. Aristotle does not elaborate or explain in any detail why this is so. But we know, e.g. from Z.16, that there are for Aristotle many things with underlying matter, such as the parts of animals and the material elements, that are not self-subsistent "thises" (1040b5ff). So the possession of underlying matter cannot explain why something is a "this," since if it did these other things would also be "thises." Some things which have matter themselves only "exist as matter" (1040b7–8). As such they are *potentially* substances but not actually substances. So having matter may explain why something is potentially a self-subsistent thing but it does not explain why anything is *actually* a self-subsistent thing (cf. H.2 1043a14ff). That Aristotle has this in mind in Z.3 seems clear from his reference in Z.13 back to the view of matter in Z.3 as what underlies, i.e. what is potentially, the *actual* substance (1038b3–6). So, at 1029a27–28, Aristotle concludes: "This is impossible [that underlying matter is what substance is] since being a self-subsistent thing and a "this" are *held most of all* to belong to *the substance* [i.e. to the particular substance which walks and sits]" (cf. Z.1. 1028a 22–28). That is, the possession of underlying matter cannot explain why such a thing as Socrates is itself a "this" or a thing that exists separately on its own.[17]

On this reading Aristotle's complaint or problem with the claim that matter as substratum is *what* substance *is*, is not that *matter* is not *itself* a "this" or a separately existing thing. On the specific version of the view that matter, as substratum, is substance which Aristotle is criticizing, it is explicitly denied that matter itself is a substratum or subject of a determinate self-subsistent sort (1029a20; cf. *Phys.* II.1 193a11). So, of course, there is no question, on this view of matter as substratum or subject, that matter itself could possibly be a self-subsistent subject. Rather, on this view, matter is the ultimate underlying subject but not thereby a self-subsistent thing, in much the way in which matter is the underlying subject for *substantial* change for Aristotle himself, without thereby being a basic self-subsistent subject. In his later reference in Z.13, back to this view in Z.3, Aristotle makes it quite clear that the notion of matter as substratum of which he earlier spoke was not a notion of matter as a self-subsistent actuality, or subject in that sense, but only as what underlies that sort of subject (1038b3–6; see also H.1 1042a26–28, b3ff). So Aristotle could hardly criticize this proposal on the basis of an assumption agreed to by his opponent that any proper answer to the question: What is substance?, must introduce an entity that *is* a self-subsistent subject. That would blatantly beg the question against his opponent who has not agreed to this and whose very position obviously involves a rejection of this, both as that position is described in Z.3 and in *Phys.* II.1. Nor could Aristotle intelligibly be taking it simply as already established, whether it is accepted by his opponent or not, that any proper answer to the question: What is substance?, must introduce an entity that is a self-subsistent subject. If he were there would be no point at all in his considering at length a theory whose whole objective is to answer the question, whatever it comes to, by producing an entity that is *not* a self-subsistent subject. He must be considering this theory on the assumption that it will at least provide an intelligible and minimally plausible answer to the question worth considering *given* the parameters for a proper answer that have already been established. If, however, Aristotle's assumption, indeed agreed to by his opponent, is that the entity offered in answer to the question: What is substance? must be the "substance of" what it belongs to, i.e. a *cause* that *explains* why the true individual substances *are* self-subsistent actualities, then Aristotle's procedure and his objection are quite in order. He can properly complain, without begging the question, that ultimate underlying matter of the sort the opponent introduces will not explain this.

Instead, as Aristotle says, it seems more likely that the fact that Socrates has a form, or a composite of form and matter, will explain this (1029a29–30). So these would be better taken to be substance (1029a29) by nature, i.e. to be what explains the initial features such as determinate subjecthood and self-subsistence which the substances which walk and sit have as substances. On the standard reading of Aristotle's aims what he is saying here is that form or shape (*morphe*) and the compound of form and matter "would be held to be" *better cases* of independently existing basic subjects than matter. This makes sense as applied to the compound, but little sense as applied to a form or, especially, a shape. Aristotle clearly indicates in Z.13, as we have noted, that his earlier interest in substratum as an answer to the question: What is substance?, was an interest in it as a *cause* (1038b6–8). The standard view of Z.3 does not fit with this. Aristotle cannot, however, without explanation, mean something quite different in Z.3 by his main question: What is substance? than he means in Z.13 and Z.17. This question has a single clear sense for Aristotle in scientific inquiry, as he indicates in *An.Po.* II.1–2 and, e.g., in Z.17 (see further, below, on Z.17).

This way of understanding the claim that substance is substratum has further advantages. It enables us to make sense of various texts which, so far, have been recalcitrant to satisfying interpretation. Consider, for instance, the following objection to the Platonic theory of Forms which we find in Z.6:

It is clear that if there are Forms, as some claim, then substratum will not be substance. For those things [the Forms] must be substances [on the Platonic theory], but they cannot be predicated of a substratum, for in that case they would exist by virtue of participation. (1031b15–18)

On the usual reading of Z.3, what Aristotle must want to argue here is that if Forms are primary substances then the primary substances cannot *be* substrata. To do this, what he *should* argue is that Forms are not substrata. But he does not argue for this. (It is hard to see how he could, since on the Platonic theory the forms are paradigms of substrata. For, roughly speaking, everything else exists only *as* an image of or participant in a Form. Forms do not depend on anything further as substrata, although all other things are dependent on them.) Rather, what Aristotle argues is that a Form cannot be *predicated of* any substratum. This hardly seems to show that a primary substance, that is a Form on the hypothesis in question, *cannot be* a substratum; instead it seems just to be a part, at least, of what might be used to *support* the claim that a form is a substratum, since a substratum *must* be something "not predicated of anything else" (1028b36–39). This muddle is avoided if Aristotle's claim is not that, given the Platonic theory, a substratum cannot *be* a primary substance, but rather that, given the Platonic theory, substratum cannot be what *explains why* the primary substances, i.e. the Forms, are primary substances, i.e. basic self-subsistent subjects. That is, it cannot be the case that *having* a substratum is what *makes* a form a primary substance or basic subject since then the Form *would* be predicated of something as substratum, as a part of its very being. This would, then, on the Platonic theory of predication, require that the substratum *participates* in the Form and so require that the Form as a substance only exists as something actually participated in, which would be inconsistent with the Platonic claim that the Forms exist quite independently of whether they are participated in or not.

## VII. Substance as Essence: Z.4–11

Let us turn now to Aristotle's discussion of the second proposal considered in Z for *what* substance *is*, namely that substance is essence (*to ti en einai*). On the standard approach Aristotle considers whether an essence, in some suitable sense of the term, *is* a primary substance without qualification, a successor to that title to Socrates who is given the title in the *Categories*. To settle this matter, on the standard approach, Aristotle should try to determine whether an essence *satisfies* both of the two supposed criteria for substance, thisness and whatness, so to speak. Now it is clear that Aristotle does in fact come to the conclusion in Z that substance, in some sense, is essence in the sense of form (Z.7 1032b1–2, 10 1035b14–16, 11 1037a5–6, a28–30, 17 1041b7–9). What this must mean, on the standard approach, is that a form, as understood by Aristotle, satisfies the criteria for both thisness and whatness. So proponents of the standard approach standardly try to show that a form, of some sort or other, does for Aristotle satisfy these two criteria. However, as we have already noted, there are very serious difficulties which arise when one does try to show this. A form does not in the least seem to be a *this* in the required sense. Of course, a form is a *this* in some sense, and Aristotle often speaks of the form as a *this* and *separate* because it is "separate in its definition," i.e. it is the subject of a proper definition (H.1 1042a29, θ.7 1049a27–36; cf. Z.4 1030a2ff). But in these passages, where he calls a form a *this*, Aristotle also makes it very clear that a form is not a *this* of the sort he had in mind in the *Categories* and Z.1, i.e. a basic subject which exists on its own, the sort of thing which walks and sits. A form, Aristotle says, is not a *this* "in that way," i.e. as "substances which exist on their own" are (Z.8 1033b21, 29). According to *Met. Δ.8*, the definable form or essence which is a "this" has the term *substance* applied to it not because it is a particular substance and self-subsistent subject, but because it is the "substance of" what it belongs to (1017b22–23). This sort of entity is the "cause of" the type of being possessed by any basic subject (b15–16).

Some defenders of the standard approach undertake to show that Aristotle does think of a form as a *this* or basic subject in the sense in question in Z.1. They argue, for instance, that this follows from the fact that for Aristotle the essence or form of a particular object, as opposed to its matter, is something like the organization of that object, which is the only thing that stays the same through various changes in its matter and other properties, and is able thus to "account for" the identity of the object over time. This, it is concluded, makes it reasonable to say that all truths about the object are ultimately truths *about* its form so that the form truly is a basic subject. But this conclusion does not follow. To say that the possession of a form *accounts for* a particular object's being a subject of various distinct attributes, or *accounts for* its being the *same* subject through various alterations over time, is not to say that the form is the basic subject but only that its presence *explains why* the *object* is a basic subject for all its attributes or alterations. Thus the form is *not* the only thing that stays the same over time. The whole composite object stays the same over time due (in part) to the form. In the *De Anima* Aristotle says of the type of essence or form which he identifies in Z with substance, namely the soul, that it is indeed that which *accounts for* the fact that some subject perceives, thinks, builds, etc. (II.2, 414a4f; cf. Z.11 1037a28ff). But he is quite emphatic that this does not mean that the form *itself* perceives or thinks or builds (I.4 408b5ff). It is *we*, i.e. particular composites of form and matter, that perceive and think and build, not the soul. The view that form, of the sort he clearly has in mind in Z, *is* a basic subject is one which Aristotle himself clearly rejects. So the attempt to show how a form can *be* a *this* in the required sense seems plainly to fail. (It fails, moreover, whether the form in question is a specific form or a particular or individual form, since a particular form or soul can no more be said to perceive or think or build for Aristotle than can a specific form.) Aristotle does sometimes suggest, of course, particularly in *Met. Λ*, that some types of forms might be, or are, capable of separate self-subsistent existence. But he also, again, denies there that the "this" which is the whole soul, i.e. the substantial form, of a perceptible substance such as a plant or animal has or is capable of self-subsistent existence (Λ.3 1070a13–26; cf. *De An.* I.1 403a3–28).

There are also difficulties for the claim that a form is a *what* in the required sense, namely the sense in question in Z.1. For one thing, as we have noted, in Z.1 Aristotle uses the term 'what something is' to designate items in the first category such as *man*, and these are not, according to the *Categories*, essences or forms but rather species and genera. A form is not a proper candidate for being a case of 'what something is' in this sense. Apart from this, the notion of essence or form which Aristotle develops in Z to characterize primary substance is a notion of essence or form as strongly opposed to matter. In Z.8 Aristotle gives as examples to illustrate what he means by such forms, the shape of a bronze sphere as opposed to its bronze, and the form in Socrates as opposed to his organic parts such as flesh, bone, etc. (1033b5, 12–14, 1034a4–7). In Z.10 he elaborates on this last example and identifies the form or the substance itself of an organic body or animal, such as a man, with its proper life function (*ergon*), as opposed to the flesh, bones, fingers and such which figure in the exercise of this function (1035b14–30). Such materials "are neither parts nor origins (*archai*) of the form" (1035a31). A particular *species* of animal or the *genus* animal does involve in its account a reference to such material parts, but the substance or substantial form does not (1035b27–30).

In addition to this, in Z.11 Aristotle says clearly, in summary of his earlier discussion, that the *account* of a primary substance does not include any mention of the material parts, i.e., the material parts which he has been discussing such as the flesh, bones, fingers, and the like. Rather, a primary substance is like the concavity which, together with a certain type of matter, the nose, constitutes the snub nose, and like the curvature which, together with a certain type of matter, constitutes the bronze sphere (1037a24–b4). Given this, it seems clear that the form which is substance in Z is not at all clear case of *what* something *is*, in the sense in question in Z.1, i.e. what some particular individual substance such as a human being is, as opposed to what it is like, etc. The reason for this, as we have already noted, is that, as Aristotle regularly emphasizes, it is necessary in saying *what* such a particular natural substance *is* to give not only its form but also its matter (see, e.g. E.1 1035a1–12). He says this in fact in Z.11, where he points out that one cannot define an animal except by mentioning its various organic parts as well as its form or active function such as perception (1036b28–32).

Some have suggested that, for Aristotle, the definition or account of a substantial form need only *imply* what the matter or material parts are, not actually mention them, and that this will satisfy his requirement that the definition of a natural substance should involve both form and matter. But elsewhere Aristotle makes it clear that he does not believe that the account of the *form* of a biological substance, which he identifies with its *telos* or goal, always implies what the matter or material parts of that substance are (*P.A.* I.1 640a34–b1). Also, in Z.11 Aristotle treats the material parts as on a par with the change or activity (*kinesis*) as what a *definition* of an animal *cannot* be without, where by the change or activity he clearly means the characteristic soul function (1035b17). His worry here is not only that someone might leave the material parts out of *the actual definition* but also that one might mention these parts without mentioning the activity. Both are treated equally (1036b28). By contrast, these parts are not mentioned in the definition of the *form*, Aristotle says, since these parts survive the animal (only homonymously, of course, but that does not affect the point here at issue) and such parts, he says, do not belong in the definition of the form (1035a17–21). It is also clear in the *De Anima* that there is some matter that is excluded from the account of the form, in the case of an ensouled or psychic entity, which, nevertheless is matter that must be included in the proper scientific account of what the thing is (I.1 403a24–b12).[18]

So the form which is Aristotle's choice for primary substance in Z is not only a very poor candidate for being a basic subject it is also a poor candidate for being *what* a particular substance is, as the latter so-called criterion is understood in Z.1 and elsewhere. One might try to resolve this latter difficulty by claiming that while for some purposes, such as the biologists's purposes, a definition based on form *and* matter might be a proper account of *what* a sensible substance *is*, nevertheless in another sense this will not do. It will not do because, as Aristotle says in Z.4 (1030a7ff), in the strictest sense of definition a definition cannot mention one element which belongs to another and definitions based on form and matter inevitably do this. So in this strict sense, but not necessarily in some more relaxed sense, a perceptible substance cannot have a *definition* or account of *what* it *is* which introduces its matter as well as its form. The thing to do if we want to a strict definition of a perceptible substance, e.g. of a human being, is to define it *qua* form or substance, i.e., to define its form, since only this form can have a strict definition. As such, only the definition of this form tells us *what* the perceptible substance *is* in the strict sense.

Now this particular distinction between stricter and weaker types of definition may be, or may not be, one which we should attribute to Aristotle on the basis of his discussion in Z.4–6. In view of what Aristotle says in H.6 one might well doubt that a definition mentioning the form and matter of a human being does mention one thing which belongs to another in a sense such as to exclude it from being a definition of the strictest sort. Even the definition of a form alone, e.g. a soul or soul function, must itself have components (cf. Z.10 1035b1–4). It is hard to see how these components will have any stricter unity than the one Aristotle attributes to the form and matter which figure in the definition of the human being. But even assuming that we do attribute this distinction, or some other similar distinction, to Aristotle it would not follow that we could solve the problem now at hand *by use* of this distinction. That we can only *strictly* define a human being in terms of its form, according to some special notion of strict definition, need not show that we can only properly say *what* it *is* by such a definition, in the sense of *what* something *is* that Aristotle has in mind in Z.1 where he says that, among predicables, a substance is *what* something *is*. Aristotle might well have the more relaxed sense (should that be the way to describe it) in mind there. His example of *what* something *is* in Z.1 as we have noted, is a type of animal such as a *human being* (1028a17). And Aristotle tells us in Z.11 that we cannot define what a type of animal is without mentioning its matter (1036b26–32).

Aristotle is, of course, happy to say in Z.10–11 that in some sense the form *is* the statue or the human being, but, he adds, only the statue or human being *qua* having form, e.g. *qua* having a soul, which is the *substance of* a living thing in the sense of its account or form (10 1035a6–9, b14–22; 11 1037a24–33). So if we are interested in defining *what* a human being *is*, *qua* having a soul or form, i.e. *qua substance*, and if we are thus interested in defining the *substance of* a human being, we might want some special strict kind of definition which omits matter. (We would still like to know, of course, *why* we should be interested in this kind of account of what a human being is. To this we shall later return.) But in Z.1 a substance, or *what* something *is*, seems clearly to be *what* a particular human being *is* without any qualification, i.e. *qua* human being not *qua* having form or *qua* substance (1028a17). And, as Aristotle makes clear in E.1 and Z.11 and elsewhere, we cannot say *what* a human being or any other sort of *animal* is (*qua* that sort of animal) without mentioning its material parts (1036b26–30). So in whatever qualified sense we might say *what* something *is* (e.g. *qua* substance) by a definition of its form alone we have not said what it is in the way required by Z.1 for saying what something is.[19]

So we remain faced with the fact that the entity on which Aristotle fixes in his discussion of substance as essence, seems not at all to be a good candidate either for being a basic subject or "this" or for being for *what* any particular natural substance *is* in the required sense. However, these problems are entirely avoided on the approach suggested here. On this approach when Aristotle says that primary substance without qualification is essence, in the sense of form, he does not mean that an essence or form is a primary substance in the sense of Z.1 (and of the *Categories*), i.e. a self-subsistent basic subject, or that it is a secondary substance, i.e. *what* some given primary substance *is* without qualification in the sense of Z.1 (or of the *Categories*). In other words, he does not mean that form *satisfies* the so-called criteria for a substance of *being* a *this* and *being what* something *is*. He means rather that form *explains* or *accounts for* these properties which those substances have as such. In specific, he means that it is the fact that individual substances, e.g. particular human beings, *have a* form (in a special sense) which explains why *they* are basic particular subjects or "thises" in the sense of Z.1. And it is the fact that a species in the category of substance (and not one in the category of quality, etc.) has such a "this-producing" form in its makeup which explains why such a species is *what* some genuine basic subject *is*. It is, I take it, one of Aristotle's objectives in Z.7–9 to bring out these points. But his clearest and simplest statement of the first point comes in Z.17, so it will be useful here to focus mainly on his discussion there.

## *VIII. Substance as Cause in Z.17*

In Z.17 Aristotle emphasizes, what he earlier had pointed out in Z.13, that by *substance* in his discussion, i.e. in his search for an answer to the question: What is substance?, he means something which is a *cause* which can be introduced to explain certain things (cf. H.1 1042a4–6). He clearly invokes the theory of scientific *inquiry* of the *Analytics* in order to make clear what he has in mind (cf. 1041a10–28 with *An.Po.* II.8 93a16–27 and II. 2 89b36ff). Without a proper understanding of some of the rather technical details of that theory of inquiry given in the *Analytics* it is not possible to understand Aristotle's highly compressed presentation of his answer in Z.17 to the question: What is substance? We have already alluded to various aspects of this theory but it is important for present purposes to be more precise about certain points. According to the theory of inquiry of *An.Po.* II (especially 1–2, 8–10, and 17) the answer to a definitional scientific question of the form: What is X?, is provided when one discovers the special *type* of definition that Aristotle calls a "syllogism of *what* a thing is." He also describes this type of definition as "like a demonstration of *what* a thing *is*" (II.10, 94a1–2, 11–12). In the syllogism and demonstration which provides the material for this type of definition or answer to the: What is X? question, the *major term* designates the entity to be defined and the middle term indicates *what* the thing in question, designated by the major term, fundamentally *is* (II.1 90a1, 8 93a37–b7). It alone indicates *what* the entity fundamentally *is* whose nature is the object of inquiry (II.17 99a21–29, II.8 93b3–7). The major premise of the relevant syllogism (i.e. the premise that connects the major term with the middle term) is, thus, an immediate indemonstrable convertible proposition that expresses what the thing in question most fundamentally is (II.10 94a9–10). Aristotle reaches this doctrine because of his identification of the question: *What* is X?, with the question: *Why* do X's *exist*? (II.2 90a15, 31–32). To answer the latter question, he holds, is just to give the *cause* (*aition*) for the *existence* of X's, and this cause *is* the middle term in the syllogism which establishes *that* X's exist (90a1, 6–7).

Thus, to establish *that* X's *exist* is not to establish an existential proposition of the form 'X's exist,' since such a proposition does not have a middle term. Rather it is to establish the fact expressed in a subject-predicate proposition which articulates what we previously understand X's to be when we know that they exist and are trying to *explain why* they exist. For instance, Aristotle says, when we are trying to explain why eclipses exist, we already know that there are eclipses and we understand an eclipse to be "a certain loss of light by the moon" (II.8 93a16–24, cf. Z.17 1041a15–16). To discover *why* eclipses exist is to discover the middle term, blockage of light by the earth, that connects the moon with its loss of light, such that by use of this as middle term we can syllogistically demonstrate that the moon loses its light. This middle term itself is *what* an eclipse is. (93b7) The syllogism that Aristotle has in mind in this case is, in effect, this:

> The moon undergoes blockage of its light by the earth.
> Blockage of its light by the earth is a loss of its light.
> _____
> So the moon undergoes a loss of its light.

In this syllogism the major term 'a loss of its light' designates the phenomenon, eclipse of the moon, whose definition (*ti esti*) we are searching for. The middle term, or cause of this phenomenon, is *what* this phenomenon *is*. So the second (major) premise states an immediate definitional identity. *What* the loss of the moon's light (= lunar eclipse) *is*, is blockage by the earth. In *Met.* H.4, where he discusses this same example again, Aristotle makes it clear that this syllogism incorporates *all* the *causes* of lunar eclipse—its formal cause, the loss of light; its efficient cause, the blockage by the earth; and its substratum or quasi-material cause, the moon. (1044b8–15. Eclipses have no final cause.) Thus, the above "syllogism of what a thing is" offers us the materials for the kind of definition that Aristotle recommends to the scientist in *De Anima* I.1, the definition which includes *all* of the causes of the entity in question (403a25–27). But its middle term, in this case the efficient cause, offers us the most fundamental cause or account of *what it is*, according to *An.Po* II.

To see how Aristotle means to apply these doctrines in Z.17 in his investigation of the question: What is substance?, it is essential to follow his own lead and to first ask what the phenomenon is, for him, by virtue of which we are presumed to grasp *that* substances exist, the phenomenon or connection between two terms whose *cause* or middle term will be *what* substance *is* (1041a10–24). Aristotle answers this question for us in a highly compressed way in the following passage:

Since it is necessary to grasp *that* the thing exists, and for this to obtain, it is clear that our inquiry [when we ask: What is substance?,] concerns *why the matter is some particular thing.* (To illustrate: Why are these [materials] a house? Because being-for-a-house belongs [to the materials]. And we ask: Why is this, i.e. this body having this character, a man?) So our inquiry [when we ask: What is substance?] is for the cause (*aition*) by virtue of which the matter is some particular thing (*ti*). This [cause] is the form. And [so] this [i.e., form] is [what] substance [is]. (1041b4–9)

Commentators sometimes suppose that what Aristotle wants to explain here (as in *Met.* H.6) is why Socrates' sort of body or matter has a certain form, namely the human form, or why Socrates' form is united with his matter. But Aristotle plainly says that the form is the *cause*, that is, in the terminology of the *Analytics*, the middle term, which connects the two other terms whose connection he wants to explain (1041b7–9). If so, then the form cannot *be* one of the other two terms. According to the general apparatus of the *Analytics* which is very much in evidence here, a cause is always a middle term connecting two other distinct terms.

Others have suggested that what Aristotle wants to explain here is why a certain sort of body or matter, such as Socrates' body, belongs to the human kind or species, on the ground that it has a certain form. But in this case, the "syllogism of what a thing is" that Aristotle has in view here would go roughly as follows:

> Socrates' body has a certain sort of form.
> What has this sort of form is a human being.
> _____
> So Socrates' body is a human being.

In this syllogism, the major term is *human being*. So if this syllogism were the one that Aristotle has in mind in Z.17, this would be the term that designates what he is trying to define. In that case the question he is trying to answer in Z.17 would be: What is a human being? But he is not trying to answer that question in Z.17 but rather the question: What is a substance? The question: What is a human being?, is a question Aristotle deals with in his biological works, not the question of *Met.* Z. If the material from Z, including Z.17, were necessary to answer the question: What is a human being? then the biologist who deals with this question would need to pay attention to metaphysics, i.e. to the study of what is *qua* being. But, as we have seen, Aristotle says in E.1 that the biologist, or other special scientist, should pay *no* attention to the study of what is *qua* being (1025b7–10). Moreover, the syllogism given above provides a very poor answer to the question: What is a human being?, in Aristotle's view. If it provided an answer to that question, the major premise in this syllogism would have to give us an immediate definitional identity. Thus, having the human form (in whatever matter) would be *sufficient* to make something a human being just as undergoing blockage by the earth of its light is sufficient to put the moon, on any occasion, into eclipse. But, as we have seen, Aristotle denies in Z.11 and in numerous other places that having human form is sufficient to make something a human being. Having human matter is also required. So the major premise of this syllogism is false on Aristotle's standard doctrine. This is quite clear in, among other places, *Metaphysics* Λ.5, where Aristotle says: "The cause (*aition*) of a human being is *both* (*te*) its elements, fire and earth, as matter, *and (kai)* its special form. Also there is something further outside, i.e. the father, and in addition to these things, the sun" (1071a13–15). More importantly, we can see in any case directly from the text of Z.17 that the major premise of the above syllogism is not the major premise of the syllogism that Aristotle has in mind in asking: What is substance? The *answer* to the question that Aristotle is asking in Z.17, as the text clearly indicates, is that substance is form (1041b7–9). So *this* is the definitional equivalence that *must* be expressed in the major premise of the syllogism that Aristotle in fact has in mind. So the major premise of the syllogism that Aristotle in fact has in mind cannot be that what has a certain sort of form is (by definition) a human being. It must rather express the proposition that what has a certain sort of form is (by definition) a substance.

It is also clear from the text that the fact that Aristotle is trying to explain, and thus the conclusion of his syllogism, is that "the matter [of a substance] is a particular thing (*ti*)" (1041b5, 8; cf.b2). Given that we know the major premise and the conclusion directly from the text, it is clear what the minor premise of Aristotle's syllogism must be and, thus, it is clear how the entire syllogism must go. It must go essentially as follows:

> The matter has form.
> What has form is a substance.
> _____
> So the matter is a particular thing.

For this to be a valid syllogism, of course, the term 'a particular thing' in the conclusion must designate the same thing as the term 'a substance' in the major premise. But it is easy to see how it can do this. The term 'a particular thing' (*ti*) for Aristotle can either designate a particular kind of thing (e.g. a human being) or it can designate a particular, i.e. a *this*, as opposed to a kind of thing (Z.3 1029a20–26, 7 1032a12–15, H.1 1042a32–b3). In the latter case it will clearly designate the same thing as the term 'substance' by use of a description of substances under which substances are best known to us before we discover the middle term that tells us *what* substance *is*. In the syllogism discussed earlier which expresses what an eclipse is, the major term 'a (certain) loss of light' designates the same thing as 'eclipse' by use a description of eclipses under which they are best known to us prior to our discovery of the middle term that indicates *what* an eclipse *is*. In just the same way 'a particular thing' (= 'a *this*') designates the same thing as the term 'substance' in the present case. In a revealing discussion of the "syllogism of what thunder is" in *An.Po.* II.8 Aristotle also shifts in the same way between the specification of the major term as 'a (certain) noise' and the specification of it as 'thunder' (93b7–12, cf. a20–23). So, more properly expressed, with just three terms, Aristotle's "syllogism of what substance is" is, in effect, this:

> The matter has form.
> What has form is a "this."
> ———————————————
> So the matter is a "this."

The causal role which Aristotle assigns to substantial form in this "syllogism of what substance is" is exactly the causal role that he assigns to it elsewhere. In *De Anima* II.1, for instance, Aristotle indicates clearly what he means by the claim that substance is form: "Substance ... understood in one way, is shape or form, i.e. that by virtue of which something is straightaway said to be a *this*." Since a natural body possessed of life has such a form, by having a soul, he goes on to argue, such a body or "matter" must be a substance of the composite type, i.e. a self-subsistent "this." So, Aristotle says, the common view that "bodies above all things are substances, especially the natural bodies," is explained and justified (412a11–22). This view is justified, of course, only with a certain qualification since Aristotle only demonstrates that natural *living* bodies are substances, or *thises*.

As we can see from this, the discussion in *De An.* II.1 also indicates to us how we should understand "the matter" to which Aristotle refers in his syllogism of what substance is in Z.17. It is natural living bodies that Aristotle has in mind and not any lower level matter. Moreover, in his demonstration in *De An.* II.1 Aristotle is not trying to explain why anything is a human being or an animal or living thing. What he wants to explain is why the natural living bodies are *substances* of a certain sort, i.e. *thises*. Similarly, in Z.17 Aristotle is asking the question: What is substance?, with a special focus on perceptible substances, that is, on the same natural living bodies that he explains the substantiality of in *De An.* II.1. He explains their substantiality or thisness in Z.17 in the same way as he does in De An. II.1, by reference to form. In Z.10 Aristotle alludes directly to the doctrine of the *De Anima* in saying that "the soul of animals (since this is the *substance of* the ensouled thing) is substance according to its definition (*logos*), i.e. form, or the essence of a certain sort of body" (1035b14–16). Here Aristotle again describes substantial form as the *substance of* the living body. He means by this, as we can see from the *De Anima*, not that the substantial form of an animal makes it an animal but that it makes it a substance. To explain what makes it an animal we need also to bring in matter as he goes on to say in Z.11 (1036b28ff) and as he also indicates in the *De Anima* (I.1 403a24–b12).

Aristotle does compare the question: What is substance?, in Z.17, to the question: What is a human being? He also compares it to the question: What is a house? But the point of the comparisons is only to emphasize that one must start in each case by properly articulating the distinct fact to be explained in answering each question (1041a23–28, a32–b7). The question: What is substance? is no more the *same* question as: What is a human being?, than it is the same question as: What is a house? These are, rather, all questions of the same type in that they all are answered by trying to explain some properly articulated previously understood fact. The question that Aristotle aims to answer in Z.17 is the question: What is substance? The answer, of course, is: Substance is form (1041b7–9). He nowhere in the chapter says anything that implies that he has *answered* the question: What is a human being?

So in Z.17, as in *De Anima* II.1, a substantial form is not treated as itself a particular basic subject or "this" but rather as something whose possession explains why certain bodies, i.e. natural living bodies, are "thises." So in answering the question: What is substance?, in Z.17, we are not abandoning the doctrine of the *Categories* but rather explaining why it is so scientifically. Given this we do not need to try to explain away Aristotle's plain statements in Z.7 and again in Z.8 that individual human beings and the like are "substances most of all," i.e. are primary substances and "thises" in the strictest sense. Aristotle's aim is never to challenge or qualify this but only to explain it and, thereby, to demonstrate and prove it.

This is not to say, of course, that the *Metaphysics* does not in any way go beyond or refine the doctrine of the *Categories*. In the *Categories*, for instance, the parts of substances, such as the head of a human being, and presumably the uniform material parts as well, are substances (5 3a29–32, 7 8b15; cf. *Met.* Δ.8 1017b10ff, Z.2 1028b8–11). So are they in the *Met.* as well, where they are referred to as matter. But there they are substances only with a qualification since strictly they turn out only to be substances and subjects *potentially* (Z.16 1040b5ff, H.1 1042a26ff, θ.7 1049a19ff). This is something which only becomes clear when it is discovered that substance is form, since these parts do not have form (= function) on their own but only as parts of a single unified living organism which does have form, and so is a substance and a subject without qualification, on its own (1040b14ff). Since the *Categories* only tells us what substance is from the point of view of what is more familiar to us, i.e. at the pre-explanatory stage, its doctrines are subject to this sort of refinement, in the *Metaphysics*, in accordance with Aristotle's standard scientific method. In the *History of Animals*, for instance, Aristotle collects data to be explained in other treatises such as the *Parts of Animals* (HA I.6

491a6ff). Some of these data turn out not to be explicable, or not to be explicable without qualification. (This has not prevented many from believing that the *History of Animals* was written, in its current version, *after* the *Parts of Animals*, in its current version.) The relation between the *Categories* and the *Metaphysics* is parallel to this.

We can see now why the specification of the form itself which is the substance of a particular substance such as a human being, cannot involve any reference to the matter of e.g., human beings, and why Aristotle goes to such lengths in Z.10–11 to see to it that the definition of a substantial form does not involve matter. Since the form is the *substance of* a *particular* substance or living body it must be able to explain *why* that body is a particular substance, or "this", and it could not properly explain that if the formula of the form itself were not independent of the matter or material parts of the body. As we have seen, for Aristotle this matter only explains, at best, why some body is potentially a substance or "this," not why it is actually a "this." So to introduce the matter as an essential part of what explains why some body is an actual "this" would undermine the effectiveness of the explanation.

## IX. Substance as the Universal in Z.13

This puts us in a position now to turn briefly to perhaps the most problematic part of Aristotle's discussion of substance, namely his consideration of the proposal that *the universal* is what *substance* is, in Z.13. Everyone agrees that Aristotle rejects this proposal. But what does this rejection amount to? As we have seen, Aristotle identifies primary substance with *form* which he identifies with a kind of *definable essence* and, in that sense, with *what* something *is*. However, the definable form of something does seem to be a universal which belongs to a number of different things since no particular individual is definable but only a universal (Z.10 1036a2–7, 11 1036a28–29, M.10 1086b33ff). So how can Aristotle deny that substances are universals if they are *definable* forms?

A standard move to deal with this is to claim that by a *form* in this context Aristotle does not mean a species form, which belongs in common to many things and so is a universal, but rather a *particular individual form* which necessarily belongs only to one thing and is a "this." Another standard move is to claim that while a substantial form is a species form and not a particular form, it still is not strictly a universal since it is only predicated of matter which is not a particular and, therefore, not predicated of a number of distinct particulars as a strict universal is. A variant of this view claims that a substantial form at least does not belong universally to the same things that it is the substance of. There are, however, numerous problem for the view that the form or essence which

Aristotle identifies with primary substance is particular or individual form, such as for instance the problem just mentioned of how this sort of entity could be strictly definable. Also, as we have seen from Z.17, Aristotle quite plainly identifies the form which he takes to be primary substance with a certain cause, namely the thing by virtue of which matter of a certain sort is a genuine basic subject or "this." Earlier in Z.7–9 he goes into some detail in spelling out what this form is which comes to be present in some matter and thereby to account for the fact that a genuine self-subsistent individual or "this" exists, for instance Callias or Socrates. One thing which Aristotle says is that this form exists before Socrates does in Socrates' father (8 1033b16–32). Given this, it is hard to see how this form can be a particular individual form which can only exist when Socrates does. Aristotle also emphasizes in Z.8 that this form is not a *this* or a self-subsistent thing, as a Platonic form would have to be. Rather it is a *such like* or sort which informs Socrates' body when *he* exists as a *this* of a certain sort, but not itself a thing which exists in its own right(b21–24).

This passage confirms the point that the form which is what substance is, in Z, is not a "this" in the sense of Z.1. It also shows, however, that this form, as a *such like* is a universal of a special type, a universal which is wholly present both in Socrates and in his father. Socrates' substantial form may be predicated of his body, as it is in Z.17, but it also belongs in common, or universally, to both his body and his father's body, and to both him and Callias (Z.8 1034a8). Aristotle makes it clear in Z.13 that what is common in this way is a universal and a *such like* rather than a "this" (1039a1–2). So it seems quite obvious that the form which is what substance is, according to Z.7–9 and 17, *is* a universal that *is* predicated universally of the things it is the substance of and is not a *this* or self-subsistent thing.[20] These facts raise very serious difficulties for the view that Aristotle's strategy in Z is to find a candidate for primary substance which is a reasonable candidate for *being* a self-subsistent *this* and not a universal or a *"such like."*

However, these problems are, once again, avoided on the reading of Z suggested here. The proposal that the universal is substance, on this reading, does not involve the claim that the universal *is* a self-subsistent subject or *this*. The proposal is rather that the universal is a cause which explains *why* all the things which are self-subsistent subjects are such. That is, the proposal is that it is the presence of a universal (rather than a substratum or a form or essence) in something which *makes it* a self-subsistent subject. This can be rejected without implying that a substantial form is not a universal. It can be rejected, for instance, on the ground that, on this view, the presence of *any* universal in *any* other thing would make it a self-subsistent subject, and this result is absurd. To reject the view on this basis leaves it quite open that *some* universals are substances, i.e. causes of self-subsistence for their possessors.

Can it be shown, then, that what Aristotle wants to do in Z.13 is to argue that the general claim that the universal is substance, i.e. *every* universal and *only* a universal *makes* its possessor a self-subsistent subject, is false, without arguing that *no* universal makes its possessor a self-subsistent subject? Aristotle introduces his topic in Z.13 as a consideration of the question whether the universal is a cause (1038b7), by which he means, as we have seen from Z.17 and other texts, a cause of the fact that certain things are self-subsistent subjects. What he takes himself to indicate by his initial exploratory arguments in the chapter is that "it seems impossible that any at all (*hotioun*) of the things which are called universals [or are predicated universally] is substance" (1038b8ff). Since all Aristotle says is that this *seems* impossible, which allows that it might *be* possible with some qualification, we need to see just what his arguments finally do establish.

Aristotle begins his rejection of the universal as substance in Z.13 by sketching an argument that raises a puzzle (1038b9ff). What he is concerned with is not the claim that a universal *is* a substance but rather, he says, with the claim that any universal is "the substance *of* each thing" (1038b10) to which it belongs. This must fit with Aristotle's remark that the universal, as substance, is a *cause* (1038b7). Aristotle's first question about this is based on the supposition that the substance *of* a thing must be unique to it. That is, it must be unique to it as a cause; it must uniquely explain *its* substantiality not that of anything else. Since a universal must be common *to* many things, it *seems* no universal can do this.

This argument gives us what we would expect on the suggestion that Aristotle's candidates for substance in Z are primarily candidates for *explaining* self-subsistence not for being instances of self-subsistence. But, nevertheless, Aristotle does use this argument to at least raise a question as to whether *any* universal can play the appropriate causal role, on the ground that it does not have the uniqueness required for this. However, it also seems clear that there is a way of dealing with this problem if the *only* universals we take to be substances, i.e. to have the appropriate explanatory power, are specific substantial forms (and not, e.g., generic forms also). For we can say that a universal *specific* form does *uniquely* account for the substantiality of its possessors. Contrary to the suggestion of the argument which Aristotle sketches to fill out his initial puzzle (1038b9ff), it can *uniquely* account for their substantiality because it does not account for the substantiality of any other particulars of any other species and there is no other competing specific or other form that could explain what it does. On the other hand, if we *also* allow universal *generic* forms to be substances, i.e. to have the requisite explanatory power, then we are in serious trouble. For, on this proposal, a universal *specific* form such as the form of man will account for the substantiality of all its possessors, and these are the individual human beings. But there is another universal, namely the generic form animal, which the individual human beings also possess which, on the proposed theory, must *also* account for their substantiality, since on this theory *every* universal accounts for substantiality on the part of all its possessors. Moreover, this generic universal will also account for the substantiality of the individual horses just as the specific form horse does (Cf. 1038b9–13). In this case explanatory uniqueness is lost, not because the specific forms taken *alone* would fail to be explanatory of substantiality or subjecthood but because the generic forms *also* must be explanatory of the subjecthood *of the same things* on the proposal in question.[21]

That this sort of line of argument is what Aristotle has in mind in the opening stretch of Z.13 which introduces the uniqueness requirement seems clear from the response to his initial arguments which he allows his opponent to give. (This is what is sometimes called the Platonist's answer, at 1038b16ff.) The opponent begins with the concession that the universal generally cannot be substance "as the essence is" (because, I take it, an essence or specific form must be *uniquely* explanatory of the self-subsistence of its possessors so the generic form cannot *also* do *that* job). Nevertheless, the opponent argues, "the universal," e.g. the generic form, can be an element *present in* this essence, as the form *animal* is present in the specific form of *man* (1038b17–18). Here the opponent *must* be excluding from his view specific forms since they are not *elements present* in essences of the sort the opponent agrees are substances of the required sort, namely specific forms. (The essences which the opponent agrees are substances are such things as *man* and *horse*, i.e. the specific form of man or horse.) Thus, the opponent claims, the generic form animal, as an element in the specific form, will be "some kind of an account of the essence," i.e. some sort of (partial) explainer of substantiality just as the specific form is (b16–19). But, Aristotle objects, this generic form, animal, as a universal, still is the "substance of" *something*, i.e. it must explain the self-subsistence of something if the theory that universals are such as to make their possessors self-subsistent subjects is to be saved. What it must explain the self-subsistence of are the things which it is in, such as the specific forms man, horse, etc. (b19–23). Aristotle takes it for granted that it cannot do this. He does not explain why, but an obvious explanation presents itself from the context. The reason why the generic form *animal* cannot explain the self-subsistence of man, horse, etc. is because these things (these specific forms) are not self-subsistent subjects at all. The presence of the generic form in these different specific forms might help to explain why they are *specific* forms (since that is what different sub-kinds *of* generic forms are made to be by, in part, their generic form) but it cannot explain why they are self-subsistent subjects because the these specific forms are still universals and no universal is a self-subsistent subject (1038b15–16).

Aristotle proceeds to an additional objection to the view that the universal is substance (1038b23ff). It is, he says, impossible for this view to avoid the result that a substance or "this" which has qualitative features (as well as essential features) will have these qualitative features not as dependent qualities but as independent basic subjects present in it, so that quality will be prior to substance and exist separate from it (b23–29). Again, Aristotle does not explain just why this result arises but the answer seems to be this. A quality such as yellow will be an instance of some higher universal such as color. If so, then as an instance of a universal it must itself *be* a self-subsistent subject since, on the theory in question, universals are always causes of self-subsistent subjecthood for their possessors. So any self-subsistent subject which is yellow cannot be qualitatively yellow but (as for Anaxagoras) it must contain its yellow color as a basic independent subject in it. But this is absurd; it makes a quality a self-subsistent thing prior to the substance it belongs to.

Aristotle adds as a further objection that on the view that the universal is substance Socrates will have a substance present in him (or present in a substance, according to some mss.) and this will be the substance *for* two things (1038b29–30). Aristotle, again, does not explain why this is so but we can see that the universal form *animal* will make both Socrates and the specific form man which is present in Socrates into self-subsistent subjects and substances since they both possess this universal form which is, thus, the substance of both Socrates and his specific form. So Socrates will possess his specific form as an independent substance in himself, which is absurd.

Aristotle next (at 1038b30ff) sums up his whole line of argument to this point in Z.13 with the following general conclusion: "To sum things up (*holos*), if man and what is predicated like man [i.e. species essences or forms] are substances *then* nothing in their formula [i.e. no more generic universal nor any quality introduced by a differentia] can be the substance of any thing" (b30–33). This general conclusion is clearly quite important since it seems to sum up what Aristotle takes himself to have shown. But what he says he has shown is not that *no* universal is a substance (i.e. a cause of self-subsistent subjecthood) but only that *if* the specific forms such as the form of man are substances, *then* none of the other universals, such as the generic forms and qualities, can be. And that is in fact all that his arguments have shown. They all turn on the supposition that the doctrine that the universal is substance requires that in addition to the specific forms, generic forms and qualities are also substances, and this combination spells disaster. Thus, Aristotle's line of argument explicitly leaves it open that some universals, namely the specific forms, are causes of substantiality and thus substances in that sense, providing that the other universals are not. If this is Aristotle's position, then there is no support to be got from Z.13 for the view that, for Aristotle, substance is particular or *individual* form or essence. That chapter will not support the doctrine that only particular or individual forms can be causes of basic subjecthood on the ground that *no* universal forms can do that job.

One might still wish to object to this reading of Z.13 on the ground that whatever Aristotle may have shown or claim he has shown by 1038b30–33, at 1038b34 he says that he has somehow made it clear that "*none(ouden)* of the things which belong universally is a substance" since none of them *is* a *this* but only a *such*. Here, at least, it seems he must be claiming that no universal *is* a basic self-subsistent subject, or primary substance *in that sense* (b35; cf. Z16 1041a3–5). As we have seen, however, this poses no difficulty. It is true that no universal is a self-subsistent subject. But this leaves it quite open that *some* universals, but not all, might be primary substances in the other sense of what *causes* the self-subsistent subjects to be such. How, then, can the conclusion that no universal is a self-subsistent subject have become clear from the preceding arguments as well as the main conclusion that the universal generally is not substance in the sense of the cause of the self-subsistence of the particular substances? The answer is that certain of the previous arguments do also make this conclusion evident, for instance the following argument which we have so far not discussed at 1038b15–16: "A [particular] substance is said to be what is not predicated of a subject, but the universal, [including the specific form] is always predicable *of* some subject. [So the specific form cannot be a particular substance, which it would have to be, as an instance of a generic form, on the view that the universal is substance.]" This does indicate that no universal is a self-subsistent subject, or substance in that sense. Nevertheless, this argument also has the function, as I take it it does in its original use, of showing why not every universal can *make* its possessor a self-subsistent subject since if it did then a specific form, as having a universal generic form predicable of it, would have to be a self-subsistent subject and as a universal it cannot be.

In Z.16 1040b16ff Aristotle offers a related argument to support his claim that "neither unity nor being can be the substance of things ... since nothing that is common is *a* substance. For the substance [of something] does not *belong to* anything except to itself and to that which has it, *of which* it is the substance" (b18–24). If unity were the *substance of* whatever it belongs to then it would make all common universals, e.g. the form of man, to be substances, since these things *have* unity. But no common universal is *a* substance, i.e. a self-subsistent thing. So *unity* cannot be the *substance of* what it belongs to and, as this argument shows again, nothing more generic than a most specific substantial form can be the *substance of* anything. Thus, specific form alone is what substance is. This argument offers a very good illustration of the difference in use of the locations 'substance of' and 'a substance' and of the importance of keeping these uses distinct.

## X. Conclusions

On the account of Aristotle's strategy in Z suggested here, then, his basic strategy conforms not to his standard dialectical procedure but to his usual procedure in scientific inquiry; and that strategy is quite successful. Aristotle's candidate for substance, specific form, does serve to uniquely *explain* the basic subjecthood of its possessors, namely the paradigmatic primary substances of the *Categories*, even though it is not itself a basic subject. It also, I take it, serves to explain why the secondary substances of the *Categories*, the species and genera of the primary substances, indicate *what* those primary substances *are*, even though *it* is not itself alone a good candidate for being *what* any of those things *is*. This is a story whose details must mainly be saved for another occasion, but the basic point is already reasonably clear. The *way* the substantial form makes Socrates into a basic subject is by informing his underlying matter so that it realizes its potential to become an individual member of a certain distinct species, which he cannot then cease to belong to without ceasing to exist, rather than by making Socrates to be of any particular accidental color, shape, etc. in a way that does not involve any such informing of his underlying matter. Thus, his *species* indicates *what* he is, and could not fail to be without ceasing to be, most of all (see Z.7 1032a28–32, 9 1034a33ff).

We can now conclude by applying the results we have reached concerning Aristotle's strategy in Z to the question which led us to investigate it. These results indicate not only that Aristotle thinks that the science of metaphysics studies a single kind or *genos*, just as the special sciences do, but also that the pattern of *inquiry* which he follows is the same as in those other sciences. His aim is to *explain* certain initially apprehended features of substances which they have not, for instance, as living things, but simply as substances. The *form* which he invokes as the primary explainer, is chosen for its ability to explain, for instance, why the particular substances, such as the particular living things, are substances, i.e. are basic self-subsistent subjects. But it is not chosen for its ability to explain all the features which they have *as living things*. This is why a *substantial* form is such a poor candidate for being *what* any living thing is *as a living thing*. A proper candidate for that job, as Aristotle makes clear in many places, would have to make reference to the particular kind of proximate matter of the particular kind of living thing in question. But a *substantial* form does not need to do this to explain the features of living substances *qua substances*. For this purpose substantial form need not and indeed cannot include proximate matter since, as we have seen, the possession of matter does not serve at all to explain why anything is an *actual* self-subsistent subject. However, the job of the *biological* essence of a human being as opposed to the *substantial* form, and essence of a human being *qua* substance, is quite different since it must explain all the attributes which a human being has, not *qua* being (i.e. *qua* substance) but *qua human* being. This shows why it is a mistake to try to identify *substantial* form with the type of *biological* essence that is explanatory in biology. This provides at least one indication of what the autonomy of metaphysics, and also of biology, involves.

It also, finally, offers us an illustration of the more general point with which we began, which deserves to be repeated now. People make mistakes, Aristotle said in *Met.* Γ.3, in trying to understand his lectures on metaphysics "due to a lack of education in the *Analytics*. For they should know these things [in the *Analytics*] already when they come [to discussions of metaphysics] and not need to inquire into them while they are listening" (1005b3–5).

NOTES

¹ This is a revised version of a paper presented first in 1990 at a conference on Aristotle on Substance sponsored by the Los Angeles Area Colloquium in Ancient Philosophy. It is based on material presented in seminars for some years prior to that. It extends to the *Metaphysics* the program, for the understanding of Aristotle's scientific works in the light of the *Posterior Analytics*, that was put forward in earlier papers and applied there to the study of the *De Anima, Generation of Animals, Physics* and other scientific works (see Bibliographical Note). There are indications that others are now beginning to follow this approach even in the study of the *Metaphysics*. Here I concentrate on my own application of this program to the *Metaphysics* in the confidence that others will, soon enough, speak for themselves. Portions of this paper have also been recently presented to the University of Texas Workshop in Ancient Philosophy, and to the Annual SSIPS/SAGP Conference on Ancient and Medieval Philosophy. I am grateful to all those who have raised questions for discussion, particularly Daniel Devereux and Frank Lewis.

² For the sense of *ta analutika* here cf. Z.12 1037b8–9. There has been a dispute since ancient times as to whether this passage (1005b2–5) is out of place. As Ross points out, following Bonitz, "it connects directly with what has been said in a29–31 and is quite in place" (W.D. Ross, *Aristotle's Metaphysics*, Oxford, 1953, Vol. I, p. 263).

³ The significance of the argument of Γ.4 for this question is discussed in "Aristotle's Conception of Metaphysics as a Science" (1994).

⁴ Some have suggested that Aristotle means to say here that metaphysics is a unified subject only in what might be called a generic, i.e. a very loose, way. But that does not fit the context. Aristotle compares the way in which metaphysics investigates one genus with the way in which grammar investigates one genus, namely because it studies one distinct kind of thing, articulate sound.

⁵ Cf. 1005a11–13 for the other attributes: opposition, completeness, unity, being in various modes, same and different.

⁶ The study of, for instance *quantity*, by metaphysics, will include the study of its proper attributes, such as large and small, and a special mode of unity (*Met.* Δ.13 1020a23–25, Γ.2 1003b22ff). These are proper attributes of quantities but, as such, they are also in their mode of being, proper attributes of substances. To be, for instance, large, or one in the relevant way, is to be a large *quantity* of a *substance*, or to be one in the *quantity* of a *substance*. This is why Aristotle can move immediately from the claim that there is one science that studies what is *qua* being and *its* proper attributes to the claim that the same single science studies substances and *their* attributes (Γ.2 1005a13–18; cf. 1003b30–36, 1004a22–33).

⁷ For the source of this terminology and line of argument see G.E.L. Owen (1960).

⁸ See H. Bonitz, *Index Aristotelicus* (Berlin, 1870), 93b56ff. Cf. Aristotle's uses of *ta phusika* for the various objects dealt with by natural science, *Index*, 834b43ff.

⁹ As the notion of focal meaning was understood by those who originally introduced it, it was supposed to apply exclusively in cases in which the same *word* is used for many different things in semantically different *senses*, where the nominal or semantic definitions which distinguish those senses are such that the term (or its semantic definition) in one sense figures in the semantic definitions of the term in the other senses. It is extremely doubtful that Aristotle has this in mind in his discussion in Γ.2 of the way in which *entities* or *the things that are* (*ta onta*) are so called "by reference to one single nature" (1003a33ff). Aristotle is not doing semantics here but metaphysics. He is not advocating the (highly dubious) doctrine that the Greek word for *entity*, i.e., *on*, has many semantically distinct definitions which would be recognized by ordinary competent speakers of Greek, in the way the English word *bank* or *hand* does. That *on* (*entity*), in Greek, has the different semantic senses, *substance, quantity, quality*, etc., which should be included in the dictionary entry under *on* (or *eimi*), is absurd. What Aristotle rather means to say is that the *real* definitions or accounts of the modes of being of the irreducibly different types of entities— quantity, quality, etc.—will all make some reference to substance.

¹⁰ The *aporia* of B.2, 997a25–32, has a complex structure, like many of the *aporiai* of B. It first poses a requirement for the view that the science of substance is "a particular demonstrative science," a requirement which, as we have seen, is met in Γ. It then poses an apparent difficulty for this result, namely that, in this case, there will be no demonstration of *what* substance *is* since a demonstrative science takes the definition of the essence of its subject genus as primitive and indemonstrable (see *An.Po.*I.10 76a31ff, *Met.*E.1 1025b10–16). This difficulty is, however, easily met. As Aristotle indicates in E.1, what is required to meet it is that though there is no proof *of* the ultimate definition of substance as the conclusion of any particular demonstration, "there is some other way in which this is made evident" in the development of the demonstrative science (1025b14–15). Here Aristotle refers again directly to the doctrine of *An.Po.* II.8–10, e.g. at 93b15–20. For the application of this to the ultimate definition of substance, see below on Z.17.

¹¹ As editors have pointed out, this passage seems out of place. It is perhaps best put at the beginning of Z.2, though this is not of much importance for present purposes.

¹² I take it that the much discussed phrase *ti esti kai tode ti* (1028a11–12) means 'what something is, i.e. [what] some *this* [is]'. This is supported by a14ff where Aristotle, without any indication that he has changed or modified the subject, speaks of "that *ti esti* which indeed indicates a substance" and of "what it [i.e. some *this*] is" by contrast with the *what* that we mention when we say "what some *this* (*tode*) is" *like*" (a15–17). He wants to fix on the *ti esti* which indicates or applies to an *ousia* or substance and the phrases "*ti esti* which indicates an *ousia*," and "what it [i.e. some *this*] is" (a17), refer to the same thing as *ti esti kai tode ti*. Aristotle needs to specify what sort of *ti esti* he has in mind, and to distinguish this from, e.g., 'the *ti esti* which indicates a quality.' The phrase *ti esti* alone does not do this, as one can see from Z.4, 1030a18ff: "The *ti esti*, in one way, indicates a substance, i.e., a *this*, in another way it indicates each of the other things predicated— quantity, quality and all other such things." Cf. *Topics* I.9 103b27–39. So the phrase *ti esti kai tode ti* does not introduce two different candidates or two different criteria for substance, any more than the phrase "*ti esti* which indicates a substance" does, but only one.

¹³ In Z.1 1028a31ff Aristotle claims that "substance is primary" in three ways. It is primary *in time* or self-subsistence, since no item in any other category is self-subsistent; only a substance is. Substance is primary *in definition* because "in the definition of any thing the account of *its* substance is present." That is, the *substance of* a thing figures in the definition of a thing. Substance is also primary *in knowledge* because we know a thing best when we know, e.g. what the species of animal is to which it belongs rather than, e.g. what the quality is which it has. In Δ.8 Aristotle claims that the use of the term 'substance' or 'a substance' to designate self-subsistent subjects is a different use

from that in which we refer to the essence or "substance *of*" a thing. The entities picked out in these different uses are not the same. So the different modes of priority for substance discussed in Z.1 do not all apply to the same entities, according to Δ.8. Nothing in Z.1 rules it out that the view of Δ.8 on this point will also turn out to be the final view of Z. See, further, below on the significance of Δ.8 for the interpretation of Z.

¹⁴ For discussion and defense of Alexander's view see J. Lennox, "Aristotelian Problems," in *Logic, Dialectic* and *Science in Aristotle*, eds. R. Bolton and R. Smith, *Ancient Philosophy*, Special Issue, 1994.

¹⁵ In any case, the view that Aristotle assigns special weight in dialectic to the views of philosophers or other experts, greater than that assigned to the views of people in general, is itself quite dubious. For discussion of this whole topic see, "The Epistemological Basis of Aristotelian Dialectic" (1990).

¹⁶ There is a good example of the mixing of dialectical and strictly causal inquiry in Aristotle's treatment of the question, "What is *sperma*?", in Books I–II of the *Generation of Animals*. On this see "Definition and Scientific Method in Aristotle's *Posterior Analytics* and *Generation of Animals*" (1987).

¹⁷ For the reference of '*the* substance' (1029a28) see a23 where the phrase designates the particular substance. At a27 substance (without article) = what substance is (cf. Z.1 1028a 22–28). Some argue that the "matter" in 1029a10ff does not include Aristotle's own matter (see, e.g. Gill, 1989, Ch. 1). But Aristotle claims to have *shown* by his argument that form and compound are better candidates for substance than matter *in his own sense* (a29ff), so this cannot be correct. The characterization of matter at a20ff does *not* require that matter here is nothing at all, contrary to Aristotle's view. Bronze (a3f) is not *in itself* a particular thing (*ti = tode ti*) nor of any quality, etc. It *is* an alloy of copper and tin. But this is not a quality, etc. of it, but *what it is*. Aristotle opposes *what* something *is* to its qualities, quantity etc. (*Top.* I.9 103b20ff). Others claim that Aristotle knows that his argument here that his own matter qualifies as substratum of which everything else is predicated is invalid since form alone is predicated of matter while qualities, etc., are predicated only of the composite substance (Lewis 1991, Ch 10). But then Aristotle could not honestly claim, as he does, to have shown by his argument that though matter does count as substratum it can be dismissed as substance on other grounds. In fact there is a natural sense in which matter does underly *as subject* form, composite, qualities, etc. since it has the *potentiality for* all these other things. This is sufficient for Aristotle's purposes in his argument.

¹⁸ For an extended discussion of this point see "The Material Cause: Matter and Explanation in Aristotle's Natural Science" (1996). Some argue (e.g. Gill, 1989, Ch.4) that the account of soul as form and essence of a certain sort of body (*De An.* II.1 412a20, cf. Z.10 1035b16) requires a mention of a type of matter in the definition of the form itself, i.e. the soul. But 403a24ff shows that the fact that psychic entities are "enmattered formulae" (*logoi enuloi*) does not entail that the form or formula itself must be defined by mention of the matter. This is ruled out by 403b2ff. Also, in II.1–2 413a9ff the account of soul at 412a20 is described as a rough sketch, not the ultimate account of soul. The latter must also cover *nous*, which is not the form of any sort of body (413b26). On this see, further, "Aristotle's Definitions of the Soul: *De Anima* II.1–3" (1978).

¹⁹ Some claim that Aristotle means to argue in Z.10–11 that *only the form* of a composite substance is definable (see, e.g., Frede/Patzig, 1988). But the text says that the composite is *itself* definable in one sense. (Z.11 1037a26ff). It is *not* definable "taken with its [particular] matter since this is indeterminate [i.e. unformulable and uncapturable in a definition]." (a27, cf.1036a2ff). That is, Callias is not definable *qua* Callias since as such he contains unformulable unique matter (1034a5–8). There is thus no scientific definition or cause of the being of Callias *qua* Callias. (1039b28ff) But Callias *is* definable "insofar as he has form" (1035a7–9), that is "with reference to his primary substance" or soul (1037a28) which is "the *substance of* a living thing" (1035b14), i.e. "that which is the cause of his being" (1017b14f). For "substance, understood in one way is form [or soul], i.e. that by virtue of

which something [e.g. Callias] is straightaway said to be a *this.*" (*De An.* II.1 412a6ff). So Callias *is definable*, i.e. there is a cause of his being, not *qua* Callias but *qua* (composite) *substance* or *this.* See further below on Z.17.

[20] Some claim that form or soul is predicated *only of* (itself and, accidentally, of) *matter*, not universally of Socrates and Callias (see Code, 1984; Lewis, 1991, Ch.6). Aristotle does say that where the subject is *not* a *this* and a substance, *form* as predicate *is* predicated of matter in the sense that (ultimate) matter *is potentially* informed or ensouled, not accidentally one should add (Z.13 1038b4ff, Θ.7 1049a27ff). But one can hardly infer from this that (human) form is *not* universally predicable of Socrates *and* Callias, in the sense that each of them *is actually* informed or ensouled. Socrates is said to be the *actual* subject for his "attributes" (*pathe*). But this does not rule it out that these include his essential attributes such as being ensouled nor, even if it should, that these are predicated of him in the same way, as *actual* not *potential* subject, as in Z.8, 17 and *De An.* II.1. The attempt to avoid this is motivated by the supposed need to construe a form, presumed to be *a substance*, as a non-universal, since no universal is *a substance*. But if form is only meant to be the *substance of*, i.e. the explainer of substantiality for, the substances, there is no need for this problematic hypothesis in the first place.

[21] If the initial argument of 1038b9ff is meant also to suggest that the *substance of* a particular substance or "this" must be unique to that *particular* substance alone, then this is a proposal that Aristotle has already rejected. This would be tantamount to the claim that what makes something a self-subsistent particular must also make it the distinct particular it is. But this Aristotle rejects. It is (universal) substantial form that makes an entity a self-subsistent particular, as we can see in Z.7–9 and 17. It is distinct concrete matter that makes any self-subsistent particular the distinct self-subsistent particular it is (Z.8 1034a5–8). Form is the principle of *particularity* not the principle of *individuation* for particulars. If the uniqueness principle (1038b10) applies only to substantial kinds then the argument is one that Aristotle can accept.

## *Bibliographical Note*

The aim of this paper has been to offer the outlines of a new approach to the understanding of Aristotle's science of substance. Various versions of the more traditional approach, with further references, are to be found in the following literature. This literature constitutes only the tip of the iceberg so far as significant discussion of *Metaphysics* Γ and Z is concerned. No fair review of this literature is at all possible within the limits of this already long paper. So I must beg to be excused for omitting specific or detailed discussion of these items or other standard literature. This has the pleasing consequence that I can avoid engaging in explicit polemic. My friends and colleagues may feel ignored but they will at least not feel attacked. With luck that could help to make Aristotle himself the main focus of attention.

Barnes, J. 1995. "Metaphysics," *The Cambridge Companion to Aristotle.* Cambridge.
Bostock, D. 1994. *Aristotle: Metaphysics Books Z and H.* Oxford.
Code, A. 1978. "No Universal is a Substance," *Paideia.*
——— 1984. "The Aporematic Approach to Primary Being in *Metaphysics* Z," *Canadian Journal of Philosophy.*
Devereux, D. 1992. "Inherence and Primary Substance in Aristotle's *Categories*," *Ancient Philosophy.*

280 ROBERT BOLTON

Frede, M. and Patzig, G. 1988. *Aristoteles, Metaphysik* Z, 2 vol. Munich.
Furth, M. 1988. *Substance, Form and Psyche: An Aristotelian Metaphysics.* Cambridge.
Gill, M.L. 1989. *Aristotle on Substance.* Princeton.
Irwin, T. 1988. *Aristotle's First Principles.* Oxford.
Lewis, F. 1991. *Substance and Predication in Aristotle.* Cambridge.
Loux, M. 1991. *Primary Ousia.* Ithaca.
Owen, G.E.L. 1986. "Logic and Metaphysics in Some Earlier Works of Aristotle" (1960), final version in *Logic, Science and Dialectic.* London and Ithaca.
Scaltsas, T. 1995. *Substances and Universals in Aristotle's Metaphysics.* Ithaca.

Earlier articles referred to above which set the framework for this discussion include:

Bolton, R. 1978. "Aristotle's Definitions of The Soul: *De Anima* II.1–3." *Phronesis.*
——1987, "Definition and Scientific Method in Aristotle's *Posterior Analytics* and *Generation of Animals*," in A. Gotthelf and J. Lennox (eds.), *Philosophical Issues in Aristotle's Biology*, Cambridge.
—— 1990. "The Epistemological Basis of Aristotelian Dialectic," in D. Devereux and P. Pellegrin (eds), *Biologie, Logique, et Metaphysique chez Aristotle.* Paris.
—— 1991. "Aristotle's Method in Natural Science," in L. Judson (ed.), *Aristotle's Physics: A Collection of Essays.* Oxford.
—— 1994. "Aristotle's Conception of Metaphysics as a Science," in T. Scaltsas *et al.* (eds.) *Unity, Identity and Explanation in Aristotle's Metaphysics*, Oxford.
—— 1996. "The Material Cause: Matter and Explanation in Aristotle's Natural Science" (forthcoming).

# INDEX OF PASSAGES

281

# GENERAL INDEX